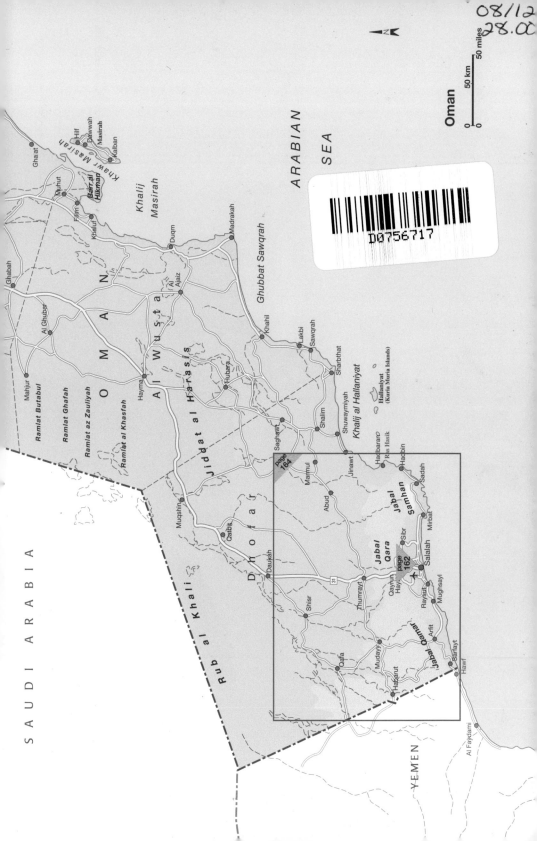

N

Oman

0   50 km
0   50 miles

ARABIAN

SEA

SAUDI ARABIA

YEMEN

Ghaat

Muhut

Barr al Hikman

Filim

Khaluf

Ghabah

Al Ghubar

Mahjur

Ramlat Butabul

Ramlat Ghafah

Ramlat az Zauliyah

Ramlat al Khasfah

O M A N

Hayma

Al Wusta

Jiddat al Harasis

Muqshin

Qatbit

Daukah

Shisr

Qafa

Mudayy

Hadarut

Arfit

Jabal Qamar

Sarfayt

Hawf

Al Faydami

Hilf
Jawwah   Masirah
Kalban

Khawr Masirah

Khalij Masirah

Duqm

Madrakah

Ghubbat Sawqrah

Al Ajaiz

Hubara

Khahil

Saghawt

Marmul

Abud

Thumrayt

31

Lakbi
Sawqrah

Sharbthat

Shalim

Shuwaymiyah

Khalij al Hallaniyat

Hallaniyat
(Kuria Maria Islands)

Hadbararo
Ras Hasik

Hacbin

Jinawt

Sadah

Dhofar

Rub al Khali

Jabal Samhan

Sibr

Qayhun
Hayma

page 162

Raysut

Salalah
Mirbat

Mughsayl

page 164

INSIGHT GUIDES

OMAN & THE UAE

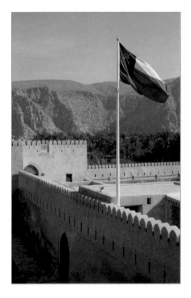

APA PUBLICATIONS L
Part of the Langenscheidt Publishing Group

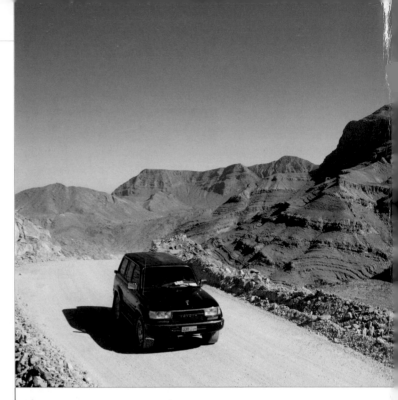

※ INSIGHT GUIDE

OMAN & THE UAE

Editorial

Project Editor
Tom Stainer
Series Manager
Rachel Lawrence
Publishing Manager
Rachel Fox
Design
Ian Spick
Map Production
**original cartography Berndtson &
Berndtson, updated by Apa
Cartography Department**
Production
Linton Donaldson

Distribution

UK
Dorling Kindersley Ltd
A Penguin Group company
80 Strand, London, WC2R 0RL
customerservice@dk.com

United States
Ingram Publisher Services
1 Ingram Boulevard, PO Box 3006,
La Vergne, TN 37086-1986
customer.service@ingrampublisher
services.com

Australia
Universal Publishers
PO Box 307
St Leonards NSW 1590
sales@universalpublishers.com.au

Worldwide
**Apa Publications GmbH & Co.
Verlag KG (Singapore branch)**
7030 Ang Mo Kio Avenue 5
08-65 Northstar @ AMK
Singapore 569880
apasin@singnet.com.sg

Printing

CTPS-China

© 2012 Apa Publications (UK) Ltd
All Rights Reserved

First Edition 1998
Second Edition 2012

CONTACTING THE EDITORS
We would appreciate it if readers
would alert us to errors or out-
dated information by writing to:
**Insight Guide s, PO Box 7910,
London SE1 1WE, England.**
insight@apaguide.co.uk
NO part of this book may be reproduced,
stored in a retrieval system or transmitted
in any form or means electronic, mech-
anical, photocopying, recording or otherwise, without prior written permission of
Apa Publications. Brief text quotations
with use of photographs are exempted
for book review purposes only. Information has been obtained from sources
believed to be reliable, but its accuracy
and completeness, and the opinions
based thereon, are not guaranteed.

www.insightguides.com

ABOUT THIS BOOK

The first Insight Guide pioneered the use of creative full-colour photography in travel guides in 1970. Since then, we have expanded our range to cater for our readers' need not only for reliable information about their chosen destination but also for a real understanding of the culture and workings of that destination. Now, when the internet can supply inexhaustible (but not always reliable) facts, our books marry text and pictures to provide those much more elusive qualities: knowledge and discernment. To achieve this, they rely heavily on the authority of locally based writers and photographers.

How to use this book

The book is carefully structured to convey an understanding of the countries and their cultures and to guide readers through their sights and attractions:

◆ To understand the region, you need to know something of its past. The **Features** section, with a pink bar, covers the states' history and culture. These lively, authoritative essays are written by specialists.
◆ The **Places** section, with a blue bar, provides full details of all the areas worth seeing. The chief places of interest are coordinated by number with full-colour maps.
◆ The **Travel Tips** listings section, with a yellow bar, offers a convenient point of reference for information on travel, hotels, restaurants, shopping etc. Information may be located quickly by using the index printed on the back cover flap – and the flaps also serve as bookmarks.

The contributors

This new edition was updated throughout by freelance travel writer **Gavin Thomas**, who specialises in

Former contributors whose work appears in the book include **Christine Osborne** (Oman's Batinah Coast, Sur and the Wahiba Sands, the Interior and Dhofar); **Tom Athey** (Muscat, the feature on forts, the Travel Tips on Oman); **Carl Phillips** (Musandam, the essay on archaeology); **Ann Verbeek** (Abu Dhabi, Dubai, Ras al Khaimah, Fujairah); **Matt Jones** (Sharjah, Ajman, Umm al Qaiwain, the feature on wadi-bashing); **William Facey** (The Maritime Heritage, Islam); **Alan Keohane** (The Bedu, the jewellery photo feature); **Geoffrey Weston** (The UAE From Rags to Riches, The Oil Boom, the short profile on Sheikh Zayed); **Michael Gallagher** (Dhofar's birdlife); **Sir Donald Hawley** (the history of Oman); **Jane Matthew** (Travel Tips on the UAE); and **Sylvia Buchanan**.

The proofreader for this edition was **Neil Titman** and the indexer was **Helen Peters**.

Map Legend

Symbol	Description
—·—	International Boundary
————	Province Boundary
——•——	National Park/Reserve
————	Ferry Route
⊖	Border Crossing
✈ ✈	Airport: International/Regional
🚍	Bus Station
✉	Post Office
❶	Tourist Information
∴	Archaeological Site
☾	Mosque
∩	Cave
1	Statue/Monument
★	Place of Interest
⸞	Beach
⚑	Lighthouse
✷	Kasbah
❆	Viewpoint
Ⓜ	Metro

The main places of interest in the Places section are coordinated by number with a full-colour map (eg ❶), and a symbol at the top of every right-hand page tells you where to find the map.

the Gulf and South Asia. He has written several guidebooks to Dubai and the UAE (including a comprehensive update of the most recent edition of Insight's *Dubai Step by Step*) and has recently made a number of extended visits to Oman. He has also worked on the Insight Guides to Sri Lanka and India.

For this edition, Gavin wrote the chapters on Food and Drink, Architecture, and Sports and Outdoor Activities from scratch, as well as the new photo feature on The Arts. He also comprehensively overhauled the chapters on Daily Life, The Expatriates, Islam and Dubai.

The guide was commissioned and managed by **Tom Stainer** at Insight Guides. It was copy-edited by Tom and **Alyse Dar**.

Contents

Maps

Inside front cover: Oman.
Inside back cover:
United Arab Emirates.

Travel Tips

THE BEST OF OMAN AND THE UAE: TOP ATTRACTIONS

From ultra-modern cities to time-warped mudbrick mountain villages, here are some of the top attractions that Oman and the UAE have to offer

▽ **Burj al Arab** The modern Gulf's most iconic landmark, the sail-shaped Burj al Arab rises majestically above the coast of southern Dubai – stunning by day, and even more spectacular after dark. *See page 209.*

△ **Sheikh Zayed Grand Mosque** Abu Dhabi's most dramatic sight: a huge snow-white mosque, topped by dozens of domes and soaring minarets, and opulently decorated inside with vast carpets and chandeliers. *See page 187.*

◁ **Old Dubai** Wander through the endless souks, traditional houses and wind towers of old Dubai, lined up along either side of the bustling Creek, still busy with old-fashioned wooden dhows. *See page 200.*

△ **Sharjah Museums and Galleries** Self-styled "cultural capital" of the UAE, Sharjah boasts an excellent array of museums and galleries, covering everything from Arabic calligraphy to antique aeroplanes. *See page 218.*

▷ **Salalah** A world away from the rest of Oman, Salalah is at its most memorable during the annual *khareef* (monsoon), when the surrounding mountains turn a verdant green. *See page 161.*

◁ **Mutrah Souk, Muscat** The biggest and most absorbing souk in the region, stuffed full of tiny shops selling all manner of traditional produce from honey to frankincense. *See page 121.*

▷ **Wahibah Desert** Magnificent stretch of untamed desert, with huge wind-blown dunes dotted with occasional hardy shrubs and trees or even hardier Bedu. *See page 154.*

△ **Jabrin Fort** The finest of Oman's 500-odd forts, with beautifully restored interiors offering a tantalising glimpse into the life of the country's former rulers. *See page 144.*

▽ **Nizwa and the Western Hajar** Oman's most historic city, with a magnificent fort and atmospheric souks tucked away in the lee of the craggy Western Hajar mountains. *See page 139.*

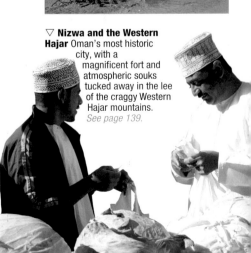

△ **Musandam Peninsula** The mountains of Arabia at their most dramatic, as the red-rock Hajar mountains go tumbling down into the sea, creating a spectacular sequence of sheer cliffs and steep-sided khors. *See page 173.*

THE BEST OF OMAN AND THE UAE: EDITOR'S CHOICE

Watch locals bargaining over goats in Nizwa, hike around Jabal Shams's spectacular Balcony Walk, or recline on the beach in Dubai sipping cocktails in the shade of a five-star palace – just a few of the region's hugely varied attractions

TOP TRADITIONAL ATTRACTIONS

Friday Market, Nizwa Colourful weekly market in historic Nizwa, with hundreds of robed locals haggling over goats, cows and other livestock. *See page 141.*
Sultan Qaboos Grand Mosque, Muscat Vast modern mosque in contemporary Islamic style, with richly decorated interiors. *See page 124.*

Dhow Wharfage, Dubai Hundreds of superb old wooden dhows moor up along the Creek, with cargo piled high on the adjacent waterfront. *See page 202.*
Women's Souk, Ibra Lively traditional women-only souk, particularly popular amongst colourfully attired local Bedu ladies. *See page 155.*

BEST SOUQS AND SHOPPING

Al Husn Souk, Salalah Fragrant souk in old Salalah, particularly famous for its superb array of local frankincense. *See page 162.*
Nizwa Souk Atmospheric cluster of neatly restored traditional souk buildings. *See page 140.*
Al Arsa Souk, Sharjah Quaint little souk in the heart of Sharjah's Heritage Quarter, with narrow alleyways lined with quirky shops. *See page 216.*
Gold and Spice Souks, Dubai Dubai's two most colourful souks, with shop windows full of gold and sacks loaded full of herbs and spices. *See pages 200 and 202.*

Ibn Battuta Mall, Dubai Weird and wonderful modern mall with extravagant decor themed after the travels of Ibn Battuta. *See page 210.*
Souk Madinat Jumeirah, Dubai. Gorgeous faux-Arabian souk in the spectacular Madinat Jumeirah complex. *See page 209.*

ABOVE: Sheikh Zayed Grand Mosque; Dubai Spice Souk.
LEFT: Friday Market, Nizwa.

BEST CULTURAL ATTRACTIONS

Dubai Museum, Dubai In the historic old Al Fahidi Fort, and offering an excellent overview of local history, culture and commerce. *See page 197.*

Jumeirah Mosque Tour, Dubai The only mosque in the city open to non-Muslims, with informative tours hosted by local Emirati guides. *See page 207.*

Sharjah Museum of Islamic Civilisation Superb modern museum highlighting Islamic contributions to science, art and architecture. *See page 218.*

Bastakiya, Dubai Wonderful old Iranian quarter, stuffed with fine old mansions topped with dozens of wind towers. *See page 198.*

Bait al Zubair, Muscat Absorbing museum covering the traditional arts and crafts of Oman. *See page 121.*

Bronze Age Tombs, Bat and Al Ayn Enigmatic clusters of beautifully preserved beehive tombs, dotted across the mountainous fringes of the Western Hajar. *See page 144.*

Sumhuram and Al Baleed The extensive remains of two of Oman's great frankincense ports, just outside Salalah. *See pages 165 and 163.*

Sheikh Zayed Grand Mosque, Abu Dhabi Monumental modern mosque, whose cluster of snow-white domes and soaring minarets rise high above southern Abu Dhabi. *See page 187.*

Jabal Akhdar Marvellous mountain plateau, dotted with a string of traditional villages sitting high above the great natural chasm of Wadi Al Ayn. *See page 138.*

Tawi Atayr and Taiq Sinkhole A pair of vast, cavernous sinkholes in the uplands of the remote Dhofar mountains. *See page 164.*

BEST MOUNTAIN SCENERY AND ADVENTURES

Wadi Tiwi Picture-perfect coastal wadi, with sheer sandstone cliffs enclosing a narrow, palm-lined canyon. *See page 150.*

Wadi Bani Awf Oman's classic off-road drive, descending from the heights of the Hajar mountains down the precipitous Wadi Bani Awf. *See page 142.*

Al Hoota Cave Venture deep inside this vast cave, strung with stalactites, in the depths of the Western Hajar mountains. *See page 141.*

The Balcony Walk The most spectacular hike in the region, running around the edge of a vast natural bowl below the towering Jabal Shams. *See page 143.*

Snake Gorge Hop over boulders and wade through pools on one of Oman's classic adventure hikes. *See page 142.*

COAST, BEACHES AND DESERT

Luxury hotels in Dubai A string of memorably opulent hotels line the coast of Dubai – perfect for a few quiet days next to the sea. *See page 259.*

Diving and snorkelling in Musandam The best diving and snorkelling in the region, amidst some of Oman's finest natural scenery. *See page 248.*

Boat trip through Khawr Sham Traditional dhows make daily tours of the stunning fjord, with pods of playful dolphins for company en route. *See page 175.*

Turtle-watching at Ras al Jinz Dozens of green turtles heave themselves up onto this beach nightly to lay their eggs. *See page 152.*

Dune-bashing in the Wahibah Desert Roll, bump and bounce across the sweeping dunes. *See page 154.*

Sur Historic Omani port, and home to the only boatyard in the country still making traditional dhows by hand. *See page 150.*

Fujairah Miles of fine golden-sand beaches, backed by the rugged Hajar mountains and offering the UAE's best snorkelling and diving. *See page 230.*

Above: beehive tombs, Bat.
Right: on a dhow cruise along the Khawr Sham, Oman.

ARABIA THEN AND NOW

Contrasting but complementary, Oman and the
UAE offer fascinating insights into Arabia's
past, present and possible future

Two of the Middle East's most absorbing destinations, Oman and the UAE offer a fascinating window into Arabia's traditional past and an exhilarating glimpse of its dynamic urban future. Images of the region are a kaleidoscopic jumble of contrasting sights, ranging from futuristic skyscrapers and super-sized shopping malls through to rustic mudbrick forts and old-fashioned wooden dhows, often within a few miles of one another.

The histories of the two countries are closely interwoven. Until recently, life in both revolved around a string of vibrant and cosmopolitan coastal ports – Muscat, Dubai, Sharjah, Sur, to name just a few – while inland, tribes of hardy Bedu eked a meagre living out of the deserts and mountains of the interior.

The discovery of oil in the 1960s changed all that, bringing modest prosperity to Oman, unimaginable wealth to Abu Dhabi, and providing the funds to help kickstart Dubai's dramatic growth. The contrasts between the two countries are now perhaps more obvious than their shared historical roots. Parts of the UAE (Dubai especially) have thrown themselves headlong into the modern world, embracing business and tourism with kamikaze gusto. Oman, by contrast, has taken a much more circumspect approach to Western values, modernising by slow and careful degrees.

For the visitor, the two countries offer contrasting but interestingly complementary experiences. The modern UAE is largely contemporary in appearance (although fascinating pockets of history remain), and many of the country's headline attractions – the ultra-modern cityscapes of Dubai in particular – are very much of our time.

By contrast, much of Oman's appeal is entirely natural: from the unforgettably dramatic Hajar mountains through to vast swathes of uninhabited desert and unspoilt beaches frequented by nesting turtles, with dolphins splashing in the waters offshore. Oman is also particularly rich in reminders of Arabia's past, with hundreds of venerable old forts, watchtowers and traditional mudbrick villages scattered across the country, nestled amidst date plantations and watered by traditional falaj irrigation channels.

PRECEDING PAGES: Sultan Qaboos Grand Mosque; Nizwa Mosque. **ABOVE, FROM LEFT:** camel on the beach in Ajman; Mutrah Corniche at night; football fans in Dubai.

LAND AND ENVIRONMENTS

From vast sand dunes to rugged mountains and
palm-fringed coast, Oman and the UAE boast a
surprisingly varied range of landscapes

The common perception of the Arabian peninsula as a vast expanse of empty desert doesn't do justice to the natural variety of the UAE and, especially, Oman, and the range of landscapes and environments can come as something of a surprise to first-time visitors – the sight of the verdant mountains of Dhofar during the annual *khareef* (monsoon), for instance, could hardly be further from the desert stereotype, while the craggy Hajar mountains and the often verdant coastlines of Oman, swathed in endless date plantations, also challenge received opinions.

The range of natural landscapes in turn support a surprisingly wide array of flora and fauna, ranging from the hardy frankincense trees of the Dhofar mountains through to the African bird-life found along the coast, and a range of elusive mammals including the Arabian oryx and the Arabian leopard, often talked about, but very rarely seen. The coastal waters, too, are rich in marine life, including pods of frolicking dolphins in Musandam, Muscat and elsewhere, through to the whales and thousands of turtles which continue to frequent the southern coast of Oman.

The deserts

Much of the interior of the UAE and Oman is desert, although this single word covers a multitude of subtly varying landscapes. The sandy deserts which are synonymous with the Arabian peninsula in the imagination of many can be found here, although they cover only a relatively small portion of the country.

LEFT: trekking up Wadi Halfayn in the Jabal Al Akhdar mountains, Oman.
RIGHT: Wahibah Desert sand dunes.

The magnificent dunes of the Wahiba Sands – known to geographers as an erg (or "sand sea", derived from the Arabic *arq*) – are the most notable example, while extensive dunes can also be found around Al Ain and in the northern UAE around Ras al Khaimah. To experience the region's finest dune formations, however, you'll have to visit the remote Rub al Khali (Empty Quarter) in the far southwest of Oman. Many of the interior deserts, however, are stony rather than sandy (technically a "hamada" or "reg"): bare, windswept plains covered in a mix of gravel and rock, supporting scant, hardy vegetation.

Coastal deserts also ring the seaboard of much of southern Oman, comprising a variety of sand, gravel and *sabkha* (salt-flats) landscapes, backed by cliff and rock formations sometimes moulded into surreal shapes by the combined effects of wind, sand and sea.

The mountains

Mountains cover only a relatively small part of the UAE and Oman, but provide many of the region's most stunning landscapes. The principal range is the mighty Hajar, which runs parallel to the coast down the east side of the peninsula, starting in Musandam, running south through Fujairah before re-entering Oman and running down past Muscat almost to the southeasternmost tip of the country – major peaks (running north to south) include Jabal Harim in Musandam (2,087 metres/ 6,487ft), Jabal Hafeet (1,249 metres/4,098ft) above Al Ain in the UAE, and Jabal Shams near Nizwa, the highest peak in either country (3,005 metres/9,859ft).

The name Hajar (meaning "stone") could hardly be more appropriate, given the mountains' lack of tree cover or any other surface vegetation, with vast slabs of rock laid bare, exposing millions of years of geological activity with textbook clarity. Most of the range is made up of various types of limestone, including

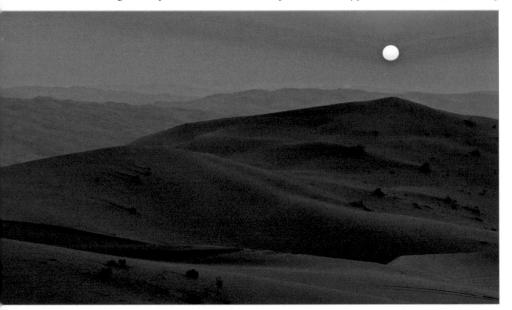

OMAN'S GEOLOGY

Oman is one of the world's most rewarding geological destinations, the Hajar mountains particularly. Much of Oman's spectacular mountain scenery derives from its location at the southeastern corner of the Arabian continental plate where it meets the Eurasian oceanic plate. As the Red Sea grows wider, Oman is being pushed slowly north and forced underneath the Eurasian plate, a massive tectonic shunt which has created the long mountainous chain of the Hajar. The various rock strata exposed on the towering cliff faces of Wadi Bani Kharous in Oman are particularly famous, showing formations spanning over 500 million years, from the Cretaceous period to the Late Proterozoic era.

Most of the rocks which now make up the Hajar mountains were actually formed underwater – as can be seen from the incongruous submarine fossils which dot the summit of Jabal Harim in Musandam. As the Arabian plate was forced beneath the Eurasian, large swathes of submarine rock were pushed up on top of the mainland. These include Oman's ophiolites: rocks formed in the oceanic crust which have been lifted above water – of particular interest to geologists as they reveal processes normally buried kilometres beneath the sea. They also provide Oman with the low, irregular, crumbling red-rock mountains which you can see along the Sumail Gap, around the Rustaq Loop and in many parts of the Eastern Hajar.

older grey and yellow formations through to outcrops of so-called geological "exotics" – pale, whitish "islands" of younger limestone, such as Jabal Misht and Jabal Khawr, respectively north and south of Al Ayn in Oman. Wadis are a characteristic feature of the Hajar, which boasts many spectacular examples, ranging from the broad wadis Sumail and Jizzi which cross the range from the coast to the interior, through to sheer-sided, needle-thin gorges such as Wadi Bimah (Snake Gorge).

In the far south of Oman lie the almost equally spectacular Dhofar mountains, encircling the city of Salalah on the coast – particularly striking during the annual *khareef*, when rain and mist descend on the heights, turning them a verdant green and creating rushing rivers and waterfalls amidst the usually parched landscape.

Human geography

The human geography of the region has been largely moulded by its physical contours. Not surprisingly, the densest population areas have grown up around the coastal areas in both Oman and the UAE, while the barren interior was (and still largely is) relatively unpopulated – the Al Ain/Buraimi conurbation straddling the border between the two countries is still the only really substantial inland city in the region, and inland towns are mainly restricted to oasis areas such as Al Ain and Liwa, or those with particular strategic military or mercantile significance, such as Nizwa and Ibra. Population levels around the coast have always been much higher, with towns developing around convenient creeks or natural harbours in places like Dubai, Sharjah, Ajman, Muscat and Sur.

Settlement into the region came from two major directions: a first wave of Arabs (known as Qahtani or Yamani – literally "Yemeni") from the Ma'rib region in what is now Yemen, and a second wave of Arabs (known as Adnani or Nizari) from the Nejd, in what is now central Saudi Arabia. Arabs of Adnani stock largely make up the current indigenous population of the UAE, while Oman is split between Adnani- and Qahtani-descended tribes. Tensions between the two ethnic groups have coloured Omani history right up until the early 20th century, and remain an important marker of cultural identity,

while physical evidence of the contrasting origins of the two groups can still be seen (compare, for instance, the faces of the Adnani-descended UAE sheikhs Zayed, Rashid and Mohammed, with their characteristically craggy, hawkish and quintessentially "Arabian" features, with the far softer and more rounded visage of Oman's Sultan Qaboos, born to a Qahtani mother in the southern province of Dhofar).

In addition, large migrations by sea from Persia resulted in extensive settlements down the Batinah coast in Oman since antiquity, whilst much more recent influxes of Iranian and Indian settlers in the UAE, and a deluge

of expats across the region, has had a further dramatic effect on the human topography of the region.

The divide between coast and interior still persists in many ways – the coast remains far more cosmopolitan, liberal and multicultural, as it always has been, while the interior remains relatively conservative.

Wildlife

Despite its largely arid and inhospitable environment, the UAE and, particularly, Oman support an unexpectedly wide range of animal life – scientific surveys have discovered no fewer than 200 species of mammal, reptile and bird even amidst the waterless dunes of the Wahibah

---

LEFT: sunset at Rub al Khali, Empty Quarter.
RIGHT: a friendly face in Oman.

Desert. The rugged Hajar mountains are where you'll find many of the region's most distinctive species, including the shaggy tahr and the legendary Arabian leopard, while inland, the desert plains are home to the majestic Arabian oryx and occasional herds of gazelle. Coastal lagoons and salt-flats support sizeable populations of migratory birds, while the offshore waters are rich in sea life, including exceptional numbers of turtles, dolphins and whales.

> Arabian oryx and other rare mammals can be seen at the Dubai Desert Conservation Reserve (www.ddcr.org), between Dubai and Al Ain, either by visiting on a day trip from Dubai or staying at the luxurious Al Maha Desert Resort, within the reserve itself.

Around 75 species of mammal can be found in the region, although almost all are rare and seldom seen in the wild. Perhaps the most famous is the Arabian leopard, while the deserts of southern Oman support populations of various small and medium-sized antelopes. Of these, the best known is the Arabian oryx (or white oryx; *Oryx leucoryx*; in Arabic, *al maha*). This has become one of the iconic animals of Oman – and, indeed, of other countries around the Gulf: one hypothesis suggests that the oryx is in fact the mythical unicorn itself, given that its two long horns can easily merge into one when the animal is seen in profile. Living in herds of around 10 to 15 animals, the remarkably strong and hardy oryx is perfectly adapted to desert life, and capable of going without water for months, surviving entirely on moisture contained in foliage. Other resident antelopes include the Arabian gazelle (or mountain gazelle; *Gazella gazella*) and the less common reem gazelle (or sand gazelle; *Gazella subgutturosa marica*).

The rare Arabian tahr (*Arabitragus jayakari*) is a mix of antelope and goat, with thick curved horns and a dense woolly fleece. It's now extremely rare in the wild, clinging to a few remote spots in the mountains. The Nubian ibex (*Capra ibex nubiana*) is another rare goat-antelope – males sport particularly impressive curved horns, reaching up to a metre in length. Other mammals (all similarly rare) include canine species such as the Arabian wolf, striped hyena and Blanford's fox, and small felines

such as the caracal, Gordon's wild cat (or sand-cat) and the prettily named but surprisingly ferocious honey badger. Rodents include the colourful Indian-crested porcupine and the small hyrax.

Birdlife is also plentiful in the region, thanks to its location on migratory routes between Europe, Asia and Africa, attracting a wide range of visiting birds, some of which also breed here – of the nearly 500 species of bird recorded in Oman, only 85 are actually permanent residents. Mountains, coast and desert all have their characteristic avian residents. Dhofar and southern Oman are particularly rich in bird-

life *(see page 158)*. Elsewhere, large numbers of migratory aquatic birds frequent the coastal lagoons and creeks, including herons, sandpipers, plovers and flamingos, which can be seen even close to central Dubai itself at the Ras al Khor bird sanctuary, as well as in many other locations around the region. Common birds of prey include the majestic Egyptian vulture, often seen surfing the thermals above the Hajar mountains. For further information about the birds of Oman, visit www.birdsoman.com, run by local experts Hanne and Jens Eriksen.

Oman's extensive coastline and relatively unspoilt marine environment also play host to an outstanding array of marine life, including numerous dolphins (spinner dolphins being the most frequently sighted, while common, bottlenose and humpback dolphins can also be found) and no fewer than 20 species of cetaceans including blue, humpback, sperm and Bryde's whales, as well as false killer whales, killer whales and whale sharks. Four of the seven main species of marine turtle also nest in Oman (green, olive ridley, hawksbill and loggerhead).

Environmental issues

The environment of the region is under increasing threat, in the UAE especially. The UAE has the largest per capita envi-

nationals hardly encourages conservation of resources either.

Major landmarks and other attractions also burn up a prodigious amount of fuel: it's been estimated that the Burj Khalifa requires cooling energy equivalent to that provided by 10,000 tonnes of melting ice per day, while Ski Dubai keeps its snow frozen in the middle of the desert at a similarly vast energy cost. Dubai and Abu Dhabi's innumerable skyscrapers are also particularly energy-inefficient, while the cost of greening large swathes of desert in Abu Dhabi emirate (a particular passion of the late Sheikh Zayed) similarly

ronmental footprint of any country in the world (slightly above the USA, almost twice that of the UK, and three times the world average). The need for year-round air-conditioning and the lack of natural water supplies (drinking water has to be created using extremely energy-intensive desalination techniques) are both partly to blame, as is the country's car-centred culture (featuring, typically, huge, petrol-hungry 4x4s) and scant public transport. The fact that utilities like water and electricty are so heavily subsidized as to be virtually free to UAE

consumes vast quantities of water, as do the myriad golf courses and swimming pools around the country. Possible environmental problems associated with the construction of the vast Palm Jumeirah in Dubai have been widely publicised, while preliminary work on the Palm Jabal Ali involved burying an entire national marine park under the island's foundations. Ironically, despite its still considerable oil reserves, Dubai now actually consumes more energy than it produces.

Ironically, it is Abu Dhabi which has for once out-thought its neighbour, headlined by the new Masdar project, a low-rise, carbon-neutral development which will eventually serve as home to some 50,000 people (see page 99).

LEFT: Arabian oryx.
ABOVE: a pair of Egyptian vultures.

DECISIVE DATES

Pre-History

c.5000–3000 BC
Evidence of coastal and inland settlements.

c.3000 BC
Magan, an area roughly corresponding with the UAE and northern Oman, supplies the city states of southern Mesopotamia with a range of raw materials, including copper.

c.2500–2000 BC
Umm an Nar period, characterised by elaborate tombs, far-reaching trade networks and sophisticated crafts.

c.2000 BC–1st millennium BC
Arab tribes arrive from southwest and central Arabia. They find coastal communities and inland wadis inhabited by people of Persian origin.

1300–300 BC
The Iron Age; development of the falaj system.

The Persian Era

563 BC
Cyrus the Great from Persia conquers Oman, founding the Achaemenid dynasty.

300 BC
The region is part of a trade network involving the whole of the Arabian peninsula, while frankincense is exported from southern Oman to Greece and Rome.

1st century AD
The *Periplus of the Erythraean Sea*, a description of trade around the coast of the Indian Ocean, designates Oman as Persian.

AD 226–640
The Sassanid period. Persian seamen control sea trade.

The Early Islamic Era

630
Islam is brought to Oman.

751
Oman elects its first Imam, Julanda bin Mas'ud.

8th–9th centuries
Arab seafaring and trading are at their height, with voyages as far as China.

10th century
Sohar in Oman is a hub of maritime trade.

14th century
Hormuz, an island off modern-day Iran, controls the mouth of the Gulf.

The Ya'aruba Dynasty in Oman

16th century
The Portuguese dominate trade in the Gulf and the Indian Ocean, capturing Muscat in 1507.

1624–1738
Ya'ruba dynasty rules Oman.

1646
Commercial treaty is signed between Oman's Imam and the British East India Company.

1650
Imam Sultan bin Saif expels the Portuguese.

1718–28
Civil war in Oman.

1730s
Saif bin Sultan II of Oman invites the Persians to help him secure his bid to be Imam.

1742
The Persians take control of Muscat.

1747
Ahmed bin Said drives the Persians from Oman and establishes the Al bu Said dynasty.

British Influence and the Founding of Dubai

1761
Abu Dhabi is founded.

1820
A British campaign to quash Qawasim "pirates" culminates in the razing of Ras al Khaimah and other Qawasim ports, including Sharjah, Umm al Qaiwain, Ajman and Lingah. British involvement in the Emirates begins.

1830s
The pearl trade is at its height.

1833
Dubai's Bani Yas sets up its own principality, ruled by the Al Maktoum family.

1853
In return for ceasing hostilities at sea, the British guarantee to protect the Trucial States from external attack.

1892
The Exclusive Agreement is signed with Britain, preventing the rulers of the Trucial Coast from forming agreements with any other foreign government.

The Trucial States, Omani Rebellions and Oil

1930s
The pearl industry declines following the arrival of the Japanese cultured pearl.

1932
Imperial Airways (later

British Airways) begins air service to Sharjah.

1936–52
The rulers of the Trucial States sign oil concessions with the Iraq Petroleum Company.

1951
A causeway is built linking Abu Dhabi to the mainland.

1952
Saudis occupy part of Buraimi, but are eventually (1955) driven out.

1954–9
Imamate rebellion under Ghalib ibn Ali in Oman.

1959
Oil is discovered in Abu Dhabi.

1962–75
Dhofar Rebellion in Oman.

1967
Oman produces oil in commercial quantities.

The Oman Renaissance and UAE Independence

1970
Accession of Sultan Qaboos bin Said in Oman.

1971
Britain withdraws from the Gulf. The United Arab Emirates is inaugurated on 2 December.

1973
Oman's first airport, Seeb International, opens.

1980
Iran–Iraq War.

1990
Iraq invades Kuwait. Gulf War ensues.

1991
Oman's Majlis Ash Shura, a consultative council with 59 elected members, is inaugurated.

1995
Oman celebrates Sultan Qaboos's silver jubilee.

2004
Death of Sheikh Zayed bin Sultan Al Nahyan, president of the UAE.

2008
Credit crunch hits the Middle East. Dubai is nearly bankrupt.

2010
Opening of Burj Khalifa, the world's tallest building.

2011
"Arab Spring" sweeps through Middle East. Clashes in Oman leave several protesters dead.

FAR LEFT: petroglyph carved into rock, Musandam. **LEFT:** overlooking Nizwa mosque. **RIGHT:** painting of Sheikh Zayed at the Al Ain Palace Museum, Abu Dhabi. **ABOVE RIGHT:** mural of Sultan Qaboos, Muscat.

ARCHAEOLOGY

Recent archaeological explorations of Oman
and the UAE have revealed a rich and varied
ancient history

If there is a general perception that the south-east corner of the Arabian peninsula has, until recent times, been relatively isolated, nothing could be further from the truth. From as early as 5000 BC, the area played an important part in the development of the ancient civilisations of the Middle East.

There are practically no historical documents originating from the UAE and Oman prior to the Islamic period, though there are references to the region by neighbouring peoples and trading partners from as early as *c.*2330 BC. Unfortunately these are few and far between, so the historical framework used by archaeologists is based primarily on the results of excavations.

Prehistoric prelude (5000–3000 BC)

Many of the earliest archaeological sites lie along the shores of the Arabian Gulf and the Gulf of Oman. Until about 16,000 years ago, when sea levels began to rise, the area now occupied by the Gulf would have formed a river valley extending as far as the Straits of Hormuz. The shoreline of the Gulf of Oman would have been distant from its present location and 100–150 metres (330–490ft) lower than the present-day mean sea level. When the sea level began to rise it attained something like its present level about 8,000 years ago, creating a variety of coastal landscapes. These varied marine habitats afforded a glut of easily obtained food such as shellfish, fish, turtle and

dugong. Mangroves attracted birdlife which could be hunted, and adjacent inland areas supported gazelle and, later on, grazing for sheep, goats and cattle.

The archaeological remains left by these early communities are distinguished by large accumulations of shells that were collected for food and then discarded. Excavation of "shell middens" at Ras al Hamra near Qurm has revealed the ground plan of small groups of circular buildings, indicated by stone foundations or arrangements of post-holes. Other finds show that the inhabitants were adept at making stone tools and shell artefacts, including personal jewellery and large shell hooks. Such items were often found amongst burials, which form large

---

LEFT: carvings at the entrance to the Grand Tomb, Hili Archaeological Park, Abu Dhabi.
RIGHT: ancient artefacts, National Museum of Ras al Khaimah.

cemeteries and hint at the social complexity of the fishing communities.

On the Gulf Coast similar shell middens are found along the margins of former lagoons, for example at Umm al Qaiwain and the Hamriyah area of Sharjah. Some of the Gulf Coast middens have also provided evidence of contact with southern Iraq from 5000–4000 BC, in particular a type of pottery called Ubaid, named after a site in southern Iraq. The pottery was clearly imported at this early date, though whether directly or indirectly has not been confirmed. However, similar finds on the island of Dalma (Abu Dhabi) suggest that the inhabitants were already accomplished sailors by this time.

Coastal midden sites were occupied up to and beyond 3000 BC. Prior to this it is probable that the arid conditions of Arabia today were not so harsh and that open grassland was available. Many of the stone tools, including finely crafted arrowheads, found in desert areas probably date from 5000–3000 BC and represent inland hunting and herding communities contemporary with the coastal communities.

The Hafit period (3000–2500 BC)

From around 3000 BC there is evidence of renewed contact between the region and southern Mesopotamia. In the late 4th millennium BC there are references in Mesopotamian texts to a place named Dilmun (now Bahrain), and towards the end of the 3rd millennium, c. 2330 BC Dilmun is mentioned along with Magan and Meluhha.

Between them, these three places supplied the city-states of southern Mesopotamia with a range of raw materials and exotic goods, including timber, stone and, above all, copper. On the basis of the abundance of copper deposits, and archaeological evidence that they were being exploited as early as the 3rd millennium BC, Magan, sometimes referred to in texts as "the Copper Mountain of Magan", is thought to be the area of southeast Arabia which loosely corresponds with the present-day UAE and Oman. Meluhha is generally identified as the Indus Valley.

Renewed contacts with Mesopotamia from the end of the 4th millennium are an indication of Magan's developing trading relations with surrounding countries, as described some

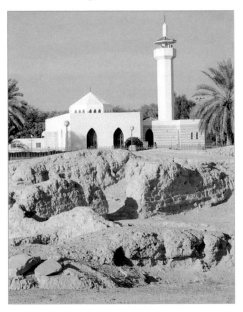

COPPER MINING

Ancient Magan was an important supplier of stone and copper. Sites in Oman such as Maysar, in the Wadi Samad area near Nizwa, have produced clear evidence for the mining, processing and export of copper on a large scale during the 3rd millennium BC, including anvil and crushing stones, a smelting oven and copper beads and rings, chisels, knives and axes. It has been estimated that up to 4,000 tonnes of copper were produced in the region in the Umm an Nar period.

Small-scale copper mining continued in northern Oman through to the late Middle Ages and beyond. However, by the late 19th century foreign competition (principally copper sheeting imported from Bombay) had extinguished the local mining industry.

Both stone and copper are still readily obtained in the UAE and Oman, and though oil and natural gas have dominated the economy for decades, recent attempts to reduce dependence on oil in Oman have seen a regeneration of the copper-mining industry. In 1983 a mine at Lasail, in Wadi al Jizzi near Sohar, was reworked for the first time since antiquity, and new deposits have since been found in Yanqul, north of Ibri, inland at Hatta, and on the Batinah Coast at Shinas. There are now a number of large-scale copper mines around Sohar, producing vast quantities of copper along with small quantities of gold and silver.

700 years later in Mesopotamian texts. Evidence includes pottery imported from Mesopotamia found in tombs.

These tombs are of a type unique to the UAE and Oman at this time, when they became a conspicuous feature of the landscape – large stone cairns, often placed in clearly visible groups along the ridges or summit of a mountain to form a dramatic skyline. Tombs of this type were first excavated at Jabal Hafit near Al Ain and are often called "Hafit tombs". Others have a characteristic beehive shape and are consequently called "beehive tombs". Both the Hafit and beehive

sufficient water for irrigation. A settlement pattern similar to that of more recent times began to emerge, and from 2500 BC there is a clear picture of what these early settlements were like.

Umm an Nar period (2500–2000 BC)

The era from 2500–2000 BC is referred to as the Umm an Nar period, named after the small island near Abu Dhabi where excavations by Danish archaeologists first produced evidence for this period. During this time a new type of tomb was introduced. Circular and averaging about 9 metres (30ft)

tombs date from the end of the 4th millennium to *c.*2500 BC.

These tombs indicate the probable distribution of settlement, and there is evidence that a farming, oasis-based economy had been introduced by this time. Excavations at the important site of Hili 8, near Al Ain, show that by 3000 BC agriculture was established, with wheat, barley and dates being cultivated. Crops and the herding of sheep, goats and cattle, introduced at an earlier date, as shown by some of the coastal midden sites, led to settlement in inland areas where there was

in diameter, it stands above ground and has a smooth exterior wall built of finely worked masonry. Some of the tombs on the island of Umm an Nar also had relief carvings on the outer wall, depicting wild animals such as gazelles and snakes, as well as domesticated animals like cattle. There are also depictions of camels, which were probably domesticated by this time.

> *Umm an Nar tombs were crowded affairs. One of the tombs at Hili is thought to have remained in use for up to two centuries, and to store the remains of several hundred people.*

LEFT: Hili Archaeological Gardens, Al Ain, Abu Dhabi.
ABOVE: Bat Tombs, Oman.

Excavation has shown that the tombs were used for multiple burials with a range of grave goods, including pottery (some imported from Mesopotamia, Iran or the Indus), stone vessels, bronze weapons, shell rings and shell and stone beads. The most spectacular Umm an Nar tomb excavated so far is displayed in Hili Archaeological Park, near Al Ain *(see page 191)*. It has carvings on the outer wall of humans as well as animals.

The excavations at Hili 8, near Hili Archaeological Park, show that settlements from this period included large defensive towers. It is probable that similar towers

were also built from the beginning of the 3rd millennium, and thus represent an established local tradition. The towers were probably surrounded by smaller buildings made from mudbricks and date palm wood. At Hili, Bat and Wadi Bahla towers are distributed over a large area. They probably defined and defended the area of habitation and cultivation.

From the beginning of the 3rd millennium local pottery had been produced, and during the Umm an Nar period pottery and other craft industries flourished. Distinctive stone vessels were manufactured and widely distributed, not only locally, but also to places in southern Iraq, Bahrain, Iran and the Indus.

Likewise, imported items continued to arrive in southeast Arabia, and the resulting distribution of exported and imported goods reflects the network of trading relations described in the Mesopotamian texts of the later 3rd millennium.

At the end of the 3rd millennium Magan ceased to be mentioned in Mesopotamian texts and Dilmun appears to have had a monopoly over the supply of goods to Mesopotamia. However, the range of exports remained much the same, with a large demand for copper, and since Dilmun had no copper sources of its own Magan probably remained the main supplier.

Recent excavations suggest that many of the 3rd-millennium settlements continued to be occupied during the 2nd millennium. However, there are radical changes in the architecture of tombs and the range of pottery and other objects produced.

Wadi Suq period (2000–1300 BC)

At the beginning of the 2nd millennium at least two types of tomb are characteristic. The first is circular, 3–4 metres (10–13ft) in diameter, with a central, below-ground, stone-lined burial chamber. Such tombs were first excavated in Wadi Suq, at the east end of Wadi Jizzi between Buraimi and Sohar in Oman. Subsequently Wadi Suq was adopted to describe the period from around 2000 to *c.* 1300 BC.

The second type of tomb characteristic of the early Wadi Suq period was first recorded at Shimmel, near Ras al Khaimah. The Shimmel-type tombs are rectangular, a few metres wide but several metres long, and stand above ground.

Imported items continue to show ongoing trading links with surrounding countries, and coastal settlements, particularly Ras al Jinz near Ras al Hadd in Oman, which appears to have flourished during the Umm an Nar and Wadi Suq periods, provide evidence for the highly developed maritime trade of this period.

The Iron Age (c.1300–300 BC)

The Iron Age saw an increase in the number and variety of settlements, which may have been due to the development of the *falaj* system of irrigation. Coastal middens continued to be occupied, villages evolved along the courses of wadis in mountainous areas, and there is evidence of larger villages of mud-brick houses, as excavated at Rumeilah and Hili 2 near Al Ain. There is also evidence of fortified hilltop settlements, such as at Lizq in Wadi Samad, Oman.

> *Wadis (the Arabic word for "valleys") are a common feature of the landscape of the UAE and Oman. Many served for millennia as important trade and migratory routes, offering relatively safe passage through otherwise perilous mountain ranges.*

important for the supply of frankincense, and by the 1st century AD maritime trade was conducted around the entire Arabian peninsula.

One of the main sites of the period is Mileiha, south of Dhaid, which appears to have been continuously occupied for 700 years, from the end of the Iron Age onwards. Excavations have recovered amphorae from Rhodes, alabaster vessels from the Yemen, and other imported goods. The town had a necropolis of monumental tombs, while traces of a fort, graves with sacrificed camels and horses have also been found. There is

As in previous periods, changes are evident in the pottery and soft-stone vessels manufactured. The discovery of distinctive vessels in neigh-bouring countries such as Bahrain indicates that maritime trade had become an important part of the regional economy.

The post-Iron Age period

From *c.*300 BC, the UAE and Oman formed part of a trade network that involved the whole of the Arabian peninsula and linked the countries of the Mediterranean with those of the Indian Ocean. Dhofar became

Left: a 5,000-year-old stone tomb at Al Ayn, Oman.
Above: the post-Iron Age site of Ad Door.

even evidence that the town was minting its own coinage.

Contemporary with this phase of occupa-tion (the first centuries AD) is Ad Door near Umm al Qaiwain, which was probably the port for inland Mileiha. Coins of the type minted at Mileiha have been found there, as well as similar graves with sacrificed camels, pottery from the eastern Mediterranean, and items from neighbouring parts of Arabia, Iraq and Iran.

In Wadi Samad there is evidence of occu-pation of the same date as Mileiha and Ad Door, and a wide range of items, some simi-lar to finds at Mileiha and Ad Door, have been excavated.

THE MARITIME HERITAGE

The UAE and Oman share an illustrious
seafaring history. As early as the 8th century,
trade vessels from the Gulf were sailing all the
way to China

The Arabian peninsula is often associated in the minds of outsiders with its desert interior and hardy tribes of wandering Bedu. In fact, much of the history, commerce and culture of the UAE and Oman has actually been played out around its coast, where a string of lively and surprisingly cosmopolitan trading towns grew up, establishing far-reaching connections with Persia, India, Africa and even as far away as China. Textiles, horses, spices and slaves were all widely traded, while the lucrative frankincense route bought enormous wealth to the ports of Dhofar. In more recent times oil has largely taken the place of more picturesque goods, while the smuggling of arms, cigarettes, gold and diamonds to Iran and India has also played a surprisingly important role in the economies of places like Dubai and the Musandam peninsula.

Maritime matters continue to play a crucial role in the contemporary life of the region, as witnessed by the huge modern container and tanker ports of Muscat, Sur, Sohar, Salalah, Fujairah and Dubai. Colourful reminders of earlier times can also be seen, most notably at the intriguing dhow wharfages in Dubai and Sharjah.

The pattern of trade

The Arabian peninsula stands between the Indian Ocean and the Mediterranean, flanked by two long seas, the Arabian Gulf (or Persian Gulf) and the Red Sea, both of which have historically served as channels down which goods have travelled from the Indian Ocean to

LEFT: dhow-building at Sur, Oman.
RIGHT: Arab passenger boat in the 13th century.

the centres of civilisation in the Near East and Mediterranean.

With the coming of Islam in the 7th century AD, both the Gulf and Red Sea were crucial to the eastern trade of the Islamic world. But it is perhaps the Gulf which has the more glorious commercial history of the two, and Oman commands the Straits of Hormuz, which join it to the Indian Ocean. As the centuries wore on, many commodities were passed on to Europe, first through the medium of Genoa and then Venice.

But not all the Indian Ocean trade was long-distance. Much of it was within the Indian Ocean itself. Over the millennia, this trading activity brought about a tremendous mixing of peoples around the coasts of the entire ocean and a lot of cultural as well as commercial exchange. The coves at Muscat and Mutrah, and the beach at Sohar, have witnessed the comings and goings of Mesopotamians, Persians, Arabs, Indians, Africans, Greeks, Jews, Turks, Italians, Portuguese and northern Europeans.

The antiquity of the sea route

By the time of the Greek and Roman empires, trade from Ethiopia, southwest Arabia and India into the Near East and Mediterranean was in full swing, much of it by camel caravan along the land routes of the Arabian pen-

The exploits of early Arabian sailors inspired the legendary stories of Sindbad the Sailor – claimed by Omanis to have been a native of the town of Sohar.

When the sea trade revived, during Sassanid rule of Persia in the 5th century, it was in the hands of Persian seamen. They controlled trade between Sri Lanka and the Gulf, to the detriment of the Red Sea. It was this tradition that the Arabs took over after the spread of Islam in the 7th century. The first named Arab

insula. Gradually this trade transferred from the land routes to the Red Sea, as seafarers from Egypt, with Mediterranean ships, began to master the monsoon routes. By c.100 BC these interlopers had discovered that in their strongly built, square-rigged ships they could sail direct from Aden to India using the southwest monsoon, something which the Indian Ocean ships with their stitched construction were too fragile to do.

A vigorous trade developed, with merchants reaching India and China, and paying for luxury goods with Roman coin. This eventually caused a serious drain of precious metals in the Roman Empire, leading to devaluation and a slump in trade in the 3rd century BC.

to make the voyage to China was an Omani in AD 750.

Medieval ships

The average Arabian seaman in pre-modern times spent his days and nights exposed to the elements, in conditions of hardship and hard work. First of all, he would have made a voyage in a smallish vessel, the planks of which were not nailed but stitched together, a mode of ship-building that came as a constant surprise to Europeans and Arabs from the Mediterranean, such as Marco Polo and the North African explorer Ibn Battuta who had first-hand experience of them.

Hull planks were stitched together edge-to-edge with coconut twine, and the ribs were fitted later – the exact opposite of European boats. Gaps were caulked with a mixture of coir and fish oil. Except in larger vessels even a partial deck or a cabin was a luxury. Ships were still pointed at both ends, and used steering oars, one on each side. The square sail had evolved into something more triangular, enabling ships to sail close to the wind, though not to tack in a modern sense.

The boat was essentially a cargo-carrying tub which needed constant maintenance. Crew and passengers accommodated themselves as

to China in such ships, and there was a huge colony of Arab merchants at Canton. By sailing all the way like this Arab merchants could cut out the middleman and make massive profits.

Gulf merchants' tales of the 8th–10th centuries describe hair-raising shipwrecks and adventures, and enormous mercantile risks. The loss of a single cargo could ruin a group of merchants and even contribute to the decline of a port. The rewards of a single successful voyage were correspondingly prodigious: a merchant could make his fortune for life. They would set out from the Omani coast in late November or early December and make the round trip to

best they could on top of the cargo, and ablutions were carried out in a precarious box slung out over the side of the boat. The main advantage of such a craft was that it was flexible in heavy surf, and therefore less likely than more robustly built ships to be smashed while coming inshore. These fragile craft could be quite large, some carrying up to 400 men.

At the height of Gulf trade, in the 9th century, Gulf and Omani seamen were sailing all the way

Left: *A View of Mutrah from the East* by R. Temple, 1809–10.
Above: *European Trading Galleons in Mutrah's Harbour,* an oil painting attributed to the Dutch painter Jan Peeters (1642–80).

China in 18 months, returning with the end of the northeast monsoon in April or May. Ships sailing to India and East Africa also made use of the northeast monsoon season. The breezes of the southwest monsoon in April to May were handy on the return from East Africa, blowing the ships back to the Omani coast.

By the 13th century the stern rudder was invented, but not the tiller: it was operated by a system of ropes, which allowed the rudder to be unshipped easily when the boat was beached.

By now Arab merchants were no longer sailing direct to China. Instead, the Chinese were sailing to the Malabar Coast and the Palk Strait between Ceylon and India, where goods were transhipped to Indian and Arab vessels. By the 13th century large junks could be seen in Malabar ports, and the 14th century saw the extraordinary Ming Voyages, when the Chinese in fleets of vast junks sailed around the shores of the Indian Ocean, reaching East Africa and the Omani coast at Dhofar.

These voyages stopped abruptly in the 1430s and the Chinese left the Indian ports. By the time of the European discovery of the East in 1498 their voyages were a distant memory.

The great ports

Medieval merchants set out from the great Islamic port of Basra on the Shatt al Arab in

Muqaddasi observed, "the hallway to China, the storehouse of the East and Iraq, and the stay of the Yemen... There is no city bigger than this on the China Sea. It is a populous and beautiful spot, where wealth and fruits are in abundance... There are wonderful markets all along the coast. Houses are high and built of teak wood and mudbricks, and there is a canal of fresh water."

Eventually Qais Island supplanted Siraf and Sohar, and by the 14th century Qais was ousted by the island of Hormuz. With its satellite ports at Qalhat in eastern Oman and Julfar near present-day Ras al Khaimah, Hormuz

For wonderful insights into the techniques of traditional Arabian dhow building and life at sea aboard one such boat, read Tim Severin's The Sindbad Voyage.

Iraq. But the large ships required to make the China run could not anchor off Basra, and so ports further down the Gulf became important points of trans-shipment – first Siraf in Persia, and then Sohar on the Omani coast.

Sohar flourished. It was at the point where trade from Aden and East Africa met the trade coming and going to India and China. Sohar was, as the 10th-century Arab geographer

completely controlled the mouth of the Gulf. By the early 1500s Muscat, with its natural harbour, had supplanted Sohar and Qalhat on the Omani coast.

Cargoes combined high-value commodities with bulk goods, because all ships need ballast. From Iraq these bulk goods were mainly dates, while the Arabian ports of the Gulf and Oman supplied dates, leather and dried fish. From East Africa the bulk goods were timber; from India, rice, dried foods, teak and other shipbuilding timber; and from China, copper cash, other metals and sugar.

But the glamour and profit were in the high-value goods, whose worth increased with every merchant and port they passed through. Oman

*The arrival of Portuguese ships in the Gulf intro-
duced profound changes to Arab shipbuilding,
including nailed instead of stitched construction,
square sterns and tiller-operated rudders –
although shipbuilding continued to be carried
out in the time-honoured way, entirely by eye.*

and the Arabian shore of the Gulf provided
horses, frankincense and pearls. From India
and Ceylon came gemstones, glass, ironware,
swords, cotton cloth, spices and aromatics
such as sandalwood and incense. China's silk,

porcelain, lacquerwork, metalwork and other
manufactures were in big demand. In exchange,
the Islamic lands sent glassware, carpets, mus-
lin, brocade, perfumes, incense, weapons and
armour – but also money.

Perhaps the most valuable raw commodities
came from East Africa: gold, slaves, ivory, rhino
horn and leopard skins. Of all the seafaring
Arabs, it was the Omanis who dominated the
rich East African trade, introducing its hugely
prized products into the economies of the
Islamic Near East.

Left: Portuguese carracks. **Above:** Vasco da Gama's
voyage around the Cape of Good Hope in 1498
changed the face of seafaring in the Gulf.

Portuguese power

It was into East Africa, in 1498, that the first
Western threat to local control of maritime
trade since Greco-Roman times arrived:
the Portuguese. Under Vasco da Gama the
Portuguese rounded the Cape of Good Hope
into the Indian Ocean in 1498, and proceeded
to dominate the international trade of the
Gulf and Indian Ocean for over a century.
Portuguese trade was a royal monopoly carried
forward by gunpowder and force of arms, and
the small Portuguese fleets had an impact on
the people of the Indian Ocean shores out of
all proportion to their numbers. They came in
search of Indian spices and the spice islands of
Indonesia, and of other luxury goods which
the Venetian monopoly had made so costly
in Europe. Their greatest colonial visionary,
Affonso d'Albuquerque, quickly realised the
strategic importance of Aden, Hormuz and
Malacca in the trade.

Hormuz, whose inhabitants were a mixture of
Arabs and Persians, commanded the Musandam
Strait, and in spite of being a waterless island
had grown immensely wealthy by raising customs dues on all cargoes passing up the Gulf.

The Portuguese took Hormuz after their
capture of Muscat in 1507. While they diverted
some of the trade from the Far East around the
Cape of Good Hope, they profited from the rest
by levying customs dues on the Gulf route just
as the Hormuzis had done before them. They
built a line of forts along the Omani, African
and Indian coasts and farther east, with Goa
as their capital. Muscat, Sohar and Hormuz
were key to their control of the Gulf. The twin
Portuguese forts dominating Muscat's old harbour were built at this time.

The Omani Empire

The Portuguese saw off Ottoman Turkish attacks
in the 16th century, but others were to come
early in the 17th century from Persia, Holland,
England and Oman. Unlike the Portuguese, the
other European nations arrived as merchant
companies wishing to trade in peace.

During the 1630s and 1640s a renascent
Omani Imamate succeeded in ejecting the
Portuguese from Muscat and their coastal
forts. The Omanis captured Portuguese ships,
and went on to establish a maritime empire.
Their ships and seamen, who often included
European renegades, were an equal match for

those of the Portuguese, English, Dutch and French. By the end of the 17th century they had also taken control of a stretch of the East African coast down to Zanzibar and Mombasa, expelling the Portuguese. Oman became a power on parts of the Persian coast, and even at times up the Gulf as far as Bahrain.

In the mid-18th century Oman fell victim to civil war and a revived Persia under Nadir Shah, who took Muscat in 1742. But after 1744 the reunited Omanis drove out the Persians. Omani fortunes began to revive again, just as a rival sea power, the Qawasim of Sharjah and Ras al Khaimah, rose up in the southern Gulf.

The Qasimi "pirates", 1722–1820

The Qawasim of Ras al Khaimah seized Lingah on the Persian shore following the death of Nadir Shah in 1747. The rise of their ports at Sharjah and at Ras al Khaimah, which had replaced ancient Julfar just to the north, was remarkably rapid and brought them into conflict with Omani maritime ambitions.

By 1780 the Qawasim were firmly established on the Persian side of the southern Gulf too. Very soon they began to threaten Muscat's control of the trade from India and East Africa into the Gulf.

By now the British East India Company was set to become involved. The Gulf was becom-

PEARLING

Up until the 20th century, the UAE's great natural resource was not oil, but pearls, gathered from the sea in conditions of extreme hardship and considerable danger. Diving took place in the hot summer months and boats were out at sea for up to four months at a time. The men would dive on empty stomachs (to avoid getting cramp) to depths of over 20 metres (65ft) and were vulnerable to attacks by jellyfish and sharks. By the turn of the 20th century there were about 1,200 pearling boats based in ports along the UAE coast, manned by some 22,000 men – a very considerable proportion of the population at that time.

ing increasingly vital to communications between London and the Company's growing possessions in India. When Napoleon's occupation of Egypt in 1798 blocked the Red Sea route one British response was to enter into treaty relations with the Omani Sultan in Muscat, a move which inevitably placed them in opposition to the Qawasim. At the same time, the British blamed the Qawasim for the piracy that then plagued the Gulf and led a series of seaborne campaigns against the so-called "Pirate Coast". These climaxed in 1820 in the destruction of the Qasimi fleets and the first of the Maritime Truces.

British officials almost certainly exaggerated the Qawasim's involvement in piracy, but their campaign against them was determined. In 1806 the British attacked Ras al Khaimah. In 1809 Ras al Khaimah, Lingah, Luft and Shinas were burnt and ships destroyed, and Ras al Khaimah was bombarded again in 1816. Finally, between 1819 and 1820, a large naval and military operation was mounted which razed Ras al Khaimah. Its ships were destroyed, along with those of Sharjah, Umm al Qaiwain, Ajman, Lingah and other Qasimi ports.

The maritime peace, 1820–53

It was only after this expedition that maritime peace became a real prospect, and

in 1820. Dubai too was included, but Dubai's real emergence as the chief trading port on the southern Gulf was due to the migration there in 1833 of the Al bu Falasah, a clan of the Bani Yas from Abu Dhabi. Its leading family, Al Maktoum, set about turning themselves into the merchant princes of the Gulf Coast, a position they have held ever since.

One long-term result of the peace was an expanding pearl trade. An ancient Gulf industry, pearling was recorded by Greek and Roman writers and probably traces its origin to the late Stone Age. Pearls are not found in abundance in Omani waters out-

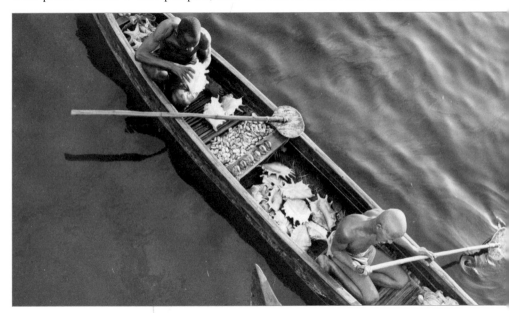

Britain's continuous and official involvement began in what are now the Emirates. The destruction of Qasimi ports and ships was followed by a "General Treaty of Peace with the Arab Tribes" in 1820. Britain's primary aim was to pacify the seas and so secure its route to India.

The decline of the Qawasim was hastened by the growth of Abu Dhabi and Dubai as competitors on the pearl banks. Abu Dhabi had emerged only in the late 18th century and its sheikh had signed the General Treaty of Peace

Left: fanciful depiction of a pirate raid.
Above: pearl divers selling seashells to the passengers of passing ships near Muscat in 1955.

side the Gulf, but the shallow southern Gulf off the Trucial Coast was rich in pearl oysters and the warm sea shallow enough to make diving feasible.

In 1835, the rulers of Sharjah, Dubai, Ajman and Abu Dhabi signed an inviolable truce under British pressure, outlawing acts of war at sea during the pearling season. Made year-round for 10 years in 1843, it became the Perpetual Treaty in 1853.

Perpetual peace

With the Perpetual Treaty of Peace of 1853, the rulers of the Gulf Coast agreed to cease hostilities at sea, and in return the British undertook to protect them against external attack.

The British were determined not to become involved in disputes on land. However, as the 1860s wore into the 1870s, the line between peace at sea and peace on land became more and more difficult to discern.

By then the Gulf's importance as a channel for imperial communications had greatly increased. In 1862 the British started a fortnightly steamer service from Bombay to Muscat and some of the Gulf ports. Equally significantly, in 1864 they laid the first submarine telegraph cable in the Gulf, running from Karachi to Bushire and Fao via the Musandam peninsula in Oman.

sons, Thuwaini and Majid, into Oman and Zanzibar.

This split was economically damaging to Oman. Other blows to its maritime prosperity followed in quick succession. Steamships were bad enough, but the Suez Canal was opened in 1869, making the Red Sea much more important than the Gulf. In addition, the British had set about suppressing the slave and arms trades, which were lucrative sources of income for merchants and rulers in Muscat, Sur and Dubai.

Oman then began a long period of economic decline which lasted right up until the 1960s,

Oman's decline

British support to Muscat continued throughout the 19th century and into the 20th. Sultan Said (ruled 1807–56) maintained a fleet of warships and merchantmen which included European ships, and even sent one of them to New York and London in 1840 and 1842.

By the time he died in 1856 the Omani maritime realm extended once again from enclaves on the Persian coast to large stretches of the East African coast. Although hampered by Britain's anti-slaving policy, Sultan Said developed the economy of Zanzibar, which became almost a second Omani capital. After his death, the Omani Empire was split between his two

and its role in the international sea trade of the Indian Ocean all but vanished.

Great power rivalry

After 1869, rivalry among the Great Powers began to threaten Britain's position in the Gulf. The Ottomans occupied Al Hasa and Qatar in 1871, and claimed eight Trucial Coast settlements, and in 1887 a resurgent Persia took over some Qasimi territory on the Persian shore. This prompted Britain to obtain from the

ABOVE: life on Dubai's Creek before the bridges were built across it.
RIGHT: the boat-building yard in Sur, the last traditional boatyard in Oman.

sheikhs of the Trucial Coast a written assurance not to correspond or agree with any other government, or to allow agents of other governments to reside in their territories.

By the early 1890s both France and Germany were trying to establish a presence in the region. In March 1892, therefore, Britain developed the 1887 assurance into an Exclusive Agreement, the basis of her relations with the Trucial States until 1971. Nonetheless, in the 1890s Russia also joined the race to seek a foothold in the Gulf.

By the end of World War I all these threats had evaporated, and Britain found itself in a position of unprecedented power in the Gulf.

20th-century developments

The first two-thirds of the 20th century were a period of long, slow decline for Oman, reflected in the steady dip in prosperity of its coastal ports – Britain's ongoing attempts to stamp out the lucrative trade in smuggled arms was particularly keenly felt. Sultan Qaboos's accession to the throne in 1970 marked a period of dramatic change and modernisation. A string of huge new modern ports were constructed at Muscat, Salalah, Sur and Sohar, both for trade and as conduits for the country's new oil exports, while more informal maritime trading networks were also established – the smuggling run between Khasab and Iran was particularly lucrative.

Smuggling also played a crucial role in the burgeoning economy of Dubai, while the country's visionary leader Sheikh Rashid commissioned vast new docks at Port Rashid and Jabal Ali, as well as a new dry dock facility – which proved particularly lucrative during the Iran–Iraq War thanks to the number of tankers damaged in the conflict which limped here for repairs. The vast new port at Fujairah, the world's third-largest oil-refuelling port after Rotterdam and Singapore, was another major development.

Vestiges of the region's seafaring past survive even so, most obviously in the dhow-wharfages of Dubai and Sharjah, and in the various dhow-building yards scattered around the coast – while the region's traditional old boats have found a new lease of life as pleasure craft for tourists and locals, offering a living link between the Gulf's historic seafaring past and burgeoning economic present.

LAST VESTIGES OF A WAY OF LIFE

The coast of the UAE and Oman was once lined with dozens of dhow-building yards, turning out hundreds of boats a year for local fishermen and traders, and providing a vital element in the region's economic life. In recent years, however, the advent of modern boat-building techniques and production lines has inevitably caused this most traditional and labour-intensive of Arabian industries to decline, almost to the point of extinction, and the high cost of commissioning a new wooden dhow means that local fishermen now generally prefer more modern, albeit more functional, vessels.

Sur is now home to the last surviving traditional boatyard in Oman *(see page 151)*, although dhow-building yards can be seen in the UAE at Dubai, Abu Dhabi, Ajman, Umm al Quwain and Ras al Khaimah (albeit in significantly reduced circumstances compared to times past). All these places continue to produce traditional wooden dhows following time-honoured designs, meticulously crafted by hand using only the simplest of tools and offering a living link with the artisanal traditions of centuries past – even if the work is now carried out by Indian craftsmen rather than by Omanis or Emiratis. Despite the boatyards' apparently bleak future, one potential lifeline has emerged in recent years with the increasing popularity of traditional dhow cruises amongst visiting tourists, providing the old boatyards with a new source of income, and meaning that the ancient traditions of Arabian boat-building may yet survive a little longer into the 21st century.

OMAN'S GREAT DYNASTIES

The Ya'ruba dynasty succeeded in uniting Oman and turning it into a place of learning and elegance. The Al Bu Said turned it into an imperial power

The history of Oman from 1624 to the present is the story of two great dynasties: the Ya'ruba (1624–1738) and the Al Bu Said (1742 to the present), whose leaders have succeeded – with varying degrees of success – in forging the disparate tribes and regions of Oman into a single unified country. These two dynasties have provided Oman with some of the most charismatic figures in its long and often turbulent history, leaders who succeeded in facing off against the Persians and Portuguese, whilst also establishing Oman as a major naval power with dominions as far away as East Africa and Pakistan.

Before the Ya'rubas

Most of the history of Oman before the coming of the Ya'rubas is one of conflict and fragmentation between rival Arab tribes and Persian settlers – even the coming of Islam in 630 AD failed to bring stability, as the Omanis and their "heretical" Ibadi creed became the target for repeated punitive attacks by the Caliphs in Damascus or Baghdad.

The origins of the Omani ruling dynasties can perhaps be traced back to the election, in 751 AD, of the country's first Imam. Elected by popular choice, the Imam served as the spiritual head of Oman's Ibadi community and enjoyed an often considerable measure of temporal authority as well, although much of the country continued to be divided along tribal lines and controlled by local governors and warlords from the string of forts which could be found dotted across the country.

LEFT: Oman's emblem of two crossed swords with a Khanjar and belt on the Palace gates, Muscat.
RIGHT: Oman's current Sultan Qaboos belongs to the Al bu Said dynasty, in power since 1747.

Twenty-six imams ruled, mainly from Nizwa, between 751 and 1154, at which point they were replaced by the kings (*maliks*) of the Nabhan dynasty, based in their gigantic fort in Bahla, from where they exercised control over much of the country. Little is known of the 350-odd years of Nabhani rule, which continued until the early 1500s and the arrival of the Portuguese, who occupied the coast and put a temporary end to Omani sovereignty.

The Ya'ruba dynasty

According to Omani chroniclers the first Imam of the Ya'ruba dynasty, Nasir bin Murshid, made the "sun of salvation" shine on the long-afflicted people of Oman. His reputation rested on unifying the country and capturing Sur and Quriyat from the Portuguese and weakening their hold on the Omani coast.

On Nasir's death in 1649 his cousin Sultan bin Saif was elected Imam and succeeded in ousting the Portuguese from Muscat, where they had been entrenched since the arrival of Affonso d'Albuquerque in 1507. He continued the unification of the country and built the great round fort at Nizwa (see page 139). At this time Oman had considerable sea power, which was used to attack the Portuguese in East Africa.

Sultan's son Bil'arub succeeded him in 1688, although the new Imam's brother, Saif bin Sultan, eventually became stronger, was elected Imam and succeeded his brother. During his reign the Omanis succeeded in considerably weakening Portuguese power in East Africa, where they had been strong since 1503. When Saif died in 1711 his son Sultan bin Saif II became Imam and was another strong ruler.

The unification of the country under these five rulers led to commercial prosperity, the encouragement of learning, and buildings of strength, beauty and elegance such as the magnificent castle at Jabrin, built by Bil'arub. The first trading agreements without the British were made during the Ya'ruba period, in 1646 and 1659.

> By the time of his death in 1711, Saif bin Sultan is said to have owned 28 ships, 700 male slaves, and a third of all the date palms in Oman.

On Sultan's death in 1718, the unity which Oman had known for nearly a century came to an end and civil war ensued. Fighting over the succession led to tribal animosity, and the whole of Oman became embroiled in desultory warfare between the two traditional factions of the Ghafiri and the Hinawi. In the late 1730s Saif bin Sultan II – one of the rival claimants to the Imamate, the other being Muhanna bin Sultan – invited the Persians under Nadir Shah to intervene on his behalf, a decision he came to regret as the Persians refused to give up their conquest.

The two rival Imams had died by 1745 and no Ya'rubi claimant came forward. Meanwhile Ahmed bin Said, who held the fort at Sohar, continued to fight the Persians, becoming both a hero and the elected Imam. In 1747 he succeeded in driving the Persians out.

The Al bu Said

Thus began the Al bu Said dynasty, which continues to rule Oman to the present day.

Ahmed himself was a man of outstanding courage, vigour, enterprise, generosity and personality. These qualities were sorely needed at the time. At home he was a good administrator of a fairly strong centralised government and he had a liberal reputation. He had in his retinue scholars, Islamic judges and notables. His bodyguard consisted of some 1,000 freemen, 1,000

Zanzibaris and 100 Nubian slaves. Abroad he led an expedition against the Persians at the request of the people of Basrah in southern Iraq, and the Mogul emperor Sha Alam sent an embassy to make a treaty to assist Ahmed against his enemies and to establish in Muscat a resident mission in what came to be known as the "Nabob's house".

Ahmed died in 1783 and his grandson Hamad became the de facto ruler, though his father, Said, had been elected Imam. On Hamad's death in 1788, Sultan – another son of Imam Ahmed bin Said – took the reins of government, though Said remained nominally Imam. Sultan was brave and of noble countenance, and both the British and the French, whose interests were in conflict in the east as well as in Europe, treated him and addressed him as if he were the Imam. He was, however, killed at Lingeh in southern Persia in 1804 by the Qawasim of Ras al Khaimah, who were at war with the Omanis over trade.

Said bin Sultan, often known as "Said the Great", succeeded his father, Sultan, and reigned for 52 years until 1856. Although some of the nobles who held the great castles were often in rebellion and there were incursions by the Wahhabis from what is now Saudi Arabia, his internal authority was in no real doubt. Europeans who met him were impressed by his

It was, however, in Africa that he made his deepest impression, and from 1829 his heart and main interests lay there. This was to have profound results later for the sultanate. He sought alliances with local queens in Madagascar and Mozambique and controlled the main Arab settlements on the east coast of Africa, making Zanzibar his second capital and transferring the Omani state archives there. He was very much the "Sailor Sayyid" and had 20 ships of his own for private trade – which he delighted in commanding himself – and paid much attention to the Omani navy. Britain and Oman had been in treaty

commanding figure, his courtly, dignified and affable manner and his kindness both to his own people and to foreign visitors.

Said's influence in the Arabian seas was considerable. Like his father he sought to control the trade passing through the Strait of Hormuz, and to this end he retained control of places on the north of the Gulf which had been acquired by Sultan. These were Hormuz, Qishm and Henjam islands together with Gwadar on the coast of Makran, which remained a part of Oman until 1958, and Chahbar.

LEFT: portrait of Sayyid Said bin Sultan Al bu Said.
ABOVE: Feisal bin Turki.
RIGHT: Taimur bin Feisal.

Said the Great enjoyed close relations with the British, giving them lavish gifts including, in 1854, the four Hallaniyat Islands off the coast of Dhofar. The British foreign secretary, unable to reciprocate such largesse, sent the Sultan a snuffbox in return.

alliance since 1800, but Said also negotiated a Treaty of Amity and Commerce with the USA in 1834.

He gave fresh life to interests in East Africa, particularly by introducing cloves as a cash crop in Zanzibar and establishing rice plantations. Many European travellers have left accounts of him, and Burton, Speke, Livingstone, Grant and Stanley all had good reason to thank the Al bu Said rulers of Zanzibar for assistance in their African explorations. He had 36 children, but a problem arose between two of his sons after his death in 1856 on a voyage to Zanzibar. Thuwaini in Muscat claimed the whole Sultanate but Majid in Zanzibar also claimed it.

The matter was referred to Lord Canning, the Viceroy and Governor-General of India – though the Sultanate had always been regarded as an independent state. With British pragmatism Lord Canning decided that Majid should rule Zanzibar and pay 40,000 crowns a year to the ruler in Muscat to adjust the inequality in

son of Said bin Sultan. Turki won the day in a battle in Wadi Dhank in 1870 and was recognised by the British. This event has present-day significance, as the Basic Law of the State issued in 1996 specifies that the Sultan of Oman "shall be a male descendant of Sayyid Turki bin Said bin Sultan", who is also "a legitimate son of Omani Muslim parents."

Turki was Sultan until 1888, although he had to cope with rivalries. He was then succeeded by his son, Feisal, who took over at the age of 23 and ruled until his death in 1913. Taimur bin Feisal followed him until 1932, when he abdicated in favour of his son Said bin Taimur.

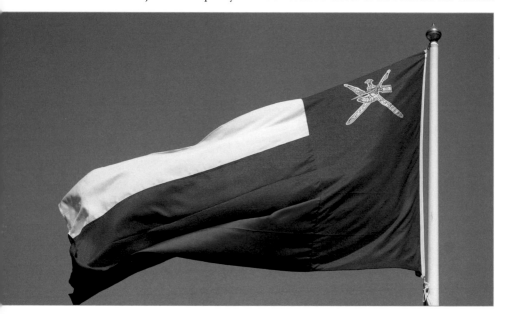

the inheritance, as Zanzibar was at this time by far the richer part. From then on the two parts remained separate, though governed by members of the same family until 1964, when Zanzibar was incorporated into Tanzania.

Thereafter the fortunes of Oman as a maritime power declined, accelerated by the introduction of steamers by the British India Steam Navigation Company in 1862. This put the Omanis at a disadvantage since their ships ceased to be competitive in the carrying trade.

Thuwaini was killed by his son Salim in 1866. A struggle for control of the Sultanate ensued between Azzan bin Qais, based in Rustaq, who headed the tribes of the interior, and Turki, who had been governor of Sohar and was another

During these reigns the interior of the country was not always at one with the Sultans and their jurisdiction on the coast. The strong sheikhs of the Harth tribe in the Sharqiyah posed a particular problem, and the very name of the country, Muscat and Oman, reflected this dichotomy.

In 1913 the tribes of the interior elected Salim bin Rashid al Kaharusi as Imam. Eventually accommodation was reached with an agreement – sometimes called (erroneously) the "Treaty of Seeb" – under which Taimur bin Feisal agreed not to interfere in the affairs of the interior, not to impose taxation in excess of 5 percent and to allow the tribes of the interior to enter Muscat and the coastal towns in safety and freedom. This administrative *modus vivendi* – although in a sense it re-emphasised the historical differences between coast and interior – worked satisfactorily until 1954, when the Imam Mohammed bin Abdulla al Kharusi died and the new Imam Ghalib, with his brother Talib, tried to establish central Oman as a separate principality. This matter was not settled on the ground until 1959, and even then the problem was of such a proportion that the "Question of Oman" came up every year at the General Assembly of the United Nations until 1971.

Sultan Said bin Taimur took over a country which was still in debt, the economic situation

In 1967 a local rebellion of the Dhofar Liberation Front in the south of the country grew into something more serious, when it received support from the Marxist People's Democratic Republic of Yemen. The intentions of the main revolutionary body were made clear in their name: "The People's Front for the Liberation of Oman and the Arabian Gulf". The situation reached such a point that Said was displaced by his son Qaboos on 23 July 1970.

The reign of Sultan Qaboos

Sultan Qaboos, the 12th member of the Al bu Said dynasty, was 30 on his accession, and he

exacerbated by the general depression of the late 1920s and early 1930s. By his own sustained and patient efforts he largely restored the situation. His stewardship ensured that when Sultan Qaboos took over in 1970 the state's finances were in a relatively flourishing state. A man of great charm and ability, Said was unable to abandon the habits of economy and careful husbandry which had become ingrained after many years of hardship, even when oil revenues began to accrue to Oman after 1967.

LEFT: Oman's flag: white represents peace and prosperity, red the struggle to liberate and unify Oman, and green Islam. ABOVE: military bands at the Omani National Day celebrations, Muscat.

proclaimed his faith in the future by announcing that his country would be known as "The Sultanate of Oman" instead of "Muscat and Oman". He also said in his first speech that under a new flag people would no longer distinguish between the coast and the interior and the southern province of Dhofar. Oman was to be a single country. The auguries were, however, not auspicious. Sultan Said had made no effort to seek international recognition, though his country was and had always been regarded as independent. He remained happy under the penumbra of the British, making it easier for the Imam Ghalib to establish relations with a number of Arab states, leading to "Imamate Offices" in Cairo, Damascus, Riyadh and Beirut.

Apart from the Omanis in rebellion in Dhofar, there were many other Omanis in opposition to Sultan Said, and young men, despairing about the limited educational facilities offered by the only three schools in the country, had sought education abroad – especially in Egypt and the Soviet Union. Thus at home the young Sultan found a country severely affected by the brain drain as well as lacking the infrastructure and services of a modern state. Abroad he had yet to acquire new friends. Only Britain and India were represented diplomatically in Muscat, each with a Consul-General.

There was a shortage of Omanis with the training to bring Oman into the modern world. But the Sultan and the Omanis themselves were undaunted, and with the help of Britain and others began the process. Ministers were appointed, and the governments structured to enable Oman to become a modern state using the gradually increasing oil revenues. The objects were to establish internal peace and security; to frustrate attacks inspired from abroad; to attract back talented but disaffected Omanis; and to gain international recognition.

Early in Sultan Qaboos's reign, Oman also revived its interest in East Africa and many

IMAM VERSUS SULTAN

Oman's history has developed around two contrasting traditions: the Imamate and the Sultanate. The country's first leaders, the Imams, were traditionally regarded as religious figureheads (although they also often wielded considerable temporal power as well). Imams were chosen by the people according to their personal qualities rather than their social origins, and could be deposed if they were deemed to be acting in an unsatisfactory manner – an early and unusual example of traditional Arabian democracy in action.

The emergence of the Ya'ruba and later Al Bu Said dynasties complicated this original picture, with leadership becoming hereditary and absolute, rather than popular and democratic. Many of the early Ya'ruba rulers took the title of

Imam, although by the beginning of the Al Bu Said dynasty the post had become increasingly irrelevant, and by the beginning of the 19th century had fallen into disuse.

Over a century passed without an Imam until 1913, when the tribes of the interior – by now in more or less constant rebellion against the sultans down on the coast in Muscat – unexpectedly elected a new Imam to serve as a figurehead for their cause. Things came to a head during the 1950s, when Imam Ghalib of Nizwa led the popular uprising known as the Jebel War against Sultan Said bin Taimur. The rebellion was eventually suppressed, however, and Ghalib was forced into exile, where he died – Oman's last Imam – in 2009.

Zanzibaris and Kenyans of Omani origin were welcomed to Oman, and subsequently played important roles in its continuing development.

Goodwill missions were despatched to Arab countries, and in 1971 applications were lodged to join the Arab League and the UN. That both were successful shows that the international community accepted that genuine change had taken place, and the "Question of Oman" was removed from the agenda of the UN.

However, the main challenge to Oman's future in 1971 lay in Dhofar. Although Sultan Qaboos had offered a general amnesty immediately on his accession, the initial effect on the

the Sultan was able, on 1 December 1975, to announce the end of the war.

The Omani renaissance

Following the resolution of the Dhofar conflict, Sultan Qaboos was able to focus entirely on the massive challenge of developing his moribund country. At the time of Qaboos's accession in 1970, Oman had become an inward-looking backwater that lagged centuries behind the modern world. There were only three schools in the whole country (in Muscat, Mutrah and Salalah), no newspapers, radio or television, no civil service and only one hospital (with just 23

rebels was minimal. Between 1972 and 1975, however, the military balance began to shift in the Sultan's favour, especially as the "hearts and minds" campaign began to carry conviction, and rebels were able to see for themselves that a new era had indeed begun. The growing physical signs of development brought an increasing number of rebels over to the government side. Thus, as a result of a hard military campaign – fought with the help of Britain, Iran and Jordan in particular – combined with civil measures,

LEFT: Omani schoolboys. Most wear the traditional embroidered Omani cap, the *kummah.*
ABOVE: Omani schoolgirls. Until the 1960s girls received no official education.

beds). The average Omani life expectancy was just 47. Muscat still closed its gates at night and, apart from the road to the little airport at Bait al Falaj, there were only two graded roads in the whole country – from Muscat to Sohar and from Muscat to Fahud.

One of the Sultan's first acts was to encourage general education, and schools in makeshift tents were immediately opened in many places. From this small beginning the Omani educational system has reached standards unimaginable earlier. At its apex is the Sultan Qaboos University, which opened to students in 1986.

Dramatic changes in public health also ensued – so much so that it is no longer complaints common to the Third World that are of most concern to Omani doctors, but illnesses of the First World, such as heart disease and cancer. The average life expectancy is now around 74. There are now over 50 hospitals and some 120 clinics all over the country.

Sultan Qaboos's achievement in building Oman into a modern state is also illustrated by the many beautiful buildings which have been erected – mosques, government buildings, palaces and private houses. Many are based on traditional buildings, which the government has done much to restore all over the country.

Modern Oman at home and abroad

Economically, modern Oman operates through a series of five-year plans with the emphasis on diversifying the economy and moving away from an over-reliance on steadily dwindling oil reserves – with the stated aim of reducing oil's contribution to GDP from the current 40 percent to less than 10 percent by 2020. Key to this diversification are the vast new industrial zones which have sprung up around the country, centred on the massive ports at Sohar, Sur and Salalah (plus, in the future, Duqm).

Politically, progress has been slower. Oman remains an absolute monarchy, with an unusually high concentration of power in the hands of Sultan Qaboos, even compared to

neighbouring states such as the UAE (where power tends to be shared more equally amongst members of the ruling families). Moves towards some form of popular representation have been made, albeit tentatively. In 1981 a State Consultative Council, the Majlis ad Dawla, was established, with 55 members directly appointed by the Sultan. Ten years later came the establishment of the larger Majlis ash Shura, with 83 members elected by popular vote – although its has no legislative powers, serving in a purely advisory role, with all final decisions still being made by Sultan Qaboos and his advisers.

> The Majlis ad Dawla, whose members are directly appointed by Sultan Qaboos, now has nine women amongst its 59 councillors; the 83-strong Majlis ash Shura, whose members are chosen by popular vote, has just two.

The role of women is also evolving. The first women members of the Majlis ad Dawla were appointed by the Sultan in 2000, while women were finally given the vote in 2003. There are now more women than men in higher education, while they also make up around a third of the country's civil service. Women are also eligible to stand for election to the Majlis ash Shura (see box above).

Oman plays an increasingly important role in regional and international affairs thanks to its geographical location on the Indian Ocean and the south side of the Strait of Hormuz, which gives it a strategic importance beyond its size and wealth. For this as well as historical reasons the Omani armed forces have benefited from a large proportion of the Omani budget.

In foreign affairs there has been an extraordinary change since 1970. After admission to the Arab League and United Nations, Omani foreign policy – which was very much that of the Sultan personally – was to reinforce its age-long connections with India and Pakistan and to develop relations with other Arab and neighbouring and friendly states, notably with the moderate states of Egypt and Jordan.

Oman's foreign policy has been empirical and pragmatic and is based on good neighbourliness, non-alignment and the encouragement of co-operation between the Gulf states and particularly those of the GCC (Gulf Co-operation Council). Oman's pragmatic policies often appeared in the past to run counter to the political wisdom of the day, but have been subsequently applauded as far-sighted.

The Arab Spring and after

Early 2011 ushered in a wave of tumultuous events – the so-called "Arab Spring" – which saw regimes toppled in Tunisia, Egypt, Yemen and Libya, and widespread clashes in Bahrain, Syria and elsewhere. Even in normally tranquil Oman repercussions were felt, with a series of nationwide protests, including clashes with police during which several demonstrators were killed. The demonstrations were uniquely Omani, however, in that without exception all the protestors pledged their unswerving loyalty to Sultan Qaboos, focusing on more local problems like ministerial nepotism and corruption, low wages and a lack of jobs.

Qaboos, in return, responded by immediately by sacking 12 ministers, raising the minimum wage and promising to create 50,000 new jobs (although no one seemed quite sure where the money or jobs were going to come from). Most interestingly, he also hinted at the possibility of the Majlis ash Shura being given real legislative powers – the first move towards genuine democracy in Oman – although exact details of how these reforms might work and when they might be introduced remain somewhat vague.

There are still significant challenges, even so. The country's burgeoning birth rate means that increasing numbers of young, educated Omanis are entering the workforce without jobs to go to, despite the government's best efforts to diversify the economy and create new industry and employment in places like Sohar, Sur and Salalah. Resentment against the number of expat workers taking jobs in the country was also a feature of the Arab Spring protests, and is unlikely to go away. And, finally, the troublesome question of who will eventually succeed Sultan Qaboos *(see box right)* is beginning to cast an increasingly long shadow over the country's future.

Despite these potential pitfalls, much has been achieved. A study in 2010 by the

United Nations Development Programme rated Oman as the "most improved" country over the past 40 years out of the 135 it surveyed, highlighting the lightning speed of progress since 1970 and the general harmony which has been created in a state once riven with faction. And meanwhile the Omanis themselves retain the courtesy and charm for which they are renowned, still justifying the words of the 19th-century traveller J.S. Buckingham: "The people seemed to me to be the cleanest, neatest, best dressed, and most gentlemanly… and inspired a feeling of confidence, goodwill and respect."

LEFT: Sultan Qaboos addresses the opening session of the Council of Oman in Muscat in 2011.
RIGHT: Grace Busaidiyah, the first woman elected to the 83-member Majlis Al Shura.

THE SUCCESSION QUESTION

One of the major questions hanging over Oman at present is the question of who will eventually succeed the ageing Sultan Qaboos – the Sultan himself remains childless, while his autocratic ruling style (in which he holds most of the principal offices of government himself) means that no strong personalities have yet emerged to take over the reins. Qaboos himself has declined to name a successor, saying that (according to established Omani tradition) it will be up to the royal family to decide – although he has also added that, if a unanimous decision cannot be reached, he has left the name of his own preferred candidate, written on two pieces of paper which are kept locked up in safes in Muscat and Salalah.

THE UAE FROM RAGS TO RICHES

How the discovery of oil and an urgent need for security persuaded seven of the Trucial sheikhdoms to put aside local rivalries and form a federation

After more than a quarter of a century of existence, the United Arab Emirates has proved to be the Arab world's most successful attempt at unity, despite widespread scepticism at its formation in 1971. Attempts by Egypt under Gamal Abdel Nasser and later by Libya under Muammar Gaddafi to merge with other states were short-lived, and the squabbles surrounding such moves made the emotive concept of the "Arab nation" something of a laughing stock among commentators outside the region. The UAE was one of the most unlikely bids for unity, but has shown itself to be the exception to the rule.

Old roots

The well-known rags-to-riches story of the Gulf states of Arabia created by the oil boom of the 1970s and 1980s caused many commentators to look upon the peoples of the region as upstarts. The UAE is quite new as a state – and its inhabitants are rather proud to be nouveaux riches – but these once largely maritime peoples can trace their roots back to prehistoric times. Excavations at Umm an Nar (now in the shadow of an oil refinery), an island off Abu Dhabi, and elsewhere show that in these early times the Gulf Arabs were under two influences – those of Mesopotamia and of the Indus civilisation in India.

The coastal dwellers were the first to deal with European travellers, but inland the Bedu (see page 69) continued their timeless nomadic existence or settled in places where they could grow a few crops, such as dates, or graze small

LEFT: former UAE president Sheikh Zayed bin Sultan Al Nahyan celebrates the end of Ramadan, 1962.
RIGHT: aerial view of Abu Dhabi town, 1962.

numbers of livestock. The Bedu in particular achieved their sense of belonging not in terms of the districts or fixed borders within which they conducted their spartan lives but through their tribal allegiances to a local sheikh. Long before the rise of Islam in the 7th century, the land that is now the UAE and the other Gulf states – Kuwait, Bahrain, Qatar, Saudi Arabia and Oman – had a tightly structured Arab society that was divided into tribes, sub-tribes and clans.

Key tribes

The Bani Yas were one such powerful federation of clans, wandering great distances in search of grazing for their camels and then returning to their date gardens around the Liwa oases on the edge of the Empty Quarter, the vast unbroken sand desert immortalised by the explorer Wilfred Thesiger in *Arabian Sands*.

As long as anyone can remember, the leader of the Bani Yas has always come from the sheikhs of the Al bu Falasah sub-tribe. One of them, called Nahyan, was the ancestor of the present ruling family of Abu Dhabi. As pearls became increasingly popular in India and then among European women in the 19th century, the Bani Yas gravitated towards the rich pearl banks of the Trucial Coast.

The town of Abu Dhabi was founded as early as 1761 after a good supply of water had been

The pearl boom collapsed in the 1930s with the arrival of the Japanese cultured pearl. The ensuing depression caused some pearl boatmen to burn their boats in desperation for fuel. But the search for a new source of energy had begun.

Oil concessions

Between 1936 and 1952 the rulers of the seven Trucial States signed oil concession agreements with the Iraq Petroleum Company, an international consortium. But oil exploration only really began in earnest after World War II.

The decline of the British Empire after the war, especially the granting of independence to India in

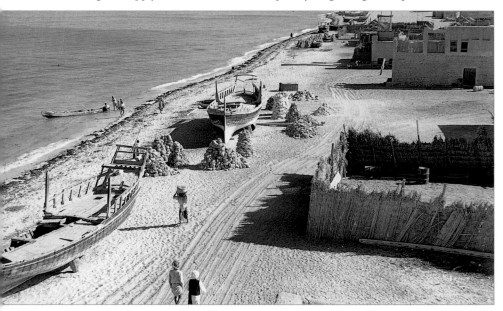

found there. A settlement grew down the coast in Dubai as a dependency of Abu Dhabi until 1833, when a faction of Bani Yas left Abu Dhabi and took control of Dubai, proclaiming their independence. The descendants of Maktoum bin Buti, leader of the breakaway, continue to rule the city to this day.

By 1900 the pearling industry was enjoying such a boom that not enough men could be found to man the 1,200 boats engaged in the trade. Control passed irrevocably to the sheikhs who ruled the coastal areas, and this power was further reinforced when the British made it clear they were only interested in the coastal areas and effectively endorsed only their rulers.

Dubai's commercial pizzazz and liberal values are nothing new. When the city unveiled its new airport in 1960 it was the first in the Gulf to have its own duty-free shop.

1947, helped to speed up changes in the Gulf. The British presence in the region was to linger a few more years. With British help the Trucial Oman Scouts (a defence force) was set up in 1951, while the following year a Trucial States Council was formed to bring a kind of unity to the coastal region through twice-yearly discussions on common problems and interests. The rulers of what became the United Arab Emirates had not met all together since 1905.

The British withdraw

The big bombshell came when Britain's cash-strapped Labour government decided that big savings must be made in defence. In February 1967 the prime minister, Harold Wilson, announced that Britain's military presence east of Suez was to be scrapped by the end of 1971. It spelt the end of British protection in the Gulf and was in breach of written agreements between Britain and the Trucial States, as well as the unwritten Arab law of trust and friendship. The British decision led directly to the formation of the UAE and speeded

the process of modernisation in the region, which had already been accelerated by the discovery of massive oil deposits. But the emirates were ill-prepared for sudden independence and had few qualified people, particularly in the spheres of defence and foreign affairs, which the British had long taken care of.

The UAE is formed

Shortly after the British decision to withdraw from the Gulf, the rulers of Abu Dhabi and Dubai announced that they would form

Left: Abu Dhabi in 1954.
Above: the Ruler's Palace, Abu Dhabi, also in 1954.

a federation and reached an agreement over offshore oil rights. The speed of their action helped to settle frontiers, even though the UAE is now a patchwork of subdivisions making up the seven emirates that form the federation – a process that had never been formalised before because of the changing tribal allegiances.

Abu Dhabi, well aware by 1970 that it was the richest oil emirate, was especially anxious to reach an overall agreement on a federation and clearly demarcated borders because of the mounting importance of oil revenues and the oil rights that would be granted once land divisions had been agreed. From the outset it adopted a policy aimed at finding a middle ground between any opposing views. Sheikh Zayed bin Sultan Al Nahyan, Abu Dhabi's ruler, repeatedly said that the resources of Abu Dhabi – which in a few years were to carry the emirate's income to the highest in the world – were "at the service of all the emirates".

Dubai and Abu Dhabi invited the other Trucial States – Sharjah, Ajman, Umm al

> The UAE boasts 7 percent of the world's proven oil reserves (with roughly 93 percent in Abu Dhabi, 5 percent in Dubai and 2 percent in Sharjah); these are estimated to last just over 90 years at current production rates.

Qaiwain, Ras al Khaimah and Fujairah – to join them in the federation, together with Qatar and Bahrain. There was clearly a strong mutual desire for security, modified by a wish for a degree of independence in each emirate, as the departure of the British drew near.

By June 1971, Bahrain had decided it was secure enough on its own and announced in August it would not join the federation, while Qatar followed suit less than three weeks later. Six of the remaining sheikhdoms had reached agreement on a federal constitution by July, and the UAE formally came into being on 2 December. In Ras al Khaimah, Ruler Sheikh Saqr bin Mohammed al Qasimi – hoping that he would find oil on Qatar's scale – held out for another two months before swallowing his pride at the prospect of massive largesse from Abu Dhabi and joined the federation too. Sheikh Zayed of Abu Dhabi became President of the Federation, with Sheikh Rashid bin

Saeed Al Maktoum, ruler of Dubai, as vice-president and prime minister.

Security was a major motive for forming the UAE, and such concern was justified in view of the massive oil deposits later discovered in the region. The possibility of a threat from the Soviet Union (particularly after its invasion of Afghanistan) always existed in the minds of the Gulf leaders and of the Western politicians whose countries depended on the Gulf's oil.

The volatility of the region was underlined by the Iran–Iraq War, which broke out in 1980, as well as the Arab-Israeli conflict. With the strategic giants of the Gulf – Iran and Iraq

– busy fighting each other, the six oil-rich Gulf monarchies (Saudi Arabia, Kuwait, the UAE, Bahrain, Qatar and Oman) seized the chance to set up their own organisation – the Arabian Gulf Co-operation Council – modelled on the lines of the European Economic Community, and which formally came into being in 1981.

Diversification and development

Meanwhile, massive changes were taking place in the emirates themselves, each of which was pursuing its own route towards development and economic security. Abu Dhabi, the largest and wealthiest of the seven statelets, followed

THE MAGNIFICENT SEVEN

The formation of the UAE presented considerable constitutional problems, as the leaders of the seven formerly independent statelets attempted to merge their territories into one, while preserving a measure of self-determination. The system adopted was a federal one, not unlike that in the USA. Each emirate gives a percentage of its income to the central government budget, which in return takes responsibility for foreign affairs, security and defence and other national issues such as immigration, currency and the postal service. Individual emirates retain a considerable level of internal autonomy and legislative power, however – which explains, for instance, why the law is so different in conservative Sharjah compared to that in liberal Dubai, just 16km (10

miles) down the road. In addition, each emirate continues to have its own ruler. Tensions inevitably arise. Dubai's close historical and commercial links with Iran, for example, have always been a source of concern for the rulers of Abu Dhabi wishing to align themselves with US policy.

Despite the seven emirates' large measure of individual autonomy, a clear pecking order applies within the federation. The ruler of Abu Dhabi, the largest and wealthiest of the emirates, is also automatically the UAE president and head of state, while the ruler of Dubai, the second-largest, serves by default as the UAE's prime minister and head of government – proving that while all seven emirates are equal, some are unquestionably more equal than others.

a cautious path towards modernity under the leadership of the canny Sheikh Zayed, its vast oil reserves freeing it from the need either to diversify or to develop its economy, given that the massive flow of petro-dollars into the city guaranteed every citizen (and their descendants) a very comfortable income for life.

Dubai found itself in a rather different position, given that its oil reserves were only ever a fraction of Abu Dhabi's. Initial revenues had already been invested by the far-sighted Sheikh Rashid into a string of infrastructure projects, including two huge new ports, an airport and the iconic World Trade Centre, laying down the economic basis for the city's subsequent dramatic rise.

Money was even tighter (and oil revenues smaller) in neighbouring Sharjah, which was also plagued with political instability. The emirate's entire banking system collapsed with debts of over US$500 million in 1989 and had to be bailed out by a Saudi consortium. Saudi influence remains strong in Sharjah to this day, accounting for the local adoption of a particularly conservative version of traditional Shariah law.

Meanwhile, the relatively small, unpopulated and oil-less emirates of Ajman, Umm Al Quwain, Ras al Khaimah (RAK) and Fujairah struggled along as best they could, helped out with grants from central government in Abu Dhabi, while the creation of large new industrial works in RAK and a vast new oil-exporting port in Fujairah also provided further economic stimulus.

Nineties and noughties

It was during the 1990s that the UAE really began to capture the world's attention, mainly thanks to a spectacular new series of developments in Dubai instigated by Sheikh Mohammed, the third son of Sheikh Rashid and the driving force behind the emirate's development from the mid-1980s onwards. It was Sheikh Mohammed who commissioned the famous Burj al Arab hotel (1999) and founded Emirates Airlines, which between them have probably done more to establish the UAE in the world's consciousness than any other projects before or since. A further

LEFT: Dubai Creekside, viewed from Bur Dubai.
RIGHT: helicopter view of the Palm Jumeirah in Dubai.

flurry of record-breaking mega-developments were swiftly inaugurated, including the Palm Jumeirah (the world's largest artificial island), Burj Khalifa (the world's tallest building) and the vast Dubailand, intended to become the planet's largest theme park and leisure attraction (although work on the development is now at a virtual standstill).

Dubai's basic aim in all of this was to become a leading global centre for tourism, transport and business – aiming not just to diversify, but also to dominate the region's economy. Not to be outdone, Abu Dhabi soon hit back with its own string of eye-catching developments,

including the Emirates Palace Hotel, Sheikh Zayed Grand Mosque and huge new Saadiyat Island complex which will come complete with new Louvre and Guggenheim museums, aiming to promote itself as a more cultured alternative to its brash neighbour.

Then, in 2008, just as it seemed the boom would never end, the UAE (Dubai in particular) was brought crashing back down to earth as the result of the global credit crunch. The real-estate market collapsed, investment fled, and Dubai, which had previously been announcing the launch of record-breaking new developments on an almost daily basis, found itself suddenly teetering on the edge of bankruptcy. Abu Dhabi eventually came to the rescue with a massive bail-out package, although many of the city's mega-projects were cancelled or put on indefinite hold, and now show little sign of being revived, for a good few years at least.

Abu Dhabi, protected by its oil revenues, remained relatively unaffected by the crunch, and even began to climb out of Dubai's lengthening shadow thanks to headline deals and events including the purchase of Manchester City football club by Sheikh Mansour (a son of Sheikh Zayed) and the staging, in 2009, of the first Abu Dhabi F1 Grand Prix. The spectacular new Sheikh Zayed Grand Mosque (2007) has also drawn increasing numbers of visitors to the emirate.

Overall, the credit crunch may have signalled the end of the UAE's rock 'n' roll years, although reports of Dubai's demise (including endless newspaper articles in the foreign press entitled "Goodbye Dubai") have been greatly exaggerated, and the city is now beginning to face the future with renewed, if somewhat chastened, optimism. Abu Dhabi, meanwhile, continues to establish itself as a genuine rival to its more glamorous neighbour, while elsewhere in the Emirates more modest industrial and tourist development continues apace.

NAMING RIGHTS

As Dubai teetered on the edge of bankruptcy in 2008, rumour abounded as to what price Abu Dhabi would extract in return for bailing out their profligate neighbour – handing over Dubai's prized Emirates Airlines was often mentioned, along with ownership of the Palm islands or other choice local real estate. In the end, Dubai wasn't obliged to relinquish any commercial crown jewels in return for the loan, but it did make one small but symbolic concession, renaming the new Burj Dubai skyscraper as the Burj Khalifa in honour of Abu Dhabi's ruler, Sheikh Khalifa bin Zayed Al Nahyan – meaning that the name of a rival ruler adorns the loftiest building in the city.

The political union between the seven emirates continues to provide a model of political harmony and stability in an often dysfunctional region, and although pro-democracy activists continue to press the government for reforms, the country escaped the widespread protests and uprisings of the Arab Spring in early 2011 almost entirely unscathed (and in stark contrast to nearby Bahrain). All of which adds up to impressive progress for a country which is barely four decades old, and which many observers thought would not last even five years.

ABOVE: Burj Khalifa and traditional architecture at sunset in downtown Dubai.

Father of the UAE

Legendary leader of Abu Dhabi and first president of the UAE, Sheikh Zayed oversaw the country's transformation from impoverished Arabian backwater to today's stable and affluent state

Governor of Al Ain, ruler of Abu Dhabi and – from its creation in 1971 until his death in November 2004 – first president of the United Arab Emirates: the charismatic figure of Sheikh Zayed bin Sultan Al Nahyan towers over the modern history of the region. A man of great charisma, intelligence and legendary generosity, it was Sheikh Zayed who oversaw Abu Dhabi's astonishing transformation from impoverished desert backwater to oil-rich super-state, as well as establishing the lasting integrity and sovereignty of the UAE in the face of considerable odds.

Born in 1918 in Al Ain, where he grew up and of which he subsequently became governor, Sheikh Zayed never lost his love for his birthplace. The explorer Wilfred Thesiger met him in the 1940s and described him in his classic book *Arabian Sands* as "a powerfully built man of about 30 with a brown beard. He had a strong intelligent face, with steady observant eyes, and his manner was quiet but masterful. He was dressed very simply, in a beige coloured shirt of Omani cloth and a waistcoat which he wore unbuttoned... He wore a dagger and cartridge belt; his rifle lay on the sand beside him."

"He had a great reputation among the Bedu," Thesiger went on. "They liked him for his easy informal ways and his friendliness, and they respected his force of character, his shrewdness and his physical strength. They said admiringly, 'Zayed is a Bedu. He knows about camels, can ride like one of us, can shoot and knows how to fight.' "

In old age Zayed's hands were still callused from the days when he used to dig, move stones and plant trees while working on restoration of the ancient falaj system of canals needed to irrigate the date groves of the Buraimi oasis near Al Ain.

It was in 1966 that his brother Shakhbut, who had ruled the emirate since 1928, was deposed,

---

RIGHT: Sheikh Zayed bin Sultan Al Nahyan, the leading light in the transformation of the UAE and father of the current ruler, Sheikh Khalifa bin Zayed Al Nahyan.

and Zayed replaced him. The first oil exports had begun only four years before, and two years later the British government was to announce its withdrawal from the Gulf, so that Abu Dhabi and the other Trucial States were free to manage their own affairs.

The new ruler quickly set about using the new oil revenues to transform Abu Dhabi itself, as well as joining forces with Sheikh Rashid of Dubai in laying the foundations of a new federal state (of which they subsequently became president and vice-president respectively).

President Zayed showed particular skill in achieving lasting harmony between the tradition-

ally rival interests of the UAE's seven emirates, each with its own ruler – particularly in the face of a chorus of sceptical observers who claimed that the federation would never work. There is no doubt that Abu Dhabi's soaring wealth helped. Zayed was always quick to help the poorer emirates financially and to spend money on vast public works throughout the country, including a welfare state that is second to none worldwide.

Sheikh Zayed is still revered throughout the UAE, and his portrait remains a common sight in public places, while his tomb, in the magnificent Sheikh Zayed Grand Mosque *(see page 187)* in Abu Dhabi, continues to draw a steady stream of visitors paying their respects to one of the modern Gulf's most accomplished statesmen.

EXPLORERS

Oman and the UAE lie on the rim of the Empty Quarter, a vast wilderness of dunes impenetrable to any but a few Bedu until as late as the 1930s

Arabia has attracted some of the world's best-known explorers, from Charles Montague Doughty to Richard Burton. Names associated with Oman and the UAE in particular include Ibn Battuta, Marco Polo, the 18th-century Danish explorer Carsten Niebuhr, whom William Gifford Palgrave called "the intelligence and courage that first opened Arabia to Europe" and, in the 20th century, Bertram Thomas and Wilfred Thesiger. There were British political agents and Western officials in the employ of the sheikhs who by the very nature of the territory – tribal and inaccessible – were often the first foreigners to set foot in a place.

Wilfred Thesiger

The explorer most fondly remembered in Oman and the UAE today is undoubtedly Wilfred Thesiger, whose two great crossings of the Rub al Khali (Empty Quarter; *see picture top centre*) are documented in his book *Arabian Sands*. Thesiger seized the opportunity to cross the Great Sands when he was offered a job in the region by the Anti-Locust Research Centre. To make himself less conspicuous in hostile country he pretended to be a Bedu from Syria, a disguise that could explain his strange looks and accent. His disguise was generally successful, and often only his closest Bedu companions knew the truth. The one thing that gave him away, they said, were his unusually large feet. They advised him never to leave footprints in the sand.

LEFT: Wilfred Thesiger in Bedu dress. Thesiger's success as an explorer was a direct result of his ability to adopt the manners, dress, language and culture of the lands through which he was travelling.

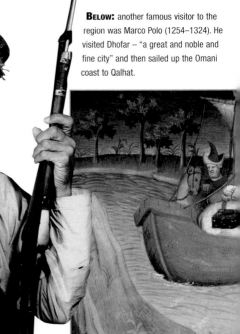

BELOW: another famous visitor to the region was Marco Polo (1254–1324). He visited Dhofar – "a great and noble and fine city" and then sailed up the Omani coast to Qalhat.

THE FIRST TO CROSS THE SANDS

Though Wilfred Thesiger's crossings of the Rub al Khali are probably the most famous, the first Western person to cross the sands was Bertram Thomas in 1931, who trekked from Salalah to Doha in 55 days.

Thomas's book about his journey, *Arabia Felix*, describes the sands as "a vast ocean of billowing sands, here tilted into sudden frowning heights, and there falling into gentle valleys... without a scrap of verdure in view. Dunes of all sizes . . . with the exquisite roundness of a girl's breasts, rise tier upon tier like a mighty mountain system." He also talked of the "roaring of the sands" which, he said, resembled a ship's foghorn.

Thomas was in Oman as Financial Adviser and Wazir to the Sultan, a post he took up in 1924 after serving as Political Officer in Iraq. Through his position he gained the respect of unpredictable tribal leaders who usually scorned, even murdered, infidels.

This proved invaluable on his journey through the Sands. Thomas claimed the Rub al Khali "obsesses every white man whose life is cast in Arabia".

RIGHT: the 11th-century North African explorer Ibn Battuta visited southeast Arabia when he was just 21. His original six-month *Haj* extended to a 24-year trip taking him as far as China.

RIGHT: when Percy Cox, British Agent in Muscat from 1899–1904, visited Tanuf, he was told that no rain had fallen since the last British agent had taken photographs there 25 years before. The sheikh demanded compensation for the crops that had perished as a result.

DAILY LIFE

In spite of the massive changes that have taken place in Oman and the UAE, everyday life remains rooted in traditional values

Contemporary life in the UAE and Oman is an intriguing blend of the traditional and the modern. Despite both countries' often outwardly contemporary appearance, old-fashioned attitudes still run deep, and social life continues to follow long-established patterns, despite the 21st-century veneer. Starbucks may have replaced the traditional coffee shop, while camels have given way to Toyota four-wheel-drives, but many of the region's immemorial attitudes and cultural norms remain largely unchanged. The oligarchical political traditions and the entrenched position of the ruling sheikhly families; the careful observance of Islamic religious practices; the role of the sexes and the conduct of family life; taboos regarding food, drink and forms of public behaviour, and so on – all these remain intact. Even in liberal and relatively permissive cities such as Dubai, visiting tourists and expats have found themselves falling foul of the authorities as a result of behaviour which would be considered unexceptional in the West, but which is considered offensive – and even illegal – in the Gulf.

Cautious signs of change are afoot. The increasing emancipation of women, who now play an increasingly important role in the business and political life of both countries, is one such development, as are the growing demands for more democratic and representative institutions which can be heard, albeit faintly, in both Oman and the UAE. Burgeoning contact with foreign countries

is also creating an increasingly cosmopolitan populace, with growing numbers of Emirati and Omani men marrying foreign women (although instances of local women marrying foreigners remain largely unknown).

Despite modest adjustments, however, traditional values remain firmly entrenched. Tribal identity is still an important marker of one's place in society, in Oman particularly, signifying one's geographical and cultural origins, and perhaps one's status in society as well. Pride in one's country and culture remains strong too, again especially in Oman, where nationals take great pleasure in the gigantic leaps their country has taken over recent decades and in the achievements of its venerated ruler Sultan Qaboos.

PRECEDING PAGES: a woman passes before a typical wrought-iron gate in Ras al Hadd.
LEFT: a Nizwa local.
RIGHT: an Omani family at a shopping mall in Muscat.

Family life and the home

The family and family home remain the core of Emirati and Omani life. Families are typically large (Oman in particular now has a rocketing birth rate and an increasingly youthful population – 10 children in one family is not uncommon). Extended families generally co-habit under the same roof, including elderly relatives who are unable to live alone, as well as young married couples, who will typically live in the house of the groom's parents until they are able to afford a home of their own. Western concepts of bachelor living or temporary residence in rented apartments are largely unknown.

walled and fortified against possible attack and shielded from the public gaze to protect the privacy of those (women particularly) within.

Food is a key ingredient of any social gathering at home. Coffee or tea is always offered as a symbol of hospitality *(see box bottom right)*, as are dates and sweetmeats. Following meals, the incense burner is filled and passed around, so that guests can fan scented smoke onto their faces. These ceremonies signify the end of the occasion.

Daily life and the social round

Daily life for Omani and Emirati men and women still revolves around the traditional

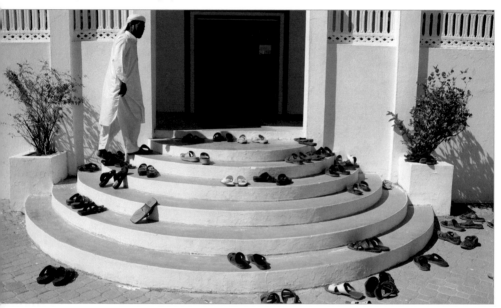

It is customary for guests to remove shoes when entering an Omani or Emirati home – a measure originally adopted for hygiene reasons when streets were dustier than they are today, but now simply a matter of politeness.

The traditional Emirati or Omani home remains something of a castle. Despite their modern appearance, houses in both the UAE and Oman continue to preserve a decidedly traditional layout, standing quite separate from one another on individual plots of lands, and often surrounded by high enclosing walls – a modern throwback to former times, when houses and settlements were typically heavily

rhythms of religious life: the five daily calls to prayer and the annual religious festivals punctuate the passing year *(see page 86)*.

Social life is also organised, to a large extent, according to traditional patterns. Omani and Emirati men and women often socialise separately – again, following an age-old traditional pattern whereby men and women would gather in separate parts of the house to exchange news and gossip. The pattern persists to this day, whether in the traditional setting of an Omani souk, with men hanging out at the local coffee shop, or in the modern malls of Dubai and Abu Dhabi, where groups of Emirati men can commonly be seen socialising over coffee in Starbucks or Costa while their wives cruise the shops looking for clothes.

Whatever its setting, social life in the Gulf retains much of its traditional courtliness and decorum, exemplified by the elaborate round of salutations and extended handshakes which can be observed whenever two nationals meet one another; close friends and relatives of the same

> Many nationals still follow traditional sports such as falconry and camel racing, although modern sports – particularly football – are popular, and televised broadcasts of major football matches from the Gulf and Europe regularly attract crowds.

– insh'allah ("God willing") and al hamdu'lillah ("Thanks be to God") are perhaps the two most common expressions in the local language.

Marriage, education and work

The large majority of young men and women still have an arranged marriage with a partner from a suitable family known to her own family. Often a girl will marry a first cousin or man from the same tribe. Muslim women always marry a Muslim, although the same is not true of men. In the UAE, increasing numbers of marriages between Emiratis and foreign women have prompted the government to offer significant cash incentives to encourage

sex may also touch or kiss cheeks or (a particularly distinctive local custom) noses. Such pleasantries typically open with the traditional *salaam aleikum* ("Peace be upon you"), followed by the response *wa aleikum a'salaam* ("And peace upon you also"), followed by a long exchange of enquiries and responses concerning one's health, one's news, the health of one's wife, children, cousins, and so on which can go on for a considerable amount of time. Invocations to God are also a characteristic feature of such exchanges (and of Emirati and Omani conversation in general)

LEFT: mosque at Job's Tomb, Dhofar, Oman.
ABOVE: a bride displays her hennaed hands, decorated the night before her wedding.

THE COFFEE CEREMONY

Every visitor to a UAE or Omani home will be offered coffee or tea. The traditional Gulf coffee – *kahwa* – is made from green coffee beans, is very strong and sometimes flavoured with cardamom or saffron. Poured from a distinctive coffee pot, it is served in tiny cups without handles, which are refilled several times until a guest "wobbles" the cup from side to side, indicating sufficiency. Three cups is considered the polite number to drink, indicating pleasure at the coffee, but not drinking to excess. The social custom of drinking coffee is also important in business.

marriages between Emirati couples. Islam allows a Muslim man to have up to four wives, provided he can support all of them. In fact, most Emirati and Omani men have only one, although a man may take a second if the first is unable to bear him children. Dowries are typically provided by the groom to the bride's family as a guarantee against possible future divorce or the death of the husband, offering a measure of financial security to the bride-to-be.

Weddings are typically large and elaborate affairs, spreading over three days or so, with vast quantities of food, music and other entertainment and guests sporting their finest traditional dress (complete with *khanjars* and possibly rifles

in Oman, *see page 67*). As with many other social events, men and women tend to congregate separately for much of the wedding until the bride and groom finally join together at the end of the festivities. On the evening before her wedding the bride will hold her henna night *(laylat al henna)*, when she will be massaged with perfumed oil and decorated with henna. For this she wears a traditional gold-embroidered green dress and elaborate gold jewellery, often part of her wedding gift.

The roles of the sexes within the family after marriage follow the usual gender patterns, with men going out to work and financing the home, while the wives and other women of the family run the house and bring up the children. The gender divide is steadily dissolving, however. Emirati

and Omani women now make up an increasingly large proportion of those in higher education in the region, generally equal to, or greater than, men at many colleges and universities, while increasing numbers of women now work in government and business. Despite this increasing sexual emancipation, women are still poorly represented in the higher echelons of the countries' ministries and corporations – although again this is something that is equally true of many other "developed" countries around the world.

Business in the UAE and Oman continues to be based more on personal relationships and mutual trust than legal contracts and corporate formalities, giving business a notably social touch – Western notions of timekeeping may, however, be somewhat lacking.

National dress

All over the Gulf region, one of the most striking features for the visitor is the very noticeable national dress of both men and women – in Oman national dress is mandatory for anyone working in the public services, while most Emiratis in the UAE also wear it as a matter of

> *A newborn baby's eyes are lined with kohl to cleanse them from infection and to help protect against the Evil Eye.*

course. National dress is an important marker of national and cultural identity, and virtually all nationals take great pride in their scrupulous personal appearance – and tend to look askance at scruffy Westerners in T-shirts and shorts, which they regard as tantamount to walking around in one's underwear (not to mention skimpy and tight clothing, which can often cause offence, even if most locals are too polite to say anything).

In both countries, the standard apparel is a *dishdasha* (also known as a *thawb* or *kandura*), a loose, ankle-length robe, usually white (although other colours, particularly in Oman, can often be seen). A small tassel *(furakha)* hanging from the neck is a typical feature of the Omani *dishdasha*, traditionally doused in scent or perfumed with frankincense. On formal occasions, men (particularly those of higher social rank) sometimes wear an over-garment, a gauzy black or brown robe *(bisht)* edged in woven gold thread.

In the UAE, the standard item of headwear is the *ghutra*, a loose piece of cotton held in place by black ropes *(iqal)* which formerly doubled as ropes for tethering camels at night. In Oman, men wear either more voluminous and colourful turbans or, more commonly, the ubiquitous "Omani cap" *(kummah)*, a richly embroidered cotton headpiece said to have been introduced from the Omani dominions in Zanzibar in the 19th century and now an important symbol of national identity. On special occasions, Omani men may also be seen wearing the traditional *khanjar* (silver dagger) tucked into their waistbands, with perhaps, in particularly traditional settings (amongst the Bedu, especially), a rifle as well.

Women cover their heads and bodies with a voluminous black overdress *(abbaya)*, under

garment sported by women in Afghanistan and often known by the same name) is becoming increasingly rare, although it may still be seen in remoter parts of the UAE and Oman. The Gulf *burqa* is a light and simple structure covering the face, with a thin strip across the forehead and over the nose, leaving the eyes and cheek areas free. The mask stops under the nose, covering the top lip but leaving the chin free. It is made from black cotton, the front covered with a gold, purple or red dye with a bluish sheen. There are several designs, and women may wear a gold one for special occasions. The mask is worn by many married women, though

which is worn a black headscarf *(shayla)* to cover the hair. The *abbaya* itself, despite its functional blackness, may often be elaborately embroidered, and edged with beads and sequins. The *abbaya* often hides brightly coloured dresses which are long-sleeved with very elaborately embroidered necklines and wrist-to-elbow decoration, sometimes embellished with crystal beading and sequins. Wealthier women may wear designer clothes under their *abbaya*.

The traditional Bedu face mask *(burqa* – not to be confused with the voluminous tent-like

LEFT: an Omani mother with her toddler.
ABOVE: wearing a traditional face mask or *burqa*.
ABOVE RIGHT: gathering outside a mosque in Muscat.

not by all women in public. Instead the headdress may be drawn across the face as a veil. To wear the *burqa* or not is a matter of personal choice, and can be dependent on the situation.

The way of death

In Islam mourning is not an important part of death. The deceased will be washed and anointed with perfumed oils and then wrapped in a white cloth and borne on a simple bier to the cemetery. The body is always buried (on its side facing Mecca), and if possible burial should take place on the day of death. Forty days after death, the close relatives of the deceased will hold a feast to mark the ascent to heaven, believed to occur after this 40-day period.

THE BEDU

The life of the Bedu used to be one of thirst and hunger, and of great journeys to find water. The lack of such hardships today is testing the strength of their culture

The Bedu of Oman and the Emirates are among the oldest tribal peoples in the world. Tracing their ancestry from a mythical hero called Kahtan in the Yemen, these southern Arabian tribesmen are sometimes referred to as the "Pure Arabs". Kahtan has been identified with Yoktan, listed in the Old Testament as a descendant of Shem, a son of Noah, making these tribes of older, purer Arab stock than the younger northern tribes that trace their ancestry from Ishmael. Of these southern tribes the Bait Kathir and Rashid are the most famous, having been Wilfred Thesiger's companions on his exploration of the Empty Quarter in the second half of the 1940s. Other tribes in the region include the Harasis, Al Wahiba, Ajman and Jenuba.

For modern Westerners concepts of tribal descent and purity of blood lines may appear somewhat irrelevant. In Arabia, family ties and tribal identity are the building blocks of society, modern as well as traditional. A citizen of any Arabian Gulf state is identified by a personal

> *Bedu is the Arabic word for nomadic tribes-people. The singular, Badawi, is little known in the West, so Bedu is used in this book. The more common Western version, Bedouin, is a double plural which does not exist in Arabic.*

name, then as the child of a father and grandfather, and then by their clan and tribal name.

This sense of being from a line of descent, of belonging to a family grouping that extends

LEFT: a Bedu man kneels on top of a sand dune in the desert. **RIGHT:** Bedu women traditionally wear the *burqa*.

through a clan and a tribe to a wider society is fundamental to Bedu life and is probably the single most important influence within the relatively young states of the Arabian peninsula.

Adapt or die

The Bedu evolved as nomadic herdsmen, living off the products of their animals, drinking their milk, weaving their hair, making leather from their skins and eating their flesh. Their lifestyle was the supreme adaptation of man to the hostile environment of some of the hottest, driest areas on earth. The land is too sterile for them to stay long in any one place. The vegetation is too thin and grows too slowly. Instead the Bedu learnt to move, following the limited rains, grazing their animals on small patches of grass wherever they could be found. It was not an easy life, but it was survival. T.E. Lawrence wrote that "the Bedouin ways were hard even for those brought up in them", that they were "a death in life". If one asks the Bedu today what life was like in the old days, their tales are of constant thirst and hunger, of great journeys to bring water from wells or to look for areas that had received some rain.

Whenever one thinks of the Bedu one imagines them with their camels and their goat-hair tents. The *bait sharar* ("house of hair") is synonymous with the Bedu. The reality is slightly different. There are tribes who have never lived

temporary shelters. These are common among the Bedu on the Jiddat al Harasis in Oman, where they resemble metal bedsteads upended and joined together to form small cabins.

The kindness of strangers

Hospitality is an essential part of Bedu life. In a land where people are few and far between and there is little to sustain life, hospitality was formerly a crucial means of exchanging news and information regarding latest tribal conflicts, the movements of friendly and hostile tribes, sources of possible grazing and areas in which rain had recently fallen – a kind of bush telegraph, with

in tents and those who have traditionally only used tents during winter when a shelter from the cold, wind and occasional rain has been a necessity. In Oman it is only the tribes of the Empty Quarter, the Bait Kathir and Rashid that have used tents. Previously the tribes of the stony plains, where trees are more plentiful, built their camps around the shade of these natural shelters, often covering them with blankets or cloth to improve them. Other tribes, especially on the coast, used palm fronds to build easily assembled and dismantled shelters called *barasti*. These are still a common sight around the Wahibah Desert in Oman and along the coasts of the Arabian Gulf. More recently the Bedu have started to use metal grilles to form

news passing by word of mouth often with remarkable speed across the vast distances. In the past any traveller seeing a tent would travel towards it, hopeful of receiving a friendly welcome, although also wary of the possibility that the inhabitants might belong to a rival tribe which whom relations were strained, or even with whom a state of open warfare existed. Thesiger's *Arabian Sands* offers several memorable descriptions of such chance meetings in the desert and the hope of meeting with friends mixed with the fear of being shot at, or worse.

Assuming no hostile relations existed, visitors would exchange for their news and in return would be greeted with tea and coffee and be invited to share a meal. Visitors knew that they would not only receive food and shelter, but also the protection of their host for the duration of their stay and for another three days after – this being the time it takes for all traces of his host's food to pass through his body. The code tying the host to his guest is called the bond of salt. Even if a visitor carried only the salt of his host in his stomach, he could call on his protection.

Camels, a crucial commodity

Up until the adoption of motor vehicles, the entire lifestyle of the Bedu relied on the camel. It was the beast of burden by which they moved

agent in Kuwait between 1929 and 1936, and author of *The Arab of the Desert*, reported how one Bedu sheikh, in about 1925, rode a camel between Riyadh and Nasriyah, in Iraq, in eight days, covering a distance of about 1,287km (800 miles). On Wilfred Thesiger's first crossing of the Empty Quarter in the winter of 1946–7, his party travelled for two weeks across the sands without finding a well where it could water its animals.

All camels in the Middle East and Arabia are domesticated, and the work of herding, breeding and milking them is traditionally the task of men. Each camel will be branded with the

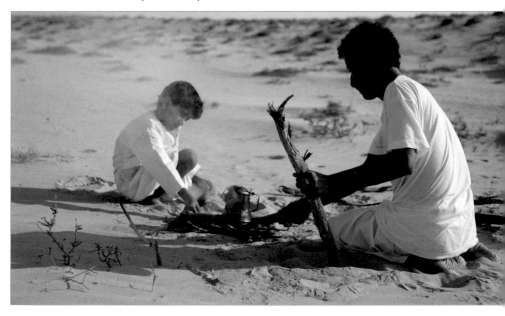

their tents and possessions as well as the mode of personal transport. The camel is still a source of milk, meat and wool. The wool, prized for its strength and warmth, is used to make cloaks and equipment such as udder bags, as well as the detailing on the tent curtain.

Under hot summer conditions the Bedu try to water their camels every day or two days, but in winter the period can be weekly or, if the grazing is good, the herds will not be watered at all. If need be, the camel can show incredible stamina. H.R.P. Dickson, a British political

Passers-by are welcomed by a set exchange of greetings and the asking of news, to which the reply is always that there is no news, or only good news.

mark, called a *wasm*, of its owner and tribe, on its neck, shoulder or hindquarters. However, even a man with over 100 animals will commonly know his own camels individually and will usually have given names to each of them.

Camels are kept by the Bedu primarily as a source of milk. Thus the majority of animals are female. The Bedu will rarely kill an adult camel, unless it is obviously sick and dying. However,

LEFT: camels are a vital commodity of Bedu life.
ABOVE: a Bedouin guide and his son build a fire to make a coffee.

they will slaughter the occasional calf, especially a male. The only time that adult camels are normally killed for food is in order to feast a large number of guests such as for a marriage or to honour a visiting sheikh.

The traditional Bedu diet consists primarily of camel milk drunk cold or hot or boiled with bread (a mix called *threat* by the Bait Kathir in Oman), or cooked with rice. Meat is an occasional luxury and more often than not is goat's meat bought in the market. Along the coasts fresh and salted fish is an important staple for people and animals, and sun-dried sardines are a traditional supplementary feed for camels.

The role of Bedu women

Whatever the impression of women in Muslim society in general, Bedu women enjoy a great deal of freedom and play an important role in desert society. In such a harsh environment, and with the heavy demands of a nomadic existence, it would be impossible for the family to survive without the women taking their share of responsibility. What segregation exists is not a reflection of lack of status. Women's separation from strangers and the use of veils is due more to a sense of modesty and the protective concern of the menfolk – a custom more akin to a code of chivalry than a regime of repression.

WEAVING

Weaving, almost entirely in the hands of women, is one of the oldest crafts of the Arabian peninsula, and the earliest illustration of the ground loom used by the Bedu is in an Egyptian fresco dating back to over 2000 BC.

Women spin using a stick with a cross-head whorl and hook before dyeing the wool and then re-spinning the material, producing a double strand of yarn. In the past, natural dyes from plants were used; modern synthetic dyes give access to brighter and more varied colours.

Most decorative motifs are geometric, but the repertoire also includes stylised representations of familiar objects and animals. The patterns are repeated to the edge of the piece.

The tent curtain, the largest decorated piece of textile made by the Bedu, is usually in black and white. The white is commonly cotton yarn but can be white camel hair. A narrow pattern, it runs the length of the textile and uses symbols and designs, including geometric representations of household objects. Designed to run from the back wall to the front, it is made extra long so that it can be extended into the open space at the entrance of the tent, creating a private space for the women. The curtain is hung with the good side facing into the men's half of the tent.

Traditional Bedu textiles can still sometimes be found in the souks around the Wahibah Desert in Oman, particularly in Sinaw and Ibra.

As children, brothers and sisters are taught to have a special sense of closeness. A young boy is encouraged to see himself as his sister's protector, to bring presents to his female siblings. He is their chaperone in public and champion of their honour. A Bedu male would not tolerate any person harming his sister's reputation, verbally or otherwise, and until his sister is married he will act as a surrogate husband. Even after her marriage he is responsible for the protection of her honour (more so than her husband) as her reputation is that of his family's, thus her honour is his honour.

Similarly young girls are their brothers' closest confidantes and are encouraged to con-

Changing times

For all their colourful history and traditions, the huge upheavals in Oman and the UAE over recent decades have largely destroyed traditional Bedu culture. The mass production of motor vehicles has irrevocably altered their formerly camel-centred way of life, as has the emergence of sovereign nation states over whose borders they were formerly wont to wander. Most of all, the growing wealth of the region has offered them the chance finally to escape the hardships and grinding poverty of former generations.

Not surprisingly, many Bedu have migrated to the towns and cities in search of work and educa-

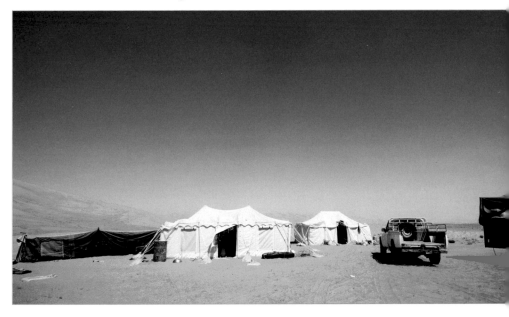

tribute to their brothers' comfort and public image. Sisters will sew and weave their brothers' clothes and camel trappings, as well as cook their favourite foods for them. From a very early age a girl takes an active part in the daily work of the family. She will herd the sheep or goats if they have any, and an unmarried teenage girl will typically be left to pasture one of the family's camel herds. Where families have no sons, the daughters will often be found herding all the animals and entertaining guests, as well as driving the family vehicles.

FAR LEFT: Bedu women of the Wahibah Desert.
LEFT: a Bedu boy in Nizwa.
ABOVE: a Bedu camp in the Rub Al Khali desert.

tion, becoming subsumed into the settled population at large. In the UAE, traditional Bedu life has now almost entirely disappeared, although some of its traditions linger on in remote corners of the country such as the Liwa oasis in Abu Dhabi emirate. In Oman, the Bedu still survive in considerable numbers, particularly around the Wahibah Desert, although former privations have been eased by the drilling of reliable wells, the provision of mobile medical centres, and regular deliveries by truck of water and animal feed. Mobile phones, too, have put an end to the traditional spreading of news by word of mouth, although the elaborate hospitality and old-fashioned salutations survive, even though the society and culture which created them has now gone for ever.

ALL THAT GLISTERS – JEWELLERY

Jewellery performs much more than a decorative purpose among the Bedu of the Middle East – it can be a talisman or even the family safe deposit

Visit any gold souk or handicraft market in the UAE or Oman and you'll see examples of the region's traditional silver jewellery – chunky rectangular bracelets or anklets and distinctively heavy necklaces, often decorated with a rustic selection of antique coins, miniature silver boxes and other ornaments.

Such traditional jewellery is no longer manufactured or worn today (except by a few Bedu in Oman), although prized antique pieces of antique Omani silver jewellery can change hands for considerable sums. Women would formerly have made up their own necklaces, adding coins, amulets and pendants either received as gifts, earned through the sale of produce, or found and kept for their magical powers. A woman's jewellery is technically her own, but she often also acts as the family bank, a custom dating from the days of raiding when women were immune from robbery. Even today, silver and gold provide a more trusted way of hoarding wealth than putting money into a bank.

Protective properties

A woman's wealth, worn as necklaces, bracelets, anklets and decorated veils, is much more than a financial reserve. Silver amulets, boxes and cylinders contain fragments of Qur'anic verse to protect the wearer against accidents, snake bites and scorpion stings. In Oman large round silver pendants called *sumt*, believed to contain an imprisoned *djinn* (demon), are popular.

LEFT: an ornately attired Omani woman from Salalah, her hands and wrist laden with traditional Bedu jewellery.

Above: Arabian golden accessories and pots.

THE RUSH FOR GOLD

Silver was originally the main metal used in Arabian jewellery – only people of importance could afford gold. All that has changed over the past 50 years, and it's now gold, rather than silver, which is the precious metal of choice for all strata of society.

The region's love affair with gold is plain to see in the glittering gold souks which can be found in most cities – those in Dubai and at Mutrah Souk in Muscat are particularly spectacular, and rank amongst the cheapest places in the world to buy the precious metal. Gold ornaments, produced mainly by expat Asian craftsmen, range from suave modern European designs through to huge and wildly extravagant Arabian-style pieces, although jewellery everywhere is still sold by weight – the quality of the design and workmanship isn't usually factored into the price.

Gold remains an essential component of the bride's price. Most brides expect to receive a full complement of gold jewellery – headdress, rings, necklaces and bracelets. Often this will be specially commissioned.

Left: gold necklace, Omani Heritage Museum. The use of gold – as shown in this finely worked necklace – was traditionally limited to the upper echelons of Arabian society, typically worn only by the ruling family and other elites.

Left: traditional Omani silver *hirz*. The thick chain is decorated with Austrian Maria Theresa Thaler coins (the standard currency of the Gulf up until the 20th century) while the central casket would probably have held a fragment of text from the Qur'an, designed to ward off the evil eye and other maleficent influences.

Above: a large selection of gold is available in the souks of Dubai.

Right: a traditional Arabic coffee pot.

THE EXPATRIATES

Expats from all over the world call the UAE and
Oman home, bringing a host of international
influences to the region's society and culture

The majority of people living in the UAE and Oman today are not local Emirati or Omani Arabs, but foreign expats – a quirk of human geography that has made this part of the Gulf one of the most ethnically diverse on the planet. Less than 20 percent of the inhabitants of the UAE are Emirati (and well under 10 percent in Dubai). The situation is less dramatic in Oman, although even there a considerable slice of the country's inhabitants are now foreign. The 2010 census revealed that of the total population of 2.6 million, over a quarter are expats, mainly from the Indian subcontinent.

Foreigners have settled around the coast of the UAE and Oman for centuries, although the massive expat influx dates from the 1960s and 1970s when the two fledgling countries – sitting on considerable oil reserves but without the sufficient native populations or technical expertise to develop their industry and infrastructure – flung open their doors, recruiting Western experts to build and run the new oil installations, financial institutions and other businesses, and subcontinental labourers to provide the manpower to achieve the dream.

The presence of huge numbers of outsiders is now an inescapable fact of life in the UAE and Oman, giving the region its unique cultural flavour, with Emiratis, Omanis, expat Arabs, Iranians, Indians, Filipinas and assorted Europeans coexisting, albeit obliquely, within the same space – the vast numbers of immigrants from India and Pakistan are particularly striking, and wandering through the streets of Bur Dubai in Dubai or Ruwi in Muscat,

for instance, you often have to pinch yourself to remember exactly where you are. For all its laudable multicultural credentials, however, the presence of such large numbers of expats continues to raise some decidedly thorny questions about the identity of the two countries themselves, their cultural past, contemporary identity and possible future.

Who are the expats?

The range of expats in the Gulf is enormous – Dubai alone is home to nationals from over 200 countries, making it one of the most truly cosmopolitan and multicultural cities on the planet. The majority (50 percent of the total number of expats in the UAE, and an even

LEFT: foreign workers walk past Dubai's Burj Khalifa.
RIGHT: dune-bashing, a favourite with expats.

higher proportion in Oman) hail from the sub-continent. India provides the biggest numbers, with a disproportionate number coming from the southern state of Kerala, while numerous Pakistanis can also be found, along with smaller numbers of Sri Lankans and Bangladeshis. Other Arabs and Iranians make up a further 23 percent in the UAE, while other nationalities (including Westerners) account for a final 8 percent. Dubai, easily the most ethnically diverse of the Emirates, is also home to a huge Filipina population, many of whom work as waitresses and cleaners in the city's tourist and leisure sectors, and also boasts a sizeable Iranian population who have played an important role in the development of the city since the early 20th century.

Expats they all might be, but a distinct pecking order generally applies (with notable exceptions). At the top of the scale come the Western technocrats and professionals who supply the UAE (and, to a lesser extent, Oman) with much of the contemporary know-how required to run the place. Expat Arabs can also be found throughout the region, including significant numbers of Lebanese, Egyptians and Syrians, while at the bottom of the heap are the legions of Indian and Pakistani labourers, taxi drivers and shopkeepers.

The various ethnic strands tend to coexist, but not communicate, each nationality and socio-economic group keeping to its own circles. This is particularly the case in the UAE, where Western expats and Indian labourers alike might go years without having any serious interaction with their Emirati hosts.

CITIZENSHIP

The issue of citizenship – or the lack of it – is a particularly vexed subject in the region. UAE citizenship, along with the considerable financial privileges it brings, is jealously guarded, and only a tiny handful of foreigners have succeeded in obtaining it. Many people who have lived all their lives in the UAE continue to carry the nationality of their parents' home country, even if they might never even have visited it, and thus have no legal right of stay in the country which is their de facto home. Obtaining Omani citizenship is only slightly less difficult, even if you were born in the country, and usually requires a minimum of 20 years' residence.

Historic roots

Foreigners are nothing new in Oman and the UAE, and have been arriving for many centuries in the guise of merchants, mercenaries or even slaves. Historically, the region enjoys particularly close links with Iran. Much of the history of coastal Oman was shaped by its contacts with Persia, and Persian settlers occupied parts of the country in antiquity, as well as periodically seizing control of parts of the coast. Dubai and Iran have also enjoyed particularly close links in more recent times. The arrival of large numbers of Iranian merchants in the city in the early 20th century played a major role in establishing it as

one of the southern Gulf's most important trading entrepôts, and the elaborate wind-towered houses they built can still be seen in the wonderful Bastakiya quarter – while the wind-tower itself has (somewhat ironically) been adopted as an important marker of national identity by the Emiratis, despite its foreign origins.

Links with Britain also run deep, dating back to the 19th century, when the location of both the UAE and Oman on shipping routes to India forced the British to take an active interest in the region. The role of British military and other advisers was a crucial factor in the so-called Omani renaissance which followed the accession of Sultan Qaboos to the throne in 1970, while the UK's post-independence influence on the

UAE – formerly the British protectorate known as the Trucial States – has also been considerable.

Other strong foreign links have also added their contribution to the region's multicultural make-up. The existence of the Omani enclave of Gwadur (in what is now the Pakistani prov-

> The UAE is perhaps unique amongst former European colonies and dependencies – not only did they not want the British to leave, they even offered to pay to keep UK armed forces on their soil following independence in 1971.

(especially) Dubai, establishing powerful trading empires, some of which survive to this day.

Executive perks

Life in the Gulf for Westerners has often been portrayed as some kind of expatriate nirvana: a heady combination of endless sunshine, superlative leisure facilities, a tax-free salary and the opportunity to enjoy a lifestyle which would never be possible back home – not to mention the region's generally liberal attitude to Western evils ranging from alcohol to (in Dubai, particularly) endemic prostitution. All of this is at least partly true, although the

ince of Baluchistan) since the late 18th century resulted in the arrival of large numbers of Baluchis in the country, where their ancestors continue to live to this day. India itself was another importance source of trade throughout the 19th and 20th centuries, thanks to a mixture of geographical proximity and the influence of the British. The Indian rupee served as the main currency of both Oman and the UAE until modern times, and many Emiratis and Omanis spent time in the subcontinent, Bombay especially. In return, Indian traders began increasingly to settle in the region, in Muscat, Abu Dhabi and

LEFT: working on the expat tan, Dubai.
ABOVE: conspicuous wealth, the Gold Souk, Dubai.

JASHANMAL'S INFLUENCE

A particularly revealing example of the early influence of Indian expats is provided by the story of Mohan Jashanmal, whose Jashanmal bookstores can still be seen in the UAE to this day. His initial department store opened in Abu Dhabi in 1964 and became a particular favourite of the legendary Sheikh Zayed, who visited regularly. Zayed was especially fascinated by Jashanmal's imported pictures of the Empire State Building, UN Headquarters and other foreign sights, saying that Abu Dhabi would soon be able to boast similar landmarks of its own – a bold but prescient claim, given that Abu Dhabi at that time was little more than a cluster of mudbrick houses and dirt-track roads.

flipside of the package are the terms under which Westerners in the region – the UAE, in particular – are allowed to enjoy such benefits. Residence in the country is permitted only so long as you hold a job with approved sponsors, with a visa renewable at three-yearly intervals and no guarantees about the future, even if you buy property in the country.

All of this gives Western expat life in the region its peculiarly transient flavour. The potential nightmare underlying the dream was made brutally clear during the 2008–9 credit crunch, when thousands of Western expats lost their jobs. Stories of Europeans fleeing Dubai

credit cards in the glove compartment and notes of apology stuck on the windscreens.

Labour rights and wrongs

Whatever the occasional travails of the region's Western expats, however, they pale into insignificance compared to the plight of the region's subcontinental expats, who have flocked to the region in search of jobs and wages which are unavailable to them at home. Particularly exploited are the hundreds of thousands of construction workers who have provided the muscle and manpower which has helped create the gleaming modern skylines of Dubai and elsewhere. Most are brought to

A side-effect of the flood of largely male expats into the UAE is the country's gender imbalance, with men outnumbering women by over two to one. In Dubai males form 75 percent of the population, making it one of the world's most sexually lopsided cities.

in the wake of the real-estate crash and abandoning their cars at the airport for fear of being arrested and thrown into prison for defaulting on loans have become the stuff of urban legend. According to a report in The Times in 2009, over 3,000 cars were found left at Dubai's international airport by Westerners fleeing the country, often with their keys in the ignition, maxed-out

the region by employment agencies in their home countries, often paying their first year's salary for the privilege. Many arrive in the region and find themselves virtual prisoners, their passports confiscated and their wages kept systematically in arrears in order to keep them in order, and confined to squalid labour camps on the margins of the cities which they have helped to build. Working conditions are little better, with labourers forced to toil through the blistering heat of the midday Gulf sun often in dangerous working conditions with little or no health and safety – construction-site fatalities occur with depressing frequency.

Other human rights abuses are also common. Expat housemaids (mainly Filipina) have also been subjected to abuse in the privacy of their employer's home, while human-trafficking and forced prostitution is another major concern, in parts of the UAE at least.

Expats, Emiratis and Omanis

The arrival of vast numbers of foreigners has, of course, had a massive impact on the lives of the people in whose countries they have landed, and although racial tensions have been remarkably absent so far, signs of changing attitudes can clearly be seen.

The virtual deluge of foreigners in the UAE has had its inevitable effect. Native Emiratis, who to begin with were happy to see foreigners arrive

"Emiratisation" aimed at increasing the involvement of local people in private enterprise, and developing the skills of the population at large – although the initiative has had relatively little impact to date, most Emiratis preferring either to live on their considerable state handouts or to take well-paid but undemanding jobs in various government ministries and other state organisations. More than 99 percent of employees in private companies remain expat to this day.

The situation in Oman is somewhat different, and relations in Oman between natives and expats are generally closer and more harmonious than those in the UAE – a reflection of the

to help develop their country, increasingly feel virtual strangers in their own land – particularly given native Emiratis' customary isolation from the expat workforce at large. Resentment at the insensitive behaviour of foreign residents (not to mention visiting tourists) has become an increasing bone of contention, added to the impending sense that their own indigenous culture is being systematically swamped by foreign influences. The government, in turn, has become increasingly concerned at the lack of involvement by native Emiratis in the economic life of the country, launching a sustained programme of

LEFT: there is a huge expat workforce in the UAE.
ABOVE: Abu Dhabi's Marina Mall.

lower overall number of foreign workers, and of the Omanis' generally lower income levels, which have compelled them to take the sort of jobs and to mix with the labour force in a way that their wealthier Emirati cousins have not been obliged to do (although, as in the UAE, the government has introduced an "Omanisation" policy designed to boost the number of nationals working for private companies). Tensions persist even so, and the taking of jobs by expats was a major bone of contention amongst protestors during the demonstrations in early 2011 that marked the Omani phase of the Arab Spring – even though many of the allegedly stolen jobs were ones which Omanis themselves were unwilling or unqualified to take on.

ISLAM IN SOUTHEAST ARABIA

Islam shapes the principles of government as well as private lives, while in Oman a particular brand of Islam, Ibadism, has played a crucial role in the country's history

Islam remains fundamental to the Gulf. Modern as it might seem, life in the UAE and Oman still revolves around traditional daily and annual religious rhythms, ranging from the five daily prayers that mark the passing of each 24-hour period through to the great festivals which punctuate the year. The dominant form of the religion nowadays in the UAE is the mainstream Sunni version of Islam. The majority of Omanis, however, continue to profess the ancient Ibadi faith, with its uniquely democratic traditions.

Islam, meaning "submission", permeates all aspects of the believer's public and private lives, laying down rules for everyday conduct and social relationships. Distinctions between religion, morality, legal affairs and politics do not exist, for they are judged to be subsumed under God's indivisible law. The faithful express their belief without self-consciousness wherever they happen to be, whether at home, in the street or in the mosque.

The coming of Islam

Islam was revealed to the Prophet Mohammed, a native of Mecca in western Arabia, in a series of revelations beginning in AD 610 and continuing until his death in AD 632. Muslims believe that God vouchsafed these utterances, of which the Qur'an is held to be a verbatim record, as the final and perfected revelation of Islam.

Islam, as the religion of Allah, is believed to have existed unchanged for all time, and to have been the religion of the patriarch Abraham.

LEFT: Sultan Qaboos Grand Mosque, the only mosque in Oman that is open to non-Muslims.
RIGHT: minaret, Bahla, Oman.

Subsequent prophets, such as Moses and Jesus, are revered but regarded as not having been in complete possession of the divine Message. Muslims do not believe that Allah is distinct from the God of the Bible and the Torah.

Oman was one of the first countries to embrace Islam, in AD 630 – part of the early spread of the new religion within Arabia during the lifetime of the Prophet Mohammed. The Prophet sent emissaries from Medina, as he did to all the tribes and settlements of Arabia, calling them to Islam. The one he sent to Oman was the general 'Amr bin al-'As, later in the 640s to be the Muslim conqueror of Egypt.

Though 'Amr targeted the flourishing Persian port and capital of Sohar on the Omani coast it was the Arab tribal ruling family, the Julanda, and not the Persian governor, who accepted his message. For the Arabs the call to Islam was the call to eject the ruling Persian colonisers of Oman out of the Batinah coastal plain of Oman.

Following the death of Mohammed in 632 a period of turbulence engulfed the new Islamic world. A series of rebellions broke out against Abu Bakr, the new caliph in Medina, leading to the so-called Ridda Wars, or Wars of Apostasy. Oman was at the forefront of the rebellion, although this was probably less to do with religious than political reasons, with the powerful Azd tribe attempting to reassert their

autonomy. According to tradition, Abu Bakr despatched a large force which clashed with the Omanis at the Battle of Dibba, resulting in the annihilation of the rebels – the large graveyard near the modern town of Dibba is said to contain the remains of those killed in the fighting.

Ibadism and Imams

Islam would thereafter remain unchallenged as the dominant faith in Oman, although the region's independent-minded and rebellious tribes adopted an unusual brand of the religion that would subsequently characterise the country's religious and political life right up to the present day. Many Omanis began to travel to the great Muslim foundation at Basra.

Here they were drawn into the political and ideological conflicts which nearly succeeded in bringing down the Umayyad Caliphate, creating enormous disorder in the early Islamic state and producing the rebel Khawarij or "Outsiders" movement.

Travellers returning to Oman over the next two centuries introduced Khawarij ideas to Oman, where they developed into the form of the religion known as Ibadism which is still practised by the majority of Omanis right up to the present. In common with other movements which would today be called fundamentalist, the aim of the Ibadis was to restore the pure Islamic state according to the teaching of the Prophet, before it had been corrupted by the third Caliph 'Uthman. Though there were several other centres of Ibadism in early Islam, notably in Yemen and Hadhramaut, today Oman is the only place where it still has a significant number of followers.

True Ibadism is distinguished from orthodox Sunni Islam at the political level in two ways. First, the hereditary principle is anathema. Ibadis believe their ruler should be chosen by an electoral college of good and learned men and proposed to the community. This Imam can be drawn from any family, for the first condition an aspiring Imam must fulfil is that of piety and learning. Second, Ibadis do not

> *A Muslim male may take up to four wives, assuming he can support them all – although in practice few take more than one.*

believe it is necessary to have an Imam at all times. During periods of political upheaval the Imamate can lapse and go into a state of secrecy, abeyance or latency known as *kitman*. This has occurred in Oman's history, sometimes for centuries.

Of all doctrines of sovereignty, this is a rather minimal one and one likely to appeal to a tribal mentality. In common with other Muslim attempts to reflect the rule of God upon earth, the ideal of the good ruler included the condition that allegiance to him should be withdrawn if, when God's law was transgressed, he showed no sign of repentance. There was no standing army under central command to enforce sovereignty, and no elaborate bodyguard: militias were raised by the Imam calling up tribal levies.

This kind of consultative system works well when everyone is in agreement, but immediately falls apart when they are not. Only rarely, therefore, has the Imamate succeeded in genuinely uniting the tribes of inner Oman. More usually the Imamate has been the political prize sought by rival tribal groupings.

While the Imamate sometimes succeeded in harnessing and harmonising tribalism, it never eradicated it: the Imam was simply a kind of supra-tribal leader, his office modelled on that of a tribal chief.

Differences between the various Emirates persist, even so. The best known is the conservative emirate of Sharjah which, as a result of strong Saudi influence, now follows a strict form of the traditional Islamic Shariah law code. Sharjah law has now banned alcohol and enacted strict "decency laws" which make it a criminal offence for two unmarried people of opposite sexes to be alone together – as well as recently banning the wearing of jewellery by men. Other emirates subscribe to a much more liberal interpretation of Islamic law, although a number of Westerners have been caught out as a result of public demonstrations of affec-

Sunni Islam on the coast

Not all Omanis are Ibadis, however. A sizeable number subscribe to the Sunni creed of Islam, along with virtually all the population of the UAE (apart from a few Shi'ites of Iranian descent). Established on the cosmopolitan coast, Sunni Islam was traditionally more liberal and outward-looking than the Ibadi creed of the interior, and religious freedoms remain carefully protected to this day – you'll find Hindu temples and Christian churches in Dubai, alongside the innumerable mosques.

LEFT: dome of the Sultan Qaboos Mosque in Muscat.
ABOVE: Muslim man praying, Dubai.

tion which would pass unnoticed in the West but which can carry a prison sentence for lewd behaviour in the UAE.

Islam in daily life

The central tenets of the religion, known as the Five Pillars of Islam, form the basis of the faith as practised by all its adherents. The first of the Five Pillars is the declaration of faith (*shahada*), which involves saying the words "There is no god but Allah, and Mohammed is the messenger of Allah". Other pillars include praying five times daily, paying the alms tax (*zakat*), fasting during the holy month of Ramadan and (if one's means allow), making the pilgrimage to Mecca (the Hajj) once in one's lifetime.

Religious invocations form a staple part of Gulf Arabic – hardly a sentence passes in most conversations without the traditional insh'allah ("God willing") or al hamdu'lillah ("Thanks be to God").

Islam permeates many levels of local life in terms of how people (women especially) dress and dietary taboos (with both pork and alcohol being forbidden), as well as providing the region with many of its most characteristic Arabic expressions and idioms.

Muslims are expected to pray five times daily at fixed times. The prayers *(salah)* are known, in order, as *fajr* (dawn), *dhuhr* (noon), *asr* (late afternoon), *maghrib* (just after sunset) and *isha'a* (between sunset and midnight). Muslims will attempt to reach a mosque in time for prayers; failing this, they will simply pray wherever they happen to be at the time, usually kneeling on a small prayer rug. The important thing is not the location, but the fact that the worshipper is in a state of ritual purity both mentally and physically – ritual pre-prayer ablutions *(wudhu)* are particularly important, and all mosques come equipped with washrooms. The stimulating

For the visitor, the most obvious sign of Islamic life are the daily calls to prayer *(adhan)*, with the soulful noise of muezzin summoning the faithful resounding from minarets across the country – Arabia's most instantly recognisable aural signature, and one that can be heard in remote mountain villages and modern shopping malls alike. In former times this would have been a person calling from the tower or roof of a mosque; nowadays prerecorded messages relayed through loudspeakers are the norm. The call to prayer itself is a précis of Islamic beliefs, rather like the *shahada*, usually centred on multiple renditions of the words *Allahu Akbar* ("God is Great"), usually sung with a rising flourish.

tours of Jumeirah Mosque in Dubai *(see page 207)* offer interesting insight into prayer rituals.

Annual festivals

Supplementing the daily round of prayer are the great annual festivals celebrated by Muslims across the world, which are conscientiously observed in both the UAE and Oman.

Pre-eminent amongst Islamic festivals is the month-long Ramadan, celebrated during the lunar month of Ramadan (exact dates vary from year to year). Ramadan is a time of fasting and religious reflection during which Muslims are

Above: prayer-book sign on the road from Quiryat, Oman. **Right:** shoes must be removed before prayer.

expected to purify mind and body and reaffirm their relationship with God. During Ramadan, Muslims are required to fast from dawn to dusk, while music and dancing is also frowned upon.

The breaking of the fast at dusk, known as *iftar*, is the highlight of the day, often with lavish amounts of food and drink being consumed to compensate for the day's efforts (ironically, it is said that many people actually gain weight during Ramadan). Special "*iftar* tents" are erected in many places, from village squares to five-star hotels, with sumptuous Arabian buffets. Things get even more colourful and busy during Eid Al Fitr, the day marking the end of Ramadan.

The region's second major festival is Eid Al Adha, the "Festival of the Sacrifice". Falling around 70 days after the end of Ramadan, this celebrates the willingness of Abraham (or Ibrahim, as he is known to Muslims) to sacrifice his son Ismail at the command of God (although having proved his obedience, he was permitted to sacrifice a ram instead). Large numbers of animals are slaughtered and the meat divided amongst the poor during the festival, making for a rather grisly sight in parts of the region, Oman especially, where huge numbers of carcasses can often be seen literally piled up by the roadside.

THE EVIL EYE AND OTHER MAGICAL BELIEFS

As in many countries across the Muslim world, the concept of the Evil Eye *(ayn al hasud)* is still very much alive and well in the UAE and Oman – the idea that an envious or hostile person can cause you bad luck or harm by a simple look or turn of speech. The concept of the Eye goes back into the depths of antiquity, and is also backed by the authority of the Qur'an, which warns against it.

There are believed to be many different ways of warding off the eye, while most traditional Arabian jewellery *(see page 74)* features protective amulets or small boxes in which pieces of Quranic text were kept to protect the wearer. The usual formula for avoiding

appearing to give the Eye is to say *masha allah*, meaning "God has willed it", rather than expressing direct praise or admiration, which might be construed as envy.

The Evil Eye is just one of many quasi-religious magical beliefs which have taken root in the Gulf. In Oman, in particular, there is also a widespread fear of jinns, powerful supernatural beings who can take possession of those unfortunate enough to offend them, causing misery, pain and even death. The jinns of the Bahla area are particularly notorious, credited with a variety of actions ranging from turning milk sour to carrying off entire mosques in the middle of the night.

FOOD AND DRINK

The UAE and Oman provide an eclectic crucible of
Arabian, Indian and European culinary traditions

The Gulf stands at something of a culinary crossroads, midway between the classic Middle Eastern cuisines of the Levant to the west and the spicier cooking of the Indian subcontinent to the east, with a dash of Iranian and European influences thrown in for good measure. Both Indian and Middle Eastern cuisines are both well represented throughout the region, as are a range of other global cooking styles, although traditional Emirati and Omani remain considerably more elusive.

Ingredients and influences

Given its largely hostile climate, food production in the UAE and Oman has traditionally been limited, with nutrition usually at subsistence levels and based around readily available foodstuffs like dates and fish. Fish was particularly important around the coast (and was also dried and sent up into the mountains both for human and animal consumption), while inland there was a heavy reliance on the ubiquitous date – an unusually rich, concentrated and durable source of food which was perfectly suited to the nomadic Bedu lifestyle, supplemented by simple flatbreads cooked over campfires and considerable quantities of coffee (see page 93). Roasted meat – wild oryx and other animals – was eaten when available, although it was usually something of an uncommon luxury, and the hunting of such animals remained a difficult and highly prized skill amongst the Bedu, at least until the advent of 4x4s and semi-automatic machine-guns. Camels were also occasionally slaughtered and

eaten on important occasions (camel remains a popular food in Dhofar to this day). Bananas, papayas, mangoes and citrus fruits were also cultivated, while the cooler heights of the Jebel Akhdar produced a supply of temperate produce – peaches, pears, grapes, apples and pomegranates, along with a wide range of vegetables and the area's famous rosewater. Such foodstuffs remained scant, however, and by and large the region had neither the wealth nor the natural produce to allow the development of a classical cuisine like that of North India, Iran or the Turkish Ottomans.

External influences brought to the coast by merchant dhows or overland by trading caravan introduced new outside elements: spices

LEFT: Sohar fish souk. ABOVE: cooking on an open-air grill at a restaurant in Salalah, Oman.

from India became an established feature in Gulf cooking, while dishes were adopted from the cuisines of other countries around the Gulf, Iran, the subcontinent and, of course, the Arab lands around the Mediterranean to the west.

Traditional regional cooking

Traditional Gulf cuisine is poorly represented in restaurants, although a few establishments are doing their best to revive local culinary traditions, such as the Bin Ateeq chain in Oman along with places like Kargeen and Ubhar in Muscat and the Khan Murjan Restaurant in Dubai.

Regional Emirati and Omani cuisine provides an interesting, lightly spiced blend of Indian and Arabian cooking traditions, most of them centred on biryani-style baked rice and meat concoctions – local offshoots of the better-known Indian biryani or Iranian *polo*. Local variants include dishes like *fouga* (a kind of Emirati-style chicken biryani) and *goboli* (rice cooked with lamb, spices, onions and raisins). Other similar biryani-style dishes you may encounter (particularly in Oman) include the Afghan-style *kabuli* (or *qabooli*), the Saudi *kabsa* (also known as *maqboos* or *machbus*) and the Yemeni *mandi*. In theory, each of these

DATES

Dates (along with coffee) provide the region with its most distinctive culinary experience – and a living link with the region's harsh history. Dates underpinned the traditional nomadic lifestyle of the desert interior, providing a concentrated, transportable and long-lasting source of nutrition which was perfectly adapted for the nomadic lifestyle of the region's Bedu – even today, local Muslims still traditionally break their daytime Ramadan fast by eating a single date as night falls.

Dates have remarkable nutritional qualities, offering an excellent source of protein, vitamins and minerals. Their high sugar content (up to 80 percent) protects them against bacterial decay and makes them extremely durable – dried

dates can last for years, making them perfectly adapted to survive in the heat of the Gulf, even without refrigeration. They can also be pressed for their juice or used to make wines and syrups. In earlier times, boiling date syrup, poured onto the heads of attackers, was even used as a military weapon. They were also the region's most important export before the discovery of oil.

Numerous different varieties of date are grown all over the Gulf, ranging dramatically in size and colour, from dark brown to pale, almost honey-coloured varieties – the best are treasured and savoured by local connoisseurs, like fine wines in France. Those from Saudi Arabia are generally reckoned to be the best.

regional variants has its own distinct character and style of preparation, although it's difficult to generalise.

Other old-fashioned recipes include *harees laham* (lamb with wheat in cow ghee); *shuwa* (slow-roasted meat cooked in a clay oven, like the classic Yemeni *mandi*); *mashuai* (whole spit-roasted kingfish served with lemon rice); and *marak* (traditional vegetable curry), although these rarely make their way onto restaurant menus.

Chicken *(dijaj)* remains the staple ingredient in most biryanis, kebabs and curries, although various other types of meat are also available going under the name *laham* (literally "meat"), which usually means beef or lamb, but might

> The Dubai Friday brunch is an institution. Many restaurants lay on all-you-can-eat (and sometimes drink) deals. It usually kicks off around midday, and can last for the remainder of the afternoon.

also conceivably mean goat or (in Salalah) camel.

There's lots of top-quality fish available along the Omani coast, although to see it done justice you'll have to shell out for a meal at one of Muscat's upmarket seafood restaurants – or go to Dubai, which is where a lot of the catch ends up. The local kingfish *(kenadh)*, shark *(qersh al samak)* and lobster *(sharkha)* are particularly good, as is the ubiquitous *hammour* (grouper), a versatile white fish which can be found on menus across the region.

Middle Eastern cuisine

Mainstream Middle Eastern cuisine – often referred to as "Lebanese" (although "Levantine" might be a more accurate description) – is widely found throughout both the UAE and Oman. Many of the most typical dishes originated in the countries of the Levant, around the eastern end of Mediterranean, during the Ottoman period.

The classic Middle Eastern meal always opens with a selection of meze – small dishes, shared amongst a group of diners, rather like Spanish tapas. Many of these have established themselves in mainstream world cuisine – bowls of olives, along with hummus, falafel

and tabouleh. Others remains less well known outside the region, including classics such as *fattoush* (a type of salad with toasted bread), *kibbeh* (deep-fried lamb balls mixed with cracked wheat), *fatayer* (triangular pastries filled with cheese or spinach), as well as dips such as *foul madamas* and *baba ghanouj* (made from fava beans and eggplant respectively, blended with lemon juice, oil, chilli and garlic).

Grilled meats, or kebabs, form the basis of more substantial dishes. Easily the most common form of Arabian food is the ubiquitous shwarma – spit-roasted chicken and/or beef carved off and served wrapped in bread with

salads – the Gulf version of the doner kebab (also served laid out on a piece of bread on a plate with chips and salad – the so-called "shwarma plate"). You'll never go far in the Gulf without seeing a local shwarma café, with dripping haunches of meat enveloped in clouds of temptingly flavoursome smoke. Other common dishes include the Lebanese *shish taouk* (chicken kebabs served with garlic sauce) and Turkish-style kofte kebabs. Most kebabs are served with Arabian-style flatbread *(khubz)* and a bowl of hummus and accompanying salad.

Lebanese food can be found across the region, from humble cafés in backwater Oman and the UAE through to glitzy establishments in Abu Dhabi and Dubai – more upscale places

FAR LEFT: tea and dates.
LEFT: *kibbeh* are lamb balls in a bulgur shell.
RIGHT: Lebanese *manakish*, a kind of pizza.

often double as impromptu party venues, with live music and the ubiquitous belly-dancer, often not getting going until past 11pm, and then cracking on until the small hours.

Subcontinental spices

Indian food, in one form or another, forms the mainstay of modern Gulf cuisine – a result of both long-standing historic links between the two regions and the presence of huge numbers of subcontinental expats in the region. In the major cities, upmarket restaurants offer superb renditions of classic North Indian dishes, on a par with anything you'll find in the West (or,

indeed, in India itself) – Indego and Nina's in Dubai *(see page 264)* offer particularly good and innovative contemporary Indian cooking, while the much-loved Mumtaz Mahal *(see page 245)* in Muscat can't be beaten for traditional classics in a relaxed atmosphere. For a true taste of Gulf-style Indian food, nothing beats a visit to one of the downmarket – but often surprisingly excellent – Indian and Pakistani cafés which cram the streets of Bur Dubai in Dubai or Ruwi in Muscat, offering a wide range of dishes stretching from classic North Indian Punjabi and Mughlai dishes through to feisty South Indian *masala dosas*, *uttapam* and thalis.

Elsewhere, a kind of low-grade pseudo-Indian style of cooking remains the staple of down-at-heel

cafés across both the UAE and, especially, Oman, featuring ubiquitous biryanis and other Indian- or Pakistani-style chicken or mutton curries – although these bear little relation to the food served up in the West, or, indeed, in the subcontinent itself.

International influences

Dubai has established itself as the Middle East's major culinary hotspot, attracting celebrity chefs ranging from Gordon Ramsay and Gary Rhodes, through to Pierre Gagnaire, Giorgio Locatelli and the late Santi Santamaria, as well as Sanjay Kapoor and Vineet Bhatia, India's first-ever Michelin-starred chef. Abu Dhabi and Muscat also boast a fair roster of top chefs, mainly based at the restaurants of top-end hotels such as the Emirates Palace in Abu Dhabi and the Al Bustan, Shangri-La and Grand Hyatt hotels in Muscat.

Thai and Chinese restaurants have also made considerable inroads into the local dining scene in the major cities, although the style of Chinese cuisine served up in many places is a hybridised Indo-Sino style of cuisine, with rather more spice than is authentic. Dubai is also good for Iranian food (evidence of the city's long-standing links with that country), featuring hearty *chelo* kebabs and *polos* (Iranian-style biryanis, traditional featuring slow-cooked

> The Arabic word for coffee, qahwah, *is thought to be the origin of the English word "coffee", via the Turkish* kahve *and the Italian* caffè – *although* qahwah *may derive from Kaffa, in Ethiopia, an original home of the coffee shrub.*

meats leavened with saffron and barberries). Moroccan food can also be found, with signature dishes including the classic spicy harira soup, *pastilla* (pigeon pie) and various tagines and couscous dishes.

Fast-food outlets have made inevitable inroads into the region, and branches of McDonald's, Subway, Domino's Pizza and suchlike are now pretty much everywhere. For a more rewarding take on local fast food, look out for branches of the Lebanese Zaatar w Zeit chain, with outlets across Dubai and Abu Dhabi, offering fast-food Lebanese-style cuisine, including the classic Lebanese *manakish* (a kind of Middle Eastern-style pizza served with thyme, yoghurt and cheese).

Desserts

No traditional meal in Oman would be complete without a portion of halwa, the rather sickly dessert which has become something of a national dish, and which can be seen piled up in china bowls and plastic tubs in shops and souks across the country. Halwa is made in a wide range of different styles, across Europe, the Middle East and Asia. Omani halwa is wheat-based, which gives it a quite different taste and texture to the nut-based halwas found in Eastern Europe, Greece and Turkey, made from a mix of semolina, ghee (clarified butter), sugar and rosewater, flavoured with cardamom and almonds and slow-boiled over a wood fire.

Umm Ali, a sweet Arabian-style bread pudding, is another favourite dessert, while you might also come across *lokhemat* – deep-fried balls of flour flavoured with cardamom and served with lime and cardamom syrup.

Drinks and shisha

Coffee remains central to life in the UAE and Oman – not just a drink, but a kind of social adhesive which oils the wheels of traditional hospitality, performed according to the traditional coffee ceremony etiquette described on page 65. Itinerant coffee-pourers can still often be seen patrolling the lobbies of upmarket hotels, government ministries and other public spaces, dispensing drinks from ornate copper pots, usually with a tray of dates to hand as well. The drink itself is notably different from that consumed in the West, served without milk and sugar but flavoured with spices including cardamom and/or cloves – intense, aromatic and slightly bitter, and traditionally drunk from tiny handle-less cups, like oversized thimbles.

Tea *(shay)* is also universally popular, although not of particularly high quality – the classic Lipton's teabag is ubiquitous, although you may hit upon a local Indian café serving up the classic subcontinental *masala chai*, sweet and heavily spiced. Fruit juices are also widely available, usually particularly good in Lebanese establishments, as are all the usual global fizzy drinks. You may also come across the traditional *laban*, a type of sour buttermilk.

Alcohol is widely available across the region (in Dubai and Abu Dhabi particularly), although punitive taxes keep prices high and local laws mean that establishments are usually only found in top-end hotels – independent pubs and licensed restaurants remain a rarity. Most establishments model themselves on ersatz English pubs, complete with faux-British wood-panelled decor and with a stereotypical range of international tipples. There's also a tempting selection of more stylish bars in Dubai, Abu Dhabi and Muscat, however, often offering superb beachside locations or high-rise settings, and with an upmarket selection of cocktails and shots aimed firmly at the expat and tourist party set.

The traditional meal concludes with shisha: Arabian-style tobacco smoked in one of the distinctive waterpipes (hookah, *narghil* or "hubbly-bubbly") which can be found across the Middle East. Shisha cafés are enormously popular in the UAE (although surprisingly rare in Oman), while many restaurants also serve shisha, although the region's smoking ban means that it can now only be served in outdoor venues. Most shisha cafés will have at least 10 types of shisha to choose from (often more), including unflavoured blends alongside various fruit-scented concoctions such as apple, lemon and grape – much gentler on the throat and infinitely more aromatic than Western cigarettes.

Left: local produce at a Muscat vegetable market.
Right: a Nizwa couple in Pizza Hut.

ARCHITECTURE

From traditional mudbrick forts and palm-thatch huts to futuristic steel-and-glass high-rises, the UAE and Oman present a kaleidoscopic array of Arabian architecture past and present

Oman and the UAE between them offer a fascinating range of architecture both ancient and modern, from the time-warped mudbrick forts and mountain villages of the Omani interior to the ultra-modern skyscrapers of Abu Dhabi and Dubai – a striking physical symbol of the whirlwind changes which have swept through the region in recent decades. The traditional architecture of Oman is as fine as anything in the Islamic world, with a staggering collection of majestic castles dotting the country's mountains, coast and desert, along with innumerable watchtowers, walled towns and villages, and intricately engi-

> Looking forward, the region's finest architectural creation will undoubtedly be the Saddiyat Island development in Abu Dhabi, with major landmarks by top architects including Norman Foster, Frank Gehry, Jean Nouvel, Tadao Ando and Zaha Hadid.

neered falaj systems – a marvellous compendium of local building traditions, making exemplary use of the very simplest building materials. The more forward-looking cities of the UAE, meanwhile, are rapidly transforming themselves into showpieces of modern architecture at its most extravagant and inventive, attracting a string of top international architects and boasting a range of iconic contemporary landmarks, including

Dubai's celebrated Burj al Arab and the recently opened Burj Khalifa, the world's tallest building.

Traditional materials

Traditional buildings in Oman and the UAE often give the marvellous impression of having grown organically out of the landscapes in which they sit, their ochre-coloured walls blending seamlessly with the surrounding mountains or desert, so that is it sometimes difficult to know where nature ends and building begins, with forts moulded around the contours of the rocks on which they sit and mudbrick villages rising out of the earth from which they were created.

LEFT: high-rises on Abu Dhabi's corniche.
ABOVE: a wind tower at Al Bateen dhow harbour, Abu Dhabi.

Much of this sense of connection between building and landscape derives from the ingenious use of locally available materials: mudbrick, coral, mountain rock, palm-thatch, mangrove wood – but little (if anything) imported or foreign. The simplest form of traditional building in the region is the *barasti* hut, fashioned from nothing but trimmed palm branches and leaves tied together to form impromptu shelters – impermanent but surprisingly effective in providing a modicum of shade, while the permeable palm-frond "walls" allowed breezes to blow through, taking advantage of

Stone was also often used, often in combination with mudbrick: either slabs of locally quarried rock in the mountains or coral-stone (*fesht*) along the coast – look closely at the walls of many of the region's lowland forts and traditional buildings and you can still make out the delicate outlines of submarine sponges and other corals. Stones were cemented together using layers of pounded gypsum, while walls were strengthened by the insertion of mangrove poles bound with rope.

More elaborate structures, whether mudbrick, stone or a mixture of both, were often faced with *sarooj*, a type of mortar-cum-plaster.

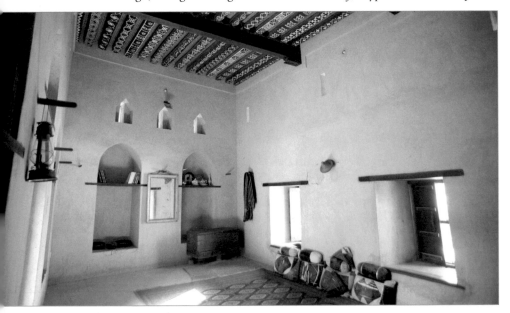

whatever breezes were available. These were the types of dwelling which most Emiratis and Omanis of the coastal regions lived in right up to the 1950s and 1960s, and replicas can be seen in various museums and forts around the region.

Larger buildings were generally fashioned from mudbrick. Mudbrick (or adobe, from the Arabic al tob, meaning "mud") was made from alluvial clay, containing fine particles of grit and silt, mixed with chopped straw to strengthen the resultant bricks. A fermenting agent, such as sugar-cane syrup, was also sometimes added. The resulting mixture was then left to "cure" for four or five days before being moulded into bricks.

Sarooj was made from a mixture of mud and limestone burnt together at extremely high temperatures for up to a week. The resultant ash was then mixed with water (again, sometimes with the addition of a fermenting agent) and the paste used to bind bricks and stone, and to provide the smooth and shiny plaster finish which can still be seen on the walls of many Omani forts today.

Imported materials were only rarely used – roofs and doors of Indian teak and other hardwoods can sometimes be found, although most timbers used are locally sourced mangrove poles, used not only to strengthen walls but also to form roofs, usually with a layer of palm leaves laid on top.

Houses and forts

Fine old traditional houses can be seen across the region, many of them now restored as museums (such as the Heritage House in Dubai, Bait al Naboodah in Sharjah and Bait al Zubair in Muscat) – although it's worth remembering that these elaborate mansions are far from typical of the living arrangements enjoyed by the former population at large, most of whom lived in simple, ephemeral *barasti* palm-thatch huts until quite recent times.

Traditional houses follow a fairly standard pattern, arranged around a central courtyard (*housh*), sometimes with a verandah (*liwan*), pro-

viding a space where inhabitants could cook, play, take the air and graze a few animals in complete privacy; some courtyards even boast a well and perhaps a couple of trees. Exterior walls are usually plain and largely windowless in order to protect the privacy of those within. Rooms usually include a *majlis* (meeting room) in which the family would have received guests and exchanged news (some larger houses have two separate *majlis* for men and women), along with assorted bedrooms, kitchens and storerooms. In the UAE, most large houses also boast

LEFT: inside Nakhal Castle on Oman's Batinah Coast.
ABOVE: looking through Al Alam Palace gates, Old Muscat.

one or more wind towers. The overall effect of most traditional houses is often understated, verging on the austere, although the overall plainness is often relieved by richly carved details including lavish wooden doors and screens, or by geometrical floral designs framing windows, doorways and arches, made from gypsum coloured with powdered charcoal.

Traditional local architecture was remarkably well adapted for its environment (unlike today's modernistic high-rises – *see page 99*). Walls were built thick and windows kept small to exclude the scorching heat outside, while both coral and adobe helped to preserve the coolness of the interiors thanks to their excellent natural insulating properties. Houses were also built close to one another, partly for security, and also to provide shade in the narrow alleyways between.

The innumerable forts of the region follow a similar pattern in terms of their overall construction and internal living arrangements, though obviously they tend to be much larger in size, and boast additional defensive features – for more on which *see page 125.*

Contemporary Islamic architecture

Despite the advent of concrete and steel, many of the region's modern buildings still follow traditional patterns. The layout of the modern Emirati and Omani villa, for instance, retains the slightly embattled appearance of an old-fashioned traditional dwelling, usually enclosed in high walls to protect the privacy of those within and standing proudly apart from its neighbours – Western terraced houses or apartment blocks being notable by their general absence. Religious architecture too remains virtually unchanged, with all mosques in the region following decidedly old-fashioned designs, such as the landmark Jumeirah Mosque in Dubai of 1978 (essentially a replica of a medieval Egyptian Fatimid mosque) or the Grand Mosque in nearby Bur Dubai, rebuilt in 1990 along decidedly traditional lines. Many modern buildings in the UAE also continue to sport emblematic wind towers, even if they no longer have any practical function.

More original reworkings of traditional regional architecture can also be seen.

Perhaps the most inventive is the flamboyant Al Alam Palace in Muscat, with its multicoloured, pseudo-Islamic tilework, stone-carving and pointed arches given a colourful contemporary makeover, or the same city's vast Sultan Qaboos Grand Mosque, a slightly minimalist reworking of the traditional Grand Mosque. The even more extravagant Sheikh Zayed Grand Mosque in Abu Dhabi follows a similar theme, with a range of international Islamic influences going into its eclectic design.

Also notable are the many striking examples of faux-Arabian kitsch which have

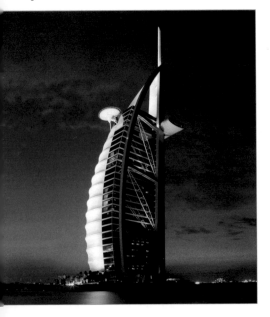

begun mushrooming across the region. Dubai has shown a particular fondness for the style – unoriginal and even rather cheesy, although the sheer extravagance with which some examples have been carried through compels reluctant admiration, as in the vast Madinat Jumeirah complex, with its hundreds of sand-coloured wind towers, or the opulently decorated interiors of the atmospheric Souk Khan Murjan – both of which present contemporary Islamic designs with a touch of Hollywood, or perhaps Disney. The landmark Emirates Palace in Abu Dhabi is another good example, the extravagant interiors being particularly fine.

Futuristic architecture in the UAE

Modern architecture has flourished in the Gulf, and the speed at which places like Dubai and Abu Dhabi have grown has resulted in one of the most spectacular building booms of modern times – at one point in the mid-noughties it was estimated that, astonishingly, a quarter of all the world's construction cranes could be found in Dubai alone. The exploding real-estate market, ready supplies of apparently limitless finance and widespread availability of large plots of unused land all conspired to turn Dubai, in particular, into an enormous building site, further heated by a general absence of the sort of zoning rules, planning permissions and conservation issues which so often haunt major new constructions in the West (and in striking contrast to Oman, where governmental restrictions have ensured that cities across the country have preserved their traditional low-rise, white-washed outline – the absence of high-rise buildings in Muscat is particularly striking).

The wide open desert spaces of Dubai and Abu Dhabi thus provided a kind of tabula rasa on which architects could doodle – and then see their doodles take shape with lightning speed. The results are inevitably mixed. Some of the modern architecture in the Gulf is spectacularly ugly, some is notable as much for its sheer quirkiness as for its ultimate success, although the region also boasts a clutch of undoubted modernist masterpieces, as well as some superb urban architectural ensembles, such as the teetering high-rises of Sheikh Zayed Road in Dubai or the shiny mass of glass-fronted high-rises looming above Abu Dhabi's corniche.

Almost all the region's finest modernist icons can be found in Dubai, a veritable encyclopaedia of contemporary design ranging from the good through to the bad, the mad and the downright ugly. Some of Dubai's most memorable buildings are decidedly quirky in inspiration: the strange Dusit Thani hotel, for example, inspired by the traditional Thai *wai* greeting, with hands placed together in welcome (although it actually looks more like an enormous upside-down tuning fork), or the landmark Etisalat Building, topped by what looks like a vast golf ball (a design now copied in other Etisalat buildings in Dubai, Abu Dhabi and elsewhere).

Many of the city's finest buildings pay oblique homage to the emirate's former maritime traditions, with various sail-shaped architectural motifs, exemplified by the celebrated clubhouse of the Dubai Creek Golf Club (1993), a fascinating sculptural creation whose

> The publicity and marketing potential of landmark buildings was recognised early by Dubai ruler Sheikh Mohammed, who commissioned the Burj al Arab to provide Dubai with an international icon to rival the Eiffel Tower or Statue of Liberty.

instantly recognisable outline (like a kind of Dubai remake of the Sydney Opera House) is inspired by the triangular shapes of the traditional *lateen* sail. The sail motif is invoked again in the superb National Bank of Dubai (designed by Carlos Ott, 1998), its towering Creekside facade comprising a single enormous "sail" surrounded by highly reflective aluminium cladding, mirroring boats on the waters below. Best of all, however, is the superlative Burj al Arab (Tom Wright, 1999), whose land-facing side provides Dubai with its largest and most magnificent architectural sail, memorably illuminated at night (and juxtaposed against the rollercoaster shape of the wonderful Jumeirah Beach Hotel next door, inspired by the shape of a breaking wave).

High-rise cities and environmental concerns

Dubai is now the tallest city in the world, outstripping traditional skyscraper hotspots like New York and Hong Kong, with no fewer than 34 of the world's 200 tallest buildings (compared to 12 in New York and 15 in Hong Kong), while Abu Dhabi, too, is looking increasingly to the clouds, with a current total of six buildings in the top 200. Pride of place goes to the jaw-dropping Burj Khalifa, far and away the world's tallest man-made structure, while other landmarks include the twin Emirates Towers (formerly the tallest buildings in the Middle East) and the soaring, pencil-thin Rose Rayhaan hotel (the tallest hotel in the world).

LEFT: Burj al Dubai. **RIGHT:** solar panels jut out from the rooftops at the Masdar City development.

Impressive though they undoubtedly are, the massed high-rises of Dubai are, as environmentalists often point out, remarkably badly suited to the Gulf. The vast quantities of glass, steel and aluminium cladding in which such buildings are characteristically wrapped act as enormous heat-traps, sucking up sunlight from the fierce desert sky and tending to overheat constantly – with the resultant need for endless air-conditioning to cool them back down again. The need for similarly energy-intensive elevators and pumping systems to move people, water and other necessities up and down such huge structures is another environmental burden.

MASDAR CITY

Oddly, it's Abu Dhabi, the most petrol-centred of the Emirates, which has taken the first steps towards addressing environmental concerns with its vast new Masdar City development, close to the international airport. Masdar is intended to house around 50,000 people and become the world's first zero-carbon, zero-waste city, relying entirely on renewable energy. Remarkably, cars will be banned inside the city, while a perimeter wall will exclude hot desert winds, and narrow shaded streets inside will funnel cool breezes across the city. The first phase of the city is slated to open in 2015.

THE ARTS

From superbly crafted traditional artefacts through to cutting-edge contemporary visual arts, Oman and the UAE offer a rich variety of artistic traditions

The modern countries and city-states of the Gulf are often derided for their rampant materialism and general lack of culture, but traditional arts and culture do survive, along with some innovative contemporary art galleries.

The region's various artisanal traditions are particularly notable, such as its striking jewellery (*see page 74*). Most are now in danger of extinction, although superb traditional antiques can still be found in shops and souks throughout the country. Oman is particularly rich in handicrafts, ranging from quaintly rustic Bahla pottery through to fabulously intricate metalwork including traditional silver *khanjars* (daggers), chunky Bedu jewellery and *mukkabbah* (the round airtight containers which were formerly used to store volatile items like frankincense). Traditional Bedu textiles can also sometimes be found in the souks around the Wahibah Desert, featuring colourful abstract geometrical designs somewhat reminiscent of India.

The region also boasts its own unique roster of performing arts. The writing and reading of poetry remains a popular pastime, commemorating the old Arabian traditions of oral recitation which date back to the Quran and beyond. Poetry recitals are held regularly in the UAE, although these are largely inaccessible to outsiders, while traditional folk music and dancing is also popular. Major poetry recitals and concerts are often broadcast on TV.

ABOVE: exhibit from Bastakiya Art Fair, 2008. Dubai's Bastakiya Art Fair has established itself as a major feature on the annual Arabian cultural calendar, showcasing an eclectic range of works by a wide range of local and international artists.

ABOVE: Algerian artist Sadek Rahim performing at the 2010 Bastakiya Art Fair.

BELOW: traditional pots on show at Jabrin Castle.

LEFT: top-quality carpets and kilims from Iran and other major rug-producing centres in Central Asia are widely available across the Gulf, particularly in Dubai and Sharjah – often at bargain prices.

Modern Art in Dubai and the UAE

Dubai might not be the most culturally cutting-edge city in the world, but in one area at least it has established itself as an unlikely crucible of contemporary creativity: the visual arts. The city is now a veritable hothouse of Arabian fine arts, providing a major international showcase for the work of leading artists from across the Middle East. Much of the credit goes to the string of innovative galleries established in the insalubrious industrial suburb of Al Quoz, off Sheikh Zayed Road near Dubai Marina, by expatriate entrepreneurs from Syria, Iran and Egypt drawn to the area's low rents and spacious warehouses, and seeing a potential market in Dubai.

These now serve (along with other galleries such as the long-established Majlis Gallery in Bastakiya and another cluster of more upmarket venues in The Gate building) as a major showcase of contemporary Arabian art, backed up by two major arts festivals: the huge Art Dubai festival at Dubai Marina (four days in mid-March; www.artdubai.ae) and the more left-field Bastakiya Art Fair (one week in mid-March; www.bastakiyaartfair.com).

Other cities in the UAE also boast a burgeoning visual arts scene. The Sharjah Art Gallery hosts regular exhibitions of new work, while the Sharjah Biennial (two months in alternate years; www.sharjahbiennial.org), is now a major fixture on the international contemporary art calendar. The arrival of the new Louvre in Abu Dhabi is likely to further accelerate the country's rise to international artistic prominence.

Above: Bastakiya's Majlis Gallery.
Below: traditional Arabian calligraphy.

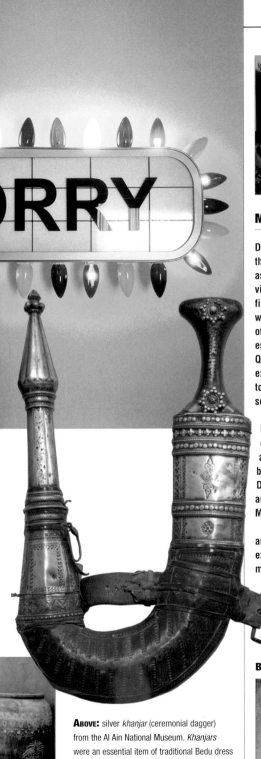

Above: silver *khanjar* (ceremonial dagger) from the Al Ain National Museum. *Khanjars* were an essential item of traditional Bedu dress up until recent times, and are still often worn on festive occasions.

SPORTS AND OUTDOOR ACTIVITIES

From traditional camel racing to Formula 1 Grand Prix, the UAE and Oman offer a wealth of spectator sports alongside myriad adventure activities and other outdoor diversions

Sport in the Gulf is booming – a combination of the region's perfect Mediterranean winter climate, the natural sporting passions of its inhabitants, and the conscious decision of its rulers to use sporting events as a way of boosting the region's international profile. Qatar's successful bid for the 2020 FIFA World Cup is the most eye-catching example to date, although the UAE has also secured hosting rights to an increasing number of top global sporting events, including the season-ending F1 Grand Prix in Abu Dhabi and the World Championship golf tournament in Dubai, as well as a host of leading tennis, rugby, running and other tournaments (while the Abu Dhabi takeover of English football club Manchester City – and subsequent multi-million-pound spending spree – has also generated enormous publicity overseas).

While the UAE (Dubai in particular) boasts the lion's share of organised sporting events, Oman comes into its own for adventure activities and other outdoor diversions, including superlative diving, wonderful mountain hiking and a range of wilderness activities including wadi- and dune-bashing, canyoning, caving and climbing – an energetic way of exploring the country's memorable landscapes.

Horse racing

Arabia has been famous for its horses since antiquity, and every thoroughbred racehorse competing in the world today can trace its lineage back to three Arab stallions – the Godolphin and Darley Arabian and the Byerley Turk – that were taken to

Britain more than three centuries ago to improve the speed and stamina of the domestic breed. Not surprisingly then, modern **horse racing** has now taken firm root in the region, particularly in Dubai, thanks to the efforts of the equine-loving Sheikh Mohammed and his brothers (*see box page 104*), who now count themselves amongst the world's most successful racehorse owners through their prestigious Godolphin stable.

Evidence of the seriousness with which Dubai takes its racing can be seen in the spectacular new Meydan Racecourse (www.meydan.ae). The racing season is held during the cooler winter months from November to March, culminating in the prestigious Dubai World Cup, the world's richest horse race, with prize money of a cool

---

LEFT: the Abu Dhabi Formula 1 Grand Prix.
RIGHT: at the Dubai World Cup, held at the Maydan Racecourse.

US$10 million. Race meets are also a major feature on the city's social calendar, attracting a lively crowd of Emiratis and expats, although no betting is allowed.

Meydan is not the only racecourse in the UAE, however, and there are also more low-key tracks at Jabal Ali (in the far south of Dubai), at Abu Dhabi and Sharjah. Details of forthcoming meetings can be found at www.emiratesracing.com.

Golf

Golf is burgeoning in the Gulf – much to the despair of environmentalists, who see the region's ever-expanding number of lush 18-hole courses, with their water-guzzling greens and fairways, as one of the prime examples of a local ecological disaster-in-the-making. Green politics aside, the region offers superb opportunities either to play or to watch top international pros in action.

Dubai, once again, takes centre stage, hosting the region's two leading tournaments. The **Dubai Desert Classic** (www.dubaidesertclassic. com), held at the Emirates Golf Club in Dubai Marina during February/March, is the region's oldest major golfing event, first held in 1993 and now established as a leading fixture on the PGA European Tour. Past winners feature a virtual who's who of golfing greats, including

KINGS OF THE TURF

Few horse-racing stories over recent decades have been as eye-catching as the rise of Dubai's Maktoum family to become one of the world's leading owners – and now breeders – of racehorses, driven by Dubai ruler Sheikh Mohammed and his brothers Hamdan and Ahmed. It was while studying at Cambridge in England in the 1960s that Sheikh Mohammed first became attracted to the atmosphere of the nearby Newmarket racecourse, and within 10 years he and his brothers all had horses in training there. Their first big win came when Hamdan's horse Touching Wood won the 1982 St Leger at Doncaster, while Hamdan followed up this success with 1989 and 1994 Derby winners Nashwan and Erhaab.

Following these triumphs, the Maktoum brothers established the remarkably successful Godolphin Racing Stables, whose various global triumphs have included the remarkable hat-trick recorded by the Lammtarra, a son of the Derby winner Nijinsky. He only ran three times as a three-year-old, but achieved the historic treble of the Derby at Epsom, the King George VI and Queen Elizabeth Stakes at Ascot, and then the Prix de l'Arc de Triomphe at Longchamp.

Today, the family has more than 1,500 racehorses in training in Dubai, Europe and North America, along with vast property interests in thoroughbred stud farms in England, Ireland and the USA – at a staggering investment of US$2.4 billion.

Ernie Els, Tiger Woods, Colin Montgomerie and Seve Ballesteros.

Newer but even more prestigious is the **Dubai World Championship** (www.dubaiworldchampionship.com; four days in December). First held in 2009, this is one of the world's richest golfing events. The championship forms the grand finale to the season-long European Tour, with the tour's 60 top players battling it out for US$7.5 million in prize money at the spectacular new Greg Norman-designed "Earth" course in Dubailand. Lee Westwood won the inaugural event in 2009, followed by Robert Karlsson in 2010.

Motorsports

Not surprisingly given the Emirati and Omani obsession with big cars and all things petrol-driven, **motorsports** have proved a big hit in the region. The leading event is the season-ending Formula 1 Abu Dhabi Grand Prix, held at Yas Island in mid-November. The race was first staged in 2009, when it was won by Red Bull's Sebastian Vettel, who repeated his victory at the dramatic 2010 race, clinching the drivers' championship in the process.

In Dubai, the state-of-the-art track at the Dubai Autodrome (www.dubaiautodrome.com) in Dubailand hosts various other international events through the year, as well as

If you want to play yourself, Dubai has a superb selection of golf courses open to visitors (although green fees can be spectacularly high), including the Emirates Golf Club, the nearby Montgomerie at Emirates Hills, the Four Seasons' Al Badia course at Dubai Festival City, the Arabian Ranches' desert course in Dubailand, the Els Club in Dubai Sports City in Dubailand, and Dubai Creek Golf & Yacht Club. There's also a growing number of courses in Abu Dhabi and elsewhere in the region.

LEFT: Abu Dhabi Golf Club.
ABOVE: Fabio Bertolacci drives his powerboat *Wind of Rome* during the 2010 UIM X-Cat Middle East Powerboat Championship in Dubai Marina.

SPORTS STARS IN DUBAI

As well as hosting more and more sporting events, Dubai has also lured increasing numbers of sports celebrities to the city. In 2002 the government offered David Beckham a free villa on the Palm Jumeirah island, after which a number of other international footballers bought properties on the island.

Not that it's all footballers. Roger Federer trains regularly in Dubai, while various top golfers – including Ernie Els, Colin Montgomerie and Greg Norman – have been involved in designing golf courses in the city. And in 2009 cricketer Andrew Flintoff moved his entire family to Dubai, adding further lustre to the city's burgeoning sporting-celebrity credentials.

offering visitors the chance to try their hand at karting, have a go at driving a F1-style single-seater car, or to take their own vehicles for a spin around the track. More challenging terrain is on offer during the Abu Dhabi Desert Challenge (www.abudhabidesertchallenge.ae), a FIA-sanctioned car and motorbike rally, held in November in the deserts around Abu Dhabi.

On the water, two rounds of the UIM Class One World Offshore **powerboat championships** (www.class-1.com) are held in the UAE, the first in Abu Dhabi in April, the last in Dubai in late October/early November. The Dubai-based Victory team are local favourites.

Other sports

Other traditionally European sports have also found an unlikely but surprisingly successful home in Dubai. The **Dubai Tennis Championship** (late Feb/early March; www. dubaitennischampionships.com) is an established fixture on the men's and women's singles circuit, attracting most of the world's top players – past winners have included Venus Wiliams, Justine Henin, Caroline Wozniacki, Andy Roddick, Rafael Nadal, Novak Djokovic (who has won the last three tournaments) and Roger Federer, who has won the men's event no less than four times.

Even more popular is the annual **Dubai Rugby Sevens** tournament (www.dubairugby7s.com). Part of the IRB Sevens World Series, this is one of the highlights of the international rugby sevens calendar, featuring all the best international teams, with recent winners including England, South Africa and New Zealand. The tournament also provides an excuse for some of the city's most raucous expat partying. Matches are played at the purpose-built The Sevens stadium, on the edge of the city next to the road to Al Ain.

Cricket, too, has found a home in Dubai, helped along by the city's large population of cricket-mad subcontinental expats. Matches are held at the 25,000-seater cricket stadium at the Dubai Sports City (www.dubaisportscity.ae) in Dubailand, which hosts occasional one-day and Twenty20 internationals between leading teams – England, Australia, New Zealand and Pakistan have all played here over the past few years.

Endurance sports can also be found. The leading event is, again, held in Dubai, whose **Dubai Marathon** (www.dubaimarathon.org) has been running (as it were) since 2006, attracting top distance athletes like three-time champion Haile Gebrselassie. Held in mid-January, the race starts and finishes in the Dubai Marina, with runners heading all the way up the coastal Jumeirah Road, and then turning around and running all the way back down again. Further up the road, the **RAK Half Marathon** (www. rakmarathon.org), held in February, is another leading event, again attracting leading competitors from around the world – Kenya's Mary Keitany set a new world record here in 2011.

Over the border, the **Tour of Oman** (www. touroforman.om) cycling race, first held in 2010, attracts a strong field of international riders and is held over six days in February at various locations around Muscat and the Western Hajar.

Traditional sports

Despite the onslaught of Western-style sports around the region, a few resolutely traditional pastimes persist. The most popular is undoubtedly **camel racing**. Racing camels are taken no less seriously than their equine counterparts, with the finest racers changing hands for over US$100,000. There are racetracks throughout the UAE and Oman. Meetings are usually held early in the morning during the cooler winter months – an entertaining sight as the camels' owners charge alongside the racetrack in trucks, exhorting their beasts to ever greater efforts. Until recently small

LEFT: cricket has grown in popularity in Dubai.

Falconry

Hawking is an old and much-loved pastime in the Gulf. Falconers pay huge sums of money for the very best birds and pamper them accordingly

Falconry is a source of great passion in the Gulf. The sport grew out of the traditional lifestyle of the Bedu, who used falcons for hunting. During winter, on the edge of any major town, it is common to see members of the local falconry club exercising and training their birds in the cool of the evening.

The main source of falcons in the Emirates is the livestock market in Sharjah, where dealers import birds from Iran and Pakistan. Aged between six months and three years, a bird can be worth anything between US$240 and US$32,000. Females are preferred over males as they are on average one-third larger.

Although it is illegal to trade in wild birds, they are favoured over more docile captive-bred falcons, which were thought to lack the natural hunting instinct. Happily, captive-bred falcons are now becoming more popular. By contrast, mature wild birds are hard to train but are exceptional hunters. These attract more experienced falconers.

The best time to capture a bird is on its first autumn migration as it passes over the desert on its way south. These immature wild birds are relatively easy to train, but already have a well-developed hunting instinct.

The saker, from the Arabic *saqr*, is the most popular bird on account of its size, toughness and versatility. Known for its intelligent hunting tactics, it predicts the movements of its prey and uses the landscape to hide its attacks.

Smaller and more fragile than the saker is the peregrine falcon *(shahin)*. Built for speed, it is designed to kill on the wing and is vulnerable on the ground. Difficult to keep in captivity, peregrines have become rare and valuable. The lanner, or *shahin wakri*, is a small falcon, like the peregrine, but with the qualities of the saker. Gyrfalcons have also appeared in Arabia in recent years. Mostly captive-bred, they are exotics, not desert falcons, adapted to live in the Arctic, and prized for their size (twice that of a peregrine) and good looks.

The hawking season is very short, from October to January and coinciding with the autumn migration of the game birds, mostly houbara. The traditional falcon species are also migratory and cannot stand the desert summer. It was once common for falconers to release their birds at the end of each hunting season. Now owners hang on to favourite or valuable birds throughout the year, keeping them in luxurious air-conditioned cages, while veterinary care is provided by dedicated falcon hospitals in Abu Dhabi and Dubai.

Falcons have also discovered an unexpected but important new role in the UAE's modern cities, being used to scare away the flocks of pigeons which are wont to perch on high-rise buildings and cover them with droppings – an effective alternative to unsightly netting or anti-roosting spikes.

Falconry displays are sometimes arranged by local tour operators or hotels (particularly desert camps). You can also visit the falcon hospital in Abu Dhabi – see www.falconhospital.com for details.

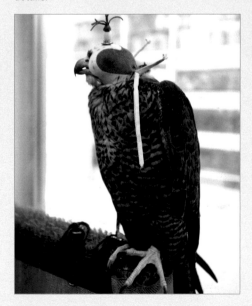

ABOVE AND RIGHT: falconry is an enduringly popular pastime.

boys, often trafficked from Pakistan or India, were employed as jockeys. Pressure from human rights organisations eventually led to the banning of this practice in both the UAE and Oman. The UAE, along with Qatar, pioneered the development of "robot" jockeys that simulate the weight and actions of young riders.

An even more antiquated sporting event is **bull-butting**, which can still be seen at various locations including Fujairah and along the Batinah Coast of Oman at Sohar, Seeb and other places. Traditional **dhow racing** is staged in Abu Dhabi and at the Dubai International Marine Cup in Dubai Marina in May and at cer-

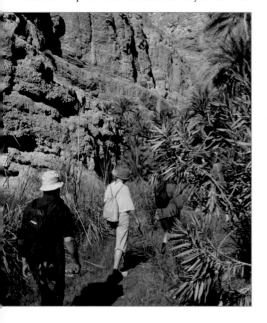

tain times other times of the year (usually over the winter months) – the only chance you'll get in the region to see traditional wooden boats under their distinctive triangular lateen sails.

Diving and watersports

The UAE and, particularly, Oman offer some superlative **diving**, with fine, and often surprisingly unspoilt underwater landscapes and a stunning array of marine life – while the relative lack of visitors means that dive sites remain refreshingly uncrowded. There's a well-developed network of dive schools across the country, often run by European expats, offering a wide range of diving, as well as the usual PADI courses. Muscat itself boasts a considerable number of

operators, with whom you can arrange trips to the wonderful Daymaniyat Islands, as well as to other locations closer to the capital. At the northern end of the country, Musandam is popularly claimed to have the country's best diving amidst the spectacular coastal scenery around the remote town of Kumzar, home to a superb range of marine life including hammerhead and leopard whale sharks, mink whales, manta, eagle rays and turtles, as well as numerous species of smaller tropical fish. There are also excellent underwater possibilities at the opposite end of the country in Dhofar, particularly around Mirbat. The presence of cold currents produced by the annual *khareef* (monsoon) create unique underwater environments here, including a mix of corals and kelp.

Diving opportunities in the UAE are mainly clustered around the east coast emirate of Fujairah – a couple of local operators, plus outfits in Dubai, can arrange trips.

Dubai is the top venue for **watersports**, with activities most easily arranged via one of the hotels in the Dubai Marina. All the marina beach hotels (apart from the Ritz-Carlton) have their own watersports centre, offering a wide range of activities including windsurfing, sailing, kayaking, water-skiing, wakeboarding and

> *Racing camels can reach speeds of 60kmph (37mph), and peak at the age of around three or four. They are nurtured on a diet of honey, ghee, barley, alfalfa, eggs and dates – along with secret concoctions devised by their trainers.*

parasailing (but not jet-skiing, which the authorities have banned). Local operators include Sky & Sea Adventure (www.watersportsdubai.com), who can be found at the Sheraton Jumeirah Beach and Hilton Jumeirah Resort.

Trekking

The mountains of Oman are **trekking** country par excellence, with dramatic paths threading their way across the windswept heights of some of the country's most spectacular ridges, or winding through sheer-sided wadis and canyons. The government has established an extensive network of (usually well-marked) hiking trails around the country, particularly in the Western Hajar. The areas around Jabal Shams and Jabal Akhdar are particularly rewarding, criss-crossed with numerous spectacular high-altitude treks, often following the routes of old donkey trails through remote traditional villages en route. Wadi walks are another popular excursion, such as the beautiful walk up Wadi Shab or the more challenging trek into Snake Gorge (Wadi Bimah) off Wadi Bani Awf – an

> Oman's most spectacular short trek is the marvellous hike, known as the "Balcony Walk", around Wadi Nakhr, the so-called Grand Canyon of Oman.

exhilarating scramble up the gorge, clambering over boulders and wading (or occasionally swimming) through rock pools.

Despite the usually benign conditions, trekking in Oman should not be attempted lightly. It's imperative to carry sufficient water and also to keep a close eye on the weather. Conditions can change with spectacular suddenness during rain, particularly in wadis, many of which are prone to potentially fatal flash-flooding. It pays to go with an experienced guide or tour company such as the Muscat Diving and Adventure Centre (www.holiday-in-oman.com), Oman's leading adventure-tour operator.

Adventure sports and activities

The UAE offers numerous opportunities to take to the air. For **hot-air ballooning** over the UAE desert contact Balloon Adventures in Dubai (www.ballooning.ae). For the ultimate views of Dubai, book yourself in for a **helicopter tour**, offering jaw-dropping views of the city's burgeoning skyline – as well as perfect views of super-sized constructions like the Palm Jumeirah and World archipelago which simply can't be seen properly from the ground. A number of tour operators offer helicopter tours – Aerogulf (based at the international airport; www.aerogulf-services.com) is one of the best established. Tours don't come cheap, as you'd expect, with prices at around US$200 for a 15-minute flight.

For an even more memorable adrenalin rush, SkyDive Dubai (www.skydivedubai.ae) offers a range of **skydiving** programmes

catering to both first-time jumpers and experienced divers. Jumps take place in the spectacular skies above southern Dubai and the Palm Jumeirah, currently costing 1750dh for a tandem jump. For the next best thing to jumping out of a plane, check out iFly Dubai indoor skydiving centre (www.iflyme.com) at Mirdif City Centre, just east of the airport, with virtual flying inside a powerful vertical wind tunnel.

Once again, Oman is the place to head to for remote wilderness adventures. **Off-road driving** is a perennial favourite, either wadi-bashing through the Hajar mountains or

dune-bashing across the Wahibah Desert (*see page 147*). Other **desert activities** are offered by camps around Wahibah, including quad-biking, sand-skiing and more low-key activities like horse and camel riding and desert hikes. Back in the mountains, there's plenty of scope of experienced **rock-climbers** to take to the craggy cliffs of the Hajar, while a trio of via ferratas, in Snake Gorge, Wadi Nakhr and Bandar Khayran, offer the chance to climb the heights without specialised skills or equipment. **Caving** is another possibility for those with the requisite experience, and suitably equipped cavers can also explore the country's remarkable though still largely unexplored subterranean wonders.

LEFT: walking up Wadi Shab, Oman. **RIGHT:** a 4x4 entering Wadi Tawi along the coast of Oman.

Oman

0   50 km
0   50 miles

PLACES: OMAN

A detailed guide to the entire country, with
principal sites clearly cross-referenced by
number to the maps

Compared with other countries around the Arabian
Gulf, Oman is a refreshing paradox: a country that has
succeeded in embracing the modern world whilst also
holding fast to its traditional cultural roots – economically
prosperous, politically stable, but also rich in reminders of times
past. For the visitor, Oman is the only country in the region that
is both accessible and authentic: safe, welcoming and easy to
explore, but offering a rich and satisfying taste of traditional
Arabia at its most memorable.

Oman is a relatively compact country by Middle Eastern or
Asian standards – roughly the size of Italy, and with most of the population
clustered along the coast. The starting point for most visitors is
the low-key capital of Muscat, a sprawling modern metropolis
which preserves some absorbing reminders of times past in the
old-fashioned districts of Mutrah and Old Muscat. Inland lie the
craggy heights of the Western Hajar mountains, centred on the
historic capital of Nizwa and covered in a fascinating patchwork
of majestic forts and mudbrick villages. East of here, the mountains roll down to the sleepy Batinah Coast, with endless fishing
villages and further forts huddled amidst dense swathes of date
palms. South of Muscat, Sharqiya province offers a varied array
of idyllic coastal scenery dotted with turtle beaches, while inland

stretch the dramatic wadis of the Eastern Hajar mountains and the magnificent
dunes of the Wahibha Desert.

At the far northern end of the country (and separated from the rest of
Oman by a swathe of UAE territory), the Musandam peninsula shows the
country at its most scenically spectacular, with huge red-rock mountains
plunging down into a tangle of sheer-sided fjords and sea cliffs, best explored
by boat amidst pods of cavorting dolphins. At the opposite end of the country,
the southern province of Dhofar is different again, visited by the annual *khareef* (monsoon) which turns the region a misty green each year from June to
September, creating impromptu rock pools and waterfalls amidst the beautiful Dhofar mountains which encircle the historic city of Salalah – and offering
a memorable conclusion to one of Arabia's most scenically spectacular and
culturally absorbing countries.

PRECEDING PAGES: sunset near Sohar; villas in Nizwa; camels in Dhofar. **ABOVE LEFT:**
Omani man in Nizwa. **ABOVE RIGHT:** wooden door at Khasab Castle.

MUSCAT

Oman's low-key capital has been transformed over the past four decades, but retains a pleasantly relaxed atmosphere, as well as many reminders of its long and cosmopolitan history

O man's understated capital, Muscat, provides a pleasant mix of traditional and modern. The city has boomed dramatically since the accession of Sultan Qaboos in 1970, transforming from a modest cluster of small, self-contained towns and villages into the sprawling modern metropolis you see today. This is now undoubtedly the heart of the nation, home to a quarter of the country's population (and four times the size of the next largest city, Salalah), the seat of government and the nation's commercial powerhouse.

Despite this, **Muscat** ❶ (Masqat) retains much of its old-fashioned charm, particularly around the historic old enclaves of Mutrah and Old Muscat, and compared to other major cities around the Gulf, the whole place remains resolutely low-key. There are no skyscrapers, and most of the large office blocks and ministries adhere to the traditional Gulf Arab style of architecture, in keeping with the Muscat Municipality's book of acceptable architectural designs, meaning that pitched roofs are forbidden, and that new buildings must be either white or sand-coloured. And presiding over it all is the image of Sultan Qaboos himself. Every shop and office has a picture of the Sultan hanging in its reception, and many homes also get the royal touch.

Although Muscat's foundation dates from the 1st century, the town didn't really get going until the 14th and 15th centuries, following the decline of Sohar. In the 16th century Muscat had the ambiguous honour of attracting the Portuguese, who occupied the city and used it as their main base in the country – and where they remained until ousted by the Omanis in 1650. The city subsequently played a leading role in national affairs, while the decision of Sultan Hamad bin Said to move his court here in 1784 (where

Main attractions

AL MIRANI AND AL JALALI FORTS
AL ALAM PALACE
BAIT AL ZUBAIR
MUTRAH SOUK
BANDAR AL JISSAH
SULTAN'S ARMED FORCES MUSEUM
QURM BEACH
SULTAN QABOOS GRAND MOSQUE

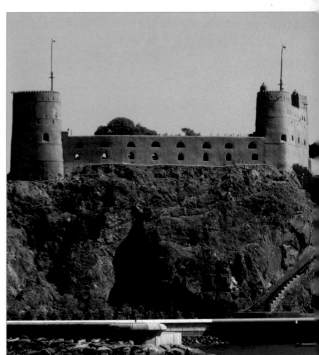

LEFT: ornate doorway in Sultan Qaboos Grand Mosque. **RIGHT:** Al Jalali Fort, Old Muscat.

Al Mirani Fort, in Old Muscat, was built by the Portuguese.

it has largely stayed ever since) effectively established it as the pre-eminent city in Oman.

Muscat can be a disorienting place at first sight. The capital was originally just two small and quite separate towns: Muscat proper – the area now known as **Old Muscat** – and the mercantile centre of Mutrah down the road. These two have now been utterly swallowed up by the surrounding suburbs, although they preserve their own distinct characters and still feel largely separate from the rest of the modern city, which stretches from the bustling central business district of Ruwi through a string of suburbs west to the international airport.

Old Muscat

Towards the southern end of the city, now rather lost within the city's ever-expanding suburban sprawl, stands the original settlement of Muscat, usually referred to as "Old Muscat", with a neat huddle of buildings ancient and modern clustered around a rocky horseshoe bay. A pair of hoary old Portuguese forts (1587–8) stand proudly on either side of the bay: **Al Mirani Ⓐ** to the west and **Al Jalali Ⓑ** opposite. Both are quite unlike the traditional Omani fort – each essentially just a narrow building perched on top of a sheer-sided rock outcrop. Neither fort is open to the public, and Al Jalali is completely off-limits, although you can get a good view of it from across the harbour. Look out too for the names of various ships on the cliffs ringing the east side of the bay, painted onto the rocks by the crews of visiting vessels – like a kind of maritime visitors' book. The young Horatio Nelson is said to have scrambled up the rocks here during a visit to Muscat in the 1770s, despite his fear of heights.

Nestled between the two forts lies the striking **Al Alam Palace** (Flag Palace) Ⓒ, one of the six official royal residences of Sultan Qaboos, built in 1972 in striking contemporary Islamic style, with towering columns in blue and gold. It's not open to the public, although you can walk right up to the main gates for a good view of the facade. Close by stands the site of the

Old Muscat

```
0        200 m
0        200 yds
```

new **National Museum**, which was due to open in early 2012. This major new attraction showcases 6,000 years of Omani heritage and history in 17 themed galleries covering the country's land, people, maritime history, arms and armour, religion and so on.

From here, it is a 10-minute walk west to **Bab al Kabir** (Kabir Gate), the main gate in the old city walls. Just inside Bab al Kabir stands the renovated 18th-century Bait Fransa, the residence of French consuls until 1920 and which now houses the **Omani-French Museum** Ⓓ (Sat–Wed 10am–1pm and 5–8pm, Thur 10am–1pm; free, although currently closed for upgrades). Built by Ghaliah bint Salim, a niece of Sultan Said bin Sultan, the house was presented to Paul Ottavi, the first French consul in Oman, to serve as the French Consulate by Sultan Feisal bin Turki al Said in 1894 and now hosts various exhibits relating to the history of the French in Oman.

South of Bab al Kabir lies Muscat's most interesting museum, the **Bait al Zubair** Ⓔ (Sat–Thur 9.30am–1pm and 4–7pm; charge). Occupying three airy traditional houses set around a garden, the museum displays an excellent selection of weapons, jewellery, costumes, household items and old photographs, while the grounds contain a re-creation of a typical Omani village, complete with *falaj* system. Next door to the museum is the **Bait Muzna art gallery**, a former royal home that has been turned into an attractive gallery showcasing modern works by international artists.

Northwest of the Bait al Zubair, one of the old city gateways, now spanning the main road to Mutrah, has been converted into the **Muscat Gate Museum** (Sat–Wed 8am–2pm; free), with detailed displays covering the history of Oman and Muscat – although not much in the way of actual exhibits.

Mutrah

The winding waterfront Corniche from Old Muscat to Mutrah is around 2km (1 mile), passing another old Portuguese stronghold along the way – **Mutrah Fort** (not open to the public) – balanced precariously atop a slender rock outcrop high above the sea.

Mutrah itself is the old commercial heart of the city, busier and considerably more built up than Old Muscat, and arranged around an attractive sweeping corniche with the huge gantries and quays of the Sultan Qaboos Port opposite. The district remains a lively hub of old-fashioned mercantile activity, most of it concentrated in the sprawling **Mutrah Souk**, easily the most popular tourist attraction in Muscat – perhaps in the whole country. Though modern – concrete shops replaced the original palm structures in the 1970s – the souk remains one of the most authentic in Arabia, its alleyways laced with the smell of frankincense and sandalwood, offering a memorable glimpse of Oman's past. It is easy to get lost if you head off the main street through the souk, although this is a large part of the fun, and you're never more than a couple of minutes' walk from the main thoroughfares. West of

Entrance of Al Alam Palace. Though listed as one of the Sultan's homes, the palace is generally used only for formal affairs.

BELOW: Bait al Zubair Museum.

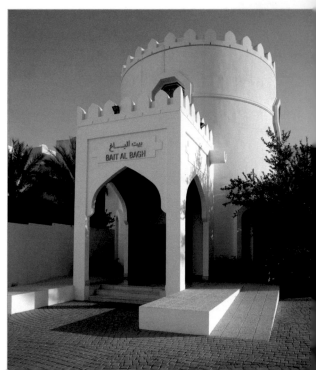

TIP

Bargaining is the order of the day in Mutrah Souk. If making a major purchase it pays to shop around and to check quality carefully.

the main section of the souk, it is also worth exploring the dazzling **Gold Souk**, reachable from slightly further west down the Corniche.

Continuing along the Corniche past the souk brings you to **Lawatiya** quarter, home to a Shi'ite merchant sect of the same name who originated from Hyderabad. Their residential area is walled and off-limits to outsiders – guards sit at the gates to make sure that only those who live there enter – but the houses backing onto the Corniche, with their lattice grilles and balconies, offer an enticing glimpse of what lies inside.

Further along, at the junction with Fish Roundabout, is the **Bait al Baranda** (Verandah House; Sat–Thur 9am–1pm and 4–6pm; charge), an attractively restored old Muscati mansion which now houses a modest museum devoted to the history of the city. Just past here is Muscat's lively **fish market**, particularly busy early in the morning when the new catch arrives on the slab and the city's restaurateurs descend to make their daily purchases.

South of Old Muscat and Mutrah

South of Old Muscat, the road winds down the coast amidst craggy ridges and areas of attractively landscaped parkland. About 4km (2½ miles) down the road, the suburb of Haramil is home to the **Marina Bander ar Rawdah**, from where many of the city's deep-water fishing charters and dolphin-watching trips depart. Don't expect too much of the **Aquarium** (Sun–Thur 8am–2.30pm, Fri 4–6pm; free), nothing but a few tankfuls of rather sorry-looking tropical fish.

Further south you reach the roundabout at the entrance to Al Bustan Palace Hotel (*see below*). The fine old wooden dhow, now marooned in the centre of the roundabout, is the famous *Sohar*, on which British adventurer Tim Severin and his Omani crew sailed from Muscat to Canton in China in 1982 – a fascinating story recounted in Severin's *The Sindbad Voyage*. The boat itself was made in Sur rather than Sohar, despite its name.

Turn left here to reach the spectacular **Al Bustan Palace Hotel**, completed in 1985 for a Gulf Co-operation Council summit, and comprehensively renovated in 2008. Formerly the top hotel in Oman (and one of the most opulent in the entire Gulf), the hotel has been somewhat upstaged by more recent openings in the city and elsewhere, but remains one of Muscat's nicest places to stay – the wonderful main atrium in soaring contemporary Islamic style is particularly fine.

Some 5km (3 miles) further south down the coast lies **Bandar al Jissah**, a beautiful bay ringed with rocky cliffs and a much-photographed "rock arch" which features on many boat tours of the capital. The formerly unspoilt beach has now been taken over by the vast **Shangri-La Barr al Jissah Resort**, comprising three Arabian-styled hotels, including the super-luxurious Al Husn, spread out along a kilometre of coastline. Despite the hotel, turtles continue to nest on the beach from

BELOW: sporting Oman's national colours.

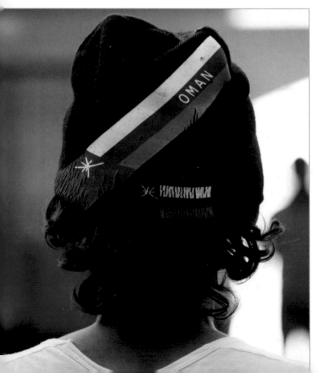

November to March, although you'll need to stay at or eat in the hotel to gain access. More laid-back and inexpensive views of the bay can be had from the nearby **Oman Dive Centre**, which has a good beachside restaurant from which to survey the waves.

Ruwi

A couple of kilometres inland from Mutrah and Old Muscat lies **Ruwi**, now the city's main business and commercial district, with a string of large-scale banks, airline offices lined up along the central Markaz Mutrah al Tijari Street. Nearby, the imposing old Bait al Falaj Fort is home to the **Sultan's Armed Forces Museum** (Sat–Wed 8am–1.30pm, Thur 9am–noon and 3–6pm, Fri 9–11am and 3–6pm; charge) – much more interesting than it might sound, with wide-ranging exhibits on Omani history backed up with impressive displays of weaponry ranging from antique swords to modern mortars. Southwest of here lies the rather grandly named **National Museum** (Sat–Wed 8am–1.30pm, Thur 9am–1pm), actually just a single large room with various traditional artefacts and other exhibits relating to the national heritage, from seafaring to fort-building – although even this will probably close following the opening of the new National Museum in Old Muscat *(see page 121)*.

A five-minute walk south of the museum down A'Noor Street brings you to **Ruwi Roundabout**, at the southwest corner of the district. This is Muscat with a decidedly subcontinental flavour, home to many expat Indians and Pakistanis and crammed with cheap curry houses. It is one of the liveliest places in the city, especially after dark and particularly along **Souk Ruwi Street**, crammed with dozens of brightly illuminated shops selling gold, textiles and electronics.

Qurm to Ghubrah

West from Ruwi stretches modern Muscat, a rather formless expanse of identikit low-rise, whitewashed suburbs stretching all the way to the international airport. **Qurm**, also west of Ruwi, is one of the city's main shopping areas (and a good place to browse for handicrafts), with a dozen or so small-scale malls clustered around Qurm Roundabout on the main Sultan Qaboos Road.

North of Qurm proper you'll find **Shati al Qurm** (Qurm Beach), a long swathe of golden sand which runs west from here for several miles, passing many of the city's most upmarket hotels en route. The beach is open to the public throughout, although you'll probably only feel comfortable sunbathing in the areas by the InterContinental and Hyatt hotels. South of the beach stretch the lush mangroves of the Qurm Natural Park (not open to the public), beyond which lies the fun **Children's Museum** (Sat–Wed 8am–1.30pm, Thur 9am–1pm; charge), with hands-on educational displays – a guaranteed hit with children, and fun for grown-ups too.

On the far side of Qurm, the suburb of Khuwayr is the city's main government and diplomatic enclave, with

Al Bustan's gold dome is actually stainless steel and was erected in a school playground in Liverpool, England, before being shipped to Oman.

BELOW: Bandar al Jissah.

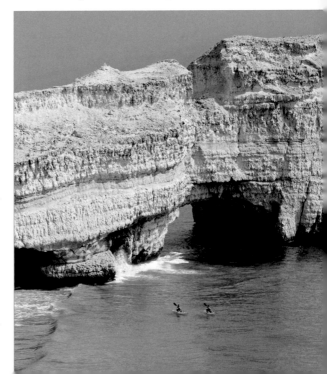

*Outside the entrance
of the Natural
History Museum are
the fossilised remains
of a 260-million-
year-old fir tree.*

dozens of impressively large ministry buildings lined up alongside the main highway. Nearby on the seafront lies the chintzy **Grand Hyatt Hotel**, one of Muscat's most extravagant buildings, its exterior designed to resemble a Yemeni castle and its interior rivalling that of Al Bustan Palace for pseudo-Arabian opulence. Khuwair is also where you'll find the city's modest **Natural History Museum** (Sat–Wed 8am–1.30pm, Sun also 4–6pm, Thur 9am–1pm; charge), offering a good overview of the country's various regions and their associated flora and fauna, including various stuffed animals and pickled snakes. The complete skeleton of a sperm whale sits in state in the adjacent Whale Hall.

Still further west, the suburb of **Ghubrah** is home to the majestic **Sultan Qaboos Grand Mosque** (open to non-Muslims Sat–Thur 8–11am; free). Opened in 2001, this is one of the largest and most spectacular mosques in the Gulf, constructed in a minimalist modern Islamic style and dressed in vast quantities of white and red-brown marble. Inside, there is room

for an estimated 20,000 worshippers in the two prayer halls and surrounding courtyard, with towering minarets at each corner. Compared to the rather chaste exterior, the interior of the main prayer hall is a riot of opulence. The carpet on the floor is the world's second-largest (it took 400 female weavers from the Iranian province of Khorasan four years to make, measures over 60 metres 196ft square, contains 1.7 million knots and weighs 21 tonnes). The huge Swarovski crystal chandelier in the centre of the hall is a staggering 14 metres (46ft) tall and was often claimed to be the largest in the world until the construction of an even bigger chandelier in Qatar in 2010.

This is also the only mosque in Oman open to non-Muslims; visitors are required to dress conservatively (no shorts or bare arms), while women will be given a scarf with which to cover their hair. Unfortunately, the mosque's popularity and limited opening times for non-Muslims mean that it tends to get overrun with tourists. Arrive early in the day for maximum tranquillity.

BELOW: the *Sohar* at
the Al Bustan
Paloeeh Hotel.

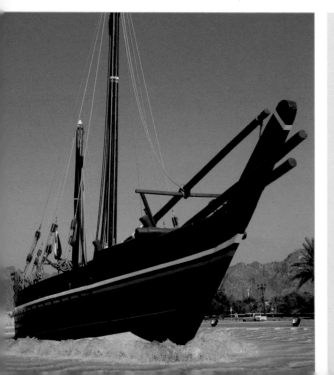

Boat Trips

A number of tour operators around Muscat run enjoyable boat trips along the coast around Bandar al Jissah, offering breezy views of the city's craggy coastline, and usually including a trip through the landmark rock arch which lies just off the beach.

Trips include daytime dolphin-spotting excursions (with an excellent chance of seeing either spinner or bottlenose dolphins), while if you are extremely lucky you might glimpse one of the whale sharks or humpback whales which occasionally visit the coast; Sidab Sea Tours' glass-bottomed boat trips (www.sidabseatours.com) offer a good view of what goes on beneath the waves. Many operators also offer popular sunset cruises (usually lasting a couple of hours, with departures at around 4.30pm) – a beautiful way of seeing the sun dip down over the coastal mountains.

Towering Strength

Oman's remarkable wealth of forts and watchtowers provides a memorable reminder of the country's turbulent past

Wherever you are in Oman, you'll never be far from some kind of traditional fortified building. There are an estimated 500 forts (*qala* or *hisn*) in the country, as well as innumerable watchtowers, fortified houses (*surs*), walled towns and villages, and other reminders of the country's turbulent and unsettled past.

Virtually every town in Oman has some kind of fort, all of which were formerly of crucial strategic importance, given that whoever controlled the local fort was usually able to command the surrounding region as well. Some forts served simply as military strongholds; others doubled as the residence of the local *wali* (governor), containing elaborate living quarters including *majlis*, bedrooms, kitchens and so on. Many combine both residential and military functions (Nizwa is a particularly good example, with its mighty round tower next to extensive residential quarters), serving both as the home base of the resident militia and seat of local government. In many cases the *majlis* in the nearest particular fort served as a kind of informal parliament for the town or village it protected – a place in which visitors were received and matters of local importance discussed. Forts also served as a refuge for local inhabitants in the event of attack.

Architectural features

Many of the country's forts exemplify Arabian military architecture at its most ingenious, with distinctive local features including slits down which boiling oil or date juice could be poured on the heads of assailants, secret passages, winding and disorienting passages to slow and confuse attackers, and other features (again, the great round tower at Nizwa is a particularly fine example). Many forts also possess their own dedicated *falaj* issuing directly into the fort, offering a guaranteed water supply in the event of a siege.

The vast forts at Bahla and Rustaq are the two largest and most physically impressive in the country (although both are currently closed for long-term renovations), while those at Nizwa and Nakhal are also impressive. The finest castle interiors are to be found at the magical fort of Jabrin and in the lovely Bait Na'aman in Barka, whose beautifully decorated interiors offer a compelling insight into life in old Oman.

Watchtowers are another characteristic feature of the Omani landscape. Generally, forts protected the towns and populated areas while watchtowers were used to guard inland trade routes and water supplies. At the sight of invaders, warning shots would be fired to alert people nearby. Other watchtowers were built close to forts for obvious reasons. The highest concentrations of watchtowers are along the main mountain passes such as Wadi Sumail and Wadi Jizzi. Elsewhere, necklaces of watchtowers can be seen atop the hills surrounding major settlements (at Ibra for example – one of the very few large towns in Oman without a fort).

By the time of the accession of Sultan Qaboos in 1970 many of the country's forts and other traditional buildings had fallen into advanced stages of dilapidation. Ongoing restoration efforts are attempting to save as much of Oman's heritage as possible – a huge project which has now succeeded in bringing many of the majestic fortifications back to life, although significant numbers of other sites – such as the spectacular fort at Jalan Bani Bu Ali – are steadily crumbling into dust.

Right: Nizwa Fort.

SOHAR AND THE BATINAH COAST

The flat and fertile Batinah Coast north of
Muscat leads to Sohar, once the most important
trading centre in the Arabian peninsula. Today
the region is famous mainly for its dates

Norch of Muscat stretches the Al
Batinah region, a narrow coastal
plain bounded by the sea on
one side and the Hajar mountains on
the other. This is one of the most fertile regions in the country, covered in
innumerable date plantations, while
fishing is another important source
of employment, with endless lines of
boats pulled up on the beaches which
dot the coast. This was formerly the
wealthiest and most cosmopolitan
part of the country, centred on the
great port of Sohar, one of the major
trading emporiums of its day. Things
are a lot quieter now, although a great
sequence of forts still stands guard
over the region, commemorating
its former economic and strategic
importance.

Getting around the Batinah is
straightforward, thanks to the fast (if
dull) dual-carriageway coastal highway which runs from Muscat via Seeb,
Barka and Sohara and on to the UAE
border, a total distance of 270km (168
miles). Unfortunately, the highway
runs a couple of kilometres inland, out
of sight of the sea, although smaller
local roads can get you down to the
coastal beaches. Inland, another major
road runs to Rustaq, as the heart of
the so-called Rustaq Loop, a rewarding inland detour in the shadow of
the Western Hajar, via some of the

country's finest forts, and with a number of exhilarating off-road routes to
explore on the way.

From Muscat to Al Sawadi

Heading north out of the capital,
the coastal highway passes **Muscat
International Airport** before reaching **Seeb ❷**, the first major settlement along the Batinah Coast
(although technically it forms part
of the Muscat Capital Area). This is
one of the most personable towns in
Oman, centred on the lively Wadi al

Main attractions

SEEB
BAIT NA'AMAN
DAYMANIYAT ISLANDS
NAKHAL FORT
WADI MISTALL
WADI ABYAD
AL AWABI
WADI BANI KHARUS
RUSTAQ
SOHAR

LEFT: Sohar moon and mosque.
RIGHT: taking cover.

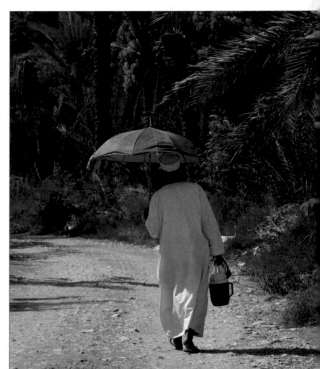

Batinah and the Interior

N

20 km
20 miles

Gulf of Oman

MASQAT (MUSCAT)
Mutrah
Qurm
Ruwi
Al Amrat
Yiti
Bawshar
Al Hajern
Muscat

Qurayyat, Sur
Sur
Ibra
As Sarin
Samad

Ash Sharqiyah
Al Hajar ash Sharqi
(Eastern Hajar)
Jabal Abyad

Ar Rusayl
Muscat International Airport
Amouage Perfumery
Seeb
Sultan Qaboos University
Al Khawd
Oman Botanic Garden
Naseem Gardens
Daymaniyat Islands Nature Reserve
Jaza'ir Daymaniyat

Bidbid
Fanja
Samail
Jabal Nakhal
Nakhal Fort
Ayn A'Thowrah
Nakhal

Ras as Sawadi
Al Sawadi
Barka
Bait Na'aman
Al-Musanaah

Wadi Abyad
Wadi Mistall
Ghubrah Bowl
Jabal Akhdar
Saiq Plateau
Birkat al Mawz
Qarut
Izki
Nizwa Fort
Nizwa
Firq

Khadra al Bu Rashyd
As Suwyq
Al Hazm
Rustaq
Al Awabi
Wadi Bani Kharus
Hat
Wadi Bani Awf
Mifsah
Misfat (Mistal al A'Abreyeen)
Al Hamra
Al Hoota Cave
Bahla
Bahla Fort
Jabrin
Jabrin Fort

Al Batinah
Wadi Hawasina
Sadam
Al Huwayl
Al Khaburah
Al Mintayfah
Ruwaila
Saham
Muqaz
Majis Jetty
Sohar Fort
Sohar

Wadi Saram
Mishkin
Yangul
Khudal
Ad Diriz
Sulaif
Bat
Bat Tombs
Al Ayn Tombs (Beehive Tombs)
Al Ayn
Kubarah
Ibri

Jabal Shams 3009
Wadi Ghul
Ghul
Jabal Kawr 2960
Hamrat Duru 1310

Shinas, Madha
Wadi Fizh
Wadi Jizzi
Afja Ziggurat
Lusayf Arch
Hayl
Ghudhayfah
Al Muqbah
Murri
Dank
Belt
Bakhabi
Al Fath
1665
1600

Al Hajar al Gharbi (Western Hajar)

Al Hilla Fort
Buraymi
Al Khandaq Fort
UAE
Al Buraymi
Wazyad
Hafit
Qabil
As Sunaynah

Ad Dhahirah
Dhahirah
Wadi Rafash

O M A N

Bahais Street which loops through the centre, flanked with a colourful selection of shops selling gold, perfumes, textiles, furniture and so on. There is also an extensive, breezy corniche, always busy after dark, beyond which lies the town's harbour, with dozens of boats moored up within a curling breakwater.

The nearby **Sultan Qaboos University**, opened in 1986, has some 15,000 students, of whom around 50 percent are women, a remarkable achievement considering that just four decades or so ago, schooling for girls was officially forbidden.

Barka ❸ (40km/25 miles from Seeb) is the next town of significance on the coast and the springboard for the Rustaq Loop *(see page 130)*. The imposing Barka Fort (Sun–Thur 8am–2pm; free), dating from the early Ya'ruba period, lies 400 metres/yds west of the main crossroads in town. The former *wali*'s quarters have been furnished as they might have appeared a century ago, while there are fine views down the coast from the terrace above.

About 5km (3 miles) beyond Barka down the main coastal highway (and then 2km/1 mile down a side road on the right) is the even more atmospheric **Bait Na'aman** ❹ (Sat–Thur 7.30am–2.30pm, closed Fri; free, although a tip is welcomed), a fortified house dating from the 1690s, which formerly served as one of the country residences of the ruling Imams. The interior is particularly interesting, beautifully restored and with a wealth of furnishings and artefacts which give a powerful sense of what life was like here back in former times.

Like Fujairah in the UAE, the Batinah is known for its bullfights. Barka is one of various towns along the coast (along with Seeb and Sohar) to host fights, which take place every Friday in winter starting around 4pm. The rules are simple – the referee pairs

An art vendor in Seeb Souk.

BELOW: an Amouage boutique.

Scents of Place

Just outside Seeb next to the Nizwa highway, the Amouage showroom and factory (www.amouage.com) welcomes visitors interested in learning more about Oman's most luxurious scent and the various traditional products with which it is made. Founded in 1983 by a member of the royal family, the Amouage factory now produces a range of scents for men and women featuring an array of traditional local ingredients, including high-quality silver frankincense and myrrh from Salalah and roses from Jabal Akhdar – a sumptuous olfactory memory of the varied fragrances of Oman. As you would probably expect, however, Amouage products don't come cheap: a bottle of the signature "Gold" perfume will set you back around OR100 (US$260) for a 100ml bottle.

A decorated room in Nakhal Fort.

BELOW: Bait Na'aman, near Barka.

animals, roughly based on equal height and weight, which are then led out and set against one another to the cheers of the exclusively male crowd. When one bull takes a tumble in the dust the other is declared victor (*see page 231*). Most contests last less than five minutes, but should the fight turn vicious, a rope secured to a front leg of each animal allows their owners to keep control.

Al Sawadi ❺ is a large fishing community 9km (5 miles) along a turn-off from the "prancing horses monument" on the coastal highway. The tarmac stops at the end of a long beach where you will find the low-key Al Sawadi Beach Resort, a good base for diving trips out to the nearby Daymaniyat Islands (Jaza'ir Daymaniyat; *see below*). Just offshore lie the rocky Sawadi Islands; boat trips out to them can be arranged with fishermen on the beach,

whilst you can walk to the one nearest the shore at low tide.

Further out to sea, 16km (10 miles) off the coast, is the **Daymaniyat Islands Nature Reserve** ❻, comprising nine limestone islets. Between April and September, thousands of migratory birds nest on the islands, including the rare sooty falcon. Large numbers of hawksbill and green turtles also nest in the sandy inlets protected by rocky overhangs. Diving and snorkelling trips to the islands can be arranged through the dive centre at the Al Sawadi Beach Resort, as well as via several dive operators in Muscat. A permit is required to land.

The Rustaq Loop

Rising majestically inland from the coast are the craggy heights of the **Hajar mountains**. Highway 13 cuts inland from Barka, travelling via the grandiose forts of Nakhal, Rustaq and Al Hazm before rejoining the coastal highway – a fine day trip popularly known as the Rustaq Loop (although the forts at Rustaq and Al Hazm were both closed for extended renovations

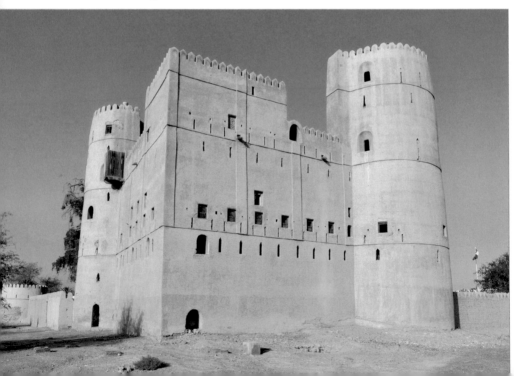

at the time of writing). Forts apart, there is also fine mountain scenery along the way, while side tracks into adjacent wadis offer some of Oman's finest off-road driving. The Rustaq Loop can easily be visited from Seeb, Al Sawadi or even Muscat.

Highway 13 turns off the main roundabout at Barkha, from where it is a 30-minute drive inland to reach the superb **Nakhal Fort** ❼ (Sat–Thur 9am–4pm, Fri 8–11am; charge), crowning a spur at the head of the wadi coming down out of the mountains. The fort's foundations are believed to pre-date Islam, though it was remodelled in the 9th, 16th, 19th and 20th centuries and now stands as an awesome tribute to the skills of ancient Omani stonemasons, soaring to a height of 30 metres (98ft). The fort was entirely self-contained, with well-water and storage rooms for stockpiling in event of a siege. The *wali* lived on the mezzanine level in winter and on the breezy upper terrace during the hot summer months. His *majlis* is lined with hand-woven carpets and rifles decorate the walls. The women's

majlis is spread with carpets and cushions while a master bedroom contains a quaint four-poster bed. A sweeping panorama can be enjoyed from the top of the fort.

The main road through Nakhal continues 2.5km (2 miles) to the **Ayn A'Thowrah hot springs**, a shady oasis with a stream running under the date palms. The water here is warm enough to poach an egg. Locals picnic around the hot spring on Friday.

Some 15km (9 miles) further along Highway 13 past Nakhal, a side road heads off south of the highway into **Wadi Mistall** ❽, a dramatic narrow gorge which opens out soon afterwards into the Ghubrah Bowl, a huge, flat gravel plain, ringed by the mountains of the **Jabal Nakhal** and **Jabal Akhdar**. On the far side of the bowl, a rough track climbs vertiginously up to the tiny village of Wekan, one of Oman's most spectacularly located mountain villages, sitting athwart the routes of some of the country's finest hiking trails.

A further 3km (2 miles) along Highway 13, the village of A'Subaikha

"My journey with Sultan was to take us through this populous province: now along the golden beaches, past little Arab ports ever associated with Sindbad the Sailor and little fishing villages whose men go forth to grope under the sea for precious pearls."

– Bertram Thomas, *Alarms and Excursions in Arabia*

LEFT: Wadi Mistall.
BELOW: women walking into Abayad.

These pots for sale near Sohar are traditionally used for storing dates.

BELOW: Wadi Bani Kharus. **RIGHT:** Rustaq.

is the starting point for another fine off-road trip, this one into the pretty **Wadi Abyad** (White Wadi), set between low red-rock hills and dotted with palm trees and rock pools. The water in some of the pools often turns a distinctive milky white due to the high concentrations of dissolved calcium it contains. This is one of Oman's more challenging wadis to drive since there's no actual track, and parts of the wadi often flood – just pick your way across the loose gravel, trying not to get bogged down en route.

A further 35km (22 miles) on from Nakhal, the town of **Al Awabi** ⑩ is home to yet another fort (Sun–Thur 8am–2pm; free), recently reopened to the public following extensive renovations. The pretty little structure is built in a mixture of stone and mudbrick with a small plain mosque standing in front. The main tower is an interesting study in traditional Omani plumbing arrangements, with no fewer than three hole-in-the-floor toilets, all carefully designed so that waste products would fall outside the castle walls and (potentially) onto the heads of the villagers outside.

Directly behind Awabi Fort, a narrow fissure in the mountains marks the start of the spectacular **Wadi Bani Kharus** ⑪, now easily accessible thanks to the construction of a new black-top road stretching all the way to the end of the wadi. A sequence of seven villages lines the floor of the wadi, with old-fashioned mudbrick houses and date plantations squeezed in below the towering cliffs. The wadi is also of particular interest to geologists, with layers of sedimentary and mineral strata spanning over 500 million years, from the Cretaceous period to the Late Proterozoic era, exposed with textbook clarity in the cliffs above.

A few kilometres west of Awabi you pass the end of the spectacular track which descends from the mountains via **Wadi Bani Awf** (see page 142).

Another 10km (6 miles) or so from here is the town of **Rustaq** ⑫, historically one of the most important in the interior, though the sprawling modern town is largely featureless and preserves disappointingly little of its history, with the exception of its mighty fort, the second-largest in the country after Bahla – although it was closed at the time of writing for extended renovations which are likely to stretch well into 2012, if not considerably further. A fort has stood on the site for more than 1,000 years, built over the site of a spring which gushes around its base. It is thought to have been founded by the Persians in the pre-Islamic period and subsequently became the first capital of the Ya'ruba dynasty under the Imam Nasir bin Murshid (died 1649). The fort was rebuilt under Imam Saif bin Sultan (died 1711), who was responsible for a massive building programme all over the interior. Saif bin Sultan also repaired the *falaj* and planted more than 30,000 date palms around Rustaq. He is buried in the western corner of the Wind Tower. The first Imam of the Al bu Said dynasty, Ahmed bin Said (died 1783), also ruled from Rustaq, where he exercised control over the interior and coast. This broke down under his

sons Said and Sultan, who split the Imamate, with Said based in Rustaq, and Sultan, the more powerful of the two brothers, ruling from Muscat.

It is a further 20km (12-mile) drive to **Al Hazm**, a modest village dominated by another huge fort (although closed for lengthy renovations at the time of writing). The three-storey limestone and wood structure with two cylindrical towers was built in 1708 by the Imam Sultan bin Saif II, who moved here from Rustaq – an inscription on the right of two decorated wooden gates identifies him as the builder.

Sohar

The approach to **Sohar** ⑬, the capital of the Batinah, is marked by a huge arch across the highway: a road to the right off the "date palm roundabout" cuts through a new business district to the old centre on the sea. Sohar is a pleasant town with clean streets lined with white houses and tropical gardens. At one time it was one of the most important trading centres on the Arabian peninsula: "Its traders and

The Batinah region is said to derive its name from an Arabic root meaning "to be hidden" – and from out at sea the tawny-coloured Hajar mountains glowering over the narrow coastal plain do indeed conceal it from sight.

BELOW: a basket of fresh dates in Rustaq.

Story of the Date

A staple food of the Bedu, a symbol of hospitality to strangers, the traditional break to the Ramadan fast, an essential ingredient at weddings, circumcisions and feasts – the date is revered throughout the Arab and Islamic world. Wilfred Thesiger, in *Arabian Sands*, recalls how when he once threw a date stone into a campfire his Bedu companion leaned over and picked it out. In the 19th century dates were Oman's biggest export, with India and the US its chief markets. Ships would leave Oman laden with dates and return with rice, coffee, sugar, spices, cloth, china, gunpowder and paper. Today, though date production is no longer essential to the economy, its potential is being reconsidered as part of ongoing efforts to wean the country away from oil. There are some 10 million date palms, occupying around 60 percent of cultivable land, and annual production is estimated at 280,000 tonnes.

BELOW: Sohar fish market **RIGHT:** Sohar's fort now houses a museum.

commerce cannot be enumerated. It is the most developed town in Oman," wrote Ibn Hawqal in *The Oriental Geography*, a 10th-century manual of the region. Sohar's fortunes have recently revived, thanks to the development of a major new port, factories and oil refineries.

Archaeological excavations date the city to the 3rd millennium BC when copper was mined in Wadi Jizzi. The city rose to prominence following the decline of the frankincense trade in Dhofar and the weakening power of the Caliphate in Baghdad, reaching its zenith in the 10th century. The city was destroyed and most of its inhabitants slain by the Buyids of Baghdad in 971. Nonetheless, a description as late as the 12th century mentions 12,000 houses elaborately constructed of brick and teak and of traders from a dozen different countries rubbing shoulders in its sprawling souks.

The seaport was absorbed into the Persian kingdom of Hormuz in the 14th century, but following capture by Portugal in 1507 its fortunes began to ebb. For the next hundred years,

Portugal maintained a trade blockade which slowly choked the commercial life out of Sohar. Even after the Portuguese left Oman in the mid-16th century, the city's fate was sealed by internecine disputes. As a result, shipping from India and East Africa discharged in Sur and Aden, and many local merchants and sea captains moved elsewhere.

The most dramatic sight in town is a whitewashed **fort** (currently closed for extended renovations) at the eastern end of the corniche in the so-called "old town" – although the original souk was demolished in the 1990s and replaced with the current modern suburban villas. The original building, believed to date from the early 14th century, is said to have been so large that it took 1,000 men to defend it – though it surrendered to Albuquerque without a single cannon being fired. A Portuguese miniature shows the fort with six towers and surrounded by palm groves, but today only a single tower rises from its courtyard.

Sohar fort is the last resting place of Sayyid Thuwaini bin Said bin Sultan

Al bu Said, one of two sons of the great Sultan Said bin Sultan under whom Oman regained prominence in the 19th century. On the demise of Sultan Said, Thuwaini became ruler of Oman and a colony on the Makran Coast of what is now Pakistan, while his brother was awarded Zanzibar and Omani possessions in East Africa. Sultan Thuwaini ruled for only a decade. In 1866 he was shot by his son while asleep in the fort during preparations for a military expedition to recapture Buraymi Oasis.

Almost next door to the fort stands the large **Sultan Qaboos Mosque**, with its eye-catching gold dome. A five-minute walk inland is the town's modest **handicrafts souk** (signed "Omani Craftsman's House"), occupying a neat little walled enclosure decorated with miniature watchtowers. There are 16 shops here, although only about a third were open at the time of writing.

Heading north along the corniche brings you to the town's striking modern **fish market**, designed in the shape of a traditional dhow. A couple of kilometres further north you will find the Sohar Beach Hotel and a spacious swathe of public **beach**, with wide, mud-coloured sands scattered with seashells. Next to the beach lies an attractively shady park arranged around a large lake.

Three roads continue from Sohar. The coastal highway continues north to the border of the UAE at **Khatmat Milahah**. Route 07 cuts off for **Buraymi** and another crossing point into the UAE. The journey along a tarmac road takes around two hours up through Wadi Jizzi, passing some of Oman's wildest and most dramatic mountain scenery en route, with jagged rock summits rising to either side of the road. Finally, the recently surfaced Highway 08 travels inland to **Yanqul** and then to **Ibri**, offering a convenient shortcut up into the Western Hajar.

The luxurious Sohar Beach Hotel.

Below: an 1865 illustration of an episode from the *1,001 Nights*.

Sindbad and Sohar

Inhabitants of Sohar like to claim that their city was the birthplace of the legendary Sindbad the Sailor, hero of the *1,001 Nights* and innumerable subsequent films and cartoons – even if there is disappointingly little concrete evidence to back the claim. According to the *1,001 Nights* themselves, Sindbad was a merchant hailing from Baghdad who set out on a series of seven voyages, surviving shipwreck and assorted incredible dangers on each one before finally making his way back to Baghdad laden with fabulous riches. In fact, Sindbad is clearly a symbolic rather than a historical figure, and his adventures derive from a long tradition of maritime yarns, tall tales and other folklore collected over the centuries by roving Arab seafarers – including, quite possibly, sailors from Oman itself.

NIZWA AND THE INTERIOR

Historically the power base of the Imamate, the Interior is a rich and rewarding region to visit, with a string of majestic forts and magnificent mountain scenery

The area of Oman historically known as the Interior refers to the region lying beyond the Hajar mountains where, from fortified strongholds, the Imams contested the authority of the sultan in Muscat. Hence the name "Muscat and Oman" which was used to describe the country prior to 1970 – Muscat being the capital enclave and Oman what an Australian might call the Outback. The Interior is the kernel of traditional Oman. The new towns growing up along Highway 15 may create an illusion of the present but only a few steps off the road lie ancient villages.

The Interior is largely made up of the provinces of Ad Dakhiliyah and Ad Dhahirah. Ibri, the regional capital, and Buraymi are the main towns in Ad Dhahirah, a sparsely populated area largely covered in waterless gravel desert (though rich in oil and gas) which sees hardly any tourists. Ad Dakhiliyah, by contrast, is the most visited part of Oman, home to three of the country's most famous forts – Nizwa, Bahla and Jabrin – and some of its finest scenery.

The Samail Gap to Nizwa

Wadi Samail, a natural break between the Western and Eastern Hajar mountains, has been the artery between the coast and the Interior for centuries.

The broad dry valley was the obvious course for the motorway from Muscat to Nizwa, providing 166km (103 miles) of relaxed driving.

The first of the many settlements along the Gap is **Fanja** (35km/22 miles from Muscat). Typically, the new town lies along the road, while the old walled village (accessible via a right-hand turn after the bridge) sits in an easily defensible position atop a large rocky hill; it is a pretty huddle of largely derelict mudbrick houses and a single watchtower,

Main attractions
SAIQ PLATEAU AND JABAL AKHDAR
NIZWA
AL HOOTA CAVE
WADI BANI AWF
AL HAMRA
JABAL SHAMS AND WADI NAKHR
MISFAH
BAHLA
JABRIN FORT
AL AYN TOMBS

LEFT: visiting Nizwa fort. **RIGHT:** the ruined village of Tanuf.

High up in the Jabal Akhdar lives the Arabian tahr, a shy goat-like creature unique to Oman. The Wadi Sarin Nature Reserve was set up to protect and increase their numbers.

commanding magnificent views over the pass below.

Further along the highway is a turn to **Bidbid,** whose quaint little restored fort (not open to the public) used to guard the junction of the old trade routes from Muscat, Nizwa and Sur. These now meet at a new flyover crossing the northern Sharqiya to Sur.

The town of **Samail** ⓮ lends its name to the pass. Modern Samail is a surprisingly large and sprawling affair. The actual wadi runs around 4km (2½ miles) east of the highway, slightly away from the new town and in complete contrast to it: an extraordinarily lush little valley full of date palms hemmed in below low-lying rocky hills. The wadi's former strategic importance is borne out by the remarkable number of fortifications that dot the area, including a long line of watchtowers on the ridges above the wadi and the neatly restored Samail Fort itself (around 3km/2 miles down the wadi from modern Samail, although it is not open to the public).

Further up the highway some 103km (64km) from Muscat lies the

venerable town of **Izki** ⓯. Once again, the disorienting modern town sprawls for a considerable distance along the highway, with the old town tucked away a few kilometres distant (most easily found if you take the back road to Birkat al Mauz). Here you'll find the collapsing remains of an impressive old stone fort and the small walled town next door overlooking the broad swathe of Wadi Halfayn. Izki is also home to the Falaj al Malki, said to be the oldest in the country and one of five Omani *falaj* now protected as a Unesco World Heritage Site.

Birkat al Mawz ⓰ (Pool of Bananas) is another of the area's traditional oasis villages, with a dense patchwork of plantations clustered around the inevitable *falaj* and fort – in this case the Unesco World Heritage-listed Falaj al Khatmeen and the impressive Bait al Ridaydha, recently restored, although not yet open to the public.

Birkat al Mawz is also the turn-off for the **Saiq Plateau,** lying at an altitude of roughly 2,000 metres (6,562ft) beneath the summit of **Jabal Akhdar** (Green Mountain). The plateau offers an invigorating escape from the lowland heat. The summer temperature does not exceed 30°C (86°F) and nights are pleasantly cool (in winter, the temperature drops as low as –5°C/23°F). Spring, when the orchards are covered by a canopy of peach, apricot, apple, pear, plum, almond and walnut blossom, is an enchanting time to visit. Indigenous olives, myrtles and pomegranates as well as ancient juniper trees are abundant. In May, the rose-picking season, the air is filled with the scent of the tiny pink Jabal Akhdar roses.

Access to the plateau is via a wide modern tarmac road, an easy drive, although only 4x4 vehicles are allowed up; you'll be turned back at the police checkpoint if you're not in a suitable vehicle. The plateau's main settlement is the surprisingly large town of **Saih Katenah,** where you'll find petrol,

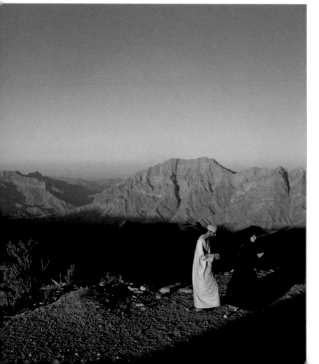

shops and the attractive Jabal Akhdar Hotel, a good base from which to explore the area. Behind Saih Katenah, the plateau falls away spectacularly, with kilometre-high cliffs dropping sheer into the dramatic Wadi al Ayn below. A series of time-warped traditional villages – **Al Aqr**, **Al Ayn** and **A'Sherageh** – are perched perilously around the rim of the cliffs, with old mudbrick houses surrounded by rose gardens and strips of agricultural terracing carved neatly out of the mountainside: a picture-perfect slice of traditional Oman, and with marvellous views over the surrounding mountains.

Nizwa

Route 15 ends at the historic town of **Nizwa** ⑰, long-time capital of the Interior and for many years also the seat of the ruling Imam – right up until the 1950s the town had a reputation for religious fanaticism and a general suspicion of outsiders – Wilfred Thesiger, passing through the area in the late 1940s, was advised to avoid the town on pain of possible arrest

and imprisonment. Ironically, in the few decades since Thesiger's aborted visit the town has reinvented itself as one the most touristed and foreigner-friendly destinations in the country.

The heart of the town itself is essentially unchanged, although extensive restoration works during the 1990s have given it a thorough scrub and polish, making it look much neater and cleaner than it probably ever did previously. The basics remain the same, however, with the huge round tower of the town's majestic fort and grand Sultan Qaboos Mosque rising out of the centre, surrounded by a neat ochre huddle of old-fashioned souks.

First point of call for most visitors is Nizwa's splendid **fort** (Sat–Thur 9am–4pm, Fri 8–11am; charge), raised over a period of 12 years by Imam Sultan bin Saif in the late 17th century. According to one source it was financed by spoils from Ras al Khaimah, while a second theory claims it was financed by an Omani attack on the tiny Portuguese colony of Diu on the Malabar Coast of India. Whichever is correct, Nizwa's importance in the long struggle

Water from Jabal Akhdar is collected by falaj, an ancient roman system of irrigation introduced by the Persians some 2,500 years ago. Underground channels transport water to villages and farmland from mother wells dug into the water table.

LEFT: a woman picking cultivated roses.

The Rose Harvest

The roses of Jabal Akhdar (the damask rose, *Rosa Damascena*) are highly prized, not only for their intrinsic beauty – most apparent during the months of April and May, when flowers bloom in gardens across the plateau, turning entire villages a delicate shade of pale pink – but also as a valuable source of local income.

The area's roses are particularly sought after thanks to their use as an ingredient in the region's highly prized rose water, generally considered the finest in the country, and with demand consistently outstripping supply. Roses (introduced to Jabal Akhdar by early Persian settlers) flourish in the mountains' temperate climate – Al Aqr is a particularly notable centre of production, packed with dozens of small rose gardens.

Rose petals are harvested in May, still following largely traditional methods. The petals are first carefully plucked (usually done during the cool early morning to help preserve their delicate aroma) and then boiled in an oven. The resultant rose-scented steam is drawn off, allowed to condense, and then filtered to produce rose water. This has various uses, being drunk with tea or coffee as well as serving as an essential ingredient in the production of traditional Omani halwa. Rose water rubbed into the scalp is also said to relieve headaches.

TIP

Thursday is the best day to stay overnight in Nizwa, allowing you the chance to rise early to see the famous livestock market in full swing near the fort.

between Muscat and the Interior is reflected in its fort, built here to serve as a residence and administrative centre for the Imams.

Big rather than aesthetically pleasing, it consists of a massive circular tower with foundations sunk 30 metres (98ft) deep to withstand vibrations from mortar fire. Several of more than 400 gun emplacements still have cannons *in situ*, one of them inscribed with the name of the Imam Sultan bin Saif and another a gift from the city of Boston to the first Omani ambassador to the US. A narrow staircase leading up to the tower is kinked at each level, leading to a false door with gun emplacements and apertures in the ceiling to pour boiling oil onto any invader who managed to penetrate this deep inside the fort.

The easy climb opens into the drum of the tower with 120 positions for askars to stand guard on the parapets. The top – 40 metres (130ft) above the souk – commands a panoramic view of the landmark brown-domed mosque next to the fort, the maze of flat-topped houses and the belt of

palms surrounding Nizwa like a cordon sanitaire. To the northeast, Jabal Akhdar is angled menacingly against the sky, with its tallest peak, Jabal Shams (3,009 metres/9,872ft), the highest point in eastern Arabia, usually swathed in cloud.

Southwest of the fort stretch the various buildings making up Nizwa's celebrated **souk**. The area around the fort is dedicated mainly to tourist souvenirs and handicrafts, providing a showcase for Nizwa's celebrated craftsmanship, including its fine silver jewellery and *khanjars*, as well as copperware and leatherwork.

Heading east from the fort, the small **East Souk** is the most atmospheric in Nizwa, and the only one to have escaped restoration. It looks incongruously ramshackle now compared to the surrounding buildings, but provides a much clearer idea of what Nizwa formerly looked like, with tiny shops clustered beneath crumbling mudbrick arches and a makeshift corrugated-iron roof propped up on weathered old wooden beams.

BELOW: an Omani man with a gun at Nizwa fort.
RIGHT: Al Hoota Cave.

At the eastern end of the East Souk lies a much-photographed miniature square usually stacked full of quaint displays of **Bahla pottery** (*see page 144*); you can also see a short section of the old **city walls** here. South of here lie the more functional food and wholesale souks, with different areas devoted to fish, meat, fruit, vegetables and dates.

Immediately south of here the open-air Goat Market is home to Nizwa's famous **Friday Market** where hundreds of traditionally attired locals come to trade goats, cows and other livestock – a lively, smelly and quintessentially Omani spectacle. The market starts at around 8am and finishes at around 11am in time for Friday prayers.

Around Nizwa

Exiting Nizwa, Route 21 passes the turn-off to the ruined town of **Tanuf**. This was one of a number of places in the area bombed by the British during the 1950s Jabal War, thanks to its connections with the rebel warlord Suleiman bin Himyar, self-styled "King of the Je Akhdar". The rather

melancholy fragments of the old mud-brick town still stand, largely ruined apart from a single small mosque. Behind the old village, the dramatic fissure in the mountains is **Wadi Tanuf**, the source of the famous Tanuf water, one of Oman's leading mineral waters, which is bottled nearby and sold nationwide.

A couple of kilometres further along Highway 21 a turn-off heads to **Al Hoota Cave ⑱** (Sat–Thur 9am–1pm and 2–6pm, Fri 9am–noon and

The pomegranate season.

BELOW: Wadi Bani Awf.

A coffee pot – a traditional symbol of hospitality all over the Middle East.

2–6pm; charge). Oman is peppered with sinkholes and caverns, but this is the only one which is currently accessible to those without specialised potholing skills and equipment. The cave extends for some 5km (3 miles) in total, of which almost 1km is accessible – an impressively large cavern dotted with clumps of stalactites and stalagmites, plus an underground lake. A small train transports passengers from the visitors' centre to the mouth of the cave.

Continuing north along the road past Al Hoota Cave brings you to the start of the spectacular descent of the Western Hajar through **Wadi Bani Awf** (or Auf), generally reckoned to be the most memorable off-road drive in the country. The scenery is dramatic throughout, while the track is likely to jangle the nerves of even experienced wadi-bashers.

The route starts at the sweeping viewpoint of **Sharaf al Alamayn** at the crest of the Western Hajar, with views across the entire range and towards the coast below. From here, a rough track descends sharply down the escarpment leading down to the famously remote village of **Balad Sayt**, hidden away in the folds of the mountainside, with a pretty little cluster of mudbrick houses standing about a sequence of tiny terraced fields. Below Balad Sayt lies Wadi Bimah, or **Snake Gorge**, as it is popularly known, a tiny fissure running between sheer high walls. This is an increasingly popular destination for adventure trips, with extreme hiking into the gorge, jumping and climbing over boulders and wading – or even swimming – through rock pools, although the whole place should be avoided if there is any hint of rain. People have drowned here in flash floods, during which the gorge can flood with frightening speed. Past here the track finally levels off, eventually joining up with Highway 13 near Al Awabi (*see page 132*).

Alternatively, heading east from Al Hoota brings you shortly afterwards to **Al Hamra** ⓳, one of the most impressive traditional towns in Oman, with streets of grand, although steadily disintegrating, three- and four-storey mudbrick houses arranged around dozens of streets and winding alleyways which roll down the hillside to the extensive date plantation and *falaj* below – although unusually for a town of this size, Al Hamra has no fort or town wall. A couple of the old houses on the main street have now been turned into museums, including the **Bait al Safah** (daily 9am–5.30pm; closed June–Aug; charge), an attractively restored old house renovated with artefacts and traditional furnishings, and the more rustic Bait al Jabal (daily 9am–5pm; charge), whose time-warped interior is filled with assorted dusty local antiques and artefacts.

Beyond Al Hamra, a road heads through Wadi Ghul before gradually climbing towards the summit of **Jabal Shams** (Sun Mountain), Oman's highest peak; the latter part of the road is unsurfaced and requires a 4x4. The summit is closed, but a track leads out onto the plateau which affords a spectacular view of **Wadi Nakhr**, popularly known as Oman's Grand Canyon, with its almost vertical, 1000-metre (3,280ft) drop to the wadi below. The memorable trek around the edge of the canyon, known as the Balcony Walk, takes about four hours including the return journey.

Accessible via a steep road from Al Hamra, **Misfah** (or Misfat al Abryeen) ⓴ is one of the country's prettiest villages, with a fascinating tangle of mudbrick houses and an idyllic *falaj*, from where steps lead down to a tiny mosque, offering spectacular views over the surrounding hills.

Bahla and Jabrin

The small town of **Bahla** ㉑, 40km (25 miles) west of Nizwa, is utterly dominated by its vast fort, the largest in Oman. The Nabahina rulers of Oman from the 12th to the 17th century raised the fort on pre-Islamic foundations and also built the 12km (7½ miles) of mudbrick town walls, large sections of which can still be seen today. The fort was closed for

In the Imam's majlis in Jabrin Fort, note the sunken recesses by the windows on the second floor. These allowed guards to fire arrows from a comfortable position and to duck any return fire.

BELOW: villas in Al Hamra.

renovations in 1987 and has yet to reopen, although work appears to be coming to a close.

The town is also known for its pottery, with workshops scattered around the area behind the souk. The Aladawi Clay Pots Factory welcomes visitors and offers you the chance to see pots being being made, and the chance to buy them at prices significantly below what you'll pay elsewhere.

Another 10km (6 miles) west lies the marvellous **Jabrin Fort ㉒** (Sat–Thur 9am–4pm, Fri 8–11am; charge), probably the most interesting in the country. Jabrin served not only as a fort but also as a retreat for the Imams and seat of learning for students of Islamic jurisprudence, medicine and astrology. Certainly its location, set back from the mountains on an open gravel plain, does not suggest that its creator, Imam Bil'arub bin Sultan al Ya'ruba (who died here in 1692 and is buried in a crypt below the fort), felt under threat of attack.

Built in 1671, the three-storey rectangular building has 4-metre (13ft) thick stone walls with north–south towers. In the high-ceilinged rooms with Moghul-style arches are traces of what must have been a sumptuously decorated palace, tastefully restored in 1983. Swirling Islamic inscriptions in the plaster walls are cut as delicately as hand-embroidered lace, rosettes cover the pine-carved ceilings, while astrological designs in what is called the Sun and Moon Room have no parallel in Oman. In contrast to the splendour are the small, plain cells used by students off the third-storey courtyard. Go up a final flight of steps to the top of the fort for a view of the *jabal* quivering in the heat haze.

Northwest to Ibri

West of Jabrin, Route 21 continues to Ibri, pulling gradually out of the Western Hajar and into the gravel plains beyond. Around halfway to Ibri, a signed turn-off to Amla leads to the village of Al Ayn, home to a remarkable cluster of **Bronze Age beehive tombs ㉓** (now Unesco-listed), dramatically situated along a ridgetop against the craggy backdrop of Jabal Misht behind.

Below: the battlements of Jabrin Fort. **Right:** the landscape around Ibri.

Even more extensive Bronze Age relics can be found a short drive beyond Al Ayn at the **Bat Tombs** . The hills around the village of Bat are littered with dozens of tombs, towers and other unidentified structures – a few have been carefully restored, although most are in an advanced stage of collapse.

Ibri ㉕, 36km (22 miles) further down Highway 21, is the heart of the Dhahirah, the northwest shoulder of Oman wedged between the Western Hajar and the Empty Quarter. Historically the town has a pronounced reputation for religious conservatism and tribal belligerence, as noted by Thesiger in *Arabian Sands*, who steered well clear of the place. Modern tourists are likely to receive a warmer welcome, although most still tend to avoid the town, despite the attractively restored old fort (Sun–Thur 8am–2pm; free) in the town centre, next to an attractive little covered souk and surrounded by the atmospheric remains of various fine old mudbrick mansions in various states of collapse.

Also worth a visit is the atmospheric fortified village of **Sulaif**, just east of Ibri. The village was deserted by its inhabitants when the *falaj* dried up some 40 years ago, but the local guardian will show you around the rabbit warren of tiny alleyways, roofless houses, mosques and other mudbrick structures, all of which are gradually returning to dust, before leading you up to the watchtower at the top of the rock outcrop on which the entire village is built.

The drive up from Ibri skirts the edge of the Empty Quarter, and sand spits across the highway. The **Dhahirah** is barren except for scattered "bag trees", so called because their thorny branches trap windblown plastic bags. Nearing Buraymi the road swings close to the rocky outcrop of Jabal Hafeet in Abu Dhabi Emirate.

Decorated tomb, Jabrin Castle.

BELOW: Bahla.

Jinns of Bahla

Bahla is famous in Omani folklore for its supernatural associations. Locals maintain that the town is a favoured haunt of powerful jinns, who are accused of various types of mischief, including flying off with various objects (including entire mosques) in the middle of the night – note the tree in the middle of the souk, decorated with symbolic chains to prevent its removal by supernatural forces. Jinns are particularly feared for their alleged ability to take possession of those who offend them in any way, often (it is said) resulting in illness, madness or even death for the unfortunate victim. Those who are thought to be possessed are entrusted to local shamans and subject to elaborate exorcism rituals in the hope (not always successful) of freeing them from the occupying spirit.

Demonstrating the traditional craft of basket weaving.

Note that approaching Buraymi from Ibri, you travel via the UAE, exiting Oman at the border post at Mazyad and then re-entering at the Hili border post in Al Ain (see page 188).

Buraymi

For centuries **Buraymi** ㉖ was an important gateway between the Gulf, Oman and Saudi Arabia. The area has been repeatedly occupied by militia from Saudi Arabia, most recently in 1952 when the Saudis, supported by the American ARAMCO oil company, claimed the oasis for themselves and sent troops to occupy it. They stayed there for three years until, diplomacy having failed, they were driven out by the British-led Trucial Oman Scouts. Not until 1975 were negotiated borderlines finally accepted.

Next to the main roundabout in town stands the **Buraymi souk** and recently restored **Al Hilla Fort** (Sun–Thur 8am–2pm; free). This is actually more of a residential complex rather than a proper fort, with relatively low walls and no towers. Inside there are two courtyards, the first large and largely empty apart from a small mosque, the second dotted with a number of unusually fine residential buildings, decorated with elaborate wooden doors and stone ornamentation.

From Al Hilla, walk down a small side road to the elegantly restored **Al Khandaq Fort** (Sat–Wed 8am–6pm, Thur–Fri 8am–1pm and 4–6pm; free). Built by the Al bu Shamis, a division of the local Na'im tribe, in about 1780, it was strengthened between 1808 and 1813 by Mutlaq al Mutairi, the leader of the occupying Saudis. The fort is surrounded by a deep (though now dry) moat and with elaborately crenellated battlements. There are no displays, but the dramatic architecture and a little imagination make a visit enjoyable.

BELOW: the charming village of Misfah.
RIGHT: springs at Misfah.

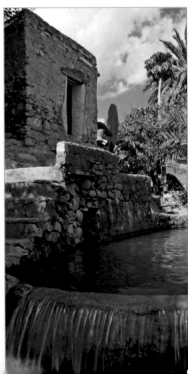

Wadi-bashing

Head out into the region's mountains and deserts for an exhilarating off-road drive

The major cities and towns of Oman and the UAE are linked by asphalt highways, but to explore fully what the region's landscape has to offer, visitors should find themselves a seat in a 4x4 and hit the dirt and the dunes.

Wadi-bashing, as off-road driving in the mountains is popularly known (or dune-bashing in the desert), is both a means to an end and an end in itself: not only will it get you from inhabited point A to isolated point B, but you'll have a lot of fun on the way.

Bouncing along a boulder-strewn wadi is like flying through bad turbulence with the "fasten seatbelt" sign on. Those who are not strapped in can become unwilling headbangers. But they usually emerge from the experience unscathed with the exuberance of children after their first spin on funfair dodgem cars.

Off-road driving should not be attempted in ordinary saloon cars. The all-terrain traction provided by four-wheel-drive vehicles is essential. It's also safer if more than one vehicle takes to the wilds at a time: that way, one can tow the other out of trouble if the need arises.

Planning and expertise

The person behind the wheel needs the handling skills of a rally driver, which is why if you're a first-time wadi-basher it's a good idea to have someone else do the work. While 4x4s can be rented, less worrisome off-road tours with experienced drivers are provided by hotels and specialist tour companies.

But even those who are most adept at judging the conditions can get stuck. A little forethought can prevent major problems, and the experienced wadi-basher hopes for the best but prepares for the worst. A long rope, shovel, tyre jack and base are musts. A small ladder or large sheet of tarpaulin can be placed under the wheels for traction. Extra fuel, a spare wheel and tyre pressure gauge are also important features of a successful trip.

Wadi- and dune-bashing depend on tyre pressure as much as skill – lower pressure for driving through sand and desert, and higher for mountain driving. When stuck in soft sand, reducing the tyre pressure and reversing over your own tracks may allow your vehicle to be driven, instead of towed, out of trouble.

To avoid getting stuck, don't change gear in soft sand, as the vehicle will lose the momentum needed to pull it through. If engines are over-revved at the first sign of trouble, the wheels dig further into the sand.

When ascending and descending sandy slopes, the wheels should be kept straight and the most vertical route taken. Attempting to cross a slope diagonally is an invitation for disaster. When going down a slope, the vehicle should be in low gear with the engine instead of the brakes used to slow it down. That way, it is less likely that the front wheels will become stuck and that the rear end will swing around, precipitating a roll.

Wadi-bashing is a great means by which to appreciate the raw beauty of the desert and mountains. It can be done year-round, but it is important to keep a close eye on the weather, especially if there's even a hint of rain in the air. Flash-floods can occur with frightening suddenness, and drownings are not unknown.

RIGHT: wadi-bashing is fun and exhilarating.

SUR, THE EAST AND THE WAHIBAH DESERT

This region offers a beautiful coastline, the characterful old shipbuilding city of Sur and the dunescapes of the Wahibah Desert, making an excellent three- or four-day excursion from Muscat

outheast of Muscat stretches **Al Sharqiyah** (The East) province, one of Oman's most diverse and colourful regions. Scenically, Sharqiyah packs in a varied range of attractions, from the wind-blown dunes of the Wahibah Desert through to the craggy heights of the Eastern Hajar mountains and long stretches of unspoilt coastline, many of them visited regularly by nesting turtles. Cultural attractions include the handsome old port of Sur, home to Oman's only surviving dhow-building yard, through to the great mudbrick castles and fortified houses of the Interior, best seen in Ibra and Jalan Bani Bu Ali. This is also where you're most likely to see traditional Bedu going about their daily life, especially in the traditional souks of Ibra and Sinaw.

It is possible to make a rewarding loop through the region, travelling down the coast through Qurayyat to Sur and then on to Ras al Jinz, before heading back inland via Jalan Bani Bu Hassan and Ibra, with a detour into the Wahibah Desert en route – an enjoyable three- or four-day excursion.

Qurayyat to Qalhat

Qurayyat ❶ (87km/54 miles) on the first, tarmacked stretch of Route 17 from Muscat, is a quiet coastal town of little interest beyond its old fort

(currently closed for renovations). It is most animated when the fishing boats return and lay their catch out on the beach. At the eastern end of the beach is a rocky outcrop crowned by a watchtower which you can wade out to at low tide. A creek, today silted up, before the turn-off to Sur was in all probability Qurayyat's old port.

South of Qurayyat on the coast lies the **Bimmah Sinkhole ❷**, now enclosed within (and signed as) the Hawiyat Najm Park. One of numerous similar sinkholes in Oman, it is around

Main attractions

WADI SHAB
SUR
RAS AL JINZ
JALAN BANI BU ALI
WAHIBAH DESERT
IBRA
MASIRAH ISLAND

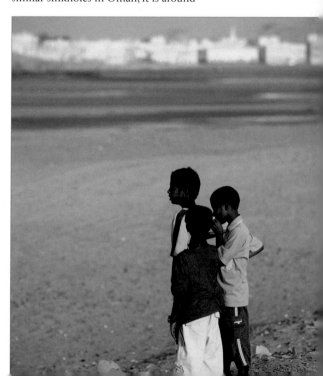

LEFT: traditional Omani coffee pot.
BELOW: view across to Al Ayjah from Sur.

The Mausoleum of Bibi Maryam in ancient Qalhat.

BELOW: a landscape of palm trees and river at Wadi Shab.

100 metres (330ft) in circumference and about 20 metres (66ft) deep. Marine life including sponges and small fish indicate a connection with the sea. Filled with blue-green water, it is a lovely place to clamber down for a swim.

Further south along the coast lie two of the country's most beautiful wadis. The first is **Wadi Shab** ❸ (76km/47 miles from Qurayyat), a narrow, palm-fringed ravine hemmed in by spectacular cliffs – the wadi is so narrow that it remains in shadow until midday. It's possible to drive (in a 4x4) a kilometre or so into the wadi over loose gravel, but after that, progress is on foot only, following the narrow footpath which winds up the gorge, past huge boulders, rock pools and the ruins of a couple of abandoned villages. A few kilometres further down the coast lies the **Wadi Tiwi**, almost identical to Wadi Shab save for the presence of a road which winds its way up the wadi through a series of tiny traditional villages.

A little further down the coast lie the remains of the ancient city of

Qalhat ❹, once one of the leading ports in the southern Gulf and visited by both Marco Polo and Ibn Battuta. The city is believed to have been founded by the Persians around the 2nd century, reaching the height of prosperity under rule from Hormuz in the 13th and 14th centuries. The extensive remains of collapsed walls, towers and assorted other structures cover the area, although it is difficult to make much sense of them. The only notable surviving structure is the Mausoleum of Bibi Maryam, last resting place of the saintly woman who, according to Ibn Battuta, had ruled the city until a few years before his visit in 1330. The mausoleum's original dome has now collapsed, though the remains of the delicately moulded arches and doorways survive more or less intact.

Sur

From Qalhat the road descends to **Sur** ❺ (150km/93 miles from Qurayyat), a major trading port with East Africa until early in the 20th century and still the biggest traditional port in Oman. Sur finally gave in to the

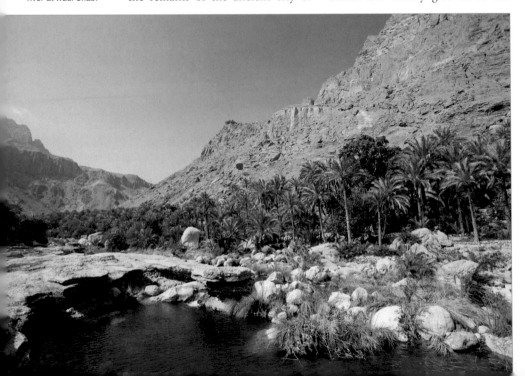

better shipping facilities of Muscat, although its economic fortunes have been revived by the construction of a huge industrial zone on the north side of town. Old Sur and the small suburb of Al Ayjah continue to provide visitors with a pastel-coloured cameo of the past.

Sur's most interesting sights are the traditional **dow-building yards**, the only surviving example in Oman (although there are several in the UAE). The yards lie on the edge of the creek, some 4km (2½ miles) east of the town centre. Access to the yards is free, and the workers, mainly Indian, do not mind being photographed.

Old merchant-style houses line the creek in **Al Ayjah**, a short drive over the bridge near the dhow yards. The little whitewashed community was founded in 1928 by rebellious sheikhs from the dissident Bani bu Ali, who established an independent customs post and ran up their own flag which took the Sultan, aided by the British Resident in the Gulf, two years to remove. At low tide the view of Al Ayjah from Sur crosses extensive mudflats and beached

bumboats, which in the evening are bathed in rose-coloured sunlight; at high tide this is one of the most charming corners of Oman.

Two forts guard Sur. The main one, **As Sunaysilah Castle** (8am–6pm; free), with its four distinctive towers, is built on a hill overlooking the sea approaches to Sur. Inside the courtyard are a mosque and a small prison, while to the far left a wooden door gives access to the water cistern. A second fort, **Bilad Sur** (currently closed for renovations) lies 6km (4 miles) south from the town centre.

Ras al Hadd and Ras al Jinz

The jutting headland known as **Ras al Hadd** is the first point in Arabia touched by the rising sun. The tiny village is dwarfed by its massive fort (Sun–Thur 8.30am–2.30pm; free), whose high walls tower over the surrounding houses, although most of the interior is simply a huge empty courtyard.

Significant numbers of green turtles come to nest along the coast around Ras al Hadd, although the biggest

The old part of Sur is known locally as "Makkah", doubtless because the wealthy owners who originally lived here were able to perform the Hajj (pilgrimage).

BELOW: a view across the lagoon to Al Ayjah.

Dhow detail.

BELOW: the dhow yard in Sur.

nesting sight lies further south, at **Ras al Jinz** ❻, 23km (14 miles) along the coast. This is one of Oman's most memorable natural spectacles, as dozens of turtles come ashore nightly to dig a hole in the sand and lay their eggs, covering them carefully before returning exhausted to the sea. The eggs, which may number up to 100 per turtle, take about 60 days to hatch, after which the tiny turtles must burrow their way to the surface and head as quickly as they can for the safety of the sea.

Turtle-watching tours depart from the modern visitor centre (www.ras-aljinz-turtlereserve.com) at 9pm and 4am, last around 60 to 90 minutes and cost OR3. There is a maximum of 100 visitors per evening and another 100 visitors per morning session; bookings either by phone or email are essential; three weeks or more in advance is recommended since places are usually booked up early.

Continuing along the coastal road past Ras al Jinz, the next sizeable settlement is the sleepy fishing town of **Al Ashkharah**. There is a choice of routes here: either south along the recently constructed tarmac road to Shanna (departure point for boats to Masirah Island) or north, heading back inland to Muscat via Jalan Bani Bu Ali and Ibra.

North from Al Ashkharah

Some 30km (19 miles) inland from Al Ashkharah the little-visited town of **Jalan Bani Bu Ali** ❼ offers an absorbing taste of traditional small-town life in provincial Oman. This is the home town of the Bani bu Ali (who also installed themselves in Al Ayjah in Sur; *see page 151*). The Bani bu Ali were the only tribe in Oman to subscribe to the conservative Wahhabism sect of Islam followed in Saudi Arabia; the town retains a certain reputation for extreme religious conservatism, and women visitors are advised to dress very modestly – although foreign visitors are also sufficiently rare to elicit an unusual measure of generally good-natured curiosity.

The main sight in town is the vast **fort**, probably the single largest unrestored mudbrick structure in the entire country: a huge, slowly disintegrating

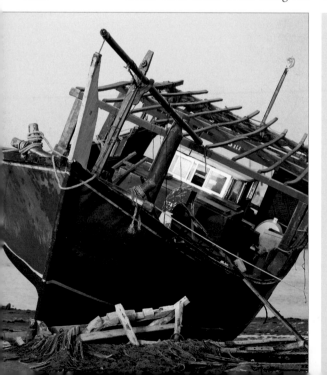

Dhows of Oman

The word "dhow" is habitually used in English as a cover-all term to describe traditional wooden Arabian boats. Locals, however, distinguish between a wide variety of different designs. Traditional Arabian dhows were curved at both ends – such as the large-scale *boom*, used for long-distance ocean crossings. Other types of vessel – such as the *sambuq* and *ghanjah* – sported high, square sterns, thought to have been inspired by the design of Portuguese galleons. Traditional dhows were also notable for their so-called "stitched" construction, whereby the planks of the boat were literally sewn together using coconut rope, and propelled by distinctive triangular *lateen* sails, although conventional nails have long since replaced traditional coconut rope, and virtually all modern vessels are powered by diesel engines rather than by sail.

edifice whose towers and battlements still rise high above the surrounding streets, although considerable sections of wall have now collapsed. Inside, the labyrinthine remains of various buildings survive, decorated in places with fine arches and arcading. There is also a small mosque, topped by a pair of flattened domes, strikingly similar to the famous old 15th-century mosque at Bidiyah *(see page 232)* in the eastern UAE.

Close to the fort stands the quaint **Al Hamooda Mosque**, an eye-catching structure topped by 52 tiny domes and with a *falaj* running in front of the main facade. Non-Muslims are prohibited from entering, although they may be able to look through the door for a glimpse of the unusual interior, filled with a dense cluster of stumpy columns.

Heading north from Jalan Bani Bu Ali, is another 10km (6 miles) to the twin town of **Jalan Bani Bu Hassan**. There's another sizeable **fort** here (Sun–Wed 7am–6pm; free), although this one has been comprehensively restored, as well as some impressively tall and large traditional houses scattered around the surrounding area, looking a bit like medieval mudbrick skyscrapers poking up above the palms.

The roadside town of **Al Kamil** lies 75km (46 miles) north of Al Ashkharah – a mainly modern affair, though a few fine old two- and three-storey mudbrick mansions can still be seen. Heading north again, it's 42km (26 miles) from Al Kamil to the turn-off east to the side road to **Wadi Bani Khalid**, one of Oman's most spectacular wadis.

Al Mintirib ❽ on the northern edge of the Wahibah Desert is about 45 minutes' drive from Al Kamil. A market depot for local Bedu, it sells everything from male stamens for pollinating female date palms to mobile phones, and is also home to the inevitable fort (Sun–Thur 8.30am–2.30pm; free). Tracks lead off from here into the Wahibah Desert, including the access routes for a couple of the sands' remote desert camps. Alternatively, **Al Qabil** has a comfortable hotel which can also be used as a base for visiting the Wahibah Desert.

Around 20,000 green turtles lay their eggs on Oman's beaches during the summer breeding season. Turtles always return to lay their eggs on the beach where they themselves were born – their so-called "natal" beach – although exactly how they navigate back to it, often covering thousands of miles of open ocean, is not yet understood.

BELOW: beach at Ras al Jinz.

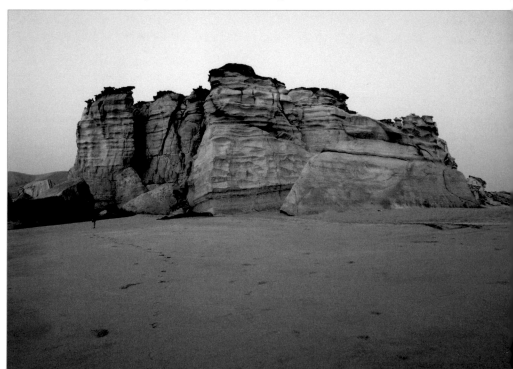

Masirah is also popular amongst windsurfers, who consider it one of the best sites in the region thanks to the offshore winds blowing down the coast, particularly during the breezy khareef (monsoon) season from June to September.

The Wahibah Desert and around

Sunset and sunrise provide spectacular photo opportunities of this unique desert covering 10,000 sq km (3,860 sq miles) of the eastern Sharqiyah, described by Nigel de Winser, the project director of a British Royal Geographic Society (RGS) expedition to the Wahibah in 1985, as "a perfect specimen of sand sea".

The 35 scientists in the expedition spent four months studying the ecosystem of the Wahibah Desert and discovered 150 species of plants, including woodlands of native ghaf inland from Al Ashkharah. Among the desert's most valuable trees is the *Proposis cinera*, which helps stabilise the shifting sands as well as provide fuel, shade and food for livestock. A hardy tree, it sends down an immensely long tap root to the water table, but most desert plants are sustained on dew.

A rare dew-drinking beetle was among 16,000 invertebrates collected by the RGS team. Two hundred species of mammals, birds, amphibians and reptiles were also logged. Early-risers

BELOW: camel in the Wahibah Desert.

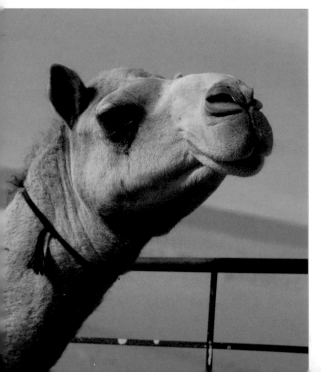

here may see patterns made by nocturnal creatures in the sand – the swishing trail of a side-winding viper, the hip-hop footprints of a hare and the pad marks of a Rüpell's sand fox to name a few. During the day the desert is devoid of life as the creatures burrow away from the intense heat.

The dune systems of the Wahibah Desert are believed to have existed before the last pluvial period in Arabia around 4,000–6,000 years ago. Aligned mainly east–west and soaring upwards of 60 to 80 metres (200 to 260ft), the dunes commence less than 1km (½ mile) off the road between Al Qabil and Al Minitrib.

Around 3,000 Bedu live on the fringes of the Wahibah Desert, mostly herders of sheep, goats and a few camels. Coastal families living south of Al Ashkharah double as fishermen, while men around Al Qabil and Al Mintirib act as guides for tour operators.

The best way to experience the sands is to spend a night or two at one of the increasing number of desert camps hidden away in various parts of the dunes. Access to most camps is via 4x4 only, although most places can arrange pick-up from the highway. The further into the dunes you go, the more pristine the scenery becomes. Most camps offer a range of desert activities, including dune-bashing and more sedate (and much quieter) camel or horse rides, sometimes guided by local Bedu. You might also find sandboarding, trekking and quad-biking trips, as well as cultural visits to local Bedu encampments. Needless to say, you shouldn't attempt to venture off into the sands without the services of a guide – the wide and uninhabited expanses of dune, with daytime temperatures nudging over 40°C (104°F), can bring ill-equipped visitors to grief very quickly.

North of Al Qabil, 1km (½ mile) east of the main highway, the village of **Mudayrib** ❾ is one of the prettiest in Sharqiyah, surrounded by a protective necklace of six watchtowers posed on top of the surrounding hills. Down in the village itself stand a number of imposing old fortified houses built by local merchants who had grown rich through the village's location on one of the main trade routes between Muscat and the coast.

Also north of Al Qabil, a side road strikes west around the top of the sand to reach the small town of **Sinaw ⑩**. The town's souk is a fascinating melting pot, as Bedu come from miles around to sell their goods and exchange news. Lining the walls around the market are shops filled with items essential to desert life, as well as silver jewellery and pottery. Before 11am on a Thursday or Friday morning are the best times to visit the souk.

Bustling **Ibra ⑪** is the main town of the region, still north of Al Qabil. There's another colourful souk here, also popular with local Bedu, although even more interesting is the famous women's souk held on a Wednesday from 9am until noon. Run by women, the souk caters to women's needs, with as many as dozens of local Bedu selling bolts of silk and satin brocades, jewellery, *kohl*, sandalwood, kitchen goods, spices and other produce.

Almost uniquely for a settlement of its size, there is no fort in Ibra, although the town preserves rich reminders of its past in the old mudbrick villages of **Al Minzahah** and **Al Kanatar** on the edge of town (and clearly signed from the main highway), two picture-perfect walled villages packed with fine old merchant houses sporting elaborately carved windows and archways. On the edge of Al Kanatar lies the venerable **Al Qablateen Mosque** (very similar to the Al Hamooda mosque in Jalan Bani Bu Ali; *see page 152*, with a dense cluster of columns inside the solid (though now roofless) rectangular structure.

Masirah Island

Lying 18km (11 miles) off the coast at the far southern end of Sharqiyah province, **Masirah Island** (Jaza'ir Masirah) is one of Oman's most remote tourist attractions and a popular destination for both locals and expatriates – though it still sees few foreign tourists. The island is roughly

TIP

Most women at Ibra's women's souk do not object to having their picture taken, but always ask first. *"Mumkin sura, min fadlich?"* ("May I take your picture?")

BELOW: men gathering on Masirah Island.

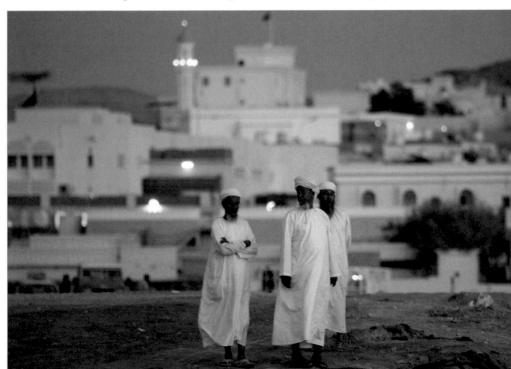

80km (50 miles) long by 18km (11 miles) wide, with a sand-fringed coast dotted with dozens of unspoilt villages climbing inland to the modest hills of the interior, rising to 274 metres (900ft) at Jabal Hamra.

Hilf, at the northern tip of the island, is Masirah's only real town, with several simple hotels, petrol stations, ATMs and a reasonable selection of shops. If you have a 4x4 and camping equipment, however, you can take your pick from any of the beaches around the coast for a memorable spot of wild camping. Car ferries run between Hilf and Shanna on the mainland; the crossing takes around 90 minutes and costs OR8 per car. Ferries leave when full – roughly every one to two hours – and normally run until around 5pm, although it is best to be at the jetty by 3pm, just in case. Note also that ferries occasionally stop running in bad weather.

Away from Hilf, Masirah remains largely untouched by the modern world. Wild camping aside, wildlife is the main attraction here, particularly the island's **turtles**. Four of the five main species of marine turtle nest here, and Masirah is believed to host the world's largest population of loggerhead turtles, while hundreds of green, hawksbill and olive ridley also visit the island. Note that turtles nest only on the east and far southwestern coasts of the island; loggerheads usually stick to the northeastern coast, while other species can be seen further south. Unfortunately, there are currently no official guided turtle watches, so you will have to ask locally to find the best places to turtle-spot – the nesting site on the beach right next to the Swiss Belhotel, 10km (6 miles) from Hilf, is a good bet at certain times of year. Dolphins and whales are also frequently seen off this coast.

Turtles aside, Masirah is also particularly rich in birdlife, with around 328 species recorded here. Additionally, the island is known for its remarkable seashells and other marine relics, including the island's celebrated endemic cowry shell (*Cypraea teulerej*).

BELOW AND RIGHT: customers and produce in Ibra's souk.

The Baron Innerdale

A small stone monument at the northern end of Masirah Island (now part of the military airbase, and out of bounds to the public) commemorates one of the more gruesome episodes in modern Omani history. In 1904 the *Baron Innerdale* steamship was travelling from Karachi to Liverpool when she ran aground near Masirah. After three days, crew and passengers took to a lifeboat, landing soon afterwards in Masirah. Subsequent events remain unclear. Arriving at Masirah, there appears to have been some misunderstanding, leading to a fight, during which the stranded crew and passengers of the *Innerdale* were massacred. The furious Sultan Faisal had nine of the killers executed, flattened Hilf village and banned the islanders from building permanent houses – a decree which remained in force until 1970.

THE BIRDLIFE ALONG DHOFAR'S COAST

The special climate of coastal Dhofar in southern Oman has made its wadis, hills and creeks particularly rich in birdlife

Dhofar's geographical location and unique monsoonal microclimate makes it one of the most rewarding birdwatching destinations in the Arabian peninsula, thanks to the presence of a wide range of indigenous and migratory species that visit the region, and which are unknown elsewhere in Oman. In spring or autumn you can expect to find many Eurasian migrants dropping in to rest and feed on their way between winter quarters in Africa and their breeding grounds to the northeast.

There are numerous rewarding birding spots throughout the regions. The coastal khors around Salalah, and ocean-side locations further afield including Mughsayl, Mirbat and Hasik, all offer rich ornithological pickings. In addition, the spectacular Tawi Atayr (the aptly named Well of Birds) is another rewarding destination, as are the various springs (*ayn*) which dot the region (such as Ayn Hamran and Ain Razat) and the dramatic Wadi Darbat. The uplands of the Jabal Samhan are also worth a visit, the haunt of majestic raptors including Egyptian vultures, the Arabian Scops owl and Verraux's eagle.

Elsewhere, commonly spotted residents include Rüppell's Weaver, Abyssinian Sunbird, African Silverbill, as well as the more mundane Graceful Warbler and Yellow-vented Bulbul. You may also see Black Kite and Fan-tailed Raven, the former perhaps nesting here in winter, the raven foraging from its cliff roosts and nests.

ABOVE: a regular sight amidst Salalah's coastal woodlands, Rüppell's Weaver is one of the region's most distinctive bird species, instantly recognizable thanks to its colourful yellow plumage and famous for its intricately woven nests.

BELOW: one of the three kingfisher species regularly sighted in Oman (along with the Common and Collared varieties), the Grey-headed Kingfisher is usually seen posed motionless on branches or overhead cables, scanning the ground for insects.

LEFT: The Glossy Ibis nests colonially in trees, often with herons. It is also gregarious when feeding in marshy wetlands; it preys on fish, frogs and occasionally on insects.

LEFT: the delicate Yellow wagtail is one of the sixteen wagtails found in Oman and the UAE, typically spotted foraging for insects amidst coastal grasslands and scrub.

BELOW: one of the region's most iconic birds of prey, the Egyptian Vulture can often be seen riding the thermals above the mountains of Oman, instantly recognisable thanks to its distinctive black-and-white wings, sometimes approaching two metres in length.

ABOVE: one of two species of kite found in Oman, the Black Kite (although it's brownish in colour, rather than black) can often be spotted hovering overhead above the Salalah mountains and lagoons.

ALONG DHOFAR'S CREEKS

Good views of waterbirds are to be had at most of the khawrs (creeks) which dot the coastline around Salalah. Khawr Salalah, right on the edge of the city, is usually thronged with resting or feeding birds, as is Khawr Rawri, a particularly magical location below the ruins of ancient Sumhuran.

Common species include visiting Greater Flamingo, egrets and herons, Glossy Ibis feeding on the grassy banks with resident moorhens and coots, gulls and terns, as well a various ducks in autumn including Cotton Teal (Indian Pygmy Goose), Pheasant-tailed Jacana, occasional lapwings, various species of snipe, roosting Yellow Wagtails, and a variety of waterbirds from the large visiting Eurasian Curlew and Black-tailed Godwit to the diminutive spring-nesting Kentish Plover.

Don't neglect the surrounds of the creeks, where Little Pratincole may roost unseen, and a flock of Alpine Swift may mill over your head, or (early on a May morning) you may find the bushes bursting with fat Marsh Warblers, dawn arrivals from wintering in Africa and now on their way to nest in Europe.

BELOW: flocks of nesting Greater and Lesser Flamingos add an incongruously African touch to parts of coastal Salalah, often seen splashing about the coastal *khors* (creeks) which fringe this part of the southern Oman coast.

DHOFAR

The only part of the Gulf that is visited by the southwest monsoon, Dhofar is a lush summer retreat for northern Omanis, with a rich history rooted in the ancient frankincense trade

Dhofar, Oman's southern province, is a ruggedly beautiful region quite different from the rest of Oman. Its mountains attract the *khareef* (southwest monsoon) blowing off the Indian Ocean, resulting in a cool, wet summer (June–September) when the rest of the country is paralysingly hot. Waterfalls pour off the *jabals* into coastal wadis, and low-hanging mists occasionally disrupt air services to the capital, Salalah. Lush woodland is sustained by rainfall of 27 to 150mm (1 to 6 inches) a year, but beyond its limits you can die of thirst. "To the south, grassy downs, green jungles and shadowy gorges fell away to the... Indian Ocean... whereas immediately to the north a landscape of black rocks and yellow sand sloped down to the Empty Quarter. I looked out over the desert. It stretched away unbroken for 1,500 miles to the orchards around Damascus," wrote Wilfred Thesiger in *Arabian Sands*.

Occupying about one-third of the total area of Oman, Dhofar adjoins the Rub al Khali (Empty Quarter), first crossed by Bertram Thomas in 1930 and then by Thesiger in the 1940s *(see page 58)*. The province shares a border with Yemen to the west (Yemen and Oman completed their demarcation

of the border in 1995), and in the northeast melts into the gravel plains of the Jiddat al Harasis.

Salalah

Most people travel to Dhofar by air, a spectacular 90-minute flight from Muscat. On the approach to **Salalah** ❶ the brown terrain is flecked with green and the drop down onto the coastal plain is sudden and exciting. Likewise 1,000km (620 miles) after leaving Muscat, the highway sweeps into Salalah, flanked by lines

Main attractions
SALALAH
JABAL SAMHAN AND WADI DARBAT
TAWI ATAYR AND TAIQ SINKHOLE
SUMHURAM AND KHAWR RAWRI
MIRBAT
JABAL QAMAR

LEFT: blowholes at Mughsayl.
RIGHT: pottery incense burners for sale in Al Husn Souk, Salalah.

of coconut palms, which here replace the date palm of the north.

Modern Salalah is now a sprawling expanse of whitewashed, low-rise buildings. The commercial centre is around As Salam Street and the parallel 23rd July Street. **As Salam Street** is usually the liveliest in the city, lined with hundreds of shops selling virtually everything under the sun; **23rd July Street** is wider and quieter, home to dozens of banks, airlines and Salalah's best selection of restaurants. The **New Souk**, off the north side of the street, is a pleasant pedestrianised complex with dozens of tea shops and traders selling locally grown tropical fruits such as coconuts, papaws and bananas.

The old town – centred on the district of Al Haffa – lies a couple of kilometres (a mile) south of here, centred on the aromatic **Al Husn Souk A**, just inland from the sea. This is undoubtedly the highlight of Salalah, with dozens of shoebox shops selling traditional products – Omani caps, walking sticks, perfumes and, especially, frankincense, of which Al Husn has probably the best selection in the country. The best time to visit is after dark, when the alleyways between the shops are perfumed with burning incense. Many of the shops are run by local women, veiled but friendly. Bags of frankincense sell for as little as OR1 (about £2/US$3), although top-quality *hojari* silver frankincense costs considerably more.

West of Al Husn Souk stretches the huge **Sultan Qaboos Palace B**, an imposing marbled building (not open to the public) which replaced the original fort in which Sultan Qaboos was born in 1940. Qaboos has always had close links with the city, having spent most of his early life here, while his mother is also Dhofari. East of the souk stretches Salalah's attractive **corniche**, with leaning coconut palms shading the beach, a wide and beautiful expanse of white sand stretching for miles down the coast. You will also find a few traditional Dhofari-style houses dotted along the beach (and Ash Sharooq Street, one block inland) with their distinctive carved windows, balconies and battlemented rooftops.

BELOW: a female goat shepherd near Salalah.

Salalah

0   500 m
0   500 yds

On the east side of the city, beyond Al Haffa, lie the extensive remains of the ancient city of Zafar, the fore-runner of modern Salalah (and the origin of the name Dhofar). Zafar's heyday came between the 12th and 16th centuries, when it was one of the leading commercial centres of southern Arabia, its fame attracting many visitors, including both Ibn Battuta and Marco Polo. The extensive ruins of the city are now protected as the **Al Baleed Archaeological Site** (Sat–Wed 8am–2pm and 4–8pm, Thur–Fri 4–8pm; charge), a large area of parkland covered in various fragmentary remains of houses, mosques, gateways, walls and other structures. The best-preserved section is the old Zafar citadel and the Grand Mosque at the western end of the site.

Next to the entrance to the archaeological site, the **Museum of the Frankincense Land** (same opening hours and ticket) offers hit-and-miss coverage of the history of Salalah and Dhofar spread over two large rooms. The Maritime Hall holds exhibits relating to Omani boat-building and maritime traditions, with assorted navigational instruments and intricate wooden models of traditional boats. The adjacent History Hall hosts a random muddle of exhibits, including finds from Al Baleed and nearby Sumhuram.

Sultan Qaboos Palace.

East of Salalah

The area east of Salalah is particularly rich in attractions, including the ancient ruins of Sumhuram, the scenic heights of Jabal Samhan and the characterful old town of Mirbat.

BELOW: tropical plants, including bananas, flourish.

Southern Tribes

About nine mountain tribes known collectively as the *Jebali* live in the coastal ranges – Jabal Qamar, Jabal Samhan and Jabal Qara – rising behind Salalah. Brown-skinned and with rounded heads, in appearance they resemble Ethiopians more than either Omanis or the long-skulled Bedu of the Jiddat al Harasis and Wahibah Desert. Most are herdsmen running stocky mountain cattle and keeping camels for prestige. During the monsoon, as the weather in the mountains cools down, they move their tents to the coastal plain around Salalah. The Jebali continue to speak a number of local languages closer to Amharic (one of the languages of modern Ethiopia and Eritrea) than Arabic, including Shehri, spoken by the Qara, and Mehri (or Mahri), spoken by the Mahra.

The lush, scenic Ain Razat.

fort (Sun–Thur 9am–4pm, Fri 8–11am; charge) in the middle of town.

Continue for 6km (4 miles) beyond Taqah to reach the turn-off on the left leading up into **Jabal Samhan**, the green coastal range which backs this section of the coast. Right next to the turning is the opening of **Wadi Darbat** ❸, marked by a huge cliff of pockmarked travertine that transforms into a spectacular waterfall during the *khareef* – probably Dhofar's most photographed sight.

Past the Wadi Darbat waterfall, the road climbs steeply up into the hills. After around 17km (11 miles) there's a signed turn-off on the left to **Tawi Atayr** (Well of Birds) ❹, one of the most dramatic of the various sinkholes that dot the porous limestones of the Salalah mountains. This enormous cavity plunges more than 100 metres (330ft). With a local guide, you can scramble down a rugged path to the bottom. A subterranean stream leads out of the sinkhole, but no one has yet managed to follow it to the end.

Some 11km (7 miles) further north lies another, and even more

Heading out of the city, the first point of interest is **Ain Razat**, a lush picnic spot around a spring, rich in birdlife. Past here, it is a further 13km (8 miles) to **Taqah** ❷ (36km/22 miles from Salalah), the second-largest town in Dhofar. The majority of its 12,000 population are fishermen netting huge catches of sardines during the winter. When the vegetation dies off, dried sardines become an important food supplement for mountain cattle. There is also a pretty little renovated impressive, sinkhole, the vast **Taiq Sinkhole ❺** (misleadingly signed as "Taiq Cave") – a vast bowl scooped out of the russet-coloured uplands. According to some estimates this is the world's third-largest sinkhole, at around 1km (½ mile) long, 750 metres (2,460 ft) across and some 200 metres (660ft) deep.

Returning to Tawi Atayr and heading east, the road climbs up to the escarpment of Jabal Samhan, the scenery becoming increasingly barren as you near the top, from where there are jaw-dropping views over the hills and down to Mirbat and the coast way below. Among the botanical wilderness, look out for the curious *Adenium obesum*, whose pink blossoms grow straight out of the trunk. The mountains around here are also said to be home to some of the country's tiny number of surviving Arabian leopards – although no one has seen any for years.

Back on the coastal highway, it's another 2km (1 mile) to the turn-off to the ruins of the town of **Sumhuram ❻** (daily 8am–6pm; charge), one of Dhofar's most important

archaeological sites. Sumhuram was formerly a major trading point on the Arabian frankincense route, but appears to have been abandoned in the 5th century AD after a sandbar (which can still be seen) formed across the mouth of Khawr Rawri, cutting off the town's access to the sea.

The remains of the town have now been meticulously restored, showing the foundations of houses, temples and streets protected by thick walls, more than 3 metres (10ft) deep in

Camels in Wadi Darbat.

BELOW: a local man at Sumhuram.

Mirbat fort.

salt content, it supports freshwater fish from small guppies to ponderous milk fish measuring almost 1 metre/yd long. Pelican, stork, spoonbill and flamingo are among 186 species of birds recorded in the vicinity.

A right turn off the tarmac road before Mirbat leads to an unusual white double-domed **Mausoleum of Bin Ali**, a 14th-century Muslim divine from Yemen. The mausoleum stands in the middle of an extensive cemetery, studded with thousands of headstones. The oldest are clustered around the mausoleum itself, often sporting elaborately carved inscriptions. Inside the mausoleum is a single darkened room, perfumed with incense, with the saint's coffin under an embroidered cloth.

A kilometre (½ mile) or so beyond lies **Mirbat ❼** (74km/46 miles from Salalah), the most picturesque town in Dhofar. Its small fort with cannon emplacements pointing seawards offers good views. Beyond the headland, the old town has some fine old houses, with the distinctive carved wooden shutters that are a particular

places. Next to the single gateway, through the walls, are two beautifully preserved inscriptions commemorating the foundation of the city, carved in the ancient South Arabic *musnad* alphabet. Inside, the considerable remains of a temple dedicated to the Mesopotamian moon god Sin can still be seen.

Immediately below Sumhuram, the idyllic **Khawr Rawri** is the largest of a dozen creeks between Salalah and Sadah. With a particularly low

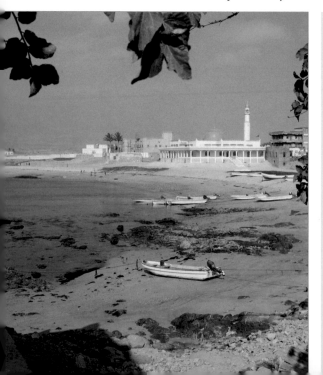

Magnetic Attraction

Just inland from the coast near Mirbat lies one of Oman's more eccentric attractions, the enigmatic Magnetic Point (or Anti-Gravity Point, as it is also known). Following a sloping track leading inland down to the beach (you will need to travel with a local tour operator to discover the exact location), you'll find that cars left in neutral will begin magically reversing themselves back up the hill, in apparent defiance of all laws of physics and common sense.

Local guides assert that this is the result of some mysterious magnetic phenomenon, although the more plausible (if prosaic) explanation is that just some kind of weird optical illusion – a local example of the type of "Gravity Hill" (or "Magnetic Hill"), of which many other examples have been recorded worldwide.

feature of the region. Anywhere else they would have been bought and restored by Europeans, but here they are falling into disrepair.

It is 64km (40 miles) from Mirbat to **Sadah** ❽. Known as the "Frankincense Highway", the road east crosses the rugged coastal plain with great views of Jabal Samhan. Sheltered from the monsoon, a few straggly frankincense trees grow in the wadis. On reaching Sadah, turn left at the Abalone Roundabout and drive down to a tiny harbour where a few boats are usually moored. Local women as well as men work as abalone divers, wearing only goggles and diving to depths of 10 metres (30ft) to prise the shells off the rocks. The season is short (Nov–Dec) to allow regeneration.

Historically, **Hadbin** (170km/105 miles east of Salalah) was linked to the export of frankincense, but today, like Sadh, it relies on fishing and occasional abalone diving. It has several small food stores, but no other facilities. Travel beyond here is strictly by 4x4 with a back-up vehicle.

West of Salalah

Leaving Salalah, the road west heads out past the enormous port and industrial complex at **Raysut**, 10km (6 miles) from Salalah. Past here the road winds inland, just out of sight of the ocean until it sweeps back to the coast and offers spectacular views of the towering sea cliffs above **Mughsayl** ❾, 45km (28 miles) from Salalah. Mughsayl is known for its giant blowholes (follow the signs on the left to Al Marneef Cave), which spurt water up to 30 metres (100ft) high during the *khareef*, although the sprays are less impressive at other times of the year, and may dry up entirely. Walking along the rock shelf, you can hear the eerie sound of the sea rushing beneath your feet. Mughsayl has a good swimming beach, and the creek at the southern end is popular for birdwatching from December to February and April to June.

Mausoleum of Bin Ali, near Mirbat.

BELOW: the dramatic coastline at Mughsayl.

TIP

On a clear day look out for dolphins, packs of sharks or even a whale or two off the coast at Mughsayl.

Past Mughsayl, the road climbs dramatically up into the barren **Jabal Qamar**. The stretch of highway here is known as the Furious Road, blasted out of sheer rock faces and climbing some 400 metres (1,312ft) in just 5km (3 miles), with endless hairpins. Some 6.4 million tonnes of rock and 160,000 tonnes of asphalt went into building the road at a cost of around £75 million (US$120 million).

Around 14km (9 miles) past Mughsayl the road finally reaches the top of the ridge, with spectacular views along the coast and down to the sea way below. On your left, a graded track (a 4x4 is usually required) winds down to the coastal village of **Fizayah**, home to a superb beach hemmed in by spectacular sea cliffs and dramatic limestone formations.

It is possible to continue west from here as far as **Rakhyut** ❿ (148km/92 miles from Salalah), a small village built in the lee of the cliffs with a couple of basic food stores and nothing else, although there is not a great deal to see en route, and you'll have to negotiate a couple of police checkpoints (bring your passport) along the way. The area beyond Rakhyut is currently off-limits due to its proximity to the Yemen border.

Job's Tomb

Job's Tomb ⓫ (open 24 hours) lies to the north of Salalah. Famed in the Old Testament for maintaining his faith in God in spite of the sufferings sent to test him, Job (Ayoub in Arabic) is revered by Muslims as well as Jews and Christians.

To reach the site held by Muslims to be the patriarch's tomb, take the Ittin road next to the Hamdan Plaza Hotel in Salalah. After about 30km (18 miles) turn left at a sign to Al Nabi Ayoub, then drive 1.5km (1 mile) to a road fork and bear left. Enter the gate beside the mosque and walk down the path to a white shrine with a gold dome. A single long grave, the tomb is covered with a green embroidered shroud, garlands and pages from the Koran left by faithful pilgrims. Non-Muslims are allowed to enter the shrine, but must cover their heads and remove their shoes first.

BELOW: the Furious Road.

The Empty Quarter and Ubar

North of Salalah and the Dhofar mountains stretch the endless deserts of the Empty Quarter (Rub al Khali), extending across northern Dhofar and into Saudi Arabia. The tarmac road to Thumrayt, part of Highway 31 to Muscat, starts climbing into Jabal Qara 5km (3 miles) outside Salalah, a gradual rise into an increasingly inhospitable landscape. The inland side of the mountains forms a plateau which dips gradually to the north, eventually giving way to gravel hills dissected by numerous wadis and the desert.

Some 35km (22 miles) north of Salalah lies the **Wadi Dawkah Frankincense Park** ⑫, on the left of the main road (there are no restrictions to visiting: simply park your car and walk over). The arid wadi contains an estimated 2,000 frankincense trees in the 9 sq km (3½ sq miles) listed by Unesco as a World Heritage Site. Those attaining the maximum height of 5 metres (16ft) are more than 200 years old. The trees are threatened by feral camels tearing off the leaves, as well as visitors making incisions in

the trunks to see the sap oozing out, as the trees cannot repair such damage and eventually dry out. The Bait Kethir Bedu, who own hereditary rights to the trees, are still allowed to collect the resin, but the way they cut the trunk does no permanent damage.

The edge of the Empty Quarter is marked by the ramshackle little town of **Thumrayt**, a popular pit-stop with passing truck drivers and crammed with cafés and petrol stations. North of here, the highway sets off on its interminable desert crossing towards Muscat, a long, flat, monotonous and hot drive. The turn-off to Ubar (*see below*) is 40km (25 miles) north of Thumrayt.

Job's Tomb, a single long grave covered with a green shroud.

The Search for Ubar

The search for the remains of Ubar was one of the great archaeological treasure hunts of recent times. The first hint that there might be more to the legend of Ubar than was previously thought was provided by English explorer Bertram Thomas, the first European to traverse the Empty Quarter in 1930–31. Travelling north of Shisr, Thomas saw a series of "well-worn tracks", described by his Bedu companions as the "Road to Ubar", which they said lay buried under the sands, although no one could say where. Thomas's great rival Harry St John Philby searched for the city without success, while Wilfred Thesiger also appears to have explored the area.

Nothing more was heard until the 1980s, when American film-maker Nicholas Clapp persuaded NASA to provide radar imaging, carried on board the US Space Shuttle, of the area in which Ubar was thought to lie. A satellite picture of the area was assembled, and in 1990 a team including Clapp, Ranulph Fiennes and archaeologist Juris Zarins set out to follow these leads on the ground. Some 18 months later, they discovered the remains of Ubar. Both Fiennes and Clapp wrote books describing the search – with each appearing to claim the leading role in the discovery of the site.

Road sign on the edge of the Empty Quarter.

Ubar or Wubar is the name of the legendary city which T.E. Lawrence dubbed the "Atlantis of the Sands". The site lies close to the village of **Shisr**, 72km (45 miles) northwest of Thumrayt via a featureless gravel road. The historian Al Hamdani, writing in AD 6, described Ubar as "a city lying astride the fabled incense routes with imposing architecture, vast orchards and fabulous wealth". The Qur'an has an account of how the citizens of "Irem" (believed to be Ubar), like the biblical inhabitants of Sodom and Gomorrah, were punished for their excessive lifestyles, and how the city, which was built over the top of a huge limestone cavern, collapsed and then was buried under drifting sand dunes.

In 1992, after a long search, the remains of what were claimed to be the ancient city of Ubar were rediscovered by an expedition led by Ranulph Fiennes and Nicholas Clapp – although controversy remains over whether or not the ruins they uncovered are really the remnants of Ubar/ Irem, or just one of many *caravanserais* dotting the overland frankincense route from southern Arabia. The remains themselves are fairly unimpressive, the fragments of a few walls and towers next to the large sinkhole into which the town suddenly collapsed some time during between AD 300 and 500.

Artefacts discovered at Ubar include a soapstone chess set dating from AD 1000, a glass bangle from AD 700 and a frankincense burner made in around AD 300. At the site itself, there is little to see beyond the ruins of a wall, several towers and the limestone cave pierced by pipes for pumping water across the desert to Thumrayt.

Beyond Ubar, tracks stretch into the increasingly impressive dunes of the Empty Quarter, a marvellous place for an overnight stay out under the stars. Needless to say, you should only venture into the desert with a competent guide and relevant equipment and provisions – a number of tour operators in Salalah can arrange this for you.

BELOW: the Empty Quarter sand dunes.

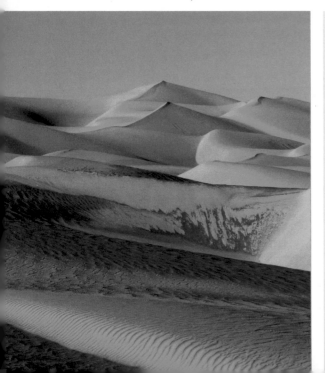

The Hallaniyat Islands

Lying 30km (18 miles) offshore from Hadbin are the four rocky and remote Hallaniyat (or Kuria Muria) Islands. A few fishermen inhabit Hallaniyat, the largest of the islands and location of their only permanent settlement, although there are no regular boat services to the archipelago. The Hallaniyat have an unusual history. In 1854, Sultan Said gifted the islands to the British after they had proposed a scheme for harvesting guano from them (the foreign secretary, Lord Clarendon, it is said, offered the Sultan a snuffbox in return). The guano scheme failed to take off, however, and the islands were soon after attached to the Aden Settlement, in what is now Yemen. They remained a British possession until 1967, when they were returned to Oman.

Frankincense – the Perfume of the Gods

Few countries in the world have as distinctive an olfactory signature as Oman's, and whether you're in a traditional souk, a mudbrick fort, a modern shopping mall or an office block, the distinctive aroma of burning frankincense is never far away

Oman has long been famous for frankincense. The frankincense trade brought enormous prosperity to the ancient cities of Dhofar, from where ships laden with the precious perfume would depart to Egypt and the Mediterranean along the Red Sea, or overland by camel via inland settlements such as the legendary Ubar (see page 169). Demand has waned somewhat since then, but frankincense remains a key ingredient in traditional Omani life. Frankincense burners are traditionally passed around after a meal to perfume clothes and hair, while the resin is also used as an ingredient in numerous perfumes, including the heady Amouage, Oman's bespoke scent *par excellence*. The smoke of frankincense also helps to repel mosquitoes, while certain types of frankincense resin are also edible, and continue to be widely used in traditional Arabian and Asian medicines to promote healthy digestion and skin – scientists are also investigating its possible uses in the treatment of chronic inflammatory diseases such as Crohn's disease, osteoarthritis and even cancer.

Frankincense (in Arabic, *luban*) is a resin obtained from one of four trees of the Boswellia genus, particularly the *Boswellia sacra*, a distinctively short

ABOVE AND RIGHT: frankincense tree, near Salalah.

and rugged species, rarely exceeding 5 metres (16ft) in height. *Boswellia sacra* can survive in the most inhospitable conditions, sometimes appearing to grow straight out of solid rock, and thrives particularly in the semi-arid mountains around Salalah.

Frankincense is collected by cutting small incisions into the bark of the tree, causing it to secrete a resin, which is allowed to dry and harden into so-called "tears". Virtually all frankincense is taken from trees growing in the wild – the difficulty of cultivating the trees means that they're not generally farmed on a commercial scale, in the manner of, say, dates.

Sourcing the finest

Most of the global supply of frankincense is now produced in Somalia, although Omani frankincense – particularly that from Dhofar – is generally considered the finest. There are many different types of frankincense, graded according to colour, purity and aroma. "Silver" (or *hojari*) frankincense is generally considered the best, with whiter and purer tears being favoured over the more yellowish, discoloured resin which is typical of Somali produce. Aficionados flock to the Al Husn Souk in Salalah, generally reckoned to stock the best frankincense in the country, though you'll find packets of resin for sale in souks and shops around the country – Mutrah Souk in Muscat has a particularly good selection, if you know what you're looking for.

THE MUSANDAM PENINSULA

Separated from the rest of Oman by the UAE, this rugged peninsula offers some of the country's most spectacular scenery, with soaring mountains falling into a series of dramatic fjords

At the northernmost tip of Oman, separated from the rest of the country by a large swathe of UAE territory, lies the Musandam peninsula, a remote region of dramatic mountains and sheer-sided *khawrs* (fjords), popularly described as the "Norway of Arabia" and widely considered to be the most scenically spectacular in Oman.

Musandam is historically one of Oman's most remote and impoverished areas, home to tribes who had little in common, either culturally or linguistically, with those further south, eking out a difficult existence amidst the region's inhospitable mountain and *khawrs*. The inhabitants of the Musandam interior, the Shehi, until recently lived largely in caves and rock shelters, speaking a form of Arabic largely unintelligible to outsiders and carrying a distinctive two-headed axe, or *jerz*, rather than the traditional Omani *khanjar*. Even more unusually, the inhabitants of Kumzar (*see page 176*) continue to speak a unique language – Kumzari – based on Iranian blended with elements of Arabic, along with numerous loan-words from Hindi, English, Spanish and French – said to be the result of sailors shipwrecked along the coast who settled in the village. The region has also enjoyed close connections with

Iran, just a short boat trip away over the Strait of Hormuz. Until recently a flourishing smuggling trade connected the two, and the influence of Iran continues to be strong to this day.

Development has been slow in coming – the first reliable road link between the peninsula and the outside world wasn't constructed until 1982 – although the area now has a decent infrastructure and basic tourist facilities, mostly found in the bustling town of Khasab, which offers the perfect base for excursions into the

Main attractions

KHASAB
THE COASTAL ROAD TO BUKHA
KHAWR SHAM
KUMZAR
JABAL HARIM

LEFT: the minaret of a mosque in Khasab.
RIGHT: an Omani girl in Musandam.

Man and daughter in Khasab.

BELOW: enjoying the scenery along the Khawr Sham.

khawrs and mountains. The region's only other major settlement is the Omani section of the town of Daba *(see page 232)* on the UAE border at the southern end of the peninsula, which is also home to a couple of hotels, although it is effectively cut off from the rest of Musandam.

Khasab

The only sizeable settlement in Musandam, the compact but bustling town of **Khasab** ❶ lies close to the northern tip of the peninsula at the head of a steep rocky wadi – an ideal base for dhow trips out onto the surrounding fjords or mountain safaris up into the Jabal Harim. The town itself divides into two parts: the New Souk, the bustling heart of modern Khasab, and, 2km (1 mile) north on the coast, the more ramshackle Old Souk. The latter is where you'll find the town's fine **fort** (Sat–Thur 9am–4pm, Fri 8–11am; charge), built by the Portuguese in the 17th century with attractively restored rooms and an unusual detached round tower standing in the middle of the courtyard, which now doubles as an interesting miniature museum on Musandam.

Directly in front of the fort stretches Khasab's extensive **harbour**, formerly the epicentre of the town's roaring smuggling trade with Iran. Various changes to customs regulations and other factors have now wiped out these contraband activities, although there are usually still plenty of Iranians in town, who pop over the Straits of Hormuz to buy up cheap household appliances for resale back home.

The coastal road to Bukha

The 28km (17-mile) coastal road from Khasab to Bukha is Musandam's only surfaced connection with the outside world, a spectacular feat of engineering which winds dramatically around the sea cliffs and *khawrs* of the coast. The first few miles out of Khasab are particularly fine, blasted out of the feet of the mountains around Khawr Qida and revealing vivid bands of sedimentary layering. On the far side of the bay, **Wadi Tawi** has petroglyphs featuring camels, sheep and hunters pecked into the rocks. From here the road climbs up to the village of **Al Harf** at the highest point of the ridge, offering spectacular views over the Strait of Hormuz – on a clear day you can see Iran.

It is another 12km (7 miles) or so from here to the quiet town of **Bukha ❷**, home to an impressive sea-front fort (Sun–Thur 8.30am–2.30pm, closed Fri and Sat; free), surrounded by a moat (formerly flooded with sea water) and an unusual tower, its distinctive tapering shape designed to reduce the impact of cannonballs. The interesting ruins of a large stone mosque stand next door. It is another 15 minutes' drive from Bukha to the UAE border at Tibat.

Khawr Sham and Kumzar

Khasab is the starting point for dhow cruises down the wonderful **Khawr Sham ❸**, the biggest fjord in

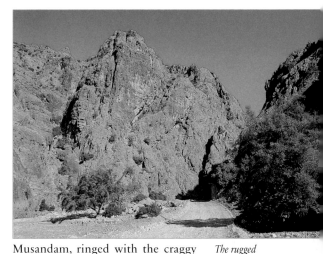

Musandam, ringed with the craggy red-rock mountains. Half a dozen tiny villages lie dotted around the *khawr*, accessible only by boat and now being steadily depopulated as the inhabitants abandon their difficult *khawr*-side existence to head off to Khasab or beyond, although some locals still spend their summers here fishing in the fjord. You're also likely to see pods of dolphins frolicking around the *khawr*, chasing boats for fun.

The rugged Musandam mountains.

BELOW: Jabal Harim.

Geology of Musandam

Just past the summit of Jabal Harim, look out for the remarkable "fossil wall" right next to the road: an extraordinary layer of sedimentary rock studded with the petrified outlines of hundreds of perfectly preserved ancient submarine creatures. These fossils attest to the remarkable geology of the peninsula, and the fact that the rock from which the towering mountains of Musandam are made up was originally formed deep under the sea. Having been originally thrust up out of the sea, Musandam is now slowly returning whence it came, with the entire peninsula falling back into the sea at the dramatic (for geologists) rate of 5mm a year, a process which has formed the spectacular *khawrs* (actually flooded valleys) which you see today.

A dhow plying the waters of the Khawr Sham.

BELOW: Jabal Harim.

next to the island at high tide; at low tide you'll have to swim across.

An even more dramatic boat trip leads out to the famously remote town of **Kumzar** ❹, the most inaccessible in Oman. There are no roads to Kumzar and the only way to reach the place is by boat – around two and a half hours by dhow or 45 minutes to an hour by speedboat. Unfortunately it is no longer possible to visit the town itself – outsiders (including Omanis not living here) have been banned since 2010 after locals complained about the intrusive behaviour of visiting tourists, but it is still well worth the trip out for the magnificent marine scenery en route. Trips head out into the open sea around the coast – unlike trips in the much more sheltered waters of Khawr Sham – passing the entrance to Khawr Ghob Ali and then past Jazirat al Ghanim (Goat Island), named for its role as a former grazing ground for sheep and goats, which were ferried here by boat from Kumzar. The journey continues into the Strait of Hormuz, with

Halfway down the *khor* lies the rocky little **Jazirat Telegraph** (Telegraph Island), named after the telegraph station established here by the British in 1864 along the route of the London-to-Bombay submarine telegraph cable, although the station lasted just four years and was abandoned in 1868. The foundations of the old British buildings can still be seen, and the island is a popular destination on dhow cruises, which often stop here for lunch. Boats can moor wonderful sea views of craggy headlands, distant islands and (generally) half a dozen oil tankers plying up and down the strait, before turning in towards Kumzar itself, a colourful huddle of buildings wedged below sheer cliffs.

The mountains

South of Khasab stretch the rugged Musandam mountains – a jagged massif of dolomite, limestone and shale, rising to the heights of the wild Jabal Harim at 2,087 metres (6,847ft) above sea level, a rewarding half- or full-day excursion from Khasab by 4x4 (count on a half-day to Jabal Harim, or a full day to reach the Rawdah Bowl). The route follows the broad Wadi Khasab behind town before climbing up into the mountains along the dirt-track road which continues all the way through to Daba (see page 232), with increasingly spectacular views of the mountains en route. Dozens of little rock dwellings can be seen along the sides of the track, now used as shelters for goats or as temporary refuges, although many were inhabited until less than 10 years ago by the reclusive Shehi.

After around 45 minutes the road reaches the **Sayh Plateau**, a rare flat piece of land in the otherwise convoluted landscape, planted with wheat and onions. Past here the road climbs again to reach the top (almost) of **Jabal Harim** (Mountain of the Women – so named because locals formerly sent their wives and daughters up here for safety in times of trouble). Rocks at the top are dotted with numerous petroglyphs along with an incongruous array of beautiful marine fossils, evidence that the entire range formerly lay below the sea.

Past here, the road descends abruptly, through some of the most memorable mountain scenery anywhere in the country to the remote **Rawdah Bowl**, a small plateau, roughly 3km (2 miles) across, encircled by mountains on all sides and home to wandering camels and various old stone buildings and other remnants of traditional life, including an unusual cemetery pre-dating the arrival of Islam.

Life was tedious for the engineers maintaining the telegraph link. The expression "going round the bend" is said to have originated on Telegraph Island, coined by crews aboard relief boats sailing around the bend into Khawr Sham.

BELOW: Arabian leopard.

Arabian Leopards

Leopards in Arabia? Indeed it is true – but for how long? Persecuted by humans as a threat to their domestic animals, the Arabian leopard is now critically endangered, with perhaps just a couple of hundred left in the wild. Reports of actual sightings are virtually unknown, and most evidence is the result of finding fresh spoors or reports from villagers of hearing the leopard's distinctive rasping cough. Most of Oman's surviving leopards are thought to live in Jabal Samham in Dhofar, though a scientific survey in 2007 found that a few still survive in the rocky recesses of Musandam – despite a systematic cull of local leopards by villagers protecting their herds back in the 1980s. Fortunately, the killing of a leopard now entails a fine of OR5,000 and up to five years in jail.

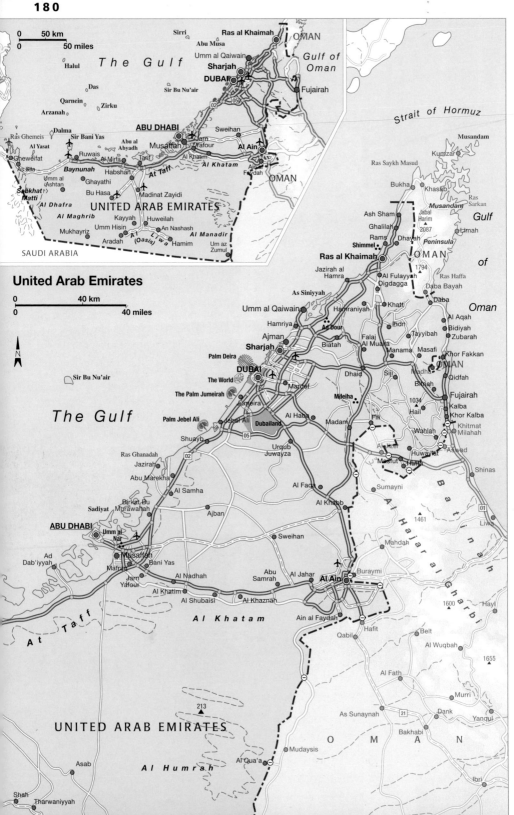

PLACES: THE UAE

A detailed guide to the entire country, with
principal sites clearly cross-referenced by
number to the maps

The modern UAE is more of a confederation than a country. Squeezed into an area roughly the size of Austria, the contrasts between the seven emirates that comprise the nation could hardly be greater, whether in terms of size, wealth, cultural outlook or general atmosphere.

Most foreign visitors head straight for the bright lights of Dubai, by far the most cosmopolitan and absorbing destination in the UAE, home to a wide range of attractions, from the bustling souks of the old city centre to jaw-dropping modern landmarks such as the gargantuan Burj Khalifa and the iconic Burj al Arab.

Visit only Dubai, however, and you will come away with a very lopsided impression of life in the modern UAE. National political life is dominated by Abu Dhabi, by far the biggest and richest of the seven statelets, covering around 85 percent of the UAE and boasting well over 90 percent of its total oil revenues. The low-key city itself has struggled to emerge from Dubai's shadow, although there are rewarding attractions here such as the majestic Sheikh Zayed Grand Mosque and opulent Emirates Palace Hotel, while it is also worth making the short side trip to the inland city of Al Ain with its rambling oases and traditional forts.

Just down the coast from Dubai, conservative Sharjah is the polar opposite of its brash neighbour, home to a string of absorbing museums and heritage attractions, including a superb new Islamic Museum and the various traditional buildings of its absorbing Heritage Area.

North of Sharjah, the tiny emirate of Ajman is notable mainly for its fine fort and traditional boat-building yards, whilst Umm al Qaiwain appears to have been largely forgotten by the modern world, with its dusty town and

mangrove-fringed coast. Further north, Ras al Khaimah sits in an attractive setting in the lee of the Hajar mountains, with a range of industrial and agricultural developments centred on the bustling RAK City. Over on the east coast, sleepy Fujairah is the most physically attractive of the emirates, with a long sandy coast backed by the craggy ranges of the Hajar mountains – a beguiling natural contrast to the vibrant cities of one of Arabia's most dynamic and multi-faceted countries.

PRECEDING PAGES: Al Ittihad Square, Abu Dhabi. **ABOVE FROM TOP:** sports fans at Al Rashid Stadium; Emirates Towers; ferry on Dubai Creek.

ABU DHABI

The sedate capital of the Emirates has plenty to offer visitors, from inspiring architecture to fabulous beaches. Two hours away by car is the oasis town of Al Ain

I n March 1948 Wilfred Thesiger emerged with four Bedu companions from the great golden dunes of Rub al Khali (the Empty Quarter) at Liwa – a fertile crescent dotted with dozens of oases – and travelled another 240km (150 miles) across "interminable blinding salt flats" to reach the coastal village of Abu Dhabi. Wading across the creek that separated Abu Dhabi from the mainland (now the site of the Maqta Bridge) they eventually arrived "at a large castle that dominated a small dilapidated town along the seashore".

Such was **Abu Dhabi ❶** until the discovery of enormous oil reserves during the late 1960s, since when this erstwhile dusty backwater has transformed into a thriving international city. Today Abu Dhabi is the capital and largest emirate of the UAE, occupying 86 percent of the country's total area.

Abu Dhabi (Father of the Gazelle) takes its name from legend. In the early 1770s, the story goes, a party of hunters from Liwa followed the tracks of a gazelle to one of the numerous coastal islands they knew in the Arabian Gulf. To their good fortune they found a freshwater spring where the animal had stopped to drink and began a settlement there in the 1790s.

The Al Nahyan, of the Al bu Falah tribe, have ruled Abu Dhabi and the Dhafrah (Liwa) since about 1690. They are a *fakhd* (sub-section) of the Bani Yas, who came originally from the desert oases of the Liwa. They owned camels, some donkeys and goats and lived in rectangular palm-frond houses built into the sand dunes above carefully tended date palm groves. During the summer many of the men would go to Abu Dhabi to join the pearling fleet as divers. In 1800, under Shakbut bin Dhiyab, the Al bu Falah collectively left the Liwa to settle on Abu Dhabi Island.

Main attractions
AL HOSN FORT
ABU DHABI CORNICHE
EMIRATES PALACE
EMIRATES HERITAGE VILLAGE
SHEIKH ZAYED GRAND MOSQUE
YAS ISLAND

LEFT: minaret of the mosque on Al Ittihad Square, Abu Dhabi.
RIGHT: banner at the Presidential Palace.

Al Hosn Fort at night.

The country's first president and so-called "father of the UAE", Sheikh Zayed *(see page 57)*, was born in 1918 in eastern Al Ain – a territory fought over for centuries but finally ruled by the Al Nahyan from about 1890. He was named after his illustrious grandfather Sheikh Zayed bin Khalifa Al Nahyan (ruler of Abu Dhabi 1855–1909), known as Zayed the Great. It is these two Zayeds who give their names to Zayed the First Street and Zayed the Second Street (otherwise referred to as Electra Street) which runs from east to west and changes name at the intersection of Sheikh Rashid bin Saeed Al Maktoum Street (Airport Road).

In 1966 Sheikh Zayed succeeded his brother Sheikh Shakhbut bin Sultan Al Nahyan as ruler. The extreme wealth generated by the discovery of oil enabled Sheikh Zayed to build first-rate public facilities for his people, but his benevolence reached beyond the UAE and was appreciated by many international charity programmes and Islamic communities.

BELOW: Emirates Palace Hotel.

His son, Sheikh Khalifa, became president following Sheikh Zayed's death in November 2004.

Al Hosn and around

At the very heart of the city lies the old **Al Hosn Fort** Ⓐ. This large white fort was built in about 1763 to protect the town's water source (the outer wall and towers were added later); at one time it was the only noteworthy building along the coast between Dubai and Doha in Qatar. Until 1972, when Sheikh Zayed moved to a new palace, it was also the ruler's residence. The entire complex is currently undergoing comprehensive redevelopment and will eventually reopen as a major new museum and cultural complex, although no one seems to know quite when this will happen. Next door to Al Hosn, the suave modern **Abu Dhabi Cultural Foundation** was developed under the patronage of Sheikh Zayed to host a range of international and local exhibitions, concerts, plays and film screenings. As with Al Hosn, the complex is currently closed for redevelopment.

Northeast of Al Hosn stretches Abu Dhabi's central commercial district, perhaps best seen from the Al Fanar revolving restaurant on top of Le Royal Méridien hotel. There's little in the way of specific things to see here apart from endless identikit glass-fronted buildings lined up along the various streets and a string of small-scale shops and malls at street level below – the most interesting is the **Madinat Zayed Gold Centre** B – the local equivalent of Dubai's famous Gold Souk – with two floors of shops stuffed with gold and silver jewellery.

North of Al Hosn lies the eye-catching **Al Ittihad Square** C, dotted with a striking sequence of five quirky oversized sculptures, including a vast cannon, an enormous perfume bottle and a gargantuan coffee pot.

North and south of Al Ittihad Square stretches Abu Dhabi's splendid waterfront **corniche**, extending along the top of the island from the Sheraton to the Hilton hotel and lined with an impressive string of high, glass-fronted towers (best seen from the Emirates Heritage Village on the Breakwater).

Notable landmarks include the elegant blue-glass **Hilton Baynunah Tower** and the folding curves of the ADIA building (opposite the British Embassy). A pleasant swathe of gardens runs alongside the road, busy every evening with joggers and families enjoying the cool sea breeze.

Looking up into the grand atrium of the Emirates Palace Hotel.

The Emirates Palace and around

At the southern end of the Corniche, about 3km (2 miles) from Al Hosn, rises the vast **Emirates Palace** D, one of the city's most eye-catching landmarks, and one of the world's most spectacularly opulent hotels. Constructed in traditional Arabian style, this red-sandstone colossus sprawls for the best part of a kilometre (½ mile) down the beach, topped with around 100 domes, while the interior is a riot of Arabian chintz, best appreciated over afternoon tea in the vast foyer or an evening meal in one of the

BELOW: the chic new Central Market.

Central Market

Nearing completion at the time of writing, the spectacular new Central Market – replacing Abu Dhabi's old city souk which was demolished in 2005 – promises to add a welcome touch of contemporary style to the city centre in a location close to Al Hosn Fort and the Cultural Foundation. Designed by Foster & Partners, the market (www.central market.ae) will comprise a magical new souk, blending elements of traditional Arabian architecture with suave modernist decor and an environmentally sensitive design. An emphasis on sustainability means shops in the souk will focus on traditional crafts and products, dotted with a range of restaurants and coffee shops and offering what promises to be a beguiling taste of traditional Arabia reinvented for the 21st century.

An elegant fountain at the corniche.

very upmarket restaurants which are scattered around the ground floor.

Beyond the hotel, the road continues south to the enormous gold-domed **Presidential Palace**, home to the ruler of Abu Dhabi (who is, of course, also the president of the UAE), although the palace is strictly off-limits to visitors. Alternatively, heading north from the Emirates Palace, a bridge leads across to the Breakwater, an area of reclaimed land which is best known as the home of the glitzy **Marina Mall** Ⓔ, one of the city's top shopping destinations, with pretty tented courtyards and fountains. Rising at the back of the mall, the Burj al Marina tower offers peerless views over the city, either from the Tiara revolving restaurant on the top (42nd) floor or, less expensively, from the coffee shop one floor below.

In front of the mall on the breakwater itself is the pleasant **Emirates Heritage Village** Ⓕ (Sat–Thur 9am–5pm, Fri 3.30–9pm; free), which commemorates life in Abu Dhabi before oil revenues changed the city for ever. Exhibits include old Bedouin tents,

a reconstruction of a *barasti* (palm-thatch) house, and a recreation of a traditional souk in which local artisans can sometimes be seen at work. There are also superb views from here to the corniche across the water, with the two distinctive Etisalat towers rising behind – immediately recognisable (like their cousins in Dubai) thanks to the enormous golf balls which sit perched on their summits.

Just past the Heritage Village rises an enormous **flagpole**, visible for miles around. Erected in 2001, this was formerly claimed to be the tallest unsupported flagpole in the world, at 123 metres (404ft) tall, although it's since been surpassed by a number of even taller flagpoles elsewhere.

Alternatively, head east for around 2km (1 mile) to reach the quiet suburb of Al Bateen and its old-fashioned **boat-building yard** Ⓖ, one of the few surviving traditional boatyards in the UAE. Visitors are welcome to wander around the yard, where piles of teak planks lie ready to be shaped into graceful wooden sailing dhows; the timber-framed outlines of one or two boats

Abu Dhabi

under construction can usually be seen propped up on wooden scaffolding.

From the boatyard it is around another 4km (2½ miles) south to the suburb of Al Mushrif, where you'll find the interesting **Women's Handicraft Centre ❶** (Sat–Wed 9am–1pm; free) in the Women's Association Complex on Karama Street. Run by the Abu Dhabi Women's Association, this government-funded project aims to help preserve traditional local arts and crafts, including jewellery and dress-making.

South of the centre

Although it is far from obvious, Abu Dhabi is actually built on an island. This stretches for around 10km (6 miles) east from the centre before rejoining the mainland via the Al Maqta Bridge (built in 1968); right next to the bridge you can see the old watchtower, which formerly guarded the entrance to the city.

Close by you can't fail to notice the monumental **Sheikh Zayed Grand Mosque ❶** (Sat–Thur 9am–9pm, Fri 4–9pm; interior closed for about 30min during prayers at 12.30pm, 3.30pm, 6pm and 7.30pm; free; free guided tours Sat–Thur at 10am), rising imperiously over the southern city. This is undoubtedly Abu Dhabi's single most worthwhile attraction: a spectacular, snow-white mass of domes and minarets visible for miles around – the vast courtyard alone is capable of accommodating some 40,000 worshippers. Completed in 2007, the mosque is one of the world's biggest – and certainly the most expensive, having cost some US\$500 million. It is also one of only two mosques in the UAE (along with the Jumeirah Mosque in Dubai; *see page 207*) open to non-Muslims. If visiting, you will be expected to dress conservatively; female visitors not suitably attired will be offered a black *abbeya* robe to wear.

Yas Island

Some 20km (12 miles) from the city centre, off the Dubai highway, **Yas Island ❶** is home to the city's new Formula 1 racetrack (which has staged the final race in the F1 season since 2010 – both of the races so far have been won by Sebastian Vettel, who clinched the F1 driver's championship

Until 1953, when a causeway was built across the Maqta, anyone wanting to cross to the other side had to wait for low tide and then wade through the shallow water.

BELOW: having fun at Ferrari World, Yas Island.

Saadiyat Island

Foremost amongst Abu Dhabi's planned mega-projects is the massive new Saadiyat Island Cultural District, located on Saadiyat Island, around 3km (2 miles) from the city centre and with attractions scheduled to start opening from 2014 onwards (although promised completion dates have been constantly pushed back ever since the project was first launched). Centrepiece of the island will be a remarkable cluster of museums and cultural institutions designed by world-famous architects, including a branch of the Guggenheim by Frank Gehry (who was responsible for the iconic Guggenheim in Bilbao), the Louvre Abu Dhabi by French architect Jean Nouvel, a performing arts centre by Iraqi architect Zaha Hadid, a maritime museum by Japanese architect Tadao Ando and a national museum by British architect Norman Foster.

TIP

For stunning views of
the city skyline, an
evening dinner cruise
aboard a traditional
wooden dhow can't be
beaten. These are
operated by various tour
agents and hotels
around the city including
Al Dhafra (www.aldhafra.
net), or the swanky
Shuja Yacht, run by Le
Royal Méridien hotel.

here in 2011). The petrolhead theme is continued with the attached Ferrari Theme Park (www.ferrariworldabu dhabi.com; Tue–Sun noon–10pm; entrance charge), a state-of-the-art entertainment complex featuring over 20 rides and other attractions, including the world's fastest rollercoaster and F1 racing simulators, plus plenty of more sedate family rides and kids' attractions, a racetrack and a driving school.

Al Ain

The fourth-largest city in the UAE, and the only major inland settlement, **Al Ain ②** is an easy 90-minute drive from Abu Dhabi down a swift modern highway – a far cry from just 50 years back, when the journey between the towns two took five days by camel. The city grew up around the string of seven oases which still dot the modern city today, making it one of the greenest in the Gulf. For much of its history, Al Ain served as a major stop on overland trading routes between Oman and the Gulf, its former strategic importance commemorated by the numerous forts that dot the town and its hinterland,

and by the archaeological remains found in the vicinity, which suggest that the area has been continuously settled for over 4,000 years. The city was awarded Unesco World Heritage status in 2011 in recognition of its rich historical significance, with listed sites including the Bronze Age tombs of Hili and Jabal Hafeet and the oases and traditional *falaj* irrigation systems of its various oases. Al Ain is also famous as the birthplace of the emirate's revered ruler, and first president of the UAE, Sheikh Zayed Bin Sultan Al Nahyan, who served as governor of Al Ain during his younger years.

Just over the border from Al Ain is the Omani city of **Buraymi** *(see page 146)* – now virtually joined up with Al Ain, although to reach it you will have to go through full border formalities (and buy an Omani visa) at the Hili checkpoint on the north side of Al Ain centre. Note that Al Ain can prove incredibly disorienting for first-time visitors, with dozens of seemingly identical roads arranged on a grid plan – fortunately, brown signs point helpfully to many of the town's major attractions.

BELOW: a decorative window at Sheikh Zayed Grand Mosque.

The old-fashioned **Al Ain National Museum** (Sat–Thur 8.30am–7.30pm, Fri 3–7.30pm, closed Mon; www.adach.ae; charge) makes a good starting point for tours of the city, with interesting displays covering various aspects of local life and displays of quaint artefacts, ranging from old Qur'ans and antique silver jewellery to farming and cooking equipment, as well as some intriguing photos of Abu Dhabi Emirate in the 1960s.

Next to the museum lies the rustic **Sultan Bin Zayed Fort** (or Eastern Fort; same hours and ticket as museum). One of 20-odd forts scattered around Al Ain and the surrounding desert, this picturesque three-towered structure is best known as the birthplace of Sheikh Zayed Bin Sultan Al Nahyan (see page 57), the much-loved ruler of Abu Dhabi and first president of the UAE, who oversaw the transformation of the emirate from impoverished Arabian backwater into today's oil-rich contemporary city-state.

Immediately behind the museum lies the city's rough-and-ready **Livestock Market**, with assorted livestock penned up in the backs of long lines of collapsed pick-up trucks. It is busiest in the early morning, up to around 9am. At other times things can be a lot slower, though it is still worth a quick look. A short walk northwest, the busy **Al Ain Souk** is home to the city's main meat, fruit and vegetable market, attracting a colourful array of local characters including visiting Omanis in big white turbans and local Bedu women in traditional metal face masks.

South of the souk stretches the idyllic **Al Ain Oasis** ❸ (daily sunrise–sunset; free), the largest of the seven oases scattered across the city (the name Al Ain, means, literally, The Spring). Various entrances lead into the oasis, with a labyrinthine network of narrow walled lanes running between densely planted thickets of palm trees, dotted with mango, fig, banana and orange trees. The plantations are watered using the traditional *falaj* irrigation method, with mud-walled channels bringing water down from the surrounding mountains.

Follow the road around the north side of the oasis behind the souk to

A Heritage Village stallholder.

BELOW: Al Ain Oasis.

Al Ain Palace Museum.

BELOW: Hili
Archaeological Park,
Al Ain.

in Al Ain, built in 1898, with a much-photographed circular tower on the northern side, consisting of four levels of diminishing size, each surmounted with a line of triangular battlements. The fort is also home to the excellent little "Mubarak bin London" exhibition, showcasing various photographs and personal effects of the legendary explorer Wilfred Thesiger (1910–2003), who stayed at the fort in the late 1940s.

Around Al Ain

There are a number of other forts and watchtowers scattered around Al Ain. The two-storey **Al Ruwailah** fortified house (off Mohammed bin Khalifa Road at the end of a small street) has an intriguing octagonal defensive wall. On the other side of Mohammed bin Khalifa Road, opposite the Al Ruwailah building, is a tower-like fort. Raised on a large mound, this circular fort provided an advanced warning post should intruders approach the palm groves from the desert. There are four more large **fortified houses** in the Qattarah

reach the the **Al Ain Palace Museum** (Sat–Thur 8.30am–7.30pm, Fri 3–7.30pm; free), an imposing complex owned by the ruling Nahyan family of Abu Dhabi. The sprawling complex is pleasant enough, with rambling, orangey-pink buildings arranged around a sequence of courtyards and small gardens, although there is not much to see.

Close by stands the rather more interesting **Jahili Fort** (Tue–Thur, Sat–Sun 9am–5pm, Fri 3–5pm; free), one of the finest traditional buildings

Umm an Nar

Just outside Abu Dhabi, the island of Umm an Nar gives its name to one of the major periods of Arabian prehistory, thanks to the treasure trove of prehistoric remains which have been uncovered here. The site was first investigated by a Danish team in 1959, with further excavations being carried out by archaeologists from Iraq and the UAE. Some 50 circular tombs have so far been unearthed, along with a variety of artefacts ranging from necklaces and jewellery to weapons and distinctive red pottery. The location of the archaeological site between a major oil refinery and a military area means that the site is currently out of bounds to the general public, although artefacts discovered here are on display at the Al Ain National Museum (see page 189).

district, south of Hili, set amongst palm groves. One offers good views from its high defensive walls (to find it from Mohammed bin Khalifa Road, pass the football stadium on the right, cross the Dolphin Roundabout and turn right into Third Street: the rear wall faces the road, but the entrance is on the right-hand side).

On the northern side of the city, the **Hili Gardens and Archaeological Park** ❺ (daily 9am–10pm; charge) is one of the most important archaeological sites in the UAE (many of the finds unearthed here are displayed in the Al Ain National Museum; *see page 189*). Pride of place goes to the so-called Great Hili Tomb, dating from the 3rd century BC: a quaint little circular structure decorated with primitive carvings of animals and humans.

Al Ain's old-fashioned **Camel Souk** ❻ is also worth a visit, with dozens of dromedaries lined up for sale and a lively crowd of local camel-fanciers haggling over the beast of their choice. The souk is busiest in the mornings around 9–10am, although low-key trading may continue throughout the

day. To reach the souk, take the road towards Mazyad from the roundabout in front of the Hilton hotel. After about 3km (2 miles) you'll see the huge new Bawadi mall on your left; the souk is just past here on the left.

Further exotic animals can be found at the **Al Ain Zoo** (also known as Al Ain Wildlife Park and Resort; opening hours vary, see website for details; www.awpr.ae; charge) in the southern part of the city, a spacious and well-run place which provides a home to a wide variety of creatures – the bird displays are particularly good.

Beyond the zoo rises the craggy **Jabal Hafit** ❼ (1,180 metres/733ft), the second-highest mountain in the UAE and a breezy retreat from the heat of the plains below. You can drive to the top from the city in under half an hour along the exhilarating modern surfaced road, from where there are huge views over the surrounding mountains. The outdoor terrace at the plush Mercure Grand Hotel, just below the summit, makes a memorable – if surprisingly chilly – spot for a drink. The area is also of particular

Beware natural hazards of the open road.

LEFT: Al Ain local.
BELOW: meerkat at Al Ain Zoo.

interest thanks to its remarkable collection of Bronze Age beehive tombs which can be found scattered around the base of the mountain, although you'll need a 4x4 and a local guide if you hope to explore them.

The Empty Quarter

The western region of Abu Dhabi encompasses the great red-sand massif of the Rub al Khali (the Empty Quarter), the oil fields of Bu Hasa, Shah and Marzuq, and the fertile Liwa oasis. In 1948 Wilfred Thesiger was the first European to explore the Liwa's 80km (50-mile) palm groves and the settlements scattered amidst its huge dunes, rising up to 90 metres (300ft) in places. Thesiger described what he saw in *Arabian Sands*: "The sands were like a garden. There were matted clumps of tribulus, three feet high, their dark green fronds covered with bright yellow flowers, bunches of karia, a species of heliotrope that was rated high as camel-food by the Bedu, and *qasis*, as well as numerous other plants which the camels scorned in the plenty that surrounded them."

Thesiger rode into the Liwa on a camel. Today the journey from Abu Dhabi is made easy with a tarmac road cutting through the desolate limestone ridges, drifts of white sand and stretches of gravel dotted with woody grass. It is a three-hour trip by road from Abu Dhabi to **Liwa ❸**. The Rumaitha oil-field route to Liwa passes an enormous pyramid in the desert, home to the Emirates National Auto Museum (www.enam.ae). Set up by the "rainbow sheikh", a well-known motor enthusiast whose logo is a rainbow, the hangar displays oversized (some six times the original) pick-up trucks and over 30 vintage vehicles.

The Liwa crescent is well served by a four-lane highway. Passing (from west to east) the villages of Aradah, Taraq, Al Hilah, Qatuf, Kayyah, Al Mariyyah, Dhafir, Huweilah, Qumidah, Shah, Tharwaniyyah, Al Nashash, Jarrah, Wedheil, Al Kris and Hamim, it is difficult to imagine how these sparsely populated villages of *barasti* (palm frond) dwellings and carefully tended date palm groves, subsisted here for hundreds of years. The concrete houses,

Southern Emirates

guesthouse and irrigated farms that you see today are a relatively recent addition, developed during the 1980s.

Any visit to the Liwa is a special experience. The effect of the remoteness and beauty of the sands is profound. Every day the dunes change and encroach on the farms nestling below. The scale of the big red dunes is best appreciated in winter, when it is possible to climb to the top of one without the heat burning through the soles of your shoes. Surprisingly, the Liwa has an extensive range of fauna. Hares, foxes, monitor lizards and other animals and reptiles flourish in the harsh, seemingly inhospitable desert environment.

West along the coast

Back on the coast west of Liwa (and some 250km/155 miles west of Abu Dhabi), Ruwais is the site of the country's largest oil refinery, established in 1978, and nearby Jabal Dhanna from where Abu Dhabi's onshore oil is piped to tanker-mooring terminals 5km (3 miles) out to sea.

Lying 9km (6 miles) off the coast roughly opposite Jabal Dhanna, the remote **Sir Bani Yas Island ④** is one of the UAE's more unusual attractions. Measuring around 16km (10 miles) long and 8km (5 miles) across, the island was formerly a private retreat of Sheikh Zayed, who established a wildlife reserve here in 1971. The reserve now protects a wide range of wildlife, including important populations of threatened local fauna including hundreds of Arabian oryx, sand gazelles and rock hyraxes – there is also an African section, home to cheetahs, giraffes, Indian blackbuck and other exotic species. Birdwatching is excellent here too, thanks to Sir Bani Yas's position on migratory routes between Europe and Asia; large flocks of flamingos are a common sight. The island is also surprisingly rich in historical remains, including a 7th-century church, the only pre-Islamic Christian site in the country. It's a rewarding destination, although also an expensive one, given that access is usually by seaplane, and the only way to visit at present is to stay overnight at the luxurious Anantara Desert Islands Resort and Spa.

Reduce your tyre pressure before venturing into the desert.

BELOW: off-road driving is not for the faint-hearted.

DUBAI

Past meets future in the Gulf's most absorbing city, with attractions ranging from traditional souks and wooden dhows through to soaring skyscrapers and artificial islands

Abu Dhabi
UNITED ARAB
EMIRATES

ontrary to popular belief, **Dubai** ⑤ wasn't born yesterday, and although much of the city – and many of its most famous landmarks – have sprung up during the past couple of decades, the city's roots go back far earlier. Archaeological sites in the metropolitan area indicate that Dubai was an important station for caravans travelling between Mesopotamia and Oman as far back as the Bronze Age. A town of sorts has existed here since the early 19th century, while by the early 20th century Dubai had already become one of the most important ports and entrepôts in this part of the Gulf, with a large Iranian and Indian population – a reminder of the city's entrepreneurial roots and historically cosmopolitan outlook, long before the discovery of oil transformed the region for ever.

The Creek

At the heart of the old city lies **Al Khor** Ⓐ (The Creek), a wide saltwater inlet which divides the two main city-centre districts of Bur Dubai and Deira and provides a scenic thoroughfare for traditional wooden dhows, *abras* (water taxis) and the occasional ship, as well as a perfect snapshot of Dubai's sometimes startling contrasts between old and new, with traditional coral-and-gypsum houses, wind

towers and minarets mixed up amidst the modern development and glassy high-rises.

The best, cheapest and most convenient way of seeing the Creek is to take the five-minute ride across it aboard one of the city's traditional *abras* – one of the most authentic and inexpensive experiences available in the Emirates. There are two main routes: the first runs between Bur Dubai Abra Station at the west end of the Textile Souk and Deira Old Souk Abra Station, in front of the Spice Souk. The second

Main attractions

AL KHOR
BASTAKIYA
SHINDAGHA
DEIRA SOUKS
AL AHMADIYA SCHOOL
WAFI AND KHAN MURJAN SOUK
EMIRATES TOWERS AND SHEIKH ZAYED ROAD
BURJ KHALIFA AND DOWNTOWN DUBAI
JUMEIRAH MOSQUE
BURJ AL ARAB
MADINAT JUMEIRAH
IBN BATTUTA MALL

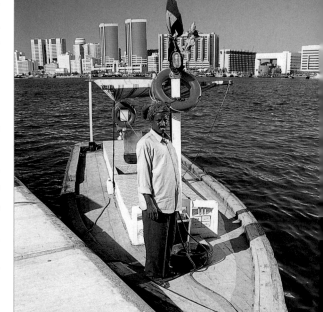

LEFT: architectural reflections.
RIGHT: an *abra* (water taxi) awaits.

Central Dubai

goes from Bur Dubai Old Souk Abra Station in the middle of the Textile Souk to Al Sabkha Abra Station, a short walk from Baniyas Square. Boats depart every couple of minutes and the fare costs a modest AED1.

Alternatively, it is also possible to charter an *abra* for longer tours up and down the Creek. This costs Dhs100 per hour, and boatmen will take you wherever you fancy, either up- or downriver – an hour's cruise will allow you to ride from the city centre down to the Dubai Creek Golf Club and back again.

A more comfortable way of seeing the Creek is to go on one of the ever-popular after-dark dinner cruises – these can be booked through any of the city's myriad tour operators, while many hotels can also arrange trips. Most cruises are aboard traditional old wooden dhows, offering a leisurely overview of the night-time city.

Bur Dubai

South of the Creek lies Bur Dubai, the oldest district in the city, and home to many of its most absorbing historical

attractions. A good place to begin is the **Dubai Museum** Ⓑ (Sat–Thur 8.30am–8.30pm, Fri 2.30–8.30pm; charge), housed in Al Fahidi Fort, the oldest building in the city. Dating from around 1787, the fort was originally built to defend the town against raiders, with large towers at three corners and a spacious central courtyard within, where you will find a traditional *barasti* (palm thatch) hut and a collection of boats formerly used for fishing and pearl diving.

The majority of the museum's exhibits are located in a series of modern underground galleries buried below the fort. These include extensive archaeological finds dating back to the Bronze Age along with wide-ranging displays on just about every aspect of traditional Emirati life, customs and culture, include a colourful little replica souk

The Dubai Museum is housed in the city's oldest building.

BELOW: Dubai Wonder Bus.

Dubai Wonder Bus

For a tour of Dubai with a difference, check out the Dubai Wonder Bus (www.wonderbustours.net), a bizarre-looking vehicle – half bus and half boat. The 90-minute tours depart from the BurJuman centre, from where you'll be driven down to Garhoud Bridge before the bus-cum-boat dives into the water and sails you up the Creek to Shindagha before emerging back onto dry land and taking you back to BurJuman by road. Other offbeat ways of enjoying the city include the helicopter tours offered by an increasing number of operators in the city, while adrenalin junkies might consider a tandem skydive above the Palm Jumeirah (see www.skydivedubai.ae for details). More sedate airborne trips over the desert outside the city are available from Balloon Adventures Dubai (www.ballooning.ae).

Colourful fabrics on display in the Textile Souk.

BELOW: an alleyway in Bastakiya.

(complete with spooky mannequins), a dhow under construction and a couple of interesting old films.

West of the museum stretches the main section of **Al Fahidi Road**, lined with shops selling a mix of electronic goods, expensive watches and colourful Indian-style fabrics. Turning east, in the opposite direction, brings you after a couple of minutes to the entrance to the historic **Bastakiya** quarter, built in the early 1900s by merchants from Bastak in southern Iran (hence the name). This is the best-preserved traditional quarter in the city: a small but surprisingly disorienting labyrinth of narrow alleyways, flanked with tall coral-and-limestone houses topped with dozens of wind towers *(barjeel)*. These were first introduced to Dubai by Iranian settlers, but have now become synonymous with the UAE. An early form of air-conditioning, these square towers capture cool air and funnel it down into the houses below, while also allowing hot air to rise and escape.

Most of the houses are fairly plain from the outside but surprisingly ornate within, usually with spacious inner courtyards, shaded with trees and surrounded by delicate arches and doorways. A number of heritage buildings have been opened as little museums (all free), giving you the chance to have a look inside, while others have been converted into small art galleries and shops.

Right next to the entrance to Bastakiya, the **Majlis Art Gallery** (Sat–Thur 10am–6pm; www.themajlisgallery.com; free) is the oldest in the city, established in 1976 to showcase the work of UAE artists, as well as international ones with UAE ties.

Beyond Bastakiya, a promenade continues east alongside the Creek, offering fine views of the high-rises of Deira over the water. A 15-minute walk past the British Consulate brings you opposite the fine cluster of modern buildings in Deira, including the landmark **National Bank of Dubai** with its instantly recognisable curved, glass-and-steel facade – particularly memorable towards dusk, when it seems to catch fire in the light of the setting sun.

From Bastakiya, walk back to the Dubai Museum and then head around the back to reach Dubai's **Grand Mosque**. This is one of the oldest mosques in Dubai (dating back to 1900, although it was rebuilt in 1998), and also boasts the city's tallest minaret (70 metres/231ft) and space for 1,200 worshippers. You can take a peek inside from the doorway, but, unless you are a Muslim, don't venture in.

Turn left at the mosque and head down any of the various little alleyways to reach the **Textile Souk** , or Old Souk, as it's sometimes known, the prettiest in Dubai, with dozens of little shops lined up in old coral-and-stone buildings under a high wooden roof; most sell cheap clothes and textiles, while a few offer souvenirs and a few antiques. Here and there the shops open up to reveal glorious views of the Creek, dotted with chuntering *abras* and old wooden dhows, with the wind-towered souks of Deira beyond.

At the southern end of the souk, hidden away behind the Grand Mosque, lies the narrow alleyway popularly known as **Hindi Lane**, stuffed full of shops selling Indian religious paraphernalia – garlands, portraits and horoscopes – and with a tiny Hindu-cum-Sikh temple halfway along. On the southern side of the souk stands the eye-catching **Ali bin Abi Taleb Mosque** (not open to non-Muslims), a Shi'ite mosque built in traditional Iranian style, and covered in a riot of colourful tilework.

Shindagha

Continuing through the Textile Souk and then along the waterfront brings you to Shindagha district. A fine cluster of old Emirati buildings line up along the Creek here, many now converted to small-scale museums, restaurants or cultural attractions.

Easily the most interesting is the **Sheikh Saeed Al Maktoum House** **E** (Sat–Thur 8am–8.30pm; Fri 3–9.30pm; charge). The former home of the ruling Maktoum family, the house was built in 1896 and offers an impressive example of traditional Emirati architecture, with elegantly cusped doorways and four fine wind-towers. The house is now home to one of Dubai's most interesting museums, documenting the social, cultural, educational and religious history of the emirate, although the undoubted highlight is the fascinating collection of old photographs from the 1940s to 1960s charting the city's transformation from modest town to modern metropolis.

Wind tower undergoing restoration. This ingenious cooling device was introduced to the region from Persia.

LEFT: at the Gold Souk.
BELOW: Sheikh Saeed Al Maktoum House.

The **Traditional Architecture Museum** (Sat–Thur 7am–7pm; free), immediately to the south, is also worth a look, occupying another fine old wind-towered house, with interesting displays on architecture in Dubai and the Emirates.

A couple of minutes' walk further along the Creekside (with marvellous views en route) brings you to the so-called **Heritage Village** (Sat–Thur 8am–10.30pm, Fri 8–11am, 4.30–10.30pm; free), a walled compound with traditional buildings arranged around a large sandy courtyard. It's usually fairly deserted during the day, but comes to life after dusk (particularly during the winter months and local festivals), with souvenir shops, food stalls (often run by local Emirati women) and occasional cultural performances. The **Diving Village** (same hours) next door is similar but smaller.

Deira

The commercial heart of the old city, life in Deira still largely revolves around the souk. The shops may be largely modern, and jazzy neon signs may have replaced the traditional hand-painted boards, but business here is still conducted more or less as it has been for over a century past, with thousands of shoebox shops wedged into the district's rambling bazaars, retailing everything from cheap toys and textiles to gold and frankincense – a far cry from the modern malls that dominate newer parts of Dubai.

The obvious place to begin any tour of Deira is at the **Gold Souk** . There are a hundred or so shops here, lined up under a wooden roof, their windows overflowing with vast quantities of gold jewellery ranging from florid Arabian designs to more understated European pieces – the traditional Emirati-style bracelets are particularly nice. Gold here remains amongst the most competitively priced in the world, attracting a colourful array of shoppers from West Africa, Russia, India and elsewhere. Jewellery is sold by weight (despite its intricacy, the quality of the workmanship isn't usually factored into the price), although bargaining is essential. Many shops also sell silver and precious stones, while the area is also a major centre for Dubai's thriving trade in designer fakes – you'll not spend long in the souk without being approached with offers of "cheap copy watch" or similar.

Walk out of the back (western) end of the Gold Souk, turn right onto Old Baladiya Street and follow it around onto Al Ahmadiya Street for a few minutes to reach the pretty **Al Ahmadiya School** ⓗ (Sat–Thur 8am–7.30pm, Fri 2.30–7.30pm; free). Established in 1912 by local pearl merchant Ahmad bin Dalmouk (after whom it is named), this was the first semi-formal school in Dubai. Pupils here were taught the Qur'an, Arabic calligraphy and arithmetic, while other subjects including history, literature and astronomy were subsequently added to the curriculum. The school itself closed in 1963, and the building was superbly restored in the 1990s and is now perhaps the most appealing traditional building in the city. The rooms around the courtyard house various low-key exhibits covering the history of the school, along with cute mannequins of pupils in traditional

dress (and one rather scary-looking teacher). There are more classrooms upstairs, still equipped with their old wooden desks and chairs.

Next to Al Ahmadiya School stands the **Heritage House** (Sat– Thur 8am–7.30pm, Fri 2.30– 7.30pm; free), dating from the late 19th century and now preserved as it would have been in the 1940s and 1950s, providing an atmospheric snapshot of the social life of Dubai's wealthier inhabitants during that period. Notable features include the men's and women's *majlis*, or meeting rooms, where guests would have sat on embroidered pillows, drinking Arabian coffee and discussing the economic, social and political issues of the day.

Turn left out of the Heritage House and follow the road around to reach the Creek, then turn left again along the waterfront, until you reach Deira Old Souk Abra Station after a couple

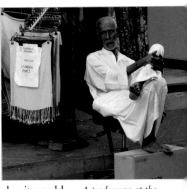

A tradesman at the Gold Souk.

Statue of an Egyptian pharaoh at the Wafi centre.

more minutes. Facing the Creek on your left is the warren of lanes and alleyways that make up Deira Old Souk (*see below*). Ahead of you, stretching down the waterfront, are the old city's **dhow moorings**, with lines of traditional old wooden cargo boats moored up along the edge of the Creek – an unexpectedly old-fashioned sight amongst the modern traffic and office blocks. Huge piles of cargo usually stand stacked up along the road here waiting to be loaded up onto boats and shipped off. Many of the dhows here head off to Iran (and many have Iranian crews), while some head further afield to India, Pakistan and East Africa.

Turning away from the Creek, head into the attractive tangle of covered alleyways making up **Deira Old Souk** ❶, although most of the souk's shops are now devoted to relatively mundane items like cheap toys, textiles and clothing. The most interesting part of the Old Souk is the **Spice Souk**, close to Deira Old Souk Abra Station: a few narrow alleyways lined with huge sacks of frankincense, saffron, crushed rose petals, dried lemons and other local produce. It is one of the prettiest corners of Deira, although unfortunately it is also steadily shrinking due to competition from local hypermarkets like the Carrefour, which is where most modern Dubaians now go for their spices.

Oud Metha

South of Bur Dubai, the district of **Oud Metha** is something of a hotchpotch – rather lacking in character or streetlife, but home to some of the inner city's biggest tourist developments, including the glitzy Wafi complex and adjacent Raffles hotel and Khan Murjan Souk.

Stretching south of Al Maktoum Bridge, the spacious **Creekside Park** ❼ (Sun–Wed 8am–11pm, Thur–Sat until 11.30pm; charge) offers one of the few sizeable open areas in the congested city centre, with fine views over

Smuggled Goods

Deira's colourful Dhow Wharfage has come under increasing fire in recent years thanks to its alleged role in the city's flourishing contraband trade with nearby Iran – where many of the boats which you'll see moored up subsequently depart. While most cargoes consist of the entirely harmless domestic items you'll see piled up by the quayside, a small but significant proportion do not. Smuggled goods range from simple contraband like scotch and cigarettes to more sophisticated items which are exported in contravention of UN sanctions such as computers and mobile phones through to more sophisticated hardware including aeroplane parts, weapons and explosives. There's been talk of moving the entire wharfage to a more secure location further down the coast, although nothing has yet materialised.

the Creek to the quaint buildings of the Park Hyatt hotel and distinctive Dubai Creek Golf Club clubhouse (inspired by the sails of a dhow and looking like a local remake of the Sydney Opera House) on the far side of the water. The park is also home to the excellent **Children's City** (Sat–Thur 9am–8pm, Fri 3–9pm; www.childrencity.ae; charge) "edu-tainment" centre for kids, with a fun, interactive range of galleries exploring various themes including science, nature, space exploration and cultures of the world. Even without kids, it's worth a peek at the City's striking buildings, painted in bright primary colours and looking a bit like some kind of supersized Lego construction.

A 10-minute walk south of the park is Oud Metha's major attraction, the glitzy **Wafi** complex **K** (Sat–Wed 10am–10pm, Thur–Fri 10am–midnight; www.waficity.com), looking like a little slice of Las Vegas dropped into the middle of the Gulf, with a comic-book Egyptian-style design featuring a zany mishmash of huge pharaonic statues, hieroglyphs, spectacular stained-glass windows and half

a dozen miniature pyramids dotted across the sprawling roof lines.

Wafi Mall interior.

Attached to the Wafi complex is the beautiful **Khan Murjan Souk** (Sat–Wed 10am–10pm, Thur–Fri 10am–midnight; www.waficity.com). This is one of Dubai's finest exercises in Orientalist kitsch, with virtually every available surface covered in lavishly detailed Arabian-style design, featuring elaborate Moroccan-style tile work, intricately carved wooden doors and ceilings, and huge hanging lamps. Next to the souk (and continuing Wafi's Egyptian theme) rises the vast postmodern pyramid of the **Raffles** hotel, Oud Metha's most dramatic landmark, visible for miles around and particularly impressive after dusk, when the glass-walled summit of the pyramid is lit up from within, glowing magically in the darkness.

BELOW: Sheikh Zayed Road skyline.

Karama and Satwa

Home to many of the low-wage Indian and Filipina expats who provide the city with its taxi drivers, waitresses, housemaids and construction workers, **Karama** offers a refreshing insight into life in the city away from the tourist fleshpots and space-age architecture. The district is centred on the low-rent **Karama Souk**, best known as the epicentre for Dubai's roaring trade in designer fakes – imitation bags, watches, sunglasses and other fake-branded items, as well as pirated DVDs – although following government crackdowns these are now kept mainly out of sight in backrooms behind the various shops. The quality of many of the fakes is surprisingly high, although prices can be unexpectedly steep.

Souvenir t-shirts at Karama Souk.

It is a short taxi ride from here to the neighbouring suburb of **Satwa**, centred on the attractive **Al Diyafah Street**, Satwa's de facto high street. This is one of the most pleasant after-dark venues in the city, with broad, tree-lined pavements dotted with a long string of cafés and restaurants, including several excellent Lebanese cafés, and attracting a refreshingly mixed crowd of Indians, Emiratis, expat Arabs and Europeans who come to stroll, and people-watch from the pavement cafés – Dubai on a refreshingly human scale.

Sheikh Zayed Road

Some 3km (2 miles) south of the old city centre – but light years distant in terms of appearance and atmosphere – the futuristic **Sheikh Zayed Road** is one of Dubai's iconic images: a huge, 12-lane highway flanked on either side by rows of densely packed skyscrapers, whose towering facades create an almost unbroken wall of glass and metal, like some kind of architectural Grand Canyon.

Standing proud above the northern end of Sheikh Zayed Road, the twin **Emirates Towers** ❶ were the

BELOW: Emirates Towers.

tallest in the city upon completion in 2000 (while the taller tower was also the highest in the Middle East at 355 metres/1,164ft). They have since been outstripped locally by both the Almas Tower in Dubai Marina and, most notably, by the gargantuan Burj Khalifa *(see page 206)* just down the road, but remain two of the most distinctive, and most beautiful, modern buildings in the city, with their unusual triangular summits and huge glass and aluminium facades, which seem to glow magically in the fierce desert light.

Immediately south of the Emirates Towers stretches the **Dubai International Financial Centre**, whose focus is the landmark Gate building, an unusual structure resembling a kind of office block-cum-triumphal archway. The building is home to the Dubai Stock Exchange, as well as a number of upmarket art galleries – one of the leading hubs of the city's burgeoning visual arts scene.

Continuing south along Sheikh Zayed Road, the highway is now hemmed in to either side by a long string of elongated skyscrapers

packed in shoulder-to-shoulder. The buildings here offer a comprehensive compendium of modern Dubaian design, ranging from the functional to the quirky and the downright bizarre. Notable landmarks include the elegant **Rose Rayhaan** hotel (the tallest hotel in the world, at 333 metres/1,093ft), having taken the record off the nearby Burj al Arab), and, opposite, the massive **Chelsea Tower**, its summit adorned with what looks like an enormous toothpick. Further south, at the end of the strip, is perhaps the most distinctive building of them all, the **Dusit Thani** hotel, a bow-legged colossus inspired by the shape of the traditional Thai *wai*, a prayer-like gesture of welcome.

Downtown Dubai

At the southern end of Sheikh Zayed Road lies the massive Downtown

There is a huge range of goods on sale, from boxes inlaid with mother-of-pearl to electronics. For many people shopping is a major reason for visiting Dubai.

BELOW: Dubai's towering skyline.

Sky-High Dubai

Dubai is now officially the tallest city on the planet – a stupendous achievement for a city which only constructed its first proper skyscraper in 1979. The city now boasts no fewer than 34 of the world's 200 highest buildings (traditional high-rise centres New York and Hong Kong, by comparison, have just 12 and 15 respectively), with new super-tall structures being constantly added to the city's skyline, despite the financial embarrassments of the past few years. These include iconic structures including the world's tallest building, the Burj Khalifa, and the magnificent Burj al Arab and Emirates Towers, as well as less high-profile landmarks (most of them located in Dubai Marina) such as the recently topped-out 23 Marina, the second-tallest building in the city at 395 metres (1,296ft).

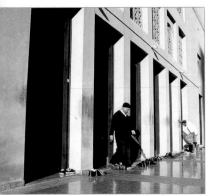

Jumeirah Mosque.

Dubai development, opened in 2010 and built at an estimated cost of a cool US$20 billion. Centrepiece of the development is the staggering **Burj Khalifa** Ⓜ, the world's tallest building, rising close to hand on your right. Opened in early 2010, the Burj Khalifa (828 metres/2,717ft) has obliterated all previous records for the world's previous tallest man-made structures, past and present, smashing the previous record for the world's tallest building (formerly held by Taipei 101 in Taiwan, at 509 metres/1,670ft) by a staggering 300 metres (984ft).

The astonishing size of the Burj Khalifa and distinctively tapering outline is hard to grasp close up – the whole thing is best appreciated from a distance, from where you can properly grasp the tower's jaw-dropping size, and the degree to which it dwarfs

BELOW: Burj Khalifa.

the surrounding high-rises, many of which are considerable structures in their own right. Expensive visits can be made to the misleadingly named At the Top observation deck (on floor 124, although there are actually 160 floors in total) – see www.burjkhalifa. ae for details.

Lying in the considerable shadow of the Burj Khalifa is the no less monumental **Dubai Mall** Ⓝ (Sun–Wed 10am–10pm, Thur–Sat 10am–midnight; www.thedubaimall.com). The entire complex covers a total area of 1.08 million sq metres (12 million sq ft), with over 1,200 shops spread across four floors, making it easily the world's largest mall measured by total area (although other malls contain more retail space) – impressively vast, even if the sheer size of the place can make a shopping trip here feel a bit like a long-distance hike. The mall is also home to the **Dubai Aquarium and Underwater Zoo** (Sun–Wed 10am–10pm, Thur–Sat 10am–midnight; www.thedubaiaquarium.com; charge), whose engaging "viewing panel" can be seen from the mall:

a huge, floor-to-ceiling transparent acrylic panel filled with an extraordinary array of marine life, ranging from sand-tiger sharks and stingrays to colourful shoals of tiny tropical fish.

Inserted into the large lake between the Burj Khalifa and Dubai Mall is spectacular **Dubai Fountain**: 275 metres (902ft) long, illuminated with over 6,000 lights and with water cannons capable of shooting jets of water up to 150 metres (492ft) high. The fountain springs into action after dark, shooting choreographed jets of water into the air which "dance" in time to a range of Arabic, Hindi and classical songs. "Performances" are staged every 20 minutes between 6pm and 10pm in the evening (until 11pm Thur–Sat) and can be watched for free from anywhere around the lake.

On the far side of the lake stretches the extensive **Old Town** development: a large swathe of low-rise, sand-coloured buildings with traditional Moorish styling – a surreal contrast to the futuristic needle of the Burj Khalifa opposite, best appreciated from the pretty forecourt of the opulent Palace hotel.

Jumeirah

One of Dubai's wealthiest residential areas, sedate Jumeirah is home to many of the city's rich European expat executives and their tanned and manicured wives (popularly, if rather disparagingly, known as Jumeirah Janes).

At the northern end of the district stands the striking **Jumeirah Mosque ⦿**. Built of stone in the Egyptian Fatimid style in the 1970s, this is one of the city's largest mosques and perhaps the most attractive, with a pair of soaring minarets and intricately filigreed domes. This is also the only mosque in Dubai that non-Muslims can visit, via tours run by the Sheikh Mohammed Centre for Cultural Understanding (tours Sat, Sun, Tue and Thur 10am; tel: 04-353 6666; www.cultures.ae; charge). Tours begin with entertaining and informative talks by a local Emirati guide on traditional religious practices, after

Jumeirah Beach Hotel.

BELOW: Wild Wadi at sunrise.

which the floor is thrown open to questions offering visitors a chance to quiz the guide on any aspect of local culture or life.

Around 4km (2½ miles) south of the mosque, **Jumeirah Beach Park** (Wed–Sun 7am–10.30pm, Thur–Sat 7am–11pm; Mon ladies and boys aged up to four only; charge) is the most attractive public beach in the city, and well worth the modest admission price. There is a fine swathe of wide, white sand to relax on, backed by an attractive palm-studded stretch of park dotted with barbecues and a couple of cafés. Shu, opposite the entrance to the park, is a good spot for lunch.

Continuing south along the Jumeirah Road again, after a further 2km (1 mile) a large brown sign points to the venerable old **Majlis Ghorfat Um Al Sheef** (Sat–Thur 8.30am–8.30pm, Fri 2.30–8.30pm; charge). Originally constructed in 1955, the two-storey *majlis* (meeting room) offers a touching throwback to earlier

Burj al Arab.

BELOW: Madinat Jumeirah.

and simpler times, with its traditional coral-stone walls, shady verandahs and teak doors and window frames. The *majlis* originally served as the summer resort of Dubai's former ruler Sheikh Rashid, serving as the venue for many of the meetings in which the visionary sheikh plotted Dubai's spectacular transformation from Arabian backwater to international super-city.

The Majlis Ghorfat Um Al Sheef marks the southern limits of Jumeirah proper, after which you enter the adjacent suburb of **Umm Suqeim** (although the entire area is usually, if inaccurately, referred to as Jumeirah), home to three of the city's most famous modern landmarks.

The first of the area's trio of supersized landmarks is the vast **Jumeirah Beach Hotel** (or JBH as it is often known). Opened in 1997, this was the first of the city's mega-hotels, a 100-metre (330ft) high colossus built in the form of a gigantic breaking wave (although from some angles it looks more like a kind of rollercoaster), a design which neatly complements that of the sail-shaped

Burj al Arab next door. Immediately behind the hotel is the perennially popular **Wild Wadi** water park, a fun place to cool off whilst being shot around waterchutes, twisting through tunnels or plummeting down the hair-raising Jumeirah Sceirah waterslide.

Towering over the coastline just beyond the JBH is the stupendous **Burj al Arab Q** (Tower of the Arabs), opened in 1999. Inspired by the shape of a huge, billowing sail, this marvellous high-rise hotel is far and away Dubai's most memorable modern landmark, its hugely distinctive, instantly recognisable outline providing the city with a defining landmark to rival the Eiffel Tower, Sydney Opera House or Big Ben.

Located just offshore on its own man-made island, the sheer size of the building is impressive enough: at 321 metres (1,053ft), taller than Paris's Eiffel Tower and a mere 60 metres (200ft) shorter than the Empire State Building in New York, although it is really the elegant simplicity, originality and sheer audacity of the design

that captures the imagination. The "sail" itself is constructed from Teflon-coated glass fibre, a dazzling white by day, lit up by spectacular light displays after dark. The building is now home to the city's most exclusive hotel, popularly dubbed the world's first "seven-star" hotel on account of the super-fuelled levels of luxury provided to guests in the hotel's 200-odd suites.

Immediately south of the Burj al Arab rises the mighty **Madinat Jumeirah R** complex, opened in 2004. This is one of modern Dubai's most memorable developments: built in a form of a self-contained faux-Arabian city, its huge sand-coloured buildings topped with innumerable wind towers and criss-crossed with miniature canals on which guests at the complex's hotels are ferried around by *abra*. The lovely Souk Madinat Jumeirah – a superb mock-Arabian bazaar with winding alleyways lined

An elephant statue at India Court in Ibn Battuta Mall.

Hatta Heritage Village.

with upmarket handicraft shops under elaborate wooden roofs and hanging lanterns – is particularly attractive.

A short drive inland from Madinat Jumeirah lies the glitzy **Mall of the Emirates**, one of the largest in the city, with an excellent selection of upmarket shops, and the attached **Ski Dubai** indoor ski slope – one of the city's more bizarre attractions, with its faux-Alpine scenery and huge expanses of (artificial) snow.

Dubai Marina

Bounding the southern end of the city is the vast new **Dubai Marina** **S** development: a swathe of densely packed skyscrapers which have mushroomed out of the desert with magical rapidity over the past five years or so. Even by Dubai standards, the speed and scale of the development here takes the breath away, especially

BELOW: Ibn Battuta Mall.

for those who remember this part of Dubai in its pre-2005 days, when the entire area was little more than untouched desert, bar a modest line of hotels fringing the coast.

At the far southern edge of the city, the **Ibn Battuta Mall** **T** (Sat–Tue 10am–10pm, Wed–Fri 10am–midnight; www.ibnbattutamall.com) is one of the city's most outlandish but engaging attractions, inspired by the travels of the famous Moroccan wanderer Ibn Battuta, with different sections themed after six of the many countries and regions he visited – Morocco, Andalusia, Tunisia, Persia, India and China – all designed with Dubai's characteristic mix of whimsy, extravagance and high kitsch.

Offshore from Dubai Marina lies the vast **Palm Jumeirah**, the world's largest artificial island. As the name suggests, the island is designed in the form of a palm tree. Driving onto the island, the main road runs down the central "trunk" of the tree (adding a whole new dimension to the expression "trunk road"), while a series of sixteen "fronds" radiate away to either side, covered in luxury villas, each with their own little slice of private beach at the end of their gardens.

At the far end of the Palm, the vast **Atlantis** resort (www.atlantisthepalm. com) rears into view above the seafront. The resort is an almost identikit copy of its sister establishment, the Atlantis Paradise Island resort in the Bahamas, with the addition of the few discreet Islamic touches, looking like some enormous Disney palace. Resort attractions include the excellent Aquaventure water park and Dolphin Bay for swimming with dolphins, plus the kooky Lost Chambers, a sequence of underwater halls and tunnels running through a huge aquarium dotted with what are claims to be the "ruins" of the legendary city of Atlantis itself.

Hatta

Some 110km (68 miles) from Dubai (around an hour's drive along the fast, modern Highway 44), lies the peaceful enclave of **Hatta ❻**, tucked up close to the border with Oman in the lee of the dramatic Hajar mountains. The road to Hatta passes through Omani territory. No visas are required, though note that if you are driving yourself your insurance won't cover you on the Omani stretch of the road, unless you have arranged additional cover.

Hatta's main attraction is the appealing **Hatta Heritage Village** (Sat–Thur 8.30am–8.30pm, Fri 2.30pm–8.30pm; free). Various styles of mountain dwellings have been rebuilt around carefully restored buildings, including the first fort in the emirate of Dubai, constructed in 1790, which now houses a weaponry museum. Check out the fascinating variety of mud and *barasti* (palm frond) houses, and a restored *falaj* irrigation system that channels water through the village to the neighbourhood's date-palm gardens. At weekends and during public holidays, local women in national dress and *burqa* face masks work away at traditional crafts and will pose for photographs

(although you should always ask their permission before snapping away). The watchtowers that loom high over the village date back to 1850.

Heritage Village aside, Hatta's main attraction for many are the **Hatta Pools** and the off-road drive that continues beyond the pools through Wadi Qahfi to the Omani village of Rayy. The dirt track that leads to the pools begins several kilometres from Hatta itself. Don't expect idyllic pools, cascading waterfalls and a brimming river at Hatta Pools and you won't be disappointed. The stunning but parched landscape around the pools bears comparison with the surface of Mars. The access track is dusty, the riverbed largely dry, while the spring pools are made up of low-level, slow-moving water. Throughout the year, there is enough water at crossing points to make a splash though.

The Hatta Fort hotel next to the main roundabout in Hatta can provide navigation sheets with directions. Alternatively, you can book a tour in a 4x4 through the hotel.

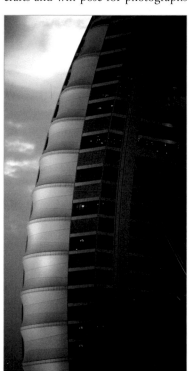

LEFT: the magnificent Burj al-Arab hotel.

Dubai's Islands

From a tourist point of view, Dubai's major physical drawback is its lack of coastline – a mere 70km (44 miles) in total. The response to this problem has been typical of Dubai. Since there's not enough beach, they have decided to build some more. The Palm Jumeirah has already added 68km (42 miles) to the emirate's coastline, although this is just the first (and smallest) of four proposed offshore developments which are intended to create up to 500km (310 miles) of new waterfront. Two further palm-shaped islands (www.thepalm.ae) are already under construction: the Palm Jabal Ali, 20km (12 miles) further down the coast, and the Palm Deira, right next to the city centre. Both are currently stalled due to financial difficulties, although large-scale reclamation works have been finished.

Even more fanciful than the two new palm islands is the extravagant World development. Lying a couple of kilometres (around 1 mile) off the coast (accessible by boat only), this vast complex of artificial islands has been constructed in the approximate shape of a map of the world, with many of the world's countries represented by their own islands within the map. As with many other mega-projects in Dubai, however, development work currently remains stalled. Only one of the islands has so far been built on, while concerns have also been raised that the entire archipelago is sinking back into the sea.

SHARJAH

In the shadow of Dubai, Sharjah is often overlooked by visitors, but it has some fine old architecture and one of the country's best selections of museums and galleries

Abu Dhabi •
UNITED ARAB
EMIRATES

Main attractions
AL ARSA SOUK
BAIT AL NABOODAH
RULER'S FORT
SHARJAH ART MUSEUM
SHARJAH MUSEUM OF ISLAMIC
   CIVILISATION
CENTRAL SOUK

It was Sharjah's good fortune to have been included in Sir Wilfred Thesiger's 1959 book *Arabian Sands*. It's just a shame that Thesiger, respected chronicler of the Arab world, didn't like it.

"We approached a small Arab town on an open beach," he wrote. "It was as drab and tumble-down as Abu Dhabi, but infinitely more squalid, for it was littered with discarded rubbish which had been mass-produced elsewhere."

It's indicative of the amazing pace of change in the UAE that less than 50 years later "drab", "tumble-down", "squalid" **Sharjah ❶** is regarded as the UAE's heritage centre, famed for its museums and traditional architecture.

Its ruler, Sheikh Dr Sultan bin Mohammed al Qasimi, instigated the restoration and reconstruction of buildings in the old city centre in the early 1990s. The resulting clusters of coral-stone museums, with their cool, high-sided alleyways and attractive wind towers, offer glimpses of what life was like here 100 years before Thesiger arrived.

Although the city, capital of the country's third-largest emirate, is now overshadowed by Abu Dhabi and Dubai, it is older than both. Recorded references to Sharjah, which means "Eastern" in Arabic, date back to at least 1490, when the Arab navigator

Ahmad Ibn Majid wrote that ships could find it if they followed the stars from the island of Tunb. On a map of 1669, the city is called Quiximi, after the Qasimi family, ancestors of the present ruler. In the 18th century, the Dutch knew Sharjah as Scharge.

By the time British interests developed in the late 18th century, the city was a stronghold from which the seafaring Qasimis, known as the Qawasim, dominated the Arabian Gulf. In 1819 the British, alarmed by the power of the Qawasim, attacked and destroyed

PRECEDING PAGES: Sharjah port. **LEFT:** by the Book. **RIGHT:** modern communication.

its fleet and bases at Sharjah and Ras
al Khaimah. Sharjah's standing did
not diminish, however. Throughout
the 19th century it remained the leading city on the Trucial Coast and the
second-most important port in the
Gulf after Kuwait. The Sheikh of the
Qawasim, Sultan Bin Saqr – great-
great grandfather of the present ruler
– chose Sharjah as his headquarters.
From 1823, Britain's resident political
agent for the Trucial States and Oman
lived here (the political agency didn't
move to Dubai until 1954).

The British built the Trucial States'
first airport on Sharjah's outskirts in
1932 and maintained a military presence there until independence in
1971. Sharjah was the headquarters of
the British-sponsored Trucial Oman
Scouts and in 1970 the staging post
for Special Air Service (SAS) opera-
tions in Oman.

The city's fortunes waned in the
1940s when Khalid Creek silted up
and sea trade was diverted to Dubai.
Fortunes improved with the discovery
of offshore oil in 1972 and the dredg-
ing of the creek, but the oil price crash
of 1985 left Sharjah in debt and the
emirate was forced to seek a massive
bail-out from a Saudi banking consortium. Saudi influence in the emirate
has remained strong ever since, leading to the introduction of the emirate's notorious "decency laws" (see
page 85) and the total prohibition of
alcohol – to the frustration of some
locals, who believe that the emirate's
conservative regime is stifling the
development of Sharjah's business
and tourism sectors, already battered
by competition from nearby Dubai.

Heritage Area and the Ruler's Fort

Sharjah served as Unesco Cultural
Capital of the Arab World in 1998,
and evidence of this can still be seen
in the beautifully restored **Heritage
Area** just west of Al Borj Avenue near
the corniche, a quaint cluster of traditional mudbrick buildings scattered
around a sequence of irregular squares
and labyrinthine alleyways.

At the centre of the district sits
the pretty **Al Arsa Souk Ⓐ** (Sat–
Thur 10am–1pm and 4.30–9pm, Fri

4.30–9pm), with rustic coral-stone walls and wooden roof. Inside, the souk's winding alleyways are lined with small antique and bric-a-brac shops selling a range of mainstream souvenirs alongside more unusual curios. In the evening the souk's coffee house is where elderly local men while away the hours between prayers at one of the district's three mosques.

Rooftops across the heritage area are dotted with wind towers, early forms of air-conditioning designed to catch and circulate breezes. The most distinctive tower is the round one above the **Majlis of Ibrahim Mohammed al Madfa** Ⓑ, the only one of its kind in the UAE, tucked away around the back of Al Arsa Souk. In addition to founding the region's first newspaper, Oman, in 1927, Ibrahim Mohammed Al Madfa acted as adviser to the ruling Al Qasimi family. His *majlis*, where he would receive business guests, is now a small museum (Sat–Thur 8am–8pm, Fri 4–8pm; free) housing some of his personal effects.

The nearby home of the wealthy Al Naboodah trading family has now

been beautifully restored as the **Bait al Naboodah** Ⓒ (Sat–Thur 8am–8pm, Fri 4–8pm; charge), an atmospheric two-storey traditional building arranged around a colonnaded courtyard. Rooms have been recreated more or less as they would have been in the early 20th century, with old wooden furniture and assorted knick-knacks.

Close by on Al Borj Avenue stands the venerable **Ruler's Fort** Ⓓ (Tue–Thur, Sat–Sun 9am–1pm and 4–8 pm, Fri 4–8pm; charge), an imposing

Al Arsa Souk is a good place to browse for antique khanjars (daggers).

BELOW: an old British cannon at the Ruler's Fort.

Detail of the exterior of the Sharjah Museum of Islamic Civilisation.

old structure which formerly served as the residence of the ruling Al Qassimi family, although it is now looking somewhat forlorn in the middle of a small canyon of banks and offices. The interior is home to an interesting museum on the history of the city, although it was closed for long-term renovations at the time of writing.

North along the corniche

Continuing west down Al Borj Avenue from the Ruler's Fort brings you to Sharjah's **corniche**, usually busy with dozens of traditional old wooden dhows moored up while their crews load and unload cargo – the wooden masts of the dhows contrasting strangely with the skeletal frames of the oil rigs in Port Khalid beyond.

A couple of minutes' walk north along the corniche brings you to **Al Souk al Shuheen** district, the trading centre of old Sharjah, busy after dark

with women shoppers dressed in flowing black robes. A sign here points inland from the corniche to the grand **Sharjah Art Museum** ❸ (Sat–Thur 8am–8pm, Fri 4–8pm; charge). The main attraction here is the "Orientalist" collection upstairs, devoted to a fine selection of paintings by 19th-century European artists depicting life in Islamic lands, including some memorable lithographs by Scottish artist David Roberts (1796–1864). The ground floor of the museum is devoted to temporary exhibitions, usually featuring local and/or Arab artists.

Another five minutes' walk north along the corniche brings you to the one of the city's highlights, the superb new **Sharjah Museum of Islamic Civilisation** ❺ (Sat–Thur 8am–8pm, Fri 4–8pm; charge), occupying the beautifully restored Souk al Majara, topped with its distinctive golden dome. The ground floor of the museum offers a wide-ranging and excellently presented overview of the various contributions made by Muslim scientists, artists and architects to world knowledge over the past 500

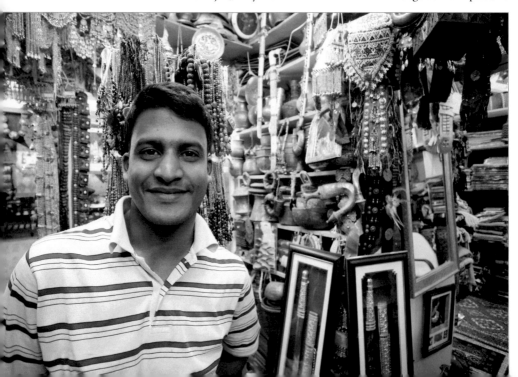

years, including absorbing displays on medieval Islamic chemistry, medicine, astronomy and navigation, backed up with quaint gadgets like armillary spheres, wall quadrants, astrolabes, equatoriums and water-clocks. Upstairs, four galleries showcase a wide range of superb Islamic arts and crafts, including beautiful historic manuscripts, ceramics, glass, armour, woodwork, textiles and jewellery.

Arouba Road and the lagoons

Return to the Ruler's Fort and continue up Al Borj Avenue to reach Arouba Road, the city's main thoroughfare, which arrows its way purposefully across the centre. At the junction of Al Borj Avenue and Arouba Road stands **Rolla Square**, a popular meeting place for Sharjah's large community of Keralan expats from India. Rolla means "banyan", commemorating a banyan tree which stood here from the early 1800s until 1978, its place now taken by a striking modern sculpture with a hollow centre in the shape of a tree. The entire

park was undergoing major redevelopment at the time of writing, due to finish in 2012.

About a 1km (½ mile) south down Arouba Road stretches the wide open expanse of Al Ittihad Square, once used as a turning circle for aircraft using the original Sharjah airport (*see below*), although it has now been attractively landscaped with rolling lawns. At the west end of the square rises the soaring **Al Ittihad (Union) Monument**, unveiled in 1989. Close by rises the impressive **King Faisal Mosque**, one of the largest in the UAE, with room for 3,000 worshippers.

The original runway of the old Sharjah airport is now King Abd al Aziz Street, while the former airport rest house, built in 1932 when Sharjah was a stopover on Imperial Airways' London to India and Australia routes, now houses the aviation-themed **Al Mahattah Museum** (Sat–Thur 8am–8pm, Fri 4–8pm; charge). Among the aircraft on display are a World War II-era Avro Anson and a Douglas DC3, which belonged to the Gulf Aviation Co., the forerunner of Gulf Air.

Sharjah Biennial

The Sharjah Art Museum is one of the major venues of the prestigious Sharjah Biennial (two months in alternate years; www.sharjahbiennial.org), a leading fixture on the international contemporary art calendar. The most recent Biennial, in 2011, was a particularly lively affair. First, Biennial director Jack Persekian was sacked by the ruler of Sharjah after it emerged that one of the artworks on display – a parody football match featuring 23 headless mannequins – contained "offensive" texts written on the shirts of the dummies. A petition against perceived censorship was subsequently issued, while soon afterwards a number of demonstrators were taken away for questioning by the authorities after protesting against the involvement of the UAE in suppressing protests in nearby Bahrain – although all were released shortly afterwards.

BELOW: inside Sharjah Art Museum.

An ornate tile at the Central Souk.

BELOW: Khalid Lagoon at dusk.

The area stretching north of Arouba Road opposite the Central Souk is home to a sequence of entertaining **wholesale markets**. The fish market is busiest in the early morning, while the nearby fruit and vegetable market is a riot of colour, especially attractive in the evening, when its outdoor stalls are lit by hissing kerosene lamps. The meat market next door is not for the squeamish. A live animal market, selling everything from falcons to cows, is tucked behind shops and restaurants on the south side of nearby Al Mina Road. Most of the falcons are imported from India or Pakistan.

Back on Arouba Street at the lagoon end of Al Ittihad Square is the superb **Central Souk G** (also known as the Blue Souk, or Souk al Markasi), a landmark building depicted on the country's Dhs5 banknote. The first-floor antique and carpet shops are particularly interesting and attract souvenir-hunting visitors staying in other emirates. Persian carpets are a speciality. Nearby, water taxis *(abra)* offer enjoyable excursions around the lagoon and to the mouth of the creek.

Continuing along Arouba Road, a bridge crosses the expansive **Khalid Lagoon**, now home to the world's fourth-largest fountains, after Geneva, Jeddah and Dubai. The 100-metre (330ft) fountain can be best enjoyed at sunset from the lagoon's northeastern shore. Southwest of the lagoon, a man-made canal feeds into Al Khan Lagoon at the attractive **Qanat al Qasba** retail and leisure development, with shops lined up along either side of the canal and the imposing **Eye of the Emirates** observation wheel.

There are a couple of further attractions about 1km (½ mile) west of Qanat al Qasba on the edge of Al Khan Lagoon, opposite Al Mamzar Park in Dubai. The state-of-the-art **Sharjah Aquarium** (www.sharjahaquarium.ae; Mon–Thur 8am–8pm, Fri 4–9pm, Sat 8am–9pm; charge) offers an interesting glimpse into the marine life of the Gulf, complete with extensive tanks and walk-through underwater tunnel. The adjacent **Sharjah Maritime Museum** (Sat–Thur 8am–8pm, Fri 4–8pm; charge) is also worth a look, exploring the emirate's former maritime traditions with displays ranging from traditional hand-crafted wooden dhows to traditional fish traps and displays on the local pearling industry.

Out of the centre

Out in the northern suburbs near the Ruler's Office stands **Sharjah Archaeology Museum** (Sat–Thur 9am–1pm and 5–8pm, Fri 5–8pm; charge). Completed in 1992, the purpose-built museum has two storeys of exhibition rooms showcasing objects from Sharjah's past – from finds at the ancient town of Mileiha through to the 1930s and more recent times, as well as Islamic antiquities. The impressive Qur'an monument at the nearby Cultural Roundabout (on the road to the international airport and the town of Dhaid) is also worth a look.

Even further out of town, the **Sharjah Natural History Museum and Desert Park** (Sat–Wed 9am–7pm, Thur noon–7pm, Fri 2–8pm; charge) lies beyond the airport on the left side of the Sharjah–Dhaid highway. The museum has five exhibition halls featuring displays on UAE geology (including a section documenting the story of oil), ecology, flora and fauna and marine life. The site also houses the Arabian Wildlife Centre and a children's farm.

Family at Central Souk.

BELOW: jewellery for sale at the Central Souk.

THE NORTHERN EMIRATES

The UAE's three northernmost emirates – Ajman, Umm al Qaiwain and Ras al Khaimah – offer a low-key alternative to life further down the coast

Main attractions
AJMAN FORT
AJMAN BOAT-BUILDING YARDS
UMM AL QAIWAIN FORT-MUSEUM
RAS AL KHAIMAH NATIONAL
MUSEUM

The trio of emirates – Ajman, Umm al Qaiwain and Ras al Khaimah – which make up the northern portion of the UAE see only a trickle of foreign visitors and boast few bona fide sights, although all three offer an absorbing glimpse of a very different side of the country – geographically close to Dubai, but surprisingly distant in atmosphere. None of the northern emirates have enjoyed the oil-and-gas bonanzas of their neighbours to the south, and despite significant funding from the government in Abu Dhabi they remain noticeably less wealthy, less populous and less developed than the big cities further south.

Ajman

The smallest of the seven emirates, somnolent **Ajman ❷** is now little more than a suburb of nearby Sharjah, strung out along a superb stretch of tranquil beach dotted with a few upmarket hotels – all that you will find here in the way of modern tourist development. Ajman town is best known for its dhow-building heritage. Pearling dhows sailed from its shores from the 3rd century BC until the 1930s, and fishing dhows are still made on Ajman's sheltered creek, though today most are made of fibreglass.

The main attraction in the town itself is the fine old **fort ❹** (Sat–Thur 9am–1pm and 4–7pm, closed Fri; charge), a pretty assortment of sand-plastered round towers, spiky parapets and a superb wind tower which still provides cooling breezes. Built around 1775, the fort served as the ruler's residence until 1970. Inside lies the interesting **Ajman Museum**, showcasing life in the region through the ages, with *barasti* houses and dhows in the courtyard and displays on policing (practised since the days of the Prophet Mohammed in the 7th century), the bedroom of Sheikh Rashid bin Humaid al Nuaimi (1928–81), a

LEFT: the fortress housing Ajman Museum.

market tableau and displays on traditional medicine.

Beyond the fort, off Leewara Street, you'll find Ajman's bustling **souks**, selling bric-a-brac, vegetables, meat and fish alongside a marina where wooden dhows jostle with modern leisure craft.

On the other side of the marina, at the northern end of Arabian Gulf Street, a couple of hotels will let you soak up the sun on their beaches for a fee – the five-star Ajman Kempinski has a particularly attractive beach, along with good restaurants and bars. South of here stretches a long swathe of superb golden sand, remarkably peaceful and undeveloped given its proximity to Sharjah and Dubai, with a solitary crumbling **watchtower** still standing guard over the shore. Most of the UAE's defensive watchtowers are round, but, unusually, this one is square.

From the coast road, Khalid bin al Waleed Street leads to the **Ruler's Palace B**, which stands on the south side of the junction with Kasr az Zahr Street and Sheikh Rashid Street. The palace, home to Sheikh Humaid bin

Rashid al Nuaimi, who succeeded his father in 1981, is not open to the public, but it's possible to peer into the leafy compound from its main gate.

On the far side of town lie Ajman's port and **boat-building yards C**, situated on the Creek a short taxi ride from the centre. Ajman's port now houses one of the UAE's largest ship-repair companies, which maintains oil-field supply boats along more than 5km (3 miles) of Creekside wharfs. Two of the most accessible are on **Tareq bin Ziyad Street** in the Mushairef district. Typically, a primitive production line of fishing dhow hulls are propped up on oil drums. Although most boats are made of fibreglass now, the deck rails that rise toward the stern are still made of wood.

Umm al Qaiwain

Umm al Qaiwain ❸ (known locally as UAQ) is the second-smallest and least populous of the emirates

A dhow and a traditional palm-frond canoe at Ajman Museum.

BELOW: building boats.

A schoolgirl caught by a camera.

–its 40,000 residents would struggle to fill Abu Dhabi's Sheikh Zayed sports stadium, and in the heat of the day there are usually more animals than people on its streets: a mix of scrawny cats, wandering goats and the occasional grazing cow.

The town itself lies on a sandy spit of land north off the main highway that links Ajman, some 20km (12 miles) southwest, with Ras al Khaimah. Approaching from the main highway, you will drive down UAQ's long, straight main shopping street (Al Moalla Road) before reaching the three defensive **watchtowers** off Al Soor Road. Round and of differing sizes, they were once joined together by a sturdy protective wall which has been partially rebuilt.

BELOW: Umm al Qaiwain's fortress.

Beyond here lies the "old" town – occupying a bulge of land at the end of the spit – although there is not much that is old about it apart from the impressive **fort-museum** (Sat–Sun, Tue–Thur 8am–1pm and 5–8pm; Fri 5–8pm; charge). The sprucely restored fort itself offers a welcome contrast to the dusty streets outside, with its pretty coral-stone buildings and a neat courtyard studded with trees. The museum is less appealing, with a dusty collection of traditional artefacts and some rather unexciting archaeological finds (pots, mainly) from the nearby site of Ad Dour.

East of the fort, the low-key **Flamingo Beach Resort** offers various activities including boat trips, crab-hunting and deep-sea fishing expeditions (advance reservations essential). Boat trips offer a nice way to see As Siniyyah (*see below*) and the various other islands which dot the coast.

Around UAQ

The island of **As Siniyyah ❹**, visible from the old town's Corniche Road, was the site of the original settlement until sweet water supplies ran out. It is now a haven for wildlife, home to herons, cormorants, flamingos, turtles and even dugong, which sailors of old mistook for mermaids. With an estimated dugong population of 1,000, the UAE is the world's second-largest sanctuary for the curious-looking mammal, known in Arabic as *arus al bahar* (sea-bride).

Permission is needed to visit As Siniyyah, but the coast either side of the town of **Khor al Beidah** holds further natural attractions, including the country's largest wintering flock of crab plover and numerous other species, while the intertidal mudflats and mangroves are bounded inland by *sabkha* (salt-flats) and dunes that host breeding larks.

Just south lie the fragmentary remains of the archaeological site of **Ad Dour,** off the coastal highway about 5km (3 miles) north of the turn-off to UAQ town. Extensive artefacts recovered from the site can be seen in the UAQ fort-museum, although there is little to see at the site itself.

About 10km (6 miles) further north along the main highway lies the **Dreamland Aqua Park** ❺ (Jan–Mar daily 10am–6pm, weekends 7/8pm; www.dreamlanduae.com; charge), an unexpectedly large and well-equipped water park in this rather out-of-the-way location. Attractions include a huge wave pool, family raft rides and twister slides – not as state-of-the-art as Wild Wadi and Aquaventure in Dubai, admittedly, but a fair bit cheaper and, during the week, a lot quieter as well.

Ras al Khaimah

The base of the Qawasim "pirates" in the 19th century, **Ras al Khaimah** ❻ (or RAK, as it's usually abbreviated) was once a powerful maritime state until being crushed by the British in the early 19th century. Modern RAK is now something of a backwater, although it is one of the UAE's most scenic and fertile areas, with extensive date palm groves and grazing plains for sheep and cattle, ringed by high mountains and rolling dunes.

RAK City

First settled in around 1500, RAK City lies right on the sea, with the oldest part of town next to the mouth of the local *khor* (creek). RAK is notably more built up and livelier than either Ajman or Umm al Qaiwain, although inconsequential compared with Dubai (or even Sharjah). The **central market area**, with gold souk, west of the fort is worth a look for its traditional street life, usually busy with robed Emiratis and their wives, veiled from head to toe in black *abbeyas* – a few still wear the traditional Bedu facemasks which have largely disappeared elsewhere in the country.

The town's main attraction is, once again, its fort, now converted into the **Ras al Khaimah National Museum** Ⓐ (Sat–Thur 8am–noon and 4–7pm, closed Fri; charge), a rather grand name for a decidedly modest museum showcasing the usual array of local artefacts and archaeological finds, although the whole collection was being reorganised at the time of writing. The 19th-century fort itself is more appealing, with a fine wind tower looming

Umm al Qaiwain's name means "Mother of the Powers", reflecting its long seafaring tradition. Fishing remains an important local activity, with lines of boats moored up near the Fish Market on Corniche Road.

BELOW: modern Ras al Khaimah.

Wind tower at Ajman Museum.

over the pleasantly shady courtyard within.

North of the fort is **Al Abrah Market**, a small group of stalls set up on the shore of the creek. On a gravel area opposite this market fish nets are prepared daily by local fishermen, and large rolls of *barasti* (palm fronds) are stored for sale to local farmers. On the same road, under the impressively long Khor Bridge, is Ras al Khaimah's colourful **fruit and vegetable market**, with its extensive range of fresh produce.

Beyond the Old Town, modern Ras al Khaimah expands. Houses and commercial buildings spread from the shore of the creek to the edge of the majestic Hajar mountains, running from here into Musandam in Oman.

Around Ras al Khaimah

South of RAK City, the coastal village of **Jazirah al Hamra** ❼ (The Red Island) was originally built on a small promontory, which at high tide became an island. The old village and

fort still stand but are abandoned, with the new village now on the mainland. This is where you'll find the impressive Al Hamra Fort Resort, designed in the form of a traditional Arabian fortress and occupying a prime slice of beachfront real estate.

A few kilometres north of Al Hamra, the new **Iceland Water Park** (daily 10/11am–7/8pm, time varies according to month; www.icelandwaterpark. com; charge) is the latest in the UAE's growing chain of state-of-the-art water parks, with an incongruously arctic theme, featuring fake ice-grottoes, penguins and snow-covered mountains towering over a variety of slides, wavepools and other attractions.

About 10km (6 miles) out of town in the inland village of **Digdagga**, the **Ras al Khaimah Camel Racing Track** offers an entertaining way to spend a Friday morning in winter. Locals enjoy the excitement and thrill of following the camels in 4x4s, so watch out for vehicles as well as unwieldly camels.

South of Digdagga, the village of **Khatt** is home to the pleasant **Khatt**

Julfar

The predecessor of modern-day Ras al Khaimah was Julfar, a flourishing port which by around 900 had established itself as one of the major trading centres in the Gulf. Arab geographers such as Al Idrisi (writing in 1154) and Yaqut Al Hamawi (c.1250) described the city and its fertile hinterlands, while it is believed that Ahmed bin Majid, one of the great Arab navigators, was born in Julfar during the 1430s. Julfar's prosperity inevitably attracted unwelcome attention. From about 1400 the city was controlled by the island of Hormuz, subsequently ousted by the Portuguese in around 1500. The Portuguese continued to occupy the city until 1633, when they were in turn overthrown by local forces, after which Julfar fell into decline, and was eventually abandoned.

Hot Springs (daily 5am–11pm; charge), with segregated enclosures offering private bathing in the pleasantly warm waters – although singularly lacking in atmosphere. The eye-catching Golden Tulip Khatt Springs hotel (www.goldentulip.com) rises impressively from a nearby hill, resembling a kind of modern remake of a traditional Arabian fort.

Excavations during the late 1980s at **Shimmel** (or Shamal) ❽, in the foothills north of Wadi Bih, about 5km (3 miles) north of Ras al Khaimah, have uncovered remnants of a settlement dating from about 3000 BC, including a large circular burial tomb dating to around 2500 BC. Shimmel is also home to **Hisn Shimmel**, popularly known as the Queen of Sheba's Palace. The stony ruins of the "palace" are believed to have been part of a large fortified hill settlement dating from around the 15th century, some 2,500 years after the death of the legendary 10th-century-BC Yemeni queen, although the view towards Ras al Khaimah and the sea is wonderful.

To reach Hisn Shimmel, head out of RAK on the Oman road heading towards Rams. Turn right after 4.5km (3 miles) at the brown sign and follow this road for 1.5km (1 mile). Turn right at the roundabout and continue continue for 2.5km (1½ miles) until you reach a fort-like building. Turn left through the village past a mosque on your left, then turn left past the mosque until a hill surrounded by a broken fence appears straight ahead. Find a convenient break in the fence and climb the hill; you will find the ruins at the top.

The small, quiet villages of **Rams** and **Dhayah**, north of Ras al Khaimah, are also worth a visit, with old watchtowers and other coral and mudbrick buildings (including, in Dhayah, an old fort) nestled amongst palm groves. British forces chose Rams as a strategic landing site for their invasion of the southern Gulf in 1819. The people of Rams fled to Dhayah Fort, where they surrendered after four days of intensive fighting.

Sunset at Ras al Khaimah.

BELOW: a camel ride on the beach in Ajman.

Northern Emirates

0   20 km
0   20 miles

N

The Gulf

Ash Sham
Ghalilah
Rams   Dhayah
❽ Shimmel
❻ Ras al Khaimah
OMAN
1794
Iceland Water Park
❼ Jazirah al Hamra
Al Fulayyah
Dreamland
Khor al Beidah   Aqua Park   Digdagga   Bayah
❹ As Siniyyah   ❺   ★ Camel Racing Track
❸ Umm al Qaiwain   Khatt
Hamraniyah   Khatt Hot Springs
Ad Dour
Hamriya   Ihdn   Tayyibah
❷ Ajman   Falaj   Al Mualla
❶ Sharjah   Biatah   Manama   Masafi
Palm Deira
The World   **DUBAI**   Mardef   Dhaid
Siji
Jumeira   Mileiha
1034
Jebel Ali   Hail
Al Haba   Fili
Dubailand   Madam
OMAN
Urqub   Huwaylat
Juwayza   Masfut
Al Jizer   Hatta

FUJAIRAH AND THE EAST COAST

Straddling the east coast of the UAE is the tranquil emirate of Fujairah, with a largely unspoilt coastline and deserted beaches backdropped by the dramatic Hajar mountains

Hugging the eastern coast of the UAE, the beautiful emirate of Fujairah offers a scenic contrast to the rest of the country, its craggy coastline, deserted beaches and dramatic wadis barely touched by tourism. The emirate as a whole remains pleasantly sleepy, bordering on comatose, with a string of low-key towns dotting the coast, backed by the dramatic chain of the rocky Hajar mountains, and with a string of secluded and largely deserted beaches between. The beach resorts of Al Aqah serve as a popular weekend retreat for stressed-out expats from Dubai, but elsewhere modern tourism has made few inroads.

The Arabs of the east coast are Sharqiyyin, who have historically controlled the route through Wadi Ham, which runs from Fujairah past Bitnah and Masafi to link with Wadi Siji where it continues out onto desert plains. Wadi Ham has been the site of many battles down the centuries. Apart from the trade route from Ras al Khaimah to Daba, it was the only means of access to the Gulf of Oman from the western regions.

Although the Persians, Portuguese and Dutch had a presence on the east coast, the remoteness of the mountains has enabled the people

of Fujairah to protect themselves against foreign rule and outside tribal influences. Even so, the emirate's rulers struggled to gain recognition of Fujairah's independence from the British, who maintained that Fujairah was part of Sharjah. In a clash with the British Royal Navy on 20 April 1925, the ruler refused to comply with the terms of the ultimatum from the Political Resident, Lt Colonel Prideaux, and British ships were ordered to bombard Fujairah castle for 90 minutes. It was not until

Main attractions
FUJAIRAH FORT
BIDIYAH MOSQUE
AL AQAH BEACH

LEFT: fishermen with their catch on an east-coast beach.
RIGHT: a dramatic sunset.

TIP

A number of tour operators in Dubai run regular tours of the east coast and Fujairah, usually covering many of the sights in this chapter – a stress-free alternative to finding your own way around the coast.

1952 that Fujairah was acknowledged by Britain as the seventh Trucial State.

Fujairah City

The little city of **Fujairah** ❶ is modest compared with Dubai and Abu Dhabi, but has enjoyed something of a boom in recent years thanks to the huge new oil-transhipment port on the edge of town, with a cluster of glass-faced high-rises now shooting up out of the neat town centre.

For visitors, the main attraction is the recently restored **fort** Ⓐ (Sun–Thur 8.30am–5pm, Fri 2–5pm; tel: 09-222 9085; charge). Dating back 500 years in places, this is the oldest fort in the UAE and perhaps the most impressive, set against a stunning mountain backdrop. To reach the fort, turn inland from the corniche down Al Nakheel Road at the Coffeepot Roundabout.

Many of the mudbrick village houses that surrounded the fort still stand. Some have been reduced to low walls, but others show signs of being inhabited – air-conditioners protrude from windows and old

cars are parked in makeshift carports. A mosque below the fort has been well maintained. It has small, decorative wooden windows and doors typical of the area.

A five-minute walk south of the fort at the intersection of Al Nakheel and Sheikh Zayed bin Sultan roads lies the old-fashioned **Fujairah Museum** Ⓑ (Sun–Thur 9am–1.30pm and 4.30–6.30pm, Fri 2–6.30pm; charge), occupying a low-walled building. The museum houses archaeological and ethnographic exhibits from the area, mostly from local sites such as Bitnah, Qidfah and Bidiyah, presenting 4,500 years of local history.

Just south of Fujairah City (and now virtually a suburb of it) is the former fishing village of **Kalba** ❷ (part of Sharjah emirate), home to a colourful fish and vegetable souk and the neatly renovated Al Ghail Fort and Bait Sheikh Said bin Hamad al Qassimi (Mon 9am–1pm, Tue–Thur and Sat 9am–1pm and 5–8pm, Fri 5–8pm; charge), comprising the old village fort and the imposing beachside residence of Sheikh Said bin Hamad.

BELOW: Fujairah Fort.

Fujairah

```
0          800 m
0          800 yds
```

N

Kuwait Rd

Al Fasseel Road

Youth Centre & National Theatre

Al Qsar Road

Al Kalaa Road

Madab Road

DATE GARDENS

King Fayssal Road

Corniche

Ⓐ Fort

AL MUDHANNAB

Fujairah Heritage Village

Fujairah Hilton Hotel

Municipality

Al Sharqi Road

Grand Majlis

Ⓑ Fujairah Museum

Al Nakheel Road

Coffeepot Roundabout

Ⓒ Great Mosque

Sheikh Zayed bin

Fahim Road

Al Muntazah Road

Gurfah Road

Fishing Harbour

Al Muntazah Rd.

NATIONAL PARK

Sultan Road

Central Market

GHURFAH

Hamad   bin   Abdullah   Road

SAFAD

MERAISHID   Kalba▼

South of the village, it is worth continuing down to the adjacent village of **Khor Kalba** to see the attractive mangrove groves fringing the entrance to the *khor* (creek). At sunset the blue water of the Gulf highlights their rich green, emphasising the natural beauty of this region.

North along the coast

Heading north along the main coastal highway from Fujairah City, it is 20km (12 miles) to the town of **Khor Fakkan ❸** (actually a part of Sharjah emirate), protected by a spur of the Hajar mountains. The attractive horseshoe-shaped harbour is constantly busy with tankers and other ships, while colourful tiers of containers lie stacked up on the quayside. Further north lies the town's breezy corniche and fine beach, along with the quirky Oceanic hotel, the town's major landmark with its distinctive round windows styled after a ship's portholes.

Heading inland just south of Khor Fakkan lies the curious little territory of **Madha**, a tiny enclave of Omani territory completely enclosed by the

UAE. The main road leads to the modern village of Madha, beyond which lies the smaller village of Nahwa – which, bizarrely enough, belongs to Sharjah. All of this creates a kind of Russian doll effect whereby a fragment of UAE territory sits within an island of Omani territory, which is itself enclosed by the UAE – a good example of the convoluted borders drawn up in an attempt to follow local

Al Aqah Beach.

BELOW: a bullfight in Fujairah.

Bullfighting

Traditional Arab sports such as falconry and camel racing are not suited to the terrain of the east coast. As a result, the large Brahmin bull, which has worked for centuries in the area, is bred to compete in a contest of strength. Two pampered bulls, each weighing a tonne or more and fed on milk, honey and meal, try to force each other to the ground. The sport was possibly introduced in the 16th century by the Portuguese, or may have its source in Persia, where the bull was once worshipped. The Fujairah contests are held on Friday in winter from roughly 4–5.30pm, on the southern edge of town, just inland from the corniche south of the Central Market roundabout (where Hamad bin Abdullah Road heads off towards Sharjah).

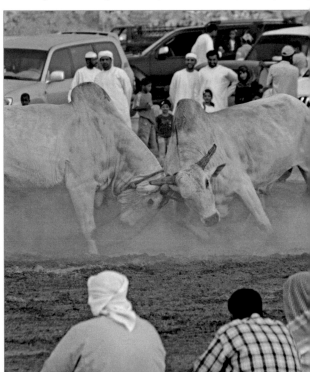

tribal allegiances during the settling of modern boundaries.

Further north along the coast, the village of **Bidiyah** is home to the the oldest mosque in the UAE, dating back to the 15th century – a rustic little structure with two flattened domes supported by a single internal pillar but no minaret. Visitors may be allowed to enter outside prayer time. It is also worth making the five-minute walk up the hill behind the mosque, with superb mountain and coastal views from the watchtower at the summit.

A few minutes' drive north of Bidiyah lies the sweeping **Al Aqah Beach** ❺, one of the most attractive in the UAE and a magnet for residents of Dubai, Abu Dhabi and Al Ain at weekends, although things are very peaceful during the week. The beach is home to a trio of upmarket hotels including the towering Le Méridien al Aqah resort, an incongruously grand structure which looks like it has been airlifted straight from Dubai, the equally vast Fujairah Rotana (www. rotana.com) and, a short distance

further on, the more homely Sandy Beach motel. All three offer an appealing spot to hole up for a night or two, enjoying the fine wide sands and swimming and snorkelling in the unspoilt coastal waters. Just off the shore from the Sandy Beach motel lies "Snoopy Island", named after the well-known cartoon character lying on his kennel, and now a popular snorkelling and diving site.

From Al Aqah, it's another 15 minutes' drive north to the Oman border and the town of **Daba** ❻, nestled in the shadow of the mountains at the southern end of the Musandam peninsula. Daba is actually three towns in one. The largest part of town, known as Daba Muhallab, belongs to the emirate of Fujairah. Next to this is the smaller area known as Daba al Hisn, administered by the emirate of Sharjah, and the even sleepier Daba Bayah, over the border in Oman.

Daba Muhallab itself is one of the most pleasant towns in the UAE, although there is not much to see apart from a couple of huge mosques, each sporting a quartet of minarets,

BELOW: a modern building in Fujairah City.

Kalba's History

Sharjah emirate is unique in having territory on both coasts of the UAE, including the east-coast enclaves of Khor Fakkan, north of Fujairah City, and Kalba, to the south. Kalba itself boasts an unusually long history, dating back to the Umm an Nar period (extensive remains from which have been discovered close to the modern town). The area fell under the control of the Portuguese during the 16th century when it was also visited by the Venetian jeweller Gasparo Balbi, who mentions Kalba ("Chelb") in his *Viaggio dell'Indie Orientali* of 1590 – also the first Western source to mention Dubai. In 1936 Britain recognised Kalba as independent from Sharjah in an attempt to persuade the local sheikh, Said bin Hamad, to grant landing rights for British planes, although Kalba subsequently rejoined the state of Sharjah in 1952.

on the seafront corniche, and the quirky sequence of oversized sculptures that adorn the town's various roundabouts, including a monster coffee pot, oil lamp and a pile of earthenware pottery.

From here, it is possible to make a pleasant side trip over the border to Daba Bayah and dip your toe into Oman. The town itself is pleasantly sleepy, fringed with a fine swathe of sand and dotted with fishing boats, often with considerable quantities of fish laid out to dry on the sand. Just inland (signed "Daba Castle") lies the town's impressive fort – a fine example of traditional Omani architecture, though it isn't open to the public.

Inland from Fujairah City

Heading inland from Fujairah along the main Sharjah highway, it is about about 12km (7 miles) to Bitnah, home to the atmospheric old Bitnah Fort (not open to the public) off on the right of the highway as it twists and turns through the mountains above the village's sprawling oasis.

Some 30km (19 miles) further down the road is the small town of **Masafi**, perhaps best known as the source of the popular brand of UAE mineral water. Masafi is also home to a lively Friday Market (open all week, despite the name) comprising a long string of shops lining the main road through town selling various souvenirs and handicrafts, including ornamental pots and huge quantities of carpets, although most are machine-made, and of rather low quality.

Friday drumming near Daba.

BELOW: the oldest mosque in the UAE at Khor Fakkan.

INSIGHT GUIDE — TRAVEL TIPS
OMAN AND THE UAE

TRANSPORT

GETTING THERE AND GETTING AROUND

GETTING THERE

By Air

Many major airlines operate direct flights to Oman; for some, it is used as a stopover on flights to and from the Far East. The national carrier, Oman Air, is expanding its network.

For a payment of £5–10 you can offset your carbon emissions at either www.climatecare.org or www.carbonneutral.com.

Major airlines in Oman

24-hour information, www.omanairports.com/liveflightinfo.asp
Air Arabia (c/o Shanfari Travels & Tours), tel: 2460 2710; www.air arabia.com
Air Canada, tel: 2456 6046; www.air canada.com

BELOW: a 4x4 at Turtle Beach Resort, Ras Al Hadd.

Air India, tel: 2452 1359; www.air india.in
American Airlines (c/o Sama Travel), tel: 2455 9941; www.aa.com
British Airways, tel: 2456 8777; www.britishairways.com
Emirates, tel: 2440 4444; www.emirates.com
Etihad, tel: 2482 3500; www.etihad airways.com
Gulf Air, tel: 2448 2777; www.gulfair.com
Oman Air, tel: 2453 1111; www.oman air.com
Qatar Airways, tel: 2416 2700; www.qatarairways.com

By Car

If you are driving from the UAE your passport will be checked at the border crossing in both Oman and the UAE; you'll need to buy additional insurance cover through your car-hire agent if you want to take a UAE hire car into Oman (or vice versa).

By Ship

There are no scheduled passenger services into Oman, but some cruise ships visit Muscat and Salalah.

GETTING AROUND

On Arrival

Muscat International Airport (www.omanairports.com) is 30km (19 miles) from the centre of old Muscat. Car hire is available from the airport, and there's also a prepaid taxi service (OR7–8 to most destinations, or OR10/13 to the Al Bustan and Shangri La hotels respectively; for full prices, see www.omanairports.com/

transport.asp). The drive to Qurum takes about 20 minutes, or around 40 minutes to get to Al Bustan Hotel, depending on traffic. There are no bus services to the airport.
Muscat International Airport
Tel: 2451 9210
Salalah International Airport
Tel: 2329 1016

Buses

Reliable bus services operate between the major towns (and between Dubai, Muscat and Salalah), usually two or three times daily. Services are inexpensive and reasonably comfortable, although getting information about timetables and departure points can be remarkably difficult – try asking at your hotel. Micros (see page 237) also run on some inter-city routes, although finding the micro you want is even more difficult than with the buses, and the vehicles themselves are much more cramped and uncomfortable, especially if you've got luggage.

Taxis

When travelling shorter distances within or around cities, the easiest option is generally to pick up a taxi (painted a distinctive orange and white). Certain caveats apply, however. Virtually all Omani taxis are unmetered, so you'll have to agree the fee before you set out. Fares generally work out surprisingly high and foreigners are almost always likely to pay significantly over the going rate, whatever their bargaining skills; it is a good idea to check with your hotel to find out what the going rate should be, so you at least have an idea as to what you're aiming for. Be aware that all taxi drivers are Omani (this being a profession reserved for nationals by the government), and outside Muscat may not speak much, or any, English, adding to the difficulties of agreeing a fare and describing your destination. Hiring a taxi directly outside an upmarket hotel or major tourist site is also likely to inflate the cost. It is also a good idea to keep plenty of small notes to hand, as drivers often claim to have no change.

In Muscat, there are a few companies offering metered cab services (Hello Taxi, tel: 2460 7011, and City Taxi, tel: 2460 2211, are two of the more reputable), although you might end up waiting ages for a cab to arrive – or it might simply not turn up at all.

Taxis also commonly operate on a "shared" basis, taking multiple passengers who split the fare between them, although most Omani taxi drivers, seeing a Westerner appear, will assume you want to hire the cab entirely for yourself ("engaged").

Micros

A cheaper alternative to taxis are microbuses, or "micros" (also known as Baisa buses), white minivans which can be seen in towns and cities all over the country. These follow fixed routes, with fixed fares, although finding the vehicle you want can be extremely difficult for casual visitors, given that micros don't carry numbers or signs indicating their route or destination. They can prove useful in Muscat, however. The hub of the network is Ruwi Roundabout, from where micros depart to Fish Roundabout in Mutrah and west along Sultan Qaboos Road as far as the international airport and Seeb. Ask around until you find what you want. Fares are typically 100–500 baisas.

Private Transport

Given the difficulties of using public transport, driving yourself is an attractive option, especially considering the cheapness of car hire and extremely low petrol costs. Most upmarket hotels have car-hire desks. Outside the major cities, driving is usually quite pleasant, with fast modern roads, usually well signposted in Arabic and English.

Omanis drive on the right-hand side of the road. Driving standards generally are not as good as in the West, so be on your guard for erratic behaviour, particularly taxis and micros

Above: taxi sign at night, Muscat.

stopping or pulling out in front of you unexpectedly, other vehicles tailgating you at speed, dangerous overtaking manoeuvres, vehicles driving at night without lights, and so on. Whatever the provocation, avoid expressing displeasure of any kind – abusive hand gestures or insulting language are both illegal under Omani law and could potentially land you in jail.

Driving in Muscat can be particularly stressful and roads often become very congested, especially during rush hour (roughly 7–9am and 1.30–3.30pm). In Dhofar, in particular, be wary of wandering camels. If an approaching vehicle displays hazard lights, this indicates camels ahead. Adopt the same procedure.

If you have an accident, you must not move the vehicles involved until a policeman arrives, unless it is only a minor accident (in this case, get the other driver's name, vehicle registration number and insurance details; if you do not agree whose fault it is, then go to the police station to report it).

Speed limits go up to 120kph (75mph) on the dual carriageways (in Muscat and between Muscat and Dubai, and Muscat and Nizwa). Other speed limits vary from 40–100kph depending on the type of road and where it is.

Car-hire companies

Avis, tel: 2440 0888; www.avis oman.com
Budget, tel: 2468 3999; www.budget oman.com
Europcar, tel: 2479 4061; www. europcar.com/car-OMAN.html
Hertz, tel: 2462 5200; www.nttoman hertz.com
Mark Rent-a-Car, tel: 2478 6885;

www.marktoursoman.com
Sixt, tel: 2451 0224; www.sixt.com/ car-rental/oman
Thrifty, tel: 2452 1189; www.thrifty oman.com
Value Plus, tel: 2451 0292; www. valueoman.com

Off-road driving

To appreciate the country fully you need to go off-road in a 4x4, but this is not for the inexperienced, as you will have to navigate steep and dangerous roads.

If you do decide to drive yourself, make sure that you go with another vehicle driven by someone with experience because it is very easy to find yourself in difficulties. You must be properly prepared before you head off into the Interior. Alternatively, tour companies can organise wadi-bashing (driving in riverbeds) trips for you.

Ferry between Muscat and Khasab

A high-speed ferry service operated by the National Ferries Company (www. nfc.om) runs four times a week from Muscat to Khasab on the Musandam peninsula, dispensing with the need for travellers to pass through UAE territory. The journey takes about five hours. Ferries were not carrying cars at the time of writing, although there are plans to change this in the near future.

All seats must be reserved in advance either through an accredited travel agent or with the National Ferries Company by email or phone (email: reservations@nfcoman. com, tel: 800 72 000, toll free); you collect your ticket from the booth at Sultan Qaboos Port one hour prior to departure.

OMAN

THE UAE

LANGUAGE

ACCOMMODATION

HOTELS, RESORTS AND DESERT CAMPS

Oman musters a reasonable spread of accommodation, although significantly less than in the UAE, and options outside Muscat and Salalah are limited. Offerings range from a string of four- and five-star beachside resort hotels (most of them rather dated, apart from a few spectacular establishments in Muscat), usually going for around US$80–100 per night and up, and more functional, but much cheaper, one- to three-star city-centre hotels aimed at locals and businesspeople (roughly US$40–80). Discounts are often available at resort hotels during the quieter summer months. Hotel prices are subject to a 17 percent government tax, which is sometimes included in quoted prices, but not always – if in doubt, check.

Camping

There are no official campsites in Oman, although opportunities abound for wild camping in the mountains, deserts and along the remoter stretches of coast. Camping equipment can be bought in Muscat, although it makes sense to bring your own.

ABOVE: the lobby of The Chedi in Muscat.

MUSCAT AND AROUND

Al Bustan Palace Hotel
Al Bustan
Tel: 2479 9666
www.albustanpalace.com
Set on its own bay on the southern edge of Muscat, the Al Bustan is the city's most famous hotel, an opulent exercise in contemporary Arabian kitsch – the spectacular interior atrium is a sight in its own right. Huge, beautifully tended grounds, a long stretch of private beach and magnificent scenery add to the appeal, as do a clutch of gorgeous eating and drinking venues. **££££**

Barasti
Oman Dive Center
Bar al Jissah
Tel: 2482 4240
www.omandivecenter.com
Set around a sandy bay not far from the Shangri-La Barr Al Jissah Resort, with accommodation in traditional *barasti* (palm-thatch) huts – pleasantly modern and comfortable inside despite their rustic appearance – opening directly onto the beach. Good licensed restaurant attached. An appealing alternative to the city's more mainstream hotels. **£££**

The Chedi
Off 18 November St, Ghubra
Tel: 2452 4400
www.GHMhotels.com
Oman's most stylish place to stay, this very cool hotel mixes Asian designer Zen with a dash of Arabian chintz to create a uniquely peaceful and tranquil atmosphere. Facilities include a gorgeous spa and superb pool, along with a pair of very smooth restaurants, including The Beach, with tables set out on the sand right next to the waves. **££££**

Crowne Plaza, Muscat
Al Qurm St,
Qurm Heights
Tel: 2466 0660
www.cpmuscat.com
Probably the best location of any hotel in the city, perched on top of a cliff overlooking the sands of Qurm beach. The hotel itself is a little dated, and rooms on the small side, although rates are often extremely competitive, while excellent facilities include good Iranian and Italian restaurants, attractive English-style pub and attractive gardens and pool. **££££**

Dawhat al Adab St
Next to Hotel Muscat Holiday, Khuwair
Tel: 2448 9890
www.ibishotel.com.
Functional chain hotel, aimed firmly at business travellers, with simple but attractive modern rooms at bargain rates, plus restaurant (unlicensed), business centre and gym. **£££**

Grand Hyatt
Off As Sarooj St,
Hayy as Saruj
Tel: 2464 1234
www.muscat.grand.hyatt.com
One of Oman's most spectacular five-stars. The rather ugly exterior is designed to resemble a kind of Yemeni castle, while the opulent interior is a riot of Arabian chintz, with huge chandeliers, soaring golden pillars, palm trees and Bedu tents. Outside there are attractive (if rather small) gardens with a nice strip of public beach at the end, while in-house facilities include Muscat's best selection of dining and drinking venues, including the excellent Tuscany restaurant, chic John Barry Bar and lively Copacabana nightclub. **££££**

Haffa House Hotel
Ruwi St,
Ruwi
Tel: 2470 7207
www.shanfarihotels.com
Perhaps the nicest of the various three- and four-star business hotels dotted around Ruwi, with cosy rooms and attractive decor. Also quieter than similar places thanks to the lack of in-house bar or live music, although there is a simple restaurant (unlicensed). **£££**

InterContinental
Al Kharjiyah St,
Shati al Qurm
Tel: 2468 0000 (UK reservations: 0870 400 9650)
www.ichotelsgroup.com
Right next to the beach, this large hotel attracts a mix of tourists and business travellers, with an excellent range of amenities including spacious gardens, two pools, health club, dive centre and an above-average selection of eating and drinking venues. **££££**

Majan Continental Hotel
Al Ghubrah St,
Ghubrah
Tel: 2459 2900
www.majanhotel.com
Medium-sized, pleasantly old-fashioned hotel with a range of rooms, including 10 family apartments with cooking facilities, several restaurants, swimming pool and pool hall. Rates include breakfast. **£££**

Marina Hotel
Muttrah Corniche
Tel: 2471 3100
A slightly more upmarket alternative to the nearby budget hotels, with good service and comfortable rooms, many with wonderful harbour views. Also home to the popular Al Boom restaurant and a couple of live-music bars. **££**

Naseem Hotel
Muttrah Corniche
Tel: 2471 2418
Easily the best of the string of budget hotels lining the Muttrah Corniche, in a briliantly central location close to Mutrah Souk. Rooms (some with wonderful harbour views) are past their best but well looked after, backed up by excellent service and very competitive rates. **££**

Ramee Guestline
Al Qurm St,
Qurm Heights
Tel: 2456 4443
www.rameehotels.com
Functional modern hotel offering reasonable value in a good location near Qurm Beach. Facilities include a pool, a pair of good North and South Indian restaurants, a pair of live-music bars and the Rock Bottom Café, one of the liveliest nightlife venues in town. **£££**

Shangri-La Barr al Jissah Resort and Spa
Tel: 2477 6666
www.shangri-la.com/muscat
This vast resort comprises three hotels (the family-centred Al Waha, the business-oriented Al Bandar, and the ultra-luxurious Al Husn), set along a kilometre of attractive private beach south of the city, although the sheer size of the development can make the whole place feel a bit overwhelming. The various buildings are attractively done out in Arabian style, and there's a vast array of facilities, including assorted pools, children's play areas, a fine spa and replica "Omani Heritage Village" and shopping mall, as well as Muscat's finest array of eating and drinking venues. Turtles can also often be seen nesting on the beach here. **££££**

PRICE CATEGORIES

Price categories are for a standard double room in high season:
£ = under OR15
££ = OR15–40
£££ = OR40–100
££££ = more than OR100

BATINAH REGION (MUSCAT TO SOHAR)

Al Sawadi

Al Sawadi Beach Resort
Tel: 2679 5545
www.alsawadibeach.com
Old-fashioned resort hotel, looking rather dated but still a pleasant enough place to hole up for a day or two, with a long swathe of beach and the Sawadi Islands just offshore. The main reason to come here, however, is to make the journey out to the nearby Daymaniyat Islands – diving and snorkelling trips can be arranged through the excellent in-house dive centre. ££££

Barka

Al Nahda Resort & Spa
4km (2½ miles) inland from Barka Roundabout
Tel: 2688 3710
www.alnahdaresort.com
Spacious and very chilled-out resort (although it is some 8km/5 miles from the actual coast), with extensive grounds and pool, as well as an extensive range of spa treatments, including Balinese, Thai, Indian and Ayurveda treatments. Very convenient base for exploring the Rustaq Loop and Batinah Coast. ££££

Buraymi

Al Buraymi Hotel
Tel: 2564 2010
The most upmarket of the various hotels in Buraymi has large and comfortable rooms, a small pool in the rather lacklustre gardens, and a passable restaurant (licensed). £££

Seeb

Al Bahjah Hotel
Wadi al Bahais Street
Tel: 2442 4400
www.rameehotels.com/seeb-hotels.html
Comfortable, old-fashioned hotel right in the thick of the colourful Seeb souk. Facilities include a good in-house Indian restaurant plus various live-music bars. Guests can also use the pool at Al Bahjah's sister resort, the rather drab Dream Resort, just outside town. ££

Sohar

Sohar Beach Hotel
Tel: 2684 1111
www.soharbeach.com
One of the nicest hotels in northern Oman, this attractive four-star sits right on the beach at the northern edge of Sohar, with attractive rooms arranged either side of the handsome gardens and pool and a main building (designed to resemble an Omani fort) with pleasant public areas plus a couple of restaurants and bars. £££–££££

DHAKILIYA REGION (NIZWA, BAHLA AREA)

Jabal Akhdar

Jabal al Akhdar Hotel
Saih Katenah
Tel: 2542 9009
www.jabalakhdharhotel.com
Situated high up in Jabal Akhdar, this is a great place to hole up for a night or two and makes an excellent base for walks or drives around the Saiq Plateau. Rooms are clean and pleasant, and there's a cosy licensed restaurant. Advance bookings during the winter strongly advised. ££–£££

Jabal Shams

Jabal Shams Resort
(signed as "Travelling and Camping Centre")
Tel: 9938 2639 (mobile)
www.jebelshamsresort.com
Not far from the summit of mighty Jabal Shams, occupying a breezy mountain location with accommodation in a range of pleasant modern chalets, some with stunning views, and a neat little restaurant (unlicensed). You can also bring your own tent and camp here for a small fee, while staff can provide information about the various magnificent walks nearby. £££

Nizwa

Al Diyar Hotel
Tel: 2541 0500
www.aldiyarhotel.com
Plain but reasonably pleasant modern hotel, the closest accommodation to the centre of Nizwa (which is about 2.5km/1½ miles down the road), with spacious rooms, a small room and reasonable in-house restaurant (unlicensed). ££–£££
Falaj Daris Hotel
Tel: 2541 0500
www.falajdarishotel.com
Easily the nicest hotel in Nizwa, around 4km (2½ miles) from the centre, in a fort-like battlemented building with discreet Omani touches. The cosy rooms are arranged around two attractive courtyards, while facilities include a pair of pools, and the best restaurant and only bar in town. £££
Golden Tulip Nizwa
Tel: 2543 1616
www.goldentulipnizwa.com
Nizwa's most upmarket option, this rather glum four-star stands in a cheerless setting 18km (11 miles) from Nizwa next to the main road to Birkat al Mawz. Interior decor has all the charm of a large hospital, although rooms are comfortable enough and there's a decent pool and courtyard gardens, plus restaurants and various bars. £££–££££
Majan Guest House
Tel: 2543 1910
www.majangh.com
Neat hotel with clean and nicely furnished rooms, next to the main road some 5km (3 miles) from Nizwa. No facilities, although there are a couple of decent cafés close by. ££

SHARQIYA REGION (SUR AREA)

Ibra

Ibra Motel
Just north of Wadi Nam roundabout on north side of town
Tel: 2557 1666
Email: ibramtl@omantel.net.om
Simple but very comfortable budget hotel with bright and spacious modern rooms at very competitive rates. No facilities, although there are a couple of cafés nearby. £

Ras al Hadd

Ras al Hadd Beach Hotel
Tel: 2556 9111
Email: surbhtl@omantel.om
Functional hotel overlooking the coast, with bright and attractive rooms plus cheaper lodgings in a line of converted portable buildings in the hotel forecourt – slighty bizarre, but reasonably comfortable, if a bit pokey. The friendly staff can arrange boat trips on the lagoon or dolphin-spotting trips out to

sea, and there's also an in-house restaurant and bar. Good base for turtle-watching at Ras al Jinz. **££–£££**

Ras al Jinz

Ras al Jinz Visitors Centre
Tel: 9655 0606
www.rasaljinz-turtlereserve.com
The smart modern turtle-watching visitor centre at Ras al Jinz also offers excellent accommodation in its 14 comfortable modern rooms, although you'll need to reserve way in advance to get one. Room rates include half-board plus evening and morning turtle watches. **££££**

Sur

Sur Beach Hotel
Qalhat Road
Tel: 2554 2031
Email: surbhtl@omantel.om
2km (1¼ miles) from the centre of Sur, this old-fashioned but well-run

resort has comfortable rooms with sea views plus more upmarket villas, a small pool and a choice of no fewer than four themed bars. **£££**

Sur Plaza Hotel
Tel: 2554 3777
www.omanhotels.com
Mid-range hotel, popular with tour groups, with attractive public areas (but rather faded rooms), pool, gym, restaurant and the pleasant Captain's Bar with nautical decor. **£££**

Wahiba Sands

Desert Nights Camp
11km (7 miles) south of Al Wasil
Tel: 9281 8388
www.desertnightscamp.com.
The most luxurious of the Wahiba desert camps, offering a real dash of Arabian style and luxury in the desert, although at a considerable price. Accommodation is in a string of chalets modelled

ABOVE: Kargeen Cafe, Muscat.

after traditional Arabian tents, and there's also an attractive licensed restaurant and a nice bar. **££££**

Nomadic Desert Camp
20km (12½ miles) south of the village of Al Wasil
Tel: 9933 6273
www.nomadicdesertcamp.com
A long-established desert

camp deep in the sands, owned and operated by a local Bedu family. Accommodation is in simple but nicely furnished *barasti* huts, with shared bathroom only and no electricity, and there's an attractive *majlis*-cum-dining area. **££**

DHOFAR/THE SOUTH

Mirbat

Salalah Marriott Resort
Tel: 2326 8245
Gleaming five-star on the coast 10km (6 miles) east of Mirbat with attractive rooms and even nicer chalets dotted around the spacious gardens, which also come with a large pool and a rather rocky stretch of beach. Facilities include a couple of restaurants and bars, the soothing Frankincense Spa by Chavana and a dive cen-

tre. **£££–££££**

Salalah

Crowne Plaza Resort
Tel: 2323 5333 (UK reservations: 0870 400 9093)
www.crowneplaza.com/salalah
Old-fashioned but attractive resort, with spacious grounds and a lovely stretch of beach. Facilities include a decent selection of restaurants and bars; there's also an in-house dive centre, and

watersports can be arranged. Good value. **£££–££££**

Al Matar Street
Tel: 2329 5444
www.shanfarihotels.com
Large, functional city-centre hotel with spacious rooms and discreet Arabian touches, plus reasonable in-house restaurant (unlicensed) and coffee shop. **££**

Hilton Salalah
Tel: 2321 1234
www.salalah.hilton.com
Salalah's flashiest hotel,

with an excellent collection of eating and drinking venues, plus dive centre, although the grounds and beach aren't as nice as those at the Crowne Plaza, and rates are usually somewhat higher. **£££–££££**

Salalah Hotel
As Suq Street
Tel: 2329 5332
Excellent central location opposite the ONTC bus station, with clean and spacious rooms at a very competitive price. **£**

MUSANDAM PENINSULA

Golden Tulip Khasab
Tel: 2673 0777
www.goldentulipkhasab.com
Khasab's most upmarket offering, set on a breezy headland 3km (2 miles) from town and with fine views, although the resort itself is rather drab. Facilities include a nice pool, small spa, upmarket (but overpriced) restaurant

and Khasab's only bar, as well as an excellent dive centre. **£££**

Khasab Hotel
Tel: 2683 0267
www.khasabhotel.net
Attractive old-fashioned hotel, with spacious rooms surrounded by gardens, plus a pool and passable restaurant. **££**

Six Senses Zighy Bay

Zighy Bay, near Daba
Tel: 2673 5555
www.sixsenses.com
Ultra-luxurious boutique resort tucked away in a remote bay north of Daba, hemmed in by mountains along a lovely stretch of unspoilt beach. Accommodation is in quaint stone villas complete with private plunge pools and all

mod-cons, and there's also a top-notch spa. Very expensive. **££££**

PRICE CATEGORIES

Price categories are for a standard double room in high season:
£ = under OR15
££ = OR15–40
£££ = OR40–100
££££ = more than OR100

EATING OUT

RECOMMENDED RESTAURANTS AND CAFÉS

Places to Eat

Compared to the UAE, Oman doesn't have a particularly well-developed dining scene, and outside the capital you'll often struggle to find anywhere to eat beyond the usual down-at-heel coffee shops and cafés which dot the centres of most towns, serving up basic Arab-Indian fare (usually a predictable range of *shwarmas*, biryanis, low-grade curries and maybe some simple seafood). More upmarket dining options can be found almost exclusively in the pricier hotels, although these are often inconveniently located, unless you're actually staying there, and even in these the standards of cooking are often surprisingly poor. The exception to

the general rule is Muscat, which now has a reasonable array of restaurants serving a wide variety of international cuisines – for latest listings, see *Oman2day* or *Time Out Muscat*, on sale in bookstores.

Reservations are usually only necessary in the most upmarket establishments – we've given phone numbers where advance booking is advised. Children are generally made to feel welcome – Omani families usually eat out with kids in tow, who are normally allowed to stay up much later than their counterparts in the West. In more expensive places a 17 percent government tax applies (which includes an 8 percent service charge). This may be factored into the menu price, or may be added afterwards, in which case this

should be clear on the menu. If in doubt, check. Tips of 10 percent are sufficient, although if a service charge has already been added to the bill it's obviously up to you whether you want to make a further contribution – although you may want to bear in mind that the waiters themselves won't necessarily receive any of the 8 percent service charge.

Alcohol is usually only available in hotel restaurants, with a very small number of exceptions, and is typically at Western prices, or sometimes significantly above.

Code to Symbols

L after the price code (eg **££L**) indicates that the restaurant is licensed to sell alcohol; **U** denotes unlicensed premises.

BELOW: Indian restaurant, Muscat.

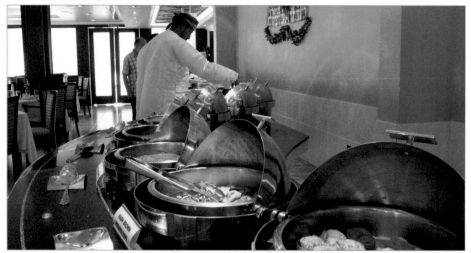

MUSCAT

Ghubrah

The Beach
The Chedi Hotel
Tel: 2452 4343
One of the most memorable places to eat in the open, located in an open-air pavilion on the beach, with the waves almost lapping against the tables – magical after dark, and with prices to match. Food is seafood fine dining, backed up by an oyster and caviar selection. Open for dinner only, apart from Friday brunch. **££££L**

The Restaurant
The Chedi Hotel
Tel: 2452 4343
The second of the Chedi's two restaurants, not quite as alluring as The Beach (see above) but still very fine. There are four separate kitchens here, serving up well-prepared Arabian, Asian, Indian and "Contemporary" (modern European/international) food, backed up by a huge wine list. Sit either indoors or in the beautiful palm-filled courtyard outside. **££££L**

Madinat Sultan Qaboos

Kargeen
Madinat Sultan Qaboos shopping complex, between Al Noor Plaza and Al Madine Plaza
Tel: 2469 2269
One of Muscat's most unusual and engaging places to eat, occupying a string of small buildings set amid large, shady gardens, with seating either inside or out. The huge menu offers a vast range of crepes, pasta, pizzas, steaks, seafood, sandwiches, grills and shwarmas, as well as some unusual Omani-style mains, including the classic shuwa. **££U**

Mutrah

Al Ahli Coffee Shop
Mutrah Souk
Lively little café tucked away inside the northern end of Mutrah Souk – perfect for a pitstop during an extended shopping trip. The menu features a big range of cheap sandwiches, burgers and shwarmas, plus more substantial dishes, and there is also a good range of juices and other drinks. **£U**

Al Boom
Marina Hotel, Mutrah Corniche
Tel: 2471 3100
Superb views of the Mutrah Corniche are the main draw at this small rooftop restaurant, with a huddle of tables crammed into the tiny outdoor terrace – arrive early to be sure of bagging a seat. Food is an unexceptional mix of Indian, Arabian, Chinese and Continental, plus some decent seafood dishes sourced fresh from the adjacent fish market. **££**

Fast Food 'n' Juice Centre
Mutrah Corniche, next to the souk entrance
Draws in steady crowds of tourists thanks to its prime corniche location, but worth paying the slightly inflated prices for the breezy harbourside views and people-watching opportunities. The menu features a big range of mainstream snacks, burgers, sandwiches and shwarmas along with more substantial grills, fish and pizza, plus juices, shakes and proper coffee. **££U**

Qurm and Shati al Qurm

Al Candle Café
On the beach behind the Grand Hyatt Hotel
Relaxed little beachside café, with sea breezes, coastal views and a very laid-back atmosphere. Popular after dark with local Omanis and other expat Arabs who come for the café's cheap shisha accompanied by Turkish coffee or Moroccan tea, while there's also a small but good menu of burgers, falafel sandwiches and a few grills. **£U**

Come Prima
Crowne Plaza Hotel
Al Qurm Street
Tel: 2466 0660
Cosy little Italian restaurant serving up a range of upmarket pasta and pizza plus more elaborate, modern Italian-style mains using fresh, authentic ingredients. **£££L**

D'Arcy's Kitchen
Jawharat A'Shati Complex
Tel: 2460 0234
Looking rather like an English country teashop, with chintzy decor and waitresses in frilly pinafores, D'Arcy's pulls in a loyal crowd of local expats for its hearty all-day breakfasts, sandwiches and soups alongside burgers, pastas and other mains ranging from fish and chips to stir-fries. **££U**

Jade Garden
Al Qurm Resort, behind the Jawaharat A'Shati Complex
Tel: 2460 5945
Cosy little restaurant attached to the tiny Al Qurm Resort and serving up a well-prepared selection of Thai and Chinese classics, alongside sushi, sashimi and teppanyaki. **££L**

Japengo
Al Shati Street, Qurm Beach
Tel: 9289 2868
In a prime beach front location midway along the main stretch of Qurm Beach, this attractive modern café serves up a shamelessly eclectic menu featuring everything from salads and sandwiches to sushi, pasta, pizza, stir-fries, Lebanese grills and fish and chips. Nothing outstanding, but reasonable value at the price. **££U**

Left Bank
Off Sultan Qaboos St, below Mumtaz Mahal (see below)
Tel: 2469 3699
Chic modern bar-restaurant, with seating on a stunning outdoor terrace overlooking the city below. Food is an eclectic range of international dishes – everything from fish and chips to curries – although prices are on the high side. There's also a good drinks list, including excellent cocktails. Alternatively, eat at the superior Mumtaz Mahal upstairs, then come here for a drink afterwards. **£££L**

Mumtaz Mahal
Near Qurm Natural Park
Tel: 2460 5907
The best Indian restaurant in Oman, perched on a hilltop overlooking Qurm Natural Park and with an airy dining room offering great views of the city below. The inventive menu features a mix of classic Mughlai and Punjabi dishes alongside some more unusual house specials and South Indian-inspired creations. Good wine list, plus superior live music Sun to Thur. **£££L**

Ruwi
Bin Ateeq
Markaz Mutrah al Tijari St
Tel: 2447 8225
Part of a nationwide chain (there's another branch in Al Khuwair, plus further outlets in Nizwa and Salalah), Bin Ateeq aims to recreate an authentic Omani dining experience, with seating in a string of self-contained, palm-walled individual dining rooms – you eat sitting on cushions on the floor, although the TVs detract

somewhat from the traditional ambience, and the rooms themselves are rather stuffy and, unless you're in a large group, not particularly sociable. Food features a decent, but not terribly inspiring, range of meat and fish curries plus assorted biryani-style dishes. A nice idea, although it just doesn't quite work. **££U**

Saravanaa Bhavan
Ruwi Street
One of Ruwi's classic budget Indian no-frills cafés (part of the global chain), offering excellent North and South Indian vegetarian cuisine at give-away prices. Usually crammed with local subcontinental expats – don't be surprised if you have to queue during busy periods. **£U**

Shiraz
Crowne Plaza Hotel
Tel: 2466 0660
This understated restaurant serves some of the best Iranian cuisine in town. Choose from a range of hearty kebabs, tasty *polos* (Iranian-style biryanis – exotic combinations including salmon and saffron, orange-flavoured chicken, and chicken and blackberry) and traditional "stews" (duck and pomegranate, shrimp and tamarind, green hammour). **£££L**

Tuscany
Grand Hyatt Muscat
Tel: 2464 1234
Regularly voted the best Italian in Oman, featuring quality authentic Italian cuisine served up under the direction of its

Piedmontese chef using a mix of authentic Italian ingredients alongside local seafood, plus a good selection of superior pasta dishes and wood-fired pizzas. **£££L**

Trader Vic's Restaurant
Intercontinental
Tel: 2468 0000
Part of an international chain, this Polynesian-themed restaurant is notable mainly for its party atmosphere, excellent drinks list (including killer cocktails) and live Cuban band (Sat–Tue). Food is an eclectic range of international dishes, although prices are a bit steep for what you get. **£££L**

Ubhar
Bareeq al Shati Mall
Tel: 8976 5555
Groundbreaking restaurant specialising in upmarket reworkings of traditional Omani classics, with dishes like camel biryani, fish *machbus*, *harees* (chicken with wheat), date ice cream and halwa in puff pastry. There's also a choice of mainstream pastas, burgers and sandwiches. **££U**

Woodlands
Bank al Markazi Street
Tel: 2470 0192
Attractive mid-range restaurant serving up superb South Indian cuisine, specialising in spicy Chettinad cooking from Tamil Nadu alongside a good selection of North and South Indian classics, as well as a reasonable wine list. **£££L**

Bait al Bahar
Tel: 2477 6565
Shangri-La Barr al Jissah Resort
Tel: 2477 6565
Soothing beachside restaurant with wonderful sea views through floor-to-ceiling windows and from the large rooftop terrace. Seafood is the order of the day, focusing on fresh local catch, attractively presented. Open for dinner only. **££££L**

Beach Pavilion
Al Bustan Palace
Tel: 2479 9666
Idyllic terrace restaurant hugging the waves on the superb beach at the Al Bustan Palace Hotel. Seafood is the speciality here, with a range of local and international offerings, although there are also some meat alternatives. Non-guests need to reserve in advance. **££££L**

Blue Marlin
Marina Bandar ar Rawdah
Tel: 2473 7286
In the smart Marina Bandar ar Rawdah, with terrace seating overlooking the posh yachts and an international menu featuring breakfasts, sandwiches, burgers and pasta dishes along with more elaborate seafood mains using catch sourced fresh from the Mutrah fish market. **££L**

Capri Court
Al Bandar Hotel, Shangri-La Barr al Jissah Resort
Tel: 2477 6565
Competing with Tuscany (see above) for the title of the best Italian in Oman, with an intimate dining room or tables on the

outside terrace and an upmarket mix of classic and contemporary Italian cuisine, plus excellent wine list. **££££L**

China Mood
Tel: 2479 9666
Beautiful Chinese restaurant with upmarket food – mainly Cantonese, along with a few Szechuan dishes plus dim sum. **££££L**

Odyssey
Oman Dive Center
Tel: 2482 4240
Attractive beachside restaurant on a sunny outdoor terrace offering well-prepared pastas, salads and sandwiches alongside international meat and fish mains, including lots of daily specials. **££L**

Shahrazad
Al Husn Hotel,
Shangri-La Barr al Jissah Resort
Tel: 2477 6565
Very upscale Moroccan restaurant, specialising in indulgent tagines and other North African classics. Dinner only. **££££L**

Sultanah
A1 Husn Hotel, Shangri-La Barr al Jissah Resort
Tel: 2477 6565
One of the top restaurants in the country, with cruise-liner decor themed after the original *Sultanah*, which in 1840 became the first Omani ship to cross the Atlantic. Food is top-notch international fine dining, plus changing specials based on the day's "port of call". Excellent but predictably expensive wine list. Dinner only. **££££L**

OUTSIDE MUSCAT

Traveller's Oasis
Tel: 2558 3235
Popular pitstop for tour parties on the main road from Muscat to Sur, close to the Wahibah Desert, with passable, reasonably priced Arabic and Asian food. **££U**

Tropicana
Buraimi Hotel
Tel: 2565 2010
Pleasant hotel restaurant with seating either in the spacious interior or the gardens outside. Food comprises a passable range of Continental,

Chinese and Indian dishes – the last are probably your best bet. **££L**

Al Shamaliah
Khasab New Souk
The best of the various cafés thronging Khasab's new souk, with lively

outdoor seating always busy with locals and expats. Food comprises an inexpensive but above-average selection of the usual kebabs, *shwarmas* and fruit juices, as well as a decent range of meze, although the Chinese and Indian

options are less inspiring. £U

Nizwa

Al Fanar Restaurant
Falaj Daris Hotel
Tel: 2541 0500
Nizwa's best restaurant, with seating either inside the plain modern dining room or, much nicer, on the pretty poolside terrace outside. The menu features a good range of international cuisine, including Lebanese and a mix of well-prepared Indian, Chinese and Continental standards, plus a few Omani specials – try the tasty *kabsa dijaj* (although some nights only buffet food is available if the hotel is full). Licensed. **££U**

Al Masharef
Next to the Tanuf Residency on the southern edge of town
Lively Turkish restaurant serving up excellent grills and *shwarmas*, backed up by Lebanese-style pastries and fruit juices. Popular evening hangout with locals – a big screen is often set up for important football matches, drawing an enthusiastic crowd. **£U**

Al Zuhly Restaurant
Next to the main car park, opposite the entrance to the Meat and Fish souks
Classic Nizwari *shwarma* café, with views of the historic Nizwa skyline, clouds of smoke from the outdoor grills and a constant stream of locals driving up and honking their horns for in-car takeaways. Food features the usual meat and fish curries, masalas and biryanis, plus cheap chicken and beef *shwarma* sandwiches. **£U**

Baalbeck Restaurant
23 July Street
Tel: 2321 1234
Excellent and inexpensive Lebanese restaurant, with friendly staff, a sociable atmosphere and tasty meze, grills and *shwarmas* served up in generous portions. There's a

ABOVE: open-air restaurant, Shatti Al Qurm, Muscat.

handful of outside tables overlooking the street – although the quaintly rustic interior is every bit as nice. **££U**

Bin Ateeq
Tel: 2541 0466
Nizwa branch of the Oman-wide chain (see above). **££U**

Bin Ateeq, Salalah
23rd July Street
The most central of the three Salalah branches of the nationwide chain – see above. **££U**

Chinese Cascade
23rd July St
The best Chinese restaurant in southern Oman, with an attractively spacious dining room and a reliable range of moderately priced Cantonese classics. **££U**

Lialy Hadrmout Restaurant
Al Husn Souk
Right next to the lovely Al Husn Souk, this lively Yemeni-style outdoor café attracts a colourful crowd of turbaned locals, with a simple but succulent range of dishes (there's no menu) including chicken or beef rice or kebabs, all served with hummus and huge, round, doughy breads. A classic slice of Dhofari life. **£U**

Palm Grove
Hilton Salalah
Tel: 2321 1234
Attractively rustic open-air beachside restaurant offering a range of

Continental, Indian, Italian and Mexican dishes. Alternatively, head indoors to the hotel's Hilton Sushi, serving fine Japanese cuisine, or the more formal Sheba's steakhouse, with succulent cuts of prime US and Australian beef. **£££U**

Woodlands
Salalah Airport
Tel: 2320 4280
In the unlikely setting of Salalah's diminutive airport, this Salalah offshoot of the excellent Muscat original (see above) serves up the city best Indian cuisine (vegetarian only), specialising in spicy South Indian fare, but with a decent range of North Indian classics to boot. **£££L**

Seeb

Keranadu
Al Bahjah Hotel
Tel: 2442 4400
An unexpected haven of authentic Indian cooking in the low-key Al Bahjah Hotel. The restaurant specialises in spicy Keralan cuisine, while there's a good spread of North Indian classic as well, including a good vegetarian selection, plus a few Chinese and Continental options. **££L**

Sohar

Sallan
Sohar Beach Hotel
Tel: 2684 1111
Suave hotel restaurant

serving up a well-prepared selection of Continental, Chinese, Indian and Arabian mains, with seating either on the attractive candlelit terrace overlooking the gardens, or inside during hotter months. **£££L**

Sur

Al Rasagh
Sur Beach Hotel
Tel: 2554 2031
Decent range of international food including Continental, Chinese and Indian dishes – the last are probably the best. **££L**

Sur Sea Restaurant
Sur Souk, in the middle of town by the Sur Hotel
Lively little Omani café with tasty, bargain-basement food and a bustling atmosphere – the street-side terrace is great for people-watching. Food features the usual mix of quasi-Indian dishes and *shwarmas*, plus some Chinese and seafood options, all inexpensively priced. The Sur Beach Restaurant, directly opposite, is very similar, and just as good. **£U**

PRICE CATEGORIES

Price categories are per meal per person. See page 3 for code to symbols.
£U = under OR6
££U/££L = OR6–12
£££U/£££L = OR12–25
££££L = more than OR25

ACTIVITIES

THE ARTS, FESTIVALS, NIGHTLIFE, SPORTS AND SHOPPING

THE ARTS

Dance, Music and Theatre

There never used to be many scheduled cultural activities in Oman – even in Muscat – but that was set to change following the long-awaited opening of the new Opera House in the capital in late 2011. It hosts a range of opera and other musical, theatrical and cultural events.

Royal Oman Symphony Concert Series
www.facebook.com/
royalomansymphonyorchestra
The country's leading musical institution – has formerly performed mainly in the auditorium of the Al Bustan Palace Hotel, though is also likely to form a mainstay of the new Opera House – check their Facebook page for details of upcoming events.

French Embassy
Jamat ad Duwal al Arabiya St, Al Khuwair
Tel: 2468 1800
www.ambafrance-om.org
Hosts a regular programme of Western classical music recitals and other cultural events.

Art Galleries

Bait Muzna Gallery
Tel: 2473 9204
Old Muscat, next to Bait al Zubair
Located in a traditional Omani house, hosting exhibitions of artworks in a variety of media, mainly by local artists, or works by international artists with a local theme.

Al Madina Art Gallery
145/6 Al Inshirah Street, Madinat Sultan Qaboos
Tel: 2469 1380
More of a shop than a gallery, selling furniture, gift items and paintings.

Omani Society for Fine Arts
Tel: 2469 2090
Near Al Sarooj roundabout, Mutrah
http://omanifinearts.com/english/
society.html
Stages exhibitions, performances and talks.

Cinemas

Cinema information lines do not usually open until after 2pm. Children under 3 years of age are not permitted, and credit card purchases must be over RO5 (US$13). A mix of English, Arabic and Hindi films are shown. For current listings see the cinema website or a local newspaper.

Muscat area

Al Bahja Cinema
Seeb, Markaz Al Bahji Mall
Tel: 2454 0855
http://albahjacinema.net
City Cinema (Al Shatti Plaza)
Shati al Qurm (near Ramada Hotel)
Tel: 2460 7360
http://citycinemaoman.com
Ruwi Cinema
Tel: 2478 0380
Star Cinema
Ruwi
Tel: 2479 1641
City Cinema (Al Nasr Cinema)
Ruwi
Tel: 2483 1358
http://citycinemaoman.com

Sur

City Cinema
Al Wafi Plaza
Tel: 2554 0666
http://citycinemaoman.com

Sohar

City Cinema
Sohar Plaza
Al Waqaibah Street (next to Bank Muscat)
Tel: 2684 4962
http://citycinemaoman.com

FESTIVALS

For details of Islamic festivals, see the Islam feature on page 83.

Muscat Festival
Month-long festival, held from late January to late February, celebrating Oman's culture and history. It includes a wide range of shopping opportunities, and activities such as dance, magic shows, music and craft demonstrations. For more details, visit www.muscat-festival.com.

Salalah Tourism Festival (formerly the Khareef Festival)
This festival (mid-June to mid-Sept) celebrates the monsoon season when the southernmost tip of Oman transforms from a dry desert to a lush green carpet. Events include sport, dance, music and handicrafts sale. For more details, visit www.salalahfestival.com.

National Day Celebration
National Day is officially 18 November, Sultan Qaboos's birthday (although the actual date is often shifted by a few days for practical reasons). Various events are held around Muscat and coloured lights are strung along the main highway for the celebrations.

NIGHTLIFE

Western-style nightlife in Oman is extremely limited – even in Muscat. Drinking options tend to be restricted to hotel bars and restaurants. Bars come in three forms: English-style pubs, "sports bars" (often with live sport on TV and pool tables), and live-music bars, usually featuring Indian or Arabian live music (usually at absolutely deafening volumes) and nubile young ladies dancing around on stage in (by Omani standards) decidedly risqué costumes. In Muscat there are also a few fine (and very expensive) hotel bars, often with beautiful decor and accomplished live music.

For a taste of real Omani nightlife, head for the nearest souk and make like a native, cruising the shops and coffee shops, which usually stay busy until around 10pm.

ABOVE: a Muscat coffee shop at night.

Bars

As well as the places listed below, a few of the restaurants listed in Eating Out *(see page 242)* are also good places for a drink, including Left Bank, Trader Vic's and Al Boom.

Al Ghazal
InterContinental, Shati al Qurm.
Quintessential Muscat-style British pub (despite the very Arabian name), with wood-panelled interior, pool tables and live sport on TV. Live music nightly except Monday, plus quiz nights, pool and darts competitions and karaoke.

Copacabana
Grand Hyatt, Hayy as Saruj
The city's top nightspot, hosting resident and visiting international DJs playing an eclectic range of music from Arabian and Bollywood tunes through to rhythm and blues and hip-hop. For latest events, check their Facebook page. Closed Fri.

John Barry Bar
Grand Hyatt, Al Khuwair
Gorgeously chic little bar (and prices to match), with nautically themed decor complete with ersatz portholes, a ceiling covered in ships' rigging and

bar staff in sailors' uniforms. Live background music is provided by a jazz duo most evenings from around 9pm.

Long Bar
Al Bandar Hotel, Shangri La's Barr al Jissah Resort & Spa
Cool bar with contemporary Arabian decor and a good range of signature cocktails, plus the usual beer and spirits. Rarely crowded.

Piano Lounge
Al Bandar Hotel, Shangri-La's Barr al Jissah Resort & Spa
Very cool little bar, with svelte modern decor and resident cocktail pianist. Alternatively, head outside to the long outdoor terrace, with beautiful sea views.

Rock Bottom Café
Ramee Guestline Hotel, Qurm Heights
Downmarket but hugely popular pub-cum-nightspot, with a noisy crowd of under-dressed teenage drinkers and a testosterone-charged atmosphere, although the band's usually pretty good.

Safari Pub
Grand Hyatt, Al Khuwair.
This poky African-themed bar isn't particularly good for a drink but is one of the best places in the city for live music, provided by a regularly changing roster of international bands.

Serai Pool Bar
The Chedi, Ghubrah

Very chic outdoor bar next to The Chedi's beautiful canopied pool – you can also order a selection of food from neighbouring The Restaurant.

SPORTS

Participant Sports
Diving, snorkelling and watersports
The relatively untouched waters off Oman offer some of the best diving in the Middle East, with warm, clear water and excellent underwater flora and fauna – the main centres are at Muscat, the nearby Daminiyat Islands, Dhofar (particularly around Mirbat) and, especially, Musandam. The long coastline also offers excellent opportunities for watersports – a number of the dive operators listed below also offer watersports.

PADI-accredited dive schools (many of which also run snorkelling and boat trips) include:

Muscat
Bluzone Diving Marina Bander al Rowdha
Tel: 2473 7293, www.bluzonediving.com
Diving, snorkelling and sunset cruises. Bluzone also has a dive shop selling a decent range of gear.
Euro Divers
Capital Area Yacht Centre, Haramil (just north of Marina Bander al Rowdhah)
Tel: 2477 6042, www.euro-divers.com
Swiss-owned company, running diving, snorkelling and dolphin-watching trips.
Oman Dive Centre
Bandar al Jissah
Tel: 2482 4040, www.extradivers.info
Part of international Extra Divers chain. Also runs snorkelling and dolphin-watching trips.
Omanta Scuba
InterContinental, Shati al Qurm
Tel: 2469 3223, www.omantascuba.com

ABOVE: snorkelling at the Khawr Sham fjord in Musandam.

Recently opened dive centre boasting a fast catamaran that can get you to the Daminiyats in just one hour. Also runs boat trips, including dolphin-watching tours with snorkelling and lunch.

Al Sawadi
Extra Divers
Al Sawadi Beach Resort
Tel: 2679 5545, www.extradivers.info
Well-run diving and watersports centre, and the closest dive school to the superb Daminiyat Islands.

Musandam
Extra Divers
Golden Tulip Hotel, Khasab
Tel: 9987 7957, www.
musandamdiving.com
Musandam's top dive centre, running trips (diving and snorkelling) all around the nearby coast and *khawrs*.

Dhofar
Extra Divers
Marriott hotel, Mirbat
Tel: 9287 3560, www.extradivers-worldwide.com
Close to some of Dhofar's prime dive sites.
Sub Aqua
Hilton Salalah Resort
Tel: 9989 4032, www.subaqua-divecenter.com
Diving and snorkelling trips, mainly around Mirbat, and also Mughsayl. Also runs fishing and dolphin-watching tours.

Golf

Muscat area
Ghallah Wentworth Golf Club
Tel: 2459 1248
www.gwgc.net
This 18-hole course in a dramatic

BELOW: decorated pottery, Bahla.

mountain setting is currently being converted from sand to grass (the front nine are now green, with work on the back nine continuing).
Muscat Hills Golf & Country Club
Seeb, close to the airport
Tel: 2451 0065, www.muscathills.com
Championship-standard 18-hole course – and the first green course in Oman.
The Wave Golf Club
The Wave, Muscat (near the international airport)
Tel: 2453 4444, www.thewavemuscat.com
Superb new 18-hole links-style course designed by Greg Norman plus golf academy, which was due to open in December 2011.

Spectator Sports

Although Oman has a number of sports stadia, there are few high-profile events. The national football team normally plays at the stadium in Wattayeh. Powerboat racing takes place at the marina.
   Traditional spectator sports are horse racing and, on the southern Batinah Coast, bullfighting (bloodless, bull-versus-bull contests of strength). Matches start around 4pm during the winter in Barka and Seeb and are free.
Camel Racing
Held at tracks in Seeb, Salalah, the Interior and Batinal regions. Usually take place during public holidays and National Day celebrations. Free.
Rally Oman
www.omanauto.org
Oman's biggest motorsport event, held in January and February.
Tour of Oman
www.tourofoman.om
First held in 2010, this cycling event draws a strong field of international riders. Held over six days in February at various locations around Muscat and the Western Hajar.

SHOPPING

Shopping in Oman still revolves around the traditional souks that can be found in every town in the country – most famously at Mutrah in Muscat, Salalah and Nizwa, which serve as showcases of traditional Omani craftsmanship and produce ranging from antique *khanjars* and Bedu jewellery to *halwa*, rose-water and frankincense. Muscat also boasts a number of modern malls, although these are rare elsewhere in the country.

Frankincense and *Bukhoor*

Available in many different grades, depending on its place of origin. The best place to buy frankincense is Al Husn Souk in Salalah, although it can be found in souks all over the country. Frankincense is also used in traditional perfumes and *bukhoor*, a characteristic Omani creation made from fine wood chips doused in various oils and spices, and available in many different "flavours" – it looks a bit like tea. It's usually sold in distinctive little golden tubs and can be burnt in a frankincense burner.

Carpets and Handicrafts

Expensive Persian carpets are available from the large shopping centres. In the same shops you'll see chests and tables with brass detail from Pakistan and India.

Gold

Oman is one of the cheapest places to buy gold. The price is determined by the weight of the article. Mutrah Souk has a huge section of gold outlets and all the shopping centres contain specialist gold stores.

Khanjars

These are the curved daggers worn by Omani men. They have intricate designs, and the handles can be made from a variety of materials. The scabbard is made of silver. Styles vary, depending on the region in which they are made. The best places to get these are Mutrah or Nizwa souks.

Pottery

Bahla is the best place to buy typical Omani pots. If you're travelling on the road to Nizwa you will see pottery for sale at the roadside in Fanja.

Silver

Oman is famous for its silver, and you can find both old and new items in the shopping malls and Mutrah Souk. But buying antique silverware is not for the inexperienced, and you may be taken for a ride by the vendor.

Shops

Omani Craftsmen's House
Opposite Sabco Centre, Qurm, Muscat
Similar to the well-known Omani Heritage Gallery *(see below)*, selling good-quality

OMAN

traditional artefacts including pottery, incense burners and rugs.

Omani Heritage Gallery
Jawaharat A'Shati Complex, Shati al Qurm, Muscat
Traditional Omani handicrafts including Bahla pottery, Dhofari frankincense burners, woollen rugs, caps, coffee pots and modern jewellery.

Sabco Centre
Qurm, Muscat
This low-key mall (and shops in the surrounding streets) has one of the country's best collections of carpet and handicrafts shops, as well as a branch of nationwide Al Haramain Perfumes chain and an outlet for the opulent Amouage perfumerie.

Tahani
Jawaharat A'Shati Complex, Shati al Qurm, Muscat
Next door to the Omani Heritage Gallery and full of an intriguing range of quality antique Bedu jewellery, *khanjars*, coffee pots and *mandoos* (traditional Omani wooden chests), plus assorted Western antiques ranging from old box cameras to wind-up telephones.

ABOVE: Mutrah Souk, Muscat.

CHILDREN'S ACTIVITIES

Unlike the UAE, Oman has few attractions specifically aimed at children (although the Children's Museum in Muscat is worth a visit). The beach is likely to be the main attraction, although older kids will probably enjoy adventure activities like dune- and wadi-bashing, boat trips around Muscat and Musandam, dolphin- and turtle-spotting trips, and the chance to explore some of the country's fairy-tale forts and the spooky Al Hoota Cave – guaranteed to fire young imaginations.

SPECIALIST TOURS

Oman offers a wide variety of tours, ranging from gentle excursions by car to challenging hiking, climbing and caving. Many places in the country can be reached as day trips from Muscat, although it's strongly recommended to leave the capital for at least a night or two at some point to get a sense of how the rest of the country lives.

Mainstream tours generally feature a predictable mix of forts, museums, easily accessible wadis and other major tourist sights. There are also other operators offering more original and challenging activities which might

include any selection from a range of activities including dune- and wadi-bashing, camel safaris, turtle-watching, dolphin-spotting, dhow cruises, hiking, climbing, caving and so on.

Arabesque Travel
www.arabesque.travel
Long-established local travel agent under mixed Omani–British ownership offering various day and overnight trips from Muscat and Salalah, including Empty Quarter tours.

Arabian Sea Safaris
Tel: 2469 3223; www.arabiansea safaris.com
Boat tours (including glass-bottomed boat trips), dolphin-spotting, sailing and fishing.

Desert Discovery Tours
Tel: 2449 3232
www.desert-discovery.com
Range of standard and more adventurous tours, specialising in the Wahiba Deseert area.

Elite Travel and Tourism
Tel: 2448 5020
www.eliteoman.com
Wide range of activities, particularly on the water, including diving, fishing, watersports, kayaking, dhow cruises and trekking.

Empty Quarter Tours
Tel: 9938 7654
www.emptyquartertours.com
General country and city tours, specialising in the Wahiba Desert.

Gulf Leisure
www.gulfleisure.com
Adventure travel specialist, particularly good for game-fishing trips but also offering a range of wadi- and dune-bashing trips, mountain-biking, climbing, trekking and canyoning.

Holiday-In-Oman (Muscat Diving and Adventure Centre)
Tel: 2454 3022
www.holiday-in-oman.com
Oman's leading adventure tour company, run by the Muscat Diving and Adventure Centre and offering a huge range of activities including

mountain-biking, climbing, trekking, diving, canyoning and caving, along with more mainstream cultural tours and self-drive itineraries.

Khasab Travel and Tours
Khasab, Musandam
Tel: 2673 0464, www.khasabtours.com
The top tour operator in the Musandam peninsula, professionally run and with excellent guides for either dhow trips along the *khawrs* or 4x4 mountain safaris, as well as city tours of Khasab itself.

Mark Tours
Al Iskan Street, Ruwi
Tel: 2478 2727
www.marktoursoman.com
Wide choice of tours includes dhow cruises, dolphin- and turtle-watching trips, city tours, safaris, wadi-bashing and self-drive tours.

Musandam Sea Adventure Tourism
Khasab
Tel: 2673 0424
www.msaoman.com
Dhow cruises, mountain safaris and other excursions around the Musandam peninsula.

Oman World Tourism
Tel: 9943 1333
www.omanworldtourism.com
Hotel packages in Muscat plus various day tours and more adventurous camping trips.

Sun & Sand Tours
Tel: 9937 3928
www.sunsandtour.com
Range of 1–11-day tours covering every part of the country, including challenging hikes through Snake Gorge and around Jabal Shams, camel safaris in Wahiba Desert and an adventurous tour overland down the coast to Salalah.

Zahara Tours
Tel: 2440 0844
www.zaharatours.com
Large and reputable company offering a range of shorts tours in the vicinity of Muscat, plus a 10-day itinerary taking in Musandam and Salalah.

THE UAE

LANGUAGE

A – Z

A HANDY SUMMARY OF PRACTICAL INFORMATION, ARRANGED ALPHABETICALLY

A

Admission Charges

Museums and fort admission prices range from 500 baisa to OR3 (US$1.30–7.80), and galleries are free. Al Hoota Cave is OR5.500 (US$14) for adults and OR3 (US$8) for children aged 6–11; free for the under-6s. Public beaches are free to use. In general, hotels do not allow non-guests to use their beaches and pools.

B

Budgeting for Your Trip

Oman is not a cheap destination, and certainly not promoted to budget

BELOW: shop sign at Bahla Fort.

travellers. Tours are fairly expensive (between OR35/US$90 for a half-day city tour to over OR100/US$260 for a full-day wadi tour). Be sure to establish whether the charge you are quoted is per person or per vehicle. Hotels are also fairly expensive. Expect to pay OR30–70 (US$80–180) for a double room per night in a three- or four-star hotel. A good dinner at a mid-range restaurant is likely to cost OR7–15 (US$18–40) per person without wine.

Car-rental costs range from OR12 to 15 (US$31–40) per day and from OR25 to 65 (US$65–170) per day for a 4x4. Most car-rental companies include insurance, but do double-check exclusions.

C

Children

Most of the five-star hotels offer babysitting services and many have separate children's areas, although some limit the number of children staying at any one time. Most can provide cribs or children's beds but these should be requested when booking.

Major supermarkets carry baby and children's products, although you may not always be able to find Western brands – bring anything essential with you.

Climate

The best time to visit Oman is from October to March. The coolest months in Muscat are December and January when nights are cool and

daytime temperatures rarely go above 30°C (86°F). May to September is the "off season", when it is hot and humid except in Dhofar, where it rains during the monsoon. July and August are the hottest months, with temperatures sometimes hitting 50°C (122°F). Rainfall is rare (except during the Dhofar monsoon), but torrential when it does occur, often causing flash floods.

What to wear

For most of the year loose-fitting cotton or linen clothes are ideal to cope with the heat. From November to March a light jacket or jumper may be needed in the evening. Swimwear or revealing clothing should only be worn on the beach. Err on the conservative side for swimwear.

Visitors are expected to cover upper arms and legs. Capri pants, shirts and skirts or shorts below the knee are all acceptable. Sunglasses, sun cream and a hat are essential, as are boots if you want to explore the mountains.

Crime and Safety

Oman is one of the safest tourist destinations in the world. Crime is rare and rape is unknown. That said, theft is not unknown and it is sensible to observe the same sort of precautions as you would at home; in particular, lock your vehicle and never leave valuables in view of passers-by.

For up-to-date advice on security in the region, see www.fco.gov.uk or call: 0845 850 2829 (UK); US citizens see http://travel.state.gov.

Traffic laws in Oman are strictly upheld, and the legal blood-alcohol level for driving is close to zero.

Customs Regulations

Oman is a Muslim state, and Islamic customs are strictly observed. Non-Muslims can import alcohol, to a maximum of 2 litres per person.

Do not bring narcotics or obscene materials into Oman. There are severe penalties even for so-called soft drugs. Possession of cannabis, even in very small quantities, will incur a minimum 12-month prison sentence followed by deportation. It's also required that travellers carrying prescription drugs take a letter from their doctor explaining that the drugs are required for health reasons.

D

Disabled Travellers

Unfortunately, Oman is poorly set up for disabled travellers. Outside the top-end hotels in Muscat, few places have accessible rooms, and getting around also presents considerable challenges – none of the country's taxis or buses are equipped for disabled travellers. It is best to contact a reputable travel agent to discuss your requirements before travelling. Muscat Diving and Adventure Centre (www.holiday-in-oman.com) and Oman Travel (www.omantravel.uk.com) are two recommended operators for travellers with disabilities, while useful tips about visiting the country can be found at www.able-travel.com.

E

Electricity

220/240 volts AC, using UK-style plugs with three square pins. UK appliances will work directly off the mains; appliances with two-pin and/or round-pin plugs will require an adaptor (widely available from any supermarket), while US appliances may also require a transformer.

Embassies and Consulates

In the event of an emergency, contact your embassy or consulate in Muscat; most are located in the suburb of Hayy as Saruj near the Grand Hyatt Hotel.
Consulate of Canada
Tel: 2478 8890; www.international.gc.ca
Consulate of Ireland
Tel: 2470 1282

Emergency Services

Ambulance, fire and police, tel: 9999
Muscat Royal Oman Police, tel: 2473 6611 (Old Muscat), 2471 2211 (Mutrah), 2470 1099 (Ruwi)
Salalah Royal Oman Police, tel: 2329 0099

Embassy of United Arab Emirates
Tel: 2460 0302; email: uaeoman@omantel.net.com
Embassy of the UK
Tel: 2460 9000; www.ukinoman.fco.gov.uk
Embassy of USA
Tel: 2469 9771; www.oman.usembassy.gov

Etiquette

Generally, Oman remains very traditional. It's fine to wear shorts on the beach, but not in the shops. Women should wear garments that cover their upper arms and their legs down to the knee. Displaying the soles of the feet is seen as insulting.

When taking photographs of local people, especially women, always ask permission first. Taking photographs of military establishments and ministry and government buildings is not allowed.

Non-Muslims are not allowed to enter mosques (with the exception of the Sultan Qaboos Mosque in Muscat and the Sheikh Zayed Grand Mosque in Abu Dhabi, along with the Jumeirah Mosque in Dubai during regular tours). During Ramadan do not eat, smoke or drink in public.

G

Gay and Lesbian Travellers

Homosexuality is illegal. Although there is a large underground gay community, nobody discusses it or even admits it exists. Any display of public affection, such as hand-holding, is frowned upon, even between heterosexual couples.

H

Health and Medical Care

Make sure you have full medical insurance. No specific vaccinations are required for Oman except a compulsory certificate against yellow fever if coming from an infected area. However, typhoid and hepatitis A vaccinations are recommended, and you should ensure your tetanus and polio injections are up to date. It is advisable to seek medical advice, as requirements do change. Tap water is safe to drink in urban areas; mineral water is available everywhere.

Medical services

There are numerous pharmacies across the UAE, all of which should be able to produce at least one English-speaking pharmacist. All the major cities have at least one 24-hour pharmacy, many of them run by the Dubai-based BinSina chain – your hotel should be able to provide details of the nearest outlet. Note that some medicines which are available over the counter in the West may not be available in the UAE, while it also helps to know the generic name of any drug you might require, in case the particular brand you're used to purchasing at home isn't available. There are good hospitals in major towns and clinics elsewhere. Pharmacies are mainly open 9am–1pm and 4–9pm, and some open 24 hours. All the following hospitals have English-speaking staff; for a complete list of hospitals in Oman see www.moh.gov.om/contactus.htm.

Hospitals in Muscat

The Royal Hospital, tel: 2459 9000, www.royalhospital.med.om
Al Nahdha Hospital, tel: 2483 7800
Muscat Private Hospital, tel: 2458 3600, muscatprivatehospital.com
Al Raffah Hospital, tel: 2461 8900, www.asterhospital.com

Outside Muscat

Nizwa Hospital, tel: 2544 9361
Sur Hospital, tel: 2556 1372
Sohar Hospital, tel: 2684 0399
Sultan Qaboos Hospital, Salalah, tel: 2321 6100

I

Internet

There are plenty of internet cafés in Muscat, especially in Mutrah and Ruwi, and in Salalah. Elsewhere, however, you might struggle to get online unless you're staying in more upmarket hotels, all of which have internet access.

Media

Print

All media is government-controlled and censored, as are books and magazines entering the country. There are four daily English-language newspapers – the *Oman Observer* (main.omanobserver.om), the *Times of Oman* (www.timesofoman.com), the *Oman Tribune* (www.omantribune.com) and the *Muscat Daily* (www.muscatdaily.com). They contain good local news and sports results and their international news coverage has improved, too. UAE papers are also available, including *The National*, published in Abu Dhabi and easily the best local news source for the region (although still subject to censorship).

Oman2day (www.omantoday.co.om), a monthly English-language leisure magazine aimed at expats and visitors, is worth buying. Along with feature articles (often including some on exploring Oman independently), it contains a comprehensive dining guide and information on the latest happenings and events. Back issues are available on the website. The same publishing house also produces the monthly Business Today (www.apexstuff.com).

Broadcast media

All hotel rooms in Oman have TVs, often offering literally hundreds of satellite

ABOVE: postbox in Muscat.

channels from across the world, almost always including BBC World and CNN for latest news plus a variety of entertainment and film channels.

The country's only English-language radio station is Hi Fm (95.9 FM; hi.yourhifm.com), broadcasting mainstream Western pop and limp chat, although you can't usually pick it up outside Muscat.

Money

Credit cards are accepted in the major hotels, but in smaller hotels and restaurants it is advisable to check first. The best rates are from foreign exchange dealers.

Currency: Rial (OMR/RO) divided into 1,000 baisas. The Omani rial is pegged to the US dollar at an exchange rate of US$1 = OR0.385 (meaning that OR1 = US$ 2.60).

Tipping

A tip of 10 percent is considered the norm in restaurants, although some places add a service charge of 10 percent to the bill, in which case tipping is not strictly necessary. It is not usual to tip custodians at museums, forts and suchlike, who are usually Omani citizens rather than immigrant workers. Fares for taxis should be agreed before you get into the car – always haggle, it's expected.

Opening Hours

Oman runs on an Islamic rather than a Western schedule, with the working week running from Saturday to Wednesday (although some businesses also open on Thursday mornings). Friday is the Islamic holy day, equivalent to the Christian Sunday.

Bear in mind there are no standard opening times and that the following are offered as a guideline only. Government offices are open 8am–2.30pm Sat–Wed. Hours of private-sector businesses vary widely. Most open 8am–1pm and 4–7pm, though not all open in the afternoon. The majority of businesses are closed on Friday. Most large malls open 10am–10pm Sat–Thur and 2–10pm Fri. Smaller shops and supermarkets are open 8am–1pm and 4–7pm.

Souks are open 8am–1pm and 4–9pm except Mutrah Souk, which closes at 7.30pm.

Banks usually open 8am–2pm Sat–Wed and 8–11am Thur.

Photography

You should always ask permission before taking photographs of people, especially women ("*mumkin sura, min fadlak?*" to a man or "*mumkin sura, min fadlik?*" to a woman) – but don't be surprised if women say no. Digital imaging services are available at photo shops around the country.

Postal and Courier Services

There are post offices in larger towns all over the country, usually opening from 8am–1.30pm Sat–Wed and 8–11am Thur. In Muscat, the most convenient branch is the main post office in Ruwi, at the northern end of Markaz Mutrah al Tijari Street.

Couriers

DHL
Qurum City Centre, Qurum, Muscat
Tel: 2447 0403
Fedex
Sinaw House, Hamriya (opposite Al Nahdha Hospital)
Tel: 2483 3311
TNT International Express
GAC Building, Al Khuwair
Tel: 2447 7870

Public Holidays

There are eight public holidays in Oman. Three of these fall on fixed dates: New Year's Day (1 Jan), Renaissance Day (23 July) and National Day (18 Nov). The other five are all religious festivals with dates fixed according to the lunar calendar (falling approximately 11 days earlier year on year). These are: the Islamic New Year, the Prophet Mohammed's birthday (Mouloud), Ascension of the Prophet (Leilat al Meiraj), Eid al Fitr (end of Ramadan) and Eid al Adha (Feast of the Sacrifice). Christian expatriates are usually allowed Christmas Day off.

Religious Services

Catholic Church of St Peter and St Paul, Darsait, tel: 2470 1893
The Protestant Church in Oman, Darsait, tel: 2479 9475
Salalah Christian Centre, Salalah, tel: 2323 5677/5727

T

Taxes

The Oman tax rate is 17 percent, which consists of municipality and tourism tax and service charge. Most prices are quoted inclusive of taxes, although not always – if in doubt, check.

Telephones

Calling from your hotel room is likely to be expensive. It is considerably cheaper to make calls home from public phone booths, although these can be hard to find (and noisy, too). Phone cards are available from supermarkets for both local and international calls. A good alternative is to bring your own mobile phone and buy a local SIM card – the main telecoms operator, Nawras, has shops nationwide wide and sells SIM cards for as little as OR3; local and international rates using a Nawras card are likely to be much lower than using your own SIM card from home.

The country code for Oman is 968. Oman telephone numbers are all eight digits, with no area codes. Muscat numbers begin with 24, Salalah with 23. Mobile numbers are also eight digits long, beginning with a 9. To phone overseas from Oman, dial 00 followed by the national code of the country you are calling. For directory assistance in Oman call 1318. Alternatively, look online at www.businessdirectoryoman.com or www.omantel-yellowpages.com.

Time Zone

GMT + 4 hours, BST + 3 hours, EST + 9 hours, PST + 12 hours.

Toilets

Public toilets are scarce. More upmarket shopping malls usually have facilities, as do the majority of museums, forts and other tourist attractions. Otherwise your best bet is to head for the nearest hotel.

Tourist Information

Tourist information offices do not exist in Oman. For information, your best bet is to try a local tour operator. Neither are there any proper Oman tourist offices overseas. In the UK, tourist enquiries are handled by PR company Representation Plus in London (tel: 020-8877 4524, email: oman@representationplus.co.uk).

Tour Operators

A number of companies operating from the UK arrange holidays, tours and activities.

Abercrombie & Kent, UK tel: 0845-618 2203, www.abercrombiekent. co.uk; USA tel: 800 554 7016, www. abercrombiekent.com.

Destination Oman, tel: 0844-482 1672; www.destinationoman.co.uk

Gane & Marshall, tel: 01822-600 600; www.ganeandmarshall.co.uk

Indian Ocean & Arabian Gateways, tel: 0161-437 4371; www.gateways.co.uk

Kuoni, tel: 01306-747002; www. kuoni.co.uk

Odyssey World, tel: 01453-883 937; www.odyssey-world.co.uk

Responsible Travel, tel: 01273-600 030; www.responsibletravel.com/ holidays/oman

Shaw Travel, tel: 01635-47055; www.shawtravel.co.uk

Steppes East Travel, tel: 01285-880 980; www.steppestravel.co.uk

Tropical Sky, tel: 0844-332 9371; www.tropicalsky.co.uk

The Ultimate Travel Company, tel: 020-7386 4646; www. theultimatetravelcompany.co.uk

Voyages Jules Verne, tel: 0845-166 7033; www.vjv.com.

V

Visas and Passports

A valid passport is required to enter Oman, plus a visa. The type of visa issued depends, in part, on your nationality, as does its cost.

Visitors from the UK, USA, Ireland, Australia and New Zealand (and many other countries: see www. omanairports.com/visaonarivals.asp – note the misspelling of "arrivals"; the correct spelling doesn't work) arriving at Muscat International Airport can obtain a tourist visa upon arrival. This can be purchased at the Travelex Foreign Exchange bureau in the immigration arrivals hall. The desk is directly in front of you as you enter the terminal. Most currencies are accepted for payment, or you can pay by credit card. Once you have paid the OR20 (around US$55) an automatic receipt will be issued; this must be presented at the immigration desk.

The tourist visa is a single-entry visa valid for one month. However, your passport must have a validity period of not less than six months after your arrival.

ABOVE: magazines on sale in Nizwa.

Residents and their families

Most people residing in a GCC (Gulf Cooperation Council) country, relatives and those travelling with them, do not need to obtain a visa to enter Oman. However, if you have members of your family travelling at a separate time, written authorisation and identification documents must be submitted.

Arriving from Dubai

Oman, Dubai and Qatar operate a common visa facility. This means visitors who already have a valid visa for Dubai or Qatar do not need to get a separate visa for Oman subject to the conditions listed at www. omanairports.com/visaonarivals.asp.

W

Weights and Measures

Oman employs the metric system.
1 inch = 2.54 centimetres (cm)
1 foot = 0.30 metres (m)
1 mile = 1.61 kilometres (km)
1 pound = 0.45 kilograms (kg)
1 American gallon = 3.79 litres (l)
1 British gallon = 4.5 litres

Women Travellers

Oman is a pretty safe place for women travelling alone, but you should still observe normal precautions. Have your shoulders and knees covered at all times. This is not law but it shows respect, and as women are stared at all the time, it makes sense to avoid unwanted attention by leaving tight-fitting or revealing clothing behind. Women do wear sleeveless tops in bars and clubs, but wear a pashmina or shawl around your shoulders until you are inside. Women get honked at when walking around, which should just be ignored.

TRANSPORT

GETTING THERE
AND GETTING AROUND

GETTING THERE

By Air

Dubai is now the Middle East's major air hub, served by most of the big international carriers and with non-stop connections to cities through Europe and Asia (as well as a few places in North America). Abu Dhabi is also increasingly well connected. Sharjah also has a sizeable airport, serving mainly other destinations around the Gulf or in the Indian subcontinent.

Abu Dhabi, tel: 02-575 7500, www. abudhabiairport.ae/english
Dubai, tel: 04-216 2525, www. dubaiairport.com
Sharjah, tel: 06-558 1111, www. sharjahairport.ae
There are smaller airports at:
Al Ain, tel: 03-785 5555
Fujairah, tel: 09-222 6222, www. fujairah-airport.com
Ras al Khaimah, tel: 07-244 8111, www.rakairport.com
Major airlines in the UAE:

Air India, tel: 02-633 4766 (Abu Dhabi), 04-227 6787 (Dubai); www. airindia.in
British Airways, tel: 02-622 5777 (Abu Dhabi), 04-307 5555 (Dubai); www.britishairways.com
Emirates, tel: 600 55 55 55; www. britishairways.com
Etihad Airways, tel: 02-599 0000; www.etihadairways.com
Gulf Air, tel: 02-651 6888; www. gulfair.com

By Ship

Arrival by ship is far less common than by plane, although a fair number of cruises stop at Dubai on their way around the Gulf.

By Train or Bus

There are no trains in the UAE apart from the Dubai metro. There are daily bus services from Muscat and Salalah in Oman.

By Car

The city and inter-emirate roads are well planned and well maintained, and are mainly dual carriageways. Visas are issued to citizens of many nationalities (including most Western countries) on the spot – if in doubt, check with your nearest UAE Consulate or Embassy (see page 273).
To Oman You can fly to Muscat, or go by bus or car from Dubai, but note that if driving a UAE hire car into Oman you'll need to take out additional insurance from your rental agency. Visitors from Western countries can obtain a visa on arrival at Muscat Airport or at the various border crossings from the UAE. If in doubt, contact the Omani Consulate in Bur Dubai, Dubai (behind the Indian Consulate, tel: 04-397 1000).

GETTING AROUND

On Arrival

There are buses and taxis available from the airports, or you can hire a car. If you are with a tour group or being met by a hotel, they will provide a free bus to your accommodation.
Abu Dhabi Bus No. 901 runs between the airport and the main bus station, 24 hours, costs Dhs3. Airport and ordinary taxis are also available. Check the fare in advance. The airport is located on the mainland, approx 40 minutes' drive from the city centre.
Al Ain The airport is on the Abu Dhabi Road, approximately 20km (12½ miles) from the centre. Bus No. 500 runs every 30 minutes, 24 hours a day. Bus No. 130 is another option. Both take approximately one hour. Airport taxis are more expensive than ordinary metered taxis.
Dubai The airport is approximately 20

BELOW: the cost of hiring a car is relatively low.

minutes from the city centre. Buses No. 401 and 402 run between the airport, Deira and Bur Dubai. Airport taxis are more expensive than ordinary metered taxis, and taxi fares are higher to Bur Dubai across the Creek.

Sharjah The airport is approximately 15km (9 miles) from the centre. There are no buses, so get a metered taxi to the town centre or to nearby Dubai.

Ras al Khaimah The airport is 23km (14 miles) from the centre. Take a taxi.

Fujairah The airport is located south of the city. Metered taxis only.

On Departure

There is no airport departure tax and the UAE's duty-free shops are some of the best in the world, so it's worth getting to the airport early. The UAE is an excellent point of transit for other destinations. Many airlines and tour operators transit through Dubai.

Public Transport

Public transport in the UAE is mainly by taxi or bus (except in Dubai, which now has its own metro system). Getting around the country's various cities is usually easiest by taxi. These are generally cheap and now metered in most emirates, and can either be called for by phone or (more usually) flagged down on the street. Women should always sit in the back of a taxi. Buses connect the various emirates.

Abu Dhabi

Bus The main bus terminal is on Al Sharqi Street, about 3km (2 miles) east of the city centre, with regular services to Dubai, Al Ain and Sharjah. Taxis are much more convenient for short trips, as bus routes cater for those living in outer suburbs and workers' camps outside the city.

Taxi All taxis should now have meters, but make sure the driver turns it on when you start the journey. You can call a cab from various companies, including Al Ghazal Taxi Service, tel: 02-444 7787, Cars Taxi, tel: 02-551 6164 or National Taxi, tel: 02-555 2212. The minimum fare is Dhs3, with Dhs1 added for every kilometre.

Al Ain

Bus Buses run regularly to Abu Dhabi and Dubai from the bus station behind the Al Ain souk.

Taxi All taxis should have meters, but, as ever, make sure the driver turns it on as you leave. Radio cabs can be summoned from Al Ghazal Taxis, tel: 03-751 6565, or Al Ghazal Express, tel: 03-766 2020.

ABOVE: a cruise ship in Abu Dhabi.

Dubai

Almost all public transport in Dubai – metro, buses and waterbuses (but not *abras*) is covered by the Nol integrated ticket system (www.nol.ae). You'll need to get a prepaid Nol card before you can use any of these forms of transport. Cards can be bought (or topped up) at any metro station, at numerous bus stops, or at branches of Carrefour, Spinneys, Waitrose and the Emirates NBD Bank. There are four different types of card/ticket. The Red Ticket has been specially designed for visitors, costing just Dhs2, although this has to be topped up with the correct fare before each journey and can only be recharged 10 times; you might prefer to invest in a more flexible Silver Card (Dhs20, including Dhs14 credit), which stores up to Dhs500 of credit and lasts five years.

Metro Dubai's state-of-the-art metro system (www.rta.ae) has revolutionised travel within the city since opening in 2009, making getting around large parts of the city far easier – and cheaper – than before. The system comprises a mix of overground and underground lines, with bright modern stations, although the popularity of the system means that it's often surprisingly difficult to get a seat. The only line currently open is the Red Line, which runs from Rashidiya via the airport and old city and then down through Karama and along Sheikh Zayed Road all the way to Jabal Ali, at the far southern edge of the city. A second line, the Green Line, opened in September 2011, providing a useful loop around the old city centre through Deira and Bur Dubai. Trains run approximately every 10 minutes from 6am to midnight Saturday to Wednesday, 6am to 1pm Thursday and 1am to 1pm Friday. Fares start at around Dhs2 up to Dhs7 in standard class, or from around Dhs4 to Dhs14 in the superior Gold Class, which offers slightly plusher carriages.

Bus Catering mainly to the needs of lower-income expat workers, Dubai's bus service isn't generally very useful for Western visitors for trips within the city. For trips to other emirates, there are regular and reliable services from Al Ghubaibah Bus Station in Bur Dubai to Abu Dhabi, Al Ain, Sharjah and (less frequently) Hatta.

Taxi This remains the best way of getting around parts of the city that the metro has not yet reached. Cabs are metered, air-conditioned, mostly reliable and can be flagged down on the street or pre-booked. Taxis from the airport start with the meter at

BELOW: catching a bus at night.

ABOVE: taxis in Abu Dhabi.

Dhs20, though in the city, meters start at Dhs3. The main operators are Dubai Taxi (tel: 04-208 0808), Cars Taxis (tel: 04-800 269 2900), Metro Taxi (tel: 04-600 267 3222) and National Taxis (tel: 04-600 339 0002).

Waterbus or _Abra_ Dubai is split in two by the Creek, which can be crossed (most memorably) by _abra_, or waterbus. Air-conditioned waterbuses serve various points on the Creek, costing Dhs4 per return journey (no single fares available), payable only with a Nol card. They're much less enjoyable than the city's _abras_, however, and at double the price have little to recommend them.

Sharjah

Bus Regular services to Dubai leave from the bus stand on Al Arouba Street, not far from the Blue Souk.
Taxi Most Sharjah taxis are now metered; it's probably best to avoid unmetered taxis – if not, make sure you agree the fare in advance. Metered taxi companies are Emirates Taxis, tel: 06-539 6666, Citi Taxis, tel: 06-533 4444, Sharjah Taxi, tel: 06-568 8444, and Union Taxi, tel: 06-532 5555.

Ajman

There is no bus service or taxi stand, although you should have little problem flagging down a taxi on the street to take you to Sharjah.

Umm al Qaiwain

Taxis only, from the stand on King Faisal Street across from Al Salam Hotel.

Ras al Khaimah

Bus Sporadic bus services connect RAK City with Ajman, Sharjah and Dubai.
Taxi Metred taxis (flag fare Dhs2.5; Dhs0.75 per km) can be flagged down on the street. Shared taxis leave from the stand near the Cove Rotana Resort, some 7km (4 miles) from the town centre, travelling to Umm al Qaiwain, Ajman, Sharjah and Dubai.

Fujairah

Bus Occasional buses connect Fujairah City with Dubai.
Taxi Metered taxis (flag-fare Dhs2.5; Dhs0.75 per km). Shared taxis leave from the stand on the Dubai/Sharjah road some 5km from the centre, for Sharjah and Dubai.

Private Transport

The UAE has a very modern road system, but the general standard of driving is poor and characterised by impatience and carelessness. Lane discipline is bad and reckless driving common. Once out on the main highways cars travel fast. Roads are mainly dual carriageway (two-lane), well signposted and in good condition. Authorities are trying to improve road safety through the use of traffic cameras monitoring speed offences.

Be aware that the penalty for drink-driving is a month in jail. It is illegal to use a mobile phone when driving, and seat belts are compulsory for drivers and front-seat passengers. Any accident, however minor, must be reported to the police. In most of the emirates you must not move the car until the police arrive. In Dubai, cars can be moved to the side of the road if they are blocking traffic and if the accident is not serious. Always wait with the car for the police.

Inter-Emirate Travel

This is unrestricted and easy by road. It is advisable to carry your papers on you while travelling in the UAE: there are no checkpoints or passport controls to go through between emirates, but occasionally the police do spot checks on the road for illegal immigrants or alcohol, although this is rare. Inter-emirate buses provide another option.

Car Hire

Hiring a car makes travelling around much easier. Most car-hire companies will accept foreign licences. Hire costs are relatively low, and there is fierce competition between companies, so a good bargain can usually be found. For insurance reasons, visitors can only drive rental cars; a temporary licence from the police is needed if you wish to drive a privately owned vehicle.

Car-hire companies

Avis
Abu Dhabi, International Airport arrivals terminal 1, tel: 02-575 7180
Dubai, International Airport arrivals terminal 1, tel: 04-224 5219
Fujairah, tel: 09-222 5384
Sharjah, International Airport arrivals, tel: 06-558 0655
www.avis.com

Budget
Abu Dhabi, International Airport terminal 3, tel: 02-599 8969
Dubai, International Airport, tel: 04-282 2727
Ras al Khaimah, Al Hamra Hotel and Beach Resort, tel: 07-244 6666
Sharjah, International Airport, tel: 06-558 0366
www.budget.com

Europcar
Abu Dhabi, tel: International Airport terminal 3, tel: 02-599 8958
Dubai, International Airport terminal 3, tel: 04-220 3933
www.europcar.com

Hertz
Abu Dhabi, International Airport terminal 1, tel: 04-224 5222, terminal 3 tel: 04-220 3013
Dubai, tel: 02-599 8939
www.hertz.com

Sixt
Ras al Khaimah, tel: 07-235 5888
www.sixt.com

Thrifty
Abu Dhabi, tel: 02-445 5011
Dubai, tel: 04-224 5404
www.thrifty.com

Rules of the road

Drive on the right-hand side of the road. No right turns at lights.
Speed limits are normally 60kph (37mph) in town and 120kph (75mph) on highways.
Speeding tickets are often issued automatically by camera, without the driver knowing. Car-rental agencies claim these from you.
Always carry your driving licence and car registration card with you.

ACCOMMODATION

HOTELS, YOUTH HOSTELS, BED AND BREAKFAST

Luxury and the UAE have become almost synonymous. Dubai boasts some of the best hotels on the planet, while Abu Dhabi also has a clutch of top-quality places to stay, including the vast Emirates Palace. Outside these places, however, options are significantly more limited, although all the emirates (apart from Umm al Qaiwain) now boast at least one five-star. Prices in these places usually start at around US$125–150 a night, climbing up to well over US$1,000 at the very best places.

Cheaper options are thinner on the ground, and you'll be pushed to find anywhere in the country for under US$75 a night. There are lots of cheap hotels in Bur Dubai and Deira in Dubai (mostly charging US$75–100 a night), plus a few in Abu Dhabi – functional, although almost always clean and comfortable, if all you want is a bed for the night.

The price guide in this section gives an indication of the rates per night charged for two people sharing a standard double room during peak season (November to April). Prices do vary according to season – rates at tourist resorts often fall considerably over the hot summer months. An extra charge of 15–20 percent (tax and service) is usually added, so it is worth checking whether this has been included in the price you are quoted.

Camping

There are no official campsites in the UAE, but it's possible to camp almost anywhere in the desert and mountain areas. It is better not to camp too close to a village or town, and to beware of camping or driving in wadi beds during the rainy season. Camping equipment is widely available, although it makes sense to bring your own.

BELOW: in the grounds of the opulent Emirates Palace Hotel.

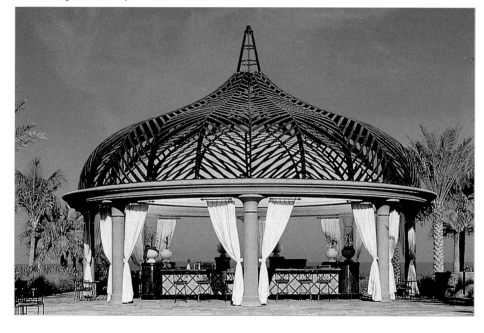

ABU DHABI

Al Ain Palace Hotel
Corniche
Tel: 02-679 4777
www.alainpalacehotel.com
One of the oldest hotels
in Abu Dhabi, although
renovations have kept it
fresh inside. The above-
average facilities include
a wide selection of in-
house bars and restau-
rants and a big pool.
£££

Al Diar Regency
Meena Road, Tourist Club
Area
Tel: 02-676 5000
www.aldiarhotels.com
Part of the Al Diar chain,
which runs a string of
inexpensive hotels across
the city – the nearest
thing to budget accommo-
dation you'll find in Abu
Dhabi, and with surpris-
ingly good amenities given
the price, including a good
selection of restaurants,
plus pub, gym, sauna and
massage treatments. The
central location is another
plus. See the website for
details of their various
other hotels and apart-
ments around the city.
£–££

Beach Rotana Hotel
10th St, Tourist Club Area
Tel: 02-697 9000
www.rotana.com
Email: beach.hotel@rotana.
com
This stylish modern resort
is one of the nicest places
to stay in the city, in the
heart of downtown next to
the Abu Dhabi Mall, with
attractive beach and gar-
dens and an excellent
selection of places to eat
and drink. **£££**

Crowne Plaza
Tel: 02-621 0000
www.ichotelsgroup.com
Functional business hotel
in the middle of town – a
slightly more upmarket
(and expensive) alterna-
tive to the nearby Novotel.
£££

Emirates Palace Hotel
Tel: 02-690 9000
www.emiratespalace.com
An iconic city landmark,
this ultra-luxurious hotel is

one of the top addresses
in the Gulf, spread over a
kilometre of private beach
and with every imaginable
luxury and a vast range of
amenities, including many
of the city's top restau-
rants. **£££**

Hilton
Corniche
Tel: 02-681 1900
www.hilton.co.uk/abudhabi
The oldest five-star in the
city, and beginning to look
its age. Plus points include
the hotel's above-average
spread of dining and
drinking options, while you
can access a decent
stretch of private beach
via the Hiltonia Beach
Club across the road.
£££

Hilton Baynunah
Corniche
Tel: 02-632 7777
www.hilton.com
Aimed at a mainly busi-
ness clientele, this soaring
blue-glass tower holds a
mix of hotel rooms and
long-stay apartments,
many with superb views.
Limited facilities, although
it does boast the city's biggest indoor pool, plus
health club. **£££**

**InterContinental Abu
Dhabi**
Al Bateen
Tel: 02-666 6888
www.intercontinental.com
One of the classier hotels
in town, in an attractively
peaceful setting on the
west side of town
(although also quite a
way from the downtown
action). Attractive rooms
come with fine views
over the city or swanky
marina below, and
there's also an enor-
mous pool and one of
the nicest hotel beaches
in the city. **£££**

Le Méridien
10th St, Tourist Club Area
Tel: 02-644 6666
www.lemeridien.com/
abudhabi
Old-fashioned but still
attractive resort in an
excellently central loca-
tion, complete with nice

gardens, a small stretch of
beach and a huge collec-
tion of restaurants.
£££

Le Royal Méridien
Khalifa St, Al Markaziyah
Tel: 02-674 2020
www.lemeridien.com/
royalabudhabi
Smart 275-room tower
hotel, overlooking the corniche, with wonderful
views from the revolving
restaurant, Al Fanar. Not
actually on the beach,
although there are attractive gardens inside, plus
indoor and outdoor pools.
£££

Millennium Hotel
Khalifa St
Tel: 02-614 6000
www.millenniumhotels.com
Aimed at business and
local travellers, with
chintzy decor and way too
much marble.
Competitive room rates
and the central location
compensate, while good
facilities include a pool,
several attractive restaurants, plus cigar and
champagne bar.
£££

Novotel Centre Hotel
Hamdan St
Tel: 02-633 3555
www.novotel.com
Functional but relatively
inexpensive lodgings right
in the middle of town
(although rates can soar if
there's a big conference or
exhibition on). Not much
in the way of facilities,
though, beyond a simple
restaurant and bar.
£££

Shangri-La
Qayrat al Beri al Maqta
Tel: 02-509 8888
www.shangri-la.com.
One of the most attractive
places to stay in town,
with lovely Moorish decor,
big gardens (complete
with four pools) and an
excellent spa, and restaurants – although the location, some 10km (6
miles) out of town close
to the Sheikh Zayed
Mosque, is inconvenient.
£££

Al Ain

Al Ain Rotana Hotel
Tel: 03-754 5111
www.rotana.com
The swankiest of Al Ain's
three five-stars, with spacious and attractive
rooms, extensive gardens
and a good selection of
restaurants. **£££**

Danat Al Ain Resort
Tel: 03-704 6000
www.danathotels.com
Old-fashioned five-star
(formerly the
InterContinental) in a very
peaceful location a few kilometres outside town –
nothing to set the pulse
racing, although rates are
often the cheapest in
town. **£££**

Hilton Al Ain
Tel: 03-768 6666
www.hilton.co.uk/alain
Dated five-star, although
rates are often very com-
petitive, and the spacious
gardens and pools are
ideal for idle lazing. **££**

**Mercure Grand Jebel
Hafeet**
Tel: 03-783 8888
www.mercure.com
Perched close to the sum-
mit of the tower Jabal
Hafeet, with stunning
views of the desert and
mountains – although
often surprisingly chilly. All
the usual five-star facilities, although it's the location which is the real draw.
££

Sir Bani Yas Island

**Anantara Desert Islands
Resort and Spa**
Tel: 02-801 5400
http://desertislands.anantara.
com
Very exclusive bolthole on
the remote Sir Bani Yas
Island, accessible by seaplane only and offering
luxurious accommoda-
tion in the Arabian-
themed hotel plus
sweeping sea views,
infinity pool, a very
upmarket spa and a
range of activities including mountain-biking, hik-
ing and kayaking.
£££

DUBAI

Al Maha Resort
Dubai–Al Ain Road (E66)
Tel: 04-832 9900
www.al-maha.com
Dubai's first eco-tourism resort – not so much a hotel as a Bedu desert encampment of 30 ultra-luxurious "tents" deep inside the Dubai Desert Conservation Reserve. Activities include camel riding, falconry displays and desert safaris. £££

Arabian Courtyard Hotel and Spa
Al Fahidi St, Bur Dubai
Tel: 04-351 9111
www.arabiancourtyard.com
Overlooking the Dubai Museum, this attractive four-star could hardly be better positioned for forays into the old city centre. Inside, there are attractive rooms with Arabian touches and some good eating and drinking spots. ££

Armani Hotel
Burj Khalifa, Downtown Dubai
Tel: 04-888 3888
http://dubai.armanihotels.com
Occupying the lower floors of the Burj Khalifa, the world's first Armani hotel offers pretty much the last word in designer minimalism – expensive, although not quite as stratospheric as you might expect. £££

Atlantis
Palm Jumeirah
Tel: 04-426 2000
www.atlantisthepalm.com
Vast mega-resort at the far end of the Palm Jumeirah – easily the most over-the-top place to stay in the city. Not as stylish as many other Dubai five-stars, although the vast array of facilities, including water park, dolphinarium, huge beach and dozens of restaurants and bars, compensate. £££

Bab al Shams Desert Resort & Spa
Endurance City
Tel: 04-809 6100
www.meydanhotels.com
Beautiful Arabian-style resort in the desert some 37km (23 miles) from Dubai located in a lovely cluster of traditional buildings – a good, and significantly cheaper, alternative to the Al Maha Resort if you want to experience some desert luxury. £££

Burj al Arab
Umm Suqeim
Tel: 04-301 7777
www.burj-al-arab.com
A stay in this iconic "seven-star" hotel offers the last word in opulence, with every mod-con and indulgence you could imagine (and several you probably couldn't), ranging from remote-control curtains to "pillow menus". Suites are huge, butlers come as standard and the whole place screams luxury – although at an inevitably stratospheric price. £££

Dubai Marine Beach Resort and Spa
Jumeirah Road, Jumeirah
Tel: 04-346 1111
www.dxbmarine.com
At the northern end of Jumeirah, Dubai Marine is the closest beach resort to the city, with attractive rooms in low-rise villas in a landscaped compound fronting onto a small beach. Also home to some of the city's posiest nightspots, including Sho Cho's and Boudoir. £££

Dusit Thani
Sheikh Zayed Road
Tel: 04-343 3333
www.dusit.com
Striking Sheikh Zayed Road landmark, designed to represent two hands pressed together in the traditional Thai *wai* greeting. Inside, the Thai-owned Dusit has plenty of understated style and the pretty Benjarong, one of the best Thai restaurants in this part of the city. ££

Fairmont Dubai
Sheikh Zayed Road
Tel: 04-332 5555
www.fairmont.com
Located at the northern end of Sheikh Zayed Road, the Fairmont is one of the most luxurious hotels along the strip, with plush rooms, a fancy spa

ABOVE: Jumeirah Beach Hotel.

and a pair of fourth-floor pools. The space-age interior boasts the popular Spectrum On One restaurant and Exchange Grills restaurants. £££

Four Points Sheraton Bur Dubai
Khalid Bin al Waleed Street, Bur Dubai
Tel: 04-397 7444
www.four_points.com/burdubai
Right in the heart of the old city, this comfortable and competitively priced four-star makes an excellent base for exploring Bur Dubai and Deira and boasts good facilities, including the lovely Antique Bazaar restaurant and cosy Viceroy Pub. ££

Golden Sands
Off Al Mankhool Street, Bur Dubai
Tel: 04-355 5553
www.goldensandsdubai.com
A vast number of pleasant self-catering studios and apartments, scattered over 11 separate buildings in the Al Mankhool area of Bur Dubai – often some of the cheapest lodgings in town, if you don't mind forgoing traditional hotel facilities. £–££

Grand Hyatt
Oud Metha
Tel: 04-317 1234
www.dubai.grand.hyatt.com
Vast hotel (the second-biggest in the city), centrally located between airport, Deira and Sheikh Zayed Road, and within walking distance of Wafi. Extravagant public areas, stunning city views from many rooms, plus an excellent spread of places to eat. £££

Grosvenor House
Dubai Marina
Tel: 04-399 8888
www.grosvenorhouse-dubai.com
One of the most alluring hotels in the Marina – not actually on the beach, although guests can use the beach facilities at the nearby Royal Méridien Beach Resort. The style is slick urban cool, while amenities include the snazzy Bar 44 at the top of the building and a selection of excellent restaurants. £££

Hilton Dubai Creek
Deira
Tel: 04-227 1111
www.hilton.co.uk/dubaicreek
The most stylish hotel in Deira, designed by architect Carlos Ott with stylishly soothing rooms and vast quantities of chrome in the foyer. Facilities include Gordon Ramsay's Verre restaurant and a breezy rooftop pool. £££

Hilton Dubai Jumeirah
Tel: 04-399 1111
www.hilton.co.uk/dubaijumeirah
Smart resort-hotel – although not as good for families as other places along the beach. £££

Ibis World Trade Centre
Sheikh Zayed Road/World Trade Centre
Tel: 04-332 4444
www.ibishotel.com

PRICE CATEGORIES

Price categories are for a standard double room in high season:
£ = less than Dhs500
££ = Dhs500–800
£££ = more than Dhs800

ABOVE: Madinat Jumeirah.

This simple but comfortable four-star is perhaps the best-value hotel in the city, although rooms can get booked up quickly if there's a big event on at the Dubai International Exhibition Centre next door. **££**

Jumeirah Beach Hotel
Umm Suqeim
Tel: 04-348 0000
www.jumeirahbeachhotel.com
One of the best beachside hotels in Dubai, this stunning wave-shaped hotel boasts superb architecture, excellent family facilities, superb grounds and a plethora of restaurants and bars. **£££**

Jumeirah Emirates Towers Hotel
Sheikh Zayed Road
Tel: 04-330 0000
www.jumeirah.com
Occupying the smaller of the two landmark Emirates Towers, and regularly voted the top business hotel in the Middle East. Rooms come with stylishly understated decor and wonderful views, while there's a superb array of restaurants and bars either in-house or in the attached Emirates Boulevard. **£££**

Le Royal Méridien Beach Resort & Spa
Dubai Marina
Tel: 04-399 5555
www.leroyalmeridien-dubai.com
Huge grounds and beach, vast pools and a good spread of leisure amenities make this one of the best family hotels in the city, although it lacks the style of other places nearby, and eating and drinking venues are rather uninspiring. **£££**

Mina A'Salam
Madinat Jumeirah, Umm Suqeim
Tel: 04-366 8888
www.madinatjumeirah.com
Grand Arabian-themed hotel with superb Moorish decor and architecture and excellent facilities (as well as being attached to the Madinat Jumeirah, with its many shops, restaurants and bars). The nearby Al Qasr hotel is similar but even more opulent. **£££**

One & Only Royal Mirage
Dubai Marina
Tel: 04-399 9999
www.oneand_only_royalmirage.com
One of Dubai's most romantic places to stay, this gorgeous Moroccan-styled resort sprawls along the beach for the best part of a kilometre, with fabulous decor, thousands of palm trees and a string of superb restaurants and bars. **£££**

The Palace
Emaar Boulevard, The Old Town Island, Downtown Dubai
Tel: 04-428 7888
www.theaddress.com.
The centrepiece of the quaint "Old Town" development, this sumptuous little hotel boasts opulent traditional Arabian styling and unrivalled views of the adjacent Burj Khalifa and Dubai Fountain. **£££**

Park Hyatt
Dubai Creek Golf & Yacht Club, Garhoud
Tel: 04-602 1234
www.dubai.park.hyatt.com
Rivalling the nearby Raffles for the title of the city centre's top place to stay, this idyllic city retreat occupies a sprawl of Moroccan-style buildings spread along the Creek between the Dubai Creek and Golf clubs, with gorgeous Arabian styling and superb views. **£££**

Radisson SAS Deira Dubai Creek
Baniyas Road, Deira
Tel: 04-222 7171
www.deiracreek.dubai.radissonsas.com
Formerly the InterContinental, this is the oldest five-star in Dubai and still one of the most appealing options in the old city, with plush decor, a superb selection of in-house restaurants and a very central location. **££–£££**

Raffles
Sheikh Rashid Rd, Oud Metha
Tel: 04-324 8888
www.raffles.com
Spectacular hotel housed in a giant pyramid, with a mix of quirky Egyptian theming and cool Asian designs, plus superb facilities including huge gardens, a gorgeous spa and some excellent restaurants and bars. **£££**

The Ritz-Carlton Dubai
Dubai Marina
Tel: 04-399 4000
www.ritzcarlton.com
A little bit of Andalusia in the Gulf, the low-lying, hacienda-style Ritz-Carlton has 138 rooms, all sea-facing. Much quieter than the larger beach resorts which surround it, although ongoing expansion may change that. **£££**

Shangri-La
Sheikh Zayed Road
Tel: 04-343 8888
www.shangri-la.com
The most appealing hotel on Sheikh Zayed Road, set in a towering, Gothamesque structure at the southern end of the strip. Inside the hotel is a model of Zen cool, with beautiful rooms (many with outstanding views) and a string of excellent restaurants. **£££**

XVA Hotel
Bastakiya
Tel: 04-353 5383
www.xvahotel.com
The only place in Dubai where you can stay in an authentic traditional house, with just a handful of rooms in this traditional old Bastakiya mansion (which doubles as an art gallery and excellent café). Rooms are smallish but full of character, and you're just footsteps from the myriad restaurants, bars and other attractions of Bur Dubai. **£–££**

Hatta

Hatta Fort Hotel
Tel: 04-852 3211
www.hattaforthotel.com
Pleasantly old-fashioned resort with fine views of the surrounding mountains, set in attractive gardens with a pool. Gets busy at weekends, but deliciously quiet at other times. **££**

SHARJAH

Note that alcohol is not served in any hotel in Sharjah emirate.

Beach Hotel
Tel: 06-528 1311
www.mhgroupsharjah.com
Port Road, Al Khan area.
Old-fashioned beach resort with a big pool, a nice strip of sand and basic facilities. **£**

Radisson Blu Sharjah
Tel: 06-565 7777
www.radissonblu.com/resort-sharjah
The top address in town,

on the coast, about 2km (1¼ miles) from the centre, with stylish modern rooms, a fine stretch of sand and a decent selection of cafés and restaurants. **£££**

Sharjah Carlton Hotel
On Port Road, Al Khan
Tel: 06-528 3711
www.mhgroupsharjah.com
One of the oldest hotels in town, although still a comfortable and inexpensive

place to stay if you want to be by the sea. Decent pool and other basic facilities. **££**
Sharjah Rotana Hotel
Al Arouba Street
Tel: 06-563 7777
www.rotana.com/

sharjahrotana
Sharjah's top business hotel, bang in the city centre, with attractive modern decor – although not much in the way of eating or drinking venues. **££**

AJMAN

Kempinski Hotel Ajman
Tel: 06-714 5555
www.ajmankempinski.com

Very peaceful resort 10 minutes' drive north of Sharjah, with relaxing gardens and a

superb stretch of sand plus attractive modern rooms and good facilities,

including spa and fitness centre, watersports and children's club. **£££**

UMM AL QAIWAIN

Flamingo Beach Resort
Tel: 06-765 0000
www.flamingoresort.ae

Pleasant, no-frills resort – nothing fancy, although offers good watersports,

as well as other activities and facilities including fishing, crab-hunting and

boat trips through local mangrove swamps, along with an Ayurvedic spa. **££**

RAS AL KHAIMAH

Al Hamra Fort Hotel
Between Ras al Khaimah and Umm al Qaiwain
Tel: 07-244 6666
www.alhamrafort.com
Luxury resort designed in the form of a traditional Arabian fortress, with accommodation either in hotel rooms or garden villas, a long stretch of pristine beach, activities including watersports, golf and kids' activities, and a good selection of restaurants and bars. **£££**
Fujairah Rotana
Al Aqah Beach
Tel: 09-244 9888
www.rotana.com

Sprawling resort on the lovely Al Aqah Beach – although it manages to feel pleasantly peaceful despite its size, with extensive grounds, spacious pool and plenty of sand to relax on. Accommodation is in crisp modern rooms, and there is also a good spa, plus diving and watersports centres. **£££**
Hilton Ras al Khaimah
Tel: 07-228 8888
www.hilton.com
RAK City's only international-standard hotel, close to the city centre, with a fine beach and attractive

ABOVE: Fujairah Rotana.

interiors featuring Moorish touches. Facilities include a Turkish hammam (steam

baths) and spa treatments, plus a good range of in-house restaurants. **££**

EAST COAST

Hilton International Fujairah
Tel: 09-222 2411
www.hilton.co.uk/Fujairah
Top option in Fujairah City, on its own fine stretch of private beach (with pleasant terrace Breezes restaurant). The rooms and interiors are attractive activities include watersports and diving. **££**
Le Méridien al Aqah
Beach Resort
Al Aqah Beach
Tel: 09-244 9000

www.lemeridien-alaqah.com
Huge high-rise resort hotel backed by the Hajar mountains – a dramatic, if incongruous, sight – offering top-notch five-star style, including spa, dive centre and kids' club, plus spacious gardens and private beach. **£££**
Oceanic Hotel, Khor Fakkan
Corniche Road, Khor Fakkan
Tel: 09-238 5111
www.oceanichotel.com
Long-established

east-coast stalwart looking a bit like a 1970s spaceship. Decidedly dated now, although current renovations will hopefully upgrade standards. There's also a dive school here, although no alcohol is served, since Khor Fakkan is actually part of Sharjah emirate. **££**
Sandy Beach Hotel
Al Aqah Beach
Tel: 09-244 5555
www.sandybm.com

Attractive low-key alternative to the nearby Le Méridien, with relaxing oceanfront accommodation in either hotel rooms or beach chalets, plus diving and watersports centres. **££**

PRICE CATEGORIES

Price categories are for a standard double room in high season:
£ = less than Dhs500
££ = Dhs500–800
£££ = more than Dhs800

EATING OUT

RECOMMENDED RESTAURANTS AND CAFÉS

A Note on Drinking

You cannot buy alcohol for home consumption in the UAE unless you hold an alcohol licence, which are only issued to non-Muslims with residence visas. However, alcohol is served in hotel bars and restaurants in most of the emirates, apart from Sharjah. There are many excellent pubs, bars and clubs (see page 267).

ABOVE: chef at Bord Eau.

WHAT TO EAT

Dubai has established itself as the Middle East's leading culinary destination, attracting a string of top international chefs, while Abu Dhabi's dining scene is also developing by leaps and bounds. Both cities offer plenty of top-notch international dining, with cuisines from around the world, often in memorable settings (and with prices to match). Arabian food is, of course, particularly excellent and well represented, and you might occasionally come across some local Gulf specialities (see page 89).

Elsewhere in the country, things are a lot less developed, and you'll often be struggling to find anything more than basic cafés serving up simple *shwarmas* or biryanis except in the few upmarket hotels.

Not that you have to spend a fortune to eat well. Streetside *shwarma* stands can be found all over the place, turning out tasty meals for less than a couple of dollars, while there are also hundreds of good and usually extremely cheap curry houses aimed at expat Indians and Pakistanis, particularly in places like

Bur Dubai and Karama in Dubai.

Alcohol is generally only served in hotel restaurants (and is banned entirely in Sharjah). It usually pays to reserve in advance at more upmarket places – we've provided phone numbers where reservations are advised. Major credit cards are accepted in all upmarket hotels.

Code to Symbols

L after the price code (eg **££L**) indicates that the restaurant is licensed to sell alcohol; **U** denotes unlicensed premises.

ABU DHABI

Al Fanar
Le Royal Méridien, Al Markaziyah
Tel: 02-674 2020
Balanced atop the roof of Le Royal Méridien hotel, Al Fanar revolving restaurant offers unrivalled views of the city below, backed up with well-prepared modern

European meat and seafood creations. **£££L**
BiCE
Hilton Hotel, Corniche
Tel: 02-681 1900
Abu Dhabi branch of the much-loved Dubai restaurant, serving up fresh and inventive classic and modern Italian fare, including

pastas, pizzas, risottos, plus meat and seafood mains. **£££L**
Bord Eau
Shangri-La Hotel
Tel: 02-509 8888
One of the best restaurants in town, serving up top-notch modern French haute cuisine, beautifully

presented, in a rather stately European-style dining room. Open dinner only. **££££L**
Emirates Palace Café
Emirates Palace Hotel, Ras al Akhdar
Tel: 02-690 7999
The magnificent lobby of the landmark Emirates

Palace provides a suitably memorable setting for superb high teas, served either in traditional English or Arabian styles. **£££L**

Finz
Beach Rotana Hotel, Tourist Club Area
Tel: 02-697 9011
Often voted the best seafood restaurant in town, with a range of fresh fish and seafood served up in an eclectic variety of international styles. Seating either inside or on the pleasant waterside terrace. **£££L**

Hakkasan
Emirates Palace Hotel
Tel: 02-690 7999
Super-swanky restaurant with opulent decor and the city's best Chinese cuisine, ranging from classics like tofu claypot to more contemporary creations like black pepper

BELOW: mint tea in style at the Grand Hyatt Hotel.

wagyu beef. **££££L**

Hanoi
Khalifa Sreet, Al Markaziyah
Tel: 02-626 1112
Excellent Vietnamese establishment, more of a café than a restaurant, but with superbly spicy and authentic cooking – vermicelli salads, chilli-salted squid and so on – at extremely modest prices. **££U**

India Palace
Al Salam St, Tourist Club Area
Tel: 02-644 8777
Abu Dhabi institution, always lively, and serving up a decent range of North Indian meat and veg curries and tandooris. **££U**

Indigo
Beach Rotana Hotel, Tourist Club Area
Tel: 02-697 9011
Suave Indian restaurant, with superior decor and a nice selection of North Indian classics, along with a few seafood options and assorted vegetarian dishes. **£££L**

Lebanese Flower
Off 26th St, Al Khalidiya
One of the city's most popular Lebanese restaurants, with a pleasantly rustic interior and a good selection of tasty grilled meat and fish dishes, plus assorted *meze*. **£U**

Mezzaluna
Emirates Palace
Tel: 02-690 7999
Suave restaurant specialising in contemporary

ABOVE: the interior of Al Nafoorah.

Italian and Mediterranean cuisine – and one of the more affordable of the Emirates Palace's many bespoke eating venues (though still far from inexpensive). **££££L**

Ocean
Le Royal Méridien, Al Markaziyah
Tel: 02-674 2020
Specialising in international seafood, with a range of ocean-fresh fish and crustacea prepared in a range of international styles, plus a decent selection of meat dishes. **£££L**

Rodeo Grill
Beach Rotana Hotel, Tourist Club Area
Tel: 02-697 9011
One of the best steakhouses in Abu Dhabi, with prime cuts of US Angus and Australian wagyu along with other meat dishes and some seafood. **£££L**

Royal Orchid

Hilton Hotel, Corniche
Tel: 02-681 1900
An old Abu Dhabi favourite, offering a wide range of well-prepared and very reasonably priced Thai and Chinese food. **££L**

Soba
Le Royal Méridien, Al Markaziyah
Tel: 02-674 2020
Cool Asian restaurant serving up a range of Japanese, Malaysian and Thai meat and seafood mains along with good sushi and sashimi. **£££L**

Talay
Le Méridien, Tourist Club Area
Tel: 02-644 6666
Fine Thai cooking, with the emphasis on seafood backed up by a decent selection of meat and a few vegetarian options. Seating either in the stylish interior or on the breezy terrace outside. **£££L**

AL AIN

Al Mallah
Near Globe Roundabout
Excellent little Lebanese café serving up hearty *shwarma*, kebabs and good juices. **£U**

Min Zaman
Al Ain Rotana

Tel: 03-754 5111
Stylish Lebanese restaurant, with a good selection of authentic *meze* and grills, plus *shisha*. **££L**

Trader Vic's
Al Ain Rotana

Tel: 03-754 5111
Local branch of the Gulf-wide chain serving up reasonable international food, potent cocktails and a lively atmosphere. **£££L**

The Wok

Danat Al Ain Resort
Tel: 03-768 6686
Good selection of pan-Oriental dishes – dim sum, sushi, Thai curries, Malaysian-style *laksas* and stir-fries. **££L**

DUBAI

Al Dawaar
Hyatt Regency Hotel, Deira
Tel: 04-209 1234
On the 25th floor of the huge Hyatt Regency, Dubai's only revolving

restaurant offers stunning city views complemented by an upmarket (if rather expensive) international buffet. **£££L**

Al Mahara

Burj al Arab, Umm Suqeim
Tel: 04-301 7600
Centred on an enormous fish tank, this spectacularly designed subterranean seafood restaurant

OMAN

THE UAE

LANGUAGE

is one of Dubai's most expensive restaurants, with sumptuous international seafood. **££££L**

Al Makan
Souk Madinat Jumeirah
Tel: 04-368 6593
Located in atmospheric Souk Madinat Jumeirah, Al Makan offers a rare chance to sample authentic Emirati cuisine in a restaurant setting, along with a good selection of more mainstream Lebanese food and grills. Outdoor terrace seating overlooks Burj al Arab Hotel. **£££U**

Al Mallah
Al Diyafah St, Satwa
One of several lively Lebanese cafés along Al Diyafah Street, with a good range of inexpensive Middle Eastern *meze*, snacks and meals (including good grills and *shwarmas*) and plenty of seating on the pavement outside – a great place to watch the nightlife of Satwa roll past. **£U**

Al Muntaha
Burj al Arab
Tel: 04-301 7600
Next to the Skyview Bar at the very top of the Burj al Arab, 200 metres/yds above the Arabian Gulf, with fantastic views and excellent (and inevitably expensive) modern European cuisine. **££££L**

Al Nafoorah
Emirates Towers, Sheikh Zayed Road
Tel: 04-319 8088
The best Lebanese restaurant in town, with an extensive range of beautifully prepared hot and cold *meze*, grills and a good wine list, including Lebanese vintages. **£££L**

At.mosphere
Burj Khalifa, 04-888 3828
On the 122nd floor of the Burj Khalifa, At.mosphere is the world's highest bar and restaurant, located almost half a kilometre above ground level. Choose between The Lounge (minimum spend Dhs200) for a drink, light meal or a pricey afternoon tea (Dhs350), or splash out on a meal at The Grill, serving upmarket international steaks in its

svelte dining room. **££££L**

Bastakiah Nights
Bastakiya, Bur Dubai
Tel: 04-353 7772
Located in a historic courtyard house in Bastakiya, this is one of the city's most atmospheric and romantic restaurants. The menu features a mix of Arabian and Iranian dishes – relatively expensive and pedestrian compared to other places in the city, but it's the setting that really seals the deal. **£££U**

Blue Elephant
Al Bustan Rotana Hotel, Garhoud
Tel: 04-282 0000
A candidate for best Thai restaurant in Dubai, located in a quaint little tropical-style "village" with a consistently good, and quite reasonably priced, selection of classic Thai fare. **£££L**

The Boardwalk
Dubai Creek Yacht Club
Tel: 04-295 6000
The mainstream menu of international food is reliable enough, but it's the terrific Creek and city views from the outdoor seating on the restaurant's eponymous boardwalk that really steal the show. **££L**

Buddha Bar
Grosvenor House, Dubai Marina
Tel: 04-317 6000
One of the best-looking restaurants in Dubai, modelled after its famous Parisian namesake, and with a fine array of Japanese, Thai and Chinese mains. Always buzzing. **£££L**

Café Chic
Le Méridien Dubai, Garhoud
Tel: 04-217 0000
One of the best French restaurants in the city, this elegant establishment wins regular plaudits for its top-notch Gallic cuisine. The desserts, including hot chocolate soufflé, are particularly good. **£££L**

Coconut Grove
Rydges Plaza Hotel, Satwa
Tel: 04-398 2222
Well off the beaten trail, but offering a genuine taste of the subcontinent, with authentically spicy dishes from Goa, Tamil Nadu and Sri Lanka. **££L**

Elements

Wafi, Oud Metha
Funky little venue in the Wafi complex serving a wide selection of reasonably priced café fare ranging from sandwiches, salads and pizzas to dim sum and sushi, plus more substantial meat and fish mains. **££U**

The Exchange Grill
Fairmont Hotel, Sheikh Zayed Rd
Tel: 04-311 8559
The city's most exclusive steakhouse, this small and very upmarket establishment serves up choice Gold Angus and wagyu cuts, backed up by one of the city's most extensive wine lists. **££££L**

Indego
Grosvenor House Hotel, Dubai Marina
Tel: 04-399 8888
Overseen by Vineet Bhatia, India's first Michelin-starred chef, this stylish restaurant showcases Bhatia's outstanding "contemporary Indian" cooking, with a seductive blend of subcontinental and international ingredients and techniques. **£££L**

Japengo Café
Palm Strip Shopping Mall, Jumeirah Road
Tel: 04-343 5028
Chic modern café-restaurant, with a shamelessly eclectic menu featuring everything from sushi and sashimi to stir-fries, pizzas, pastas, *meze* and good old-fashioned lamb chops, plus sandwiches and salads. There's another branch overlooking the canal in the Souk Madinat Jumeirah. **££U**

Kan Zaman
Creekside, Shindagha
Tel: 04-393 9913
In a fine location near the mouth of the Creek, Kanzaman ("once upon a time") has breezy outdoor and waterside seating and a good selection of Lebanese *meze*, Turkish coffee and shisha (hubbly bubbly pipes). **££U**

Khan Murjan Restaurant
Khan Murjan Souk, Oud Metha
Beautiful courtyard restaurant at the heart of the Souk Khan Murjan. The menu features an

unusually wide range of Middle Eastern dishes, from mainstream Lebanese grills and *meze* to traditional Gulf dishes like *fouga* and *goboli*. **££U**

Lime Tree Café
Near Spinneys, Jumeira Road
Tel: 04-349 8498
Set in an attractive modern villa, this neat little café offers a classic slice of expat Jumeirah life. Healthy specialities include outstanding carrot cake, tasty wraps and delicious smoothies. **£U**

More
Behind Lifco Supermarket, near Welcare Hospital, Garhoud
Tel: 04-283 0224
A funky Dutch-owned bistro with a wide range of superior international café fare. A difficult place to beat for its combination of excellent atmosphere, quality, value and service. **££U**

Nina
Arabian Courtyard, One&Only Royal Mirage
Tel: 04-399 9999
Innovative modern Indian restaurant, combining subcontinental flavours with international ingredients and cooking techniques – anything from traditional butter chicken to frogs' legs and rambutan. **£££L**

Noodle House
Emirates Towers Boulevard, Emirates Towers, Sheikh Zayed Road
Something of a local institution, this cheerful noodle bar is a kind of Dubai Wagamama, with good, reasonably priced Thai, Chinese, Malay, Singaporean, Indonesian and Japanese dishes served up at long communal tables. Reservations aren't accepted, so you might have to queue at busy times. **££L**

Pars Iranian Kitchen
Al Dhiyafa Road, Satwa Roundabout
Tel: 04-398 4000
Pleasant garden restaurant next to Satwa Roundabout serving up excellent and authentic Iranian fare – grills, *polos* (biryanis) and the like – at very competitive prices. **££U**

Pierchic
Al Qasr Hotel, Madinat Jumeirah
Tel: 04-366 6730
Fabulous, very romantic international seafood restaurant at the end of its own wooden pier with stunning views of Burj al Arab and the Madinat Jumeirah resort. **££££L**

Ravi Restaurant
Just off Satwa Roundabout, Satwa
This legendary little café remains enduringly popular with locals, expats and tourists alike for its cheap and tasty Pakistani-style chicken, mutton and vegetable curries, while the outdoor seating offers a good (if noisy) perch from which to enjoy the passing streetlife. **£U**

Rhodes Mezzanine
Grosvenor House Hotel
Tel: 04-399 8888
Dubai outpost of UK celebrity chef Gary Rhodes, with a short but inventive menu showcasing Rhodes's distinctive brand of modern European cuisine, accompanied by classic British puddings like jam roly-poly and bread-and-butter pudding. **££££L**

Shakespeare & Co
Al Attar Business Tower, 37th St, Sheikh Zayed Road
Chintzy little

European-style café tucked away halfway down Sheikh Zayed Road and a nice place for a coffee or light lunch, with soups, salads, sandwiches and crepes along with substantial mains. **££U**

Shu
Jumeirah Road, opposite Jumeirah Beach Park
Tel: 04-349 1303
Chic Lebanese café with seating either in the cool interior or on the relaxed outside terrace. If you're feeling adventurous, try the house speciality: fried sparrow with pomegranate syrup. **££U**

Spectrum on One
The Fairmont Dubai, Sheikh Zayed Road
Tel: 04-311 8101
Suave multi-cuisine restaurant serving up a vast range of top-notch international fare – including Indian, Chinese, Japanese, Arabian and European – from its six different show kitchens. **£££L**

Tagine
The Palace, One&Only Royal Mirage
Tel: 04-399 9999
This exquisitely decorated little Moroccan restaurant is one of the most appealing in the city, with *Arabian Nights* decor and a fine

array of traditional Moroccan cuisine, including a delicious selection of tagines and traditional dishes like spicy *harira* soup, lamb's brain and pigeon pie. **£££L**

Teatro
Towers Rotana, Sheikh Zayed Road
Tel: 04-343 8000
This long-established restaurant is usually one of the liveliest along Sheikh Zayed Road, with theatrically themed decor and an eclectic menu featuring Italian, Indian, Chinese and Thai, plus a bit of sushi – generally well-cooked and reasonably priced. **££L**

The Thai Kitchen
Park Hyatt, Garhoud
Tel: 04-317 2222
One of the best and most romantic Thai restaurants in town, set on the Park Hyatt's idyllic Creekside terrace and offering a sumptuous range of unusual regional specialities served in tapas-size portions. **£££L**

Verre
Hilton Creek, Deira
Tel: 04-212 7551
www.hilton.co.uk/dubaicreek
Dubai outpost of UK celebrity chef Gordon Ramsay, and regularly voted the top restaurant in

the city, Verre is highly recommended if you want to splash out on Ramsay's superb French-inspired modern European culinary creations. **££££L**

Vu's
Emirates Towers Hotel, Sheikh Zayed Road
Tel: 04-319 8088
Inventive fusion fine dining, with a mix of European and Asian influence, plus stunning views from the 50th floor of the landmark Emirates Towers hotel. Vu's bar, downstairs, is a fine place for a pre- or post-prandial drink. **££££L**

XVA Café
Bastakiya, Bur Dubai
Tel: 04-353 5383
Delightful courtyard café in a historic house that is now an art gallery and boutique hotel. The menu offers fresh and healthy vegetarian fare including salads, soups and sandwiches. **£U**

Zaatar W Zeit
The Walk, Dubai Marina
Cheery Lebanese-style fast-food joint, with salads, wraps and pizzas alongside various kinds of *manakish* (a kind of Middle Eastern-style pizza) and other Lebanese snacks. **£U**

SHARJAH

Canton Chinese Restaurant
Radisson Blu Hotel, Corniche
Tel: 06-565 7777
Cantonese Chinese classics in an attractive dining room in Sharjah's top hotel. **£££U**

Danial
Crystal Plaza
Tel: 06-574 4668

Chintzy Iranian restaurant, in a convenient location just behind the Central Souk, serving a reasonable buffet spread at lunchtime along with a selection of Middle Eastern and Iranian dishes. **££U**

Sanobar
Al Khan Road, near the

Sharjah Aquarium
Tel: 06-528 3501
Lebanese restaurant specialising in seafood, freshly grilled, plus assorted *meze*, with seating either in the quaint interior or on the sea-facing terrace. **££U**

Souk al Arsah Coffee

Shop
Souk al Arsah, Heritage Area
Cute little café next to the pretty courtyard at the heart of the Souk al Arsah – a good place to grab a tea or coffee or to try one of the café's spicy chicken, mutton and fish biryanis. **£U**

EAST COAST

Neptunia
Hilton Fujairah Resort, Fujairah City
Tel: 09-222 2411
The best restaurant in Fujairah City, with terrace seating overlook-

ing the sea and a mainly Mediterranean and Arabian menu. **£££L**

The Views
Le Méridien Al Aqah Beach Resort,

Al Aqah
Tel: 09-244 9000
Fine sea views and international food from the brasserie-style menu. **£££L**

OMAN
THE UAE
LANGUAGE

ACTIVITIES

THE ARTS, NIGHTLIFE, SPORTS, SHOPPING, CHILDREN'S ACTIVITIES AND TOUR OPERATORS

THE ARTS

Dance, Music and Theatre

Although the UAE has few concert and dance performances, big-name rock and pop acts do visit now and then, usually in Dubai. The Amphitheatre in Dubai Media City is the usual venue for big-name events. Otherwise, the venues below sometimes host performances.

Dubai Community and Arts Centre (DUCTAC)
Mall of the Emirates, Sheikh Zayed Road, tel: 04-341 4777; www. ductac.org
Home to a trio of lively little venues: the Centrepoint Theatre, Kilachand Studio Theatre and Manu Chhabria Arts Centre, which host a wide range of productions, including film, music and theatre, with the emphasis on local and community-based projects.

Madinat Theatre
Madinat Jumeirah, tel: 04-366 6546; www.madinattheatre.com
Dubai's first proper theatre when it opened in the mid-noughties, although don't expect much beyond a fairly predictable range of mainstream musicals, children's shows and other stereotypical crowd-pleasers.

The Palladium Dubai
Media City, tel: 04-363 6897; www. thepalladiumdubai.com
State-of-the-art new entertainment venue hosting a very mixed range of events, including regular stand-up comedy and live-music shows through to international seminars and awards ceremonies.

Art Galleries

Abu Dhabi

Ghaf Gallery
Al Khaleej al Arabi St, near Khalidiya Gardens, off the corniche, tel: 02-665 5332; http://ghafgallery.blogspot.com
Solo shows and mixed exhibitions featuring work by local and international artists.

Qibab Gallery
26th Street, Al Bateen, tel: 02-665 2350; www.qibabgallery.com
Specialises in Iraqi art, but also exhibits works by a wide range of other international artists.

Salwa Zeidan Gallery
Al Khaleej al Arabi St, near Khalidiya Gardens, off the corniche, tel: 02-666 9656; www.salwazeidangallery.com
Works by leading Middle Eastern artists and emerging local talent in a range of media.

Dubai

Artspace
The Gate Village Building 3, Podium Level, DIFC, Sheikh Zayed Road, tel: 04-323 0820; www.artspace-dubai.com
Upmarket gallery specialising in established Middle Eastern artists.

The Courtyard
Al Quoz, off Sheikh Zayed Road, tel: 04-347 9090; www. courtyardgallerydubai.com
One of Dubai's oldest galleries, in an entertainingly quirky development off Sheikh Zayed Road and showcasing the work of leading regional and international artists.

Gallery Isabelle van den Eynde
(formerly the B21 Gallery)
Sheikh Zayed Road, off Interchange 3 (exit 43), Al Quoz, tel: 04-323 5052; www.ivde.net
Showcases work by up-and-coming Arab artists.

Green Art Gallery
Al Serkal Avenue, Al Quoz, tel: 04-346 9305; www.gagallery.com
Exhibits and sells quality paintings.

Majlis Gallery
Bastakiya, Bur Dubai, tel: 04-353 6233; www.themajlisgallery.com
The UAE's oldest gallery, showing original art by well-known artists for sale in old wind-towered house.

thejamjar
Sheikh Zayed Road, off Interchange 4 (exit 39), Al Quoz, tel: 04-341 7303; www.thejamjardubai.com
Exhibits work by local and international artists and also runs assorted community projects and art classes.

The Third Line
Al Quoz, next to The Courtyard, tel: 04-341 1367; www.thethirdline.com
Displays work by contemporary Middle Eastern artists.

XVA Gallery
Bastakiya, Bur Dubai, tel: 04-358 5117; www.xvagallery.com
Long-established gallery-café in fine traditional building.

Sharjah

Sharjah Art Museum
Tel: 06-568 8222, www. sharjahmuseums.ae
Exhibitions of cutting-edge new Middle Eastern art.

Cinema

Note that films are commonly censored, with anything of a remotely sexual nature (or featuring anything approaching nudity) removed.

Abu Dhabi

Cine Royal
Khalidiya Mall, tel: 02-681 9444; www.cineroyal.ae

Grand Abu Dhabi Mall
Abu Dhabi Mall, tel: 02-645 8988;
www.grandcinemas.com
Grand al Mariah
Al Mariah Center, tel: 02-678 5000;
www.grandcinemas.com
Vox Cinema
Marina Mall, tel: 02-681 8484; www.
voxcinemas.com

Dubai

Grand Cinemas
www.grandcinemas.com. The city's
largest cinema chain, with a range
of multiplexes, including the Grand
Cineplex at Wafi (tel: 04-324 2000),
the Grand in the Mercato Mall in
Jumeirah (tel: 04-349 9713), Cinecity
at Al Ghurair City (tel: 04-228 9898),
the Megaplex at Ibn Battuta Mall (tel:
04-366 9898), and the Grand Festival
at Festival City (tel: 04-232 8329).
Movies Under the Stars
Rooftop Gardens, Wafi, Oud Metha;
www.wafi.com
Free open-air movie screening on Sunday
evenings from October to May (starting at
8pm), with seating on beanbags.
Vox Cinemas
www.voxcinemas.com. Two large
modern mulitplexes, at Deira City
Centre (tel: 04-294 9000) and the Mall
of the Emirates (tel: 04-341 4222).

Sharjah

Sahara
Sahara Mall, tel: 06-531 6500; www.
grandcinemas.com

NIGHTLIFE

The UAE boasts a fair selection of
Western-style nightlife, mainly in
Dubai, while Abu Dhabi is gradually
catching up, based around a mix of
British-style pubs, elegant bars and a
small number of clubs.

Pubs and Bars

Abu Dhabi

Belgian Cafe
InterContinental Hotel, Al Bateen
Convivial Belgian style café-bar, with
speciality beers and good food.
Brauhaus
Beach Rotana Hotel, Tourist Club Area
Lively German-style pub-cum-
restaurant, with speciality beers
on tap or by the bottle, plus a good
selection of German-style food.
Captain's Arms
Le Méridien Hotel, Tourist Club Area
Popular British-style pub with good
array of draught beers and outdoor
seating overlooking the hotel gardens.

ABOVE: Madinat Theatre.

Jazzbar
Hilton Hotel, Corniche
Long-established nightspot with good
live jazz (nightly), candlelit tables and
cocktails. Usually fairly chilled-out,
although can get lively later on.
Left Bank
Souk Qaryat al Beri
This chic new bar-restaurant is a bit of
a hike from the centre, although worth
it for the superb views, cool decor
and good music, with nightly DJ and
dance floor.
P.J. O'Reillys
Le Royal Méridien, Al Markaziyah
Perennially popular Irish pub, often
with the best – or at least noisiest –
atmosphere in town, with regular DJs
or live bands and a bit of a dance floor.
Sax Club
Le Royal Méridien, Al Markaziyah
One of the city's more glamorous
drinking venues, with moody lighting,
swanky cocktails and one of Abu
Dhabi's more fashionable crowds.
Live band and DJ nightly.
Yacht Club
InterContinental Hotel, Al Bateen
Smooth modern bar and terrace
overlooking the marina with a fancy
drinks lists and good food.

Dubai

360°
Jumeirah Beach Hotel
Dubai's ultimate chill-out bar, on a
breakwater amidst the waves facing
the Burj al Arab with a very cool crowd
and regular DJs.
The Agency
Emirates Towers Boulevard, Sheikh
Zayed Road
The city's top wine bar, with a huge list
of international tipples.
Bahri Bar
Mina A'Salam Hotel, Madinat Jumeirah
Seductive little bar with Moroccan-
style decor and peerless views of the
Burj al Arab from the outside terrace.
Bar 44
Grosvenor House, Dubai Marina

Cool cocktail bar atop the soaring
Grosvenor House hotel, with
unrivalled Marina views, fancy drinks
and a dressy crowd.
Barasti Bar
Le Méridien Mina Sehayi, Dubai Marina
Enduringly popular nightspot on the
beach, with a lively pub-style deck
upstairs and a cooler chill-out area on
the beach below. Regular live DJs.
Belgium Beer Café
Crowne Plaza Hotel, Festival City
Surprisingly authentic Belgian-style
pub-cum-restaurant, with an excellent
range of speciality beers and good
traditional Belgian cuisine.
Blue Bar
Novotel, World Trade Centre,
Sheikh Zayed Road
Cool bar with a good selection of
speciality Belgian beers and live music
(mainly blues and soul) later on.
Cin Cin
Fairmont Hotel, Sheikh Zayed Road
Very exclusive bar boasting soothing
decor, a huge list of wines, vodkas
and whiskies, plus cigar bar. Live DJ
some nights.
Eclipse
InterContinental Hotel, Festival City
Smooth modern bar at the top of the
Festival City InterContinental, with a
good drinks list and sweeping city views.
Long's Bar
Towers Rotana Hotel, Sheikh Zayed Road
Lively pub with the longest bar in the
Middle East.
Neos
The Address, Downtown Dubai
The second-highest bar in Dubai, with
vertiginous views over the surrounding
Downtown Dubai and Burj Khalifa.
Rooftop Bar
Arabian Courtyard, One&Only Royal
Mirage, Dubai Marina
Opulent Arabian-style rooftop bar.
Skyview Bar
Burj al Arab
At the top of the Burj al Arab, with
psychedelic decor and vast sea
and city views. Minimum spend of

ABOVE: AD Golf Club.

Dhs275 per person, and you'll need to reserve in advance on tel: 04-301 7600 or BAArestaurants@jumeirah. com.

Sho-Cho
Dubai Marine Beach Resort, Jumeirah
Chic and very posey little bar-cum-Japanese restaurant, eternally popular amongst the city's Lebanese and Bollywood party crowd. Live DJ most nights.

The Terrace
Park Hyatt, Garhoud
Alluring, upmarket Creekside terrace-bar, with lovely waterside views and a very chilled-out atmosphere.

Viceroy Bar
Four Points Sheraton, Khalid Bin al Waleed Road, Bur Dubai
One of the nicest English-style pubs in town, with cosy wood-panelled interior and decent drinks and food.

Vu's Bar
Emirates Towers
Cool chrome-and-glass bar at the summit of the Emirates Tower with huge views and an almost equally big drinks list.

Clubs

Abu Dhabi

Al Ain
Luce, Danat Al Ain Resort
Al Ain's most stylish venue mixes upmarket Italian restaurant with stylish lounge bar which kicks on into the small hours, ably assisted by live Latin band.

Allure
Yas Island, www.nightcluballure.com
Uber-chic new nightclub, currently the hottest place in town – or, rather, 20km (12½ miles) out of town on Yas Island. Dress to impress.

Rock Bottom Café
Al Diar Capital Hotel, Al Markaziyah
Unashamedly downmarket venue, always lively, with nightly DJ and/or live band.

Dubai

Boudoir
Dubai Marine Beach Resort, Jumeirah
Chintzy bar-cum-nightclub – it looks a bit like a 19th-century French brothel – attracting a cashed-up selection of expats and the city's Lebanese party crowd drowning in cocktails and champagne. Live DJs nightly.

Chi@The Lodge
Oud Metha, next to Al Nasr Leisureland, www.chinightclubdubai. com
The biggest club in the Middle East, with room for 3,500 revellers. Hosts regular big-name international DJs and occasional bands.

Zinc
Crowne Plaza Hotel, Sheikh Zayed Road, www.myspace.com/zincdubai
The longest-running club in Dubai, kept afloat by its relatively attitude-free atmosphere, eclectic soundtrack and general reputation for unpretentious dancing and partying.

SPORTS

The UAE offers numerous choices for summer sports: there are long, deserted beaches open to the public, desert and mountains to explore, and pools, sports facilities and clubs in the cities. Many independent sports clubs and hotels have gymnasiums, swimming pools and tennis courts where daily entrance rates are usually available.

Other sports available include abseiling, aqua-biking, deep-sea fishing, dune-buggy driving, fishing, golf, polo, ice-skating, go-karting, sailing, sand-skiing, skiing, water sports of all kinds and more. Horse and camel races usually take place on Thursday and Friday during the cooler winter months, and are open to everyone.

Dhow sailing and racing are memorable sights – see press for details.

Major tournaments that attract world-class players, including golf, tennis, powerboat racing and horse racing, are also held throughout the winter – see the Sports and Outdoor Activities chapter on page 103 for more information.

Diving and Watersports

In Dubai, the beachfront resort hotels are the easiest places to arrange watersports. All the marina beach hotels (apart from the Ritz-Carlton) have their own watersports centres, with activities including windsurfing, sailing, kayaking, water-skiing, wakeboarding and parasailing. Local operators include **Sky & Sea Adventure** (tel: 04-399 9005, www. watersportsdubai.com), who can be found at the Sheraton Jumeirah Beach and Hilton Jumeirah Resort.

Watersports can also be arranged in Abu Dhabi through **Blue Dolphin** (tel: 02-666 9392) and in Fujairah through the **Sandy Beach Hotel** (tel: 09-244 5555, www.sandybm.com).

The best diving in the UAE is off the east coast; alternatively, the superb dive sites of the Musandam peninsula in Oman are also within easy striking distance.

Al Boom Diving
Tel: 04-342 2993, www. alboomdiving.com
Runs dive centres at the Jebel Ali Golf Resort and Spa in the far south of Dubai, and at the Al Aqah Méridien hotel in Fujairah, offering a range of PADI courses and dives, plus Musandam excursions.

Pavilion Dive Centre
Jumeirah Beach Hotel, Dubai, tel: 04-406 8828, www.jumeirah.com
PADI courses and introductory dives, plus trips to nearby wrecks and to Musandam.

BELOW: you can even learn to ski in Dubai, as shown here at Ski Dubai.

Sandy Beach Hotel
Al Aqah Beach, Fujairah, tel: 09-244 5555, www.sandybm.com/diving.htm
Excellent base for east-coast dive sites.

Golf Courses

Abu Dhabi

AD City Golf Club
Al Mushrif, tel: 02-445 9600, www.adcitygolf.ae
Verdant nine-hole course close to city centre.

AD Golf Club
Umm an Nar, tel: 02-558 8990, www.adgolfclub.com
Championship-standard course and home to the Abu Dhabi Golf Championship.

Al Ghazal Golf Club
Near Airport, tel: 02-575 8044, www.alghazalgolf.ae
One of the world's finest sand courses.

Yas Links
Yas Island, tel: 02-810 7777, www.yaslinks.com
Superb new 18-hole course (plus floodlit 9-hole par-3course).

Dubai

Al Badia Golf Course
Festival City, tel: 04-601 0111, www.albadiagolfclub.ae
Attractive Creekside course designed by Robert Trent Jones II with numerous water features.

Arabian Ranches Golf Club
Arabian Ranches, Dubailand, tel: 04-366 3000, www.arabianranchesgolfdubai.com
Links-style grass course set in the middle of natural desert.

Dubai Creek Golf Club
Garhoud, tel: 04-380 1234, www.dubaigolf.com
Superb Creekside course (designed by Thomas Bjorn). Also has a floodlit 9-hole par-3 course.

The Els Club
Dubai Sports City, Dubailand, tel: 04-425 1010, www.elsclubdubai.com
"Desert links" course with greens and fairways surrounded by rolling dunes and untouched desert.

Emirates Golf Club
Dubai Marina, tel: 04-380 1234, www.dubaigolf.com
The oldest all-grass championship course in the Gulf, and current home of the Dubai Desert Classic.

Jumeirah Golf Estates
Dubai Marina, tel: 04-390 3333, www.jumeirahgolfestates.com
Four separate state-of-the-art courses – "Fire", "Earth", "Water" and "Wind" (designed by Greg Norman, Vijay Singh, Sergio Garcia and Pete Dye) – set amidst dramatic desert scenery.

ABOVE: there are great views from the restaurant at the top of Marina Mall in Abu Dhabi.

The Montgomerie Dubai
Dubai Marina, tel: 04-390 5600, www.themontgomerie.com
Links-style course designed by Colin Montgomerie.

Skiing

Ski Dubai
Mall of the Emirates, www.skidxb.com
The first indoor ski resort in the Middle East, with real snow and five runs.

Sports Clubs

Abu Dhabi

AD Chess Club
Tel: 02-633 1110, www.abudhabichess.com

AD Country Club
Tel: 02-657 7777, www.adcountryclub.com
Gym, fitness classes, tennis, squash and other sports.

AD Equestrian Club
Tel: 02-445 5500, www.adec-web.com.

AD Harlequins Rugby Club
www.abudhabiquins.com

The Club
Tel: 02-673 1111, www.the-club.com
Wide range of sports including tennis, squash, sailing, kayaking and climbing.

Dubai

Desert Sport Diving Club
www.desertsportsdivingclub.net

Dubai Archers
www.dubaiarchers.com

Dubai Exiles RFC (rugby)
Tel: 050-459 8603, www.dubaiexiles.com

Dubai International Marine Club (sailing)
Tel: 04-399 5777, www.dimc.ae

Dubai Polo and Equestrian Club
Tel: 04-361 8111, www.poloclubdubai.com

Dubai Roadsters (cycling)
www.dubairoadsters.com

Jebel Ali Equestrian Club
Tel: 04-884 5101

Jebel Ali Shooting Club
Tel: 04-883 6555

SHOPPING

Shopping in the UAE is an intriguing blend of the contemporary and traditional, and although the country is increasingly being taken over by vast modern shopping malls, traditional souks survive in many places. Dubai is far and away the best place to shop (and even has its own shopping festival), with a string of landmark shopping complexes, including the vast Dubai Mall, as well fascinating souks of Deira and Bur Dubai. Abu Dhabi is less well equipped, although there are a couple of good malls and some other interesting shops, while Sharjah boasts a pair of wonderful souks. Elsewhere, shopping opportunities are rather limited.

Goods on offer are similarly diverse, ranging from top-fashion designer-label fashion and cutting-edge electronics to traditional jewellery, perfumes, dates and spices. Bargaining is expected in the souks, but in the shopping malls prices are usually fixed.

What to Buy

Good buys in the country include **gold** and other **precious stones** (particularly diamonds), which sell here for considerably less than in the West. Antique Bedu **silver jewellery** can also be found, at a price. **Carpets**

ABOVE: shoppers at the Gold Souk.

can be a good buy, too – the cheapest are at the Blue Souk in Sharjah, and there is also a reasonable selection in Deira Tower on Baniyas Square. **Spices** of all kinds are notably cheaper here than in the West. It is also fun to buy some **perfume** – most shops will help you mix up your own personalised bespoke scent if you don't like any of the brands on offer. Colourful souvenirs range from traditional Arabian **coffee pots** to kitsch Burj al Arab **paperweights**.

Abu Dhabi

Souks

The central souk (at Khalifa Street) was demolished in 2005 and replaced as the stunning new **Central Market** (www.centralmarket.ae/souk) by Foster + Partners, housing a range of upmarket boutiques and smaller crafts shops.

Madinat Zayed (on East Road, near the Post Office) is where you'll find Abu Dhabi's **Gold Souk**, with two storeys of shops inside a modern mall.

A string of low-key markets can be found dotted around **Al Mina district** – Abu Dhabi's nearest equivalent to a traditional souk. The Carpet Souk is a square of shops selling a mix of low-grade factory rugs and more collectable items, while the nearby Food Souk boasts a good selection of little date shops. Past here the **Iranian Souk** – despite its colourful name – is mainly devoted to the sale of household goods and plants.

At the **Emirates Heritage Village**, you can see craftsmen making glassware, leather goods and silverware, all of which are for sale.

At the far western end of the city, between Maqta and Musaffah bridges (not far from the Sheikh Zayed Grand Mosque), the new waterside **Souk Qaryat al Beri** (http://soukqaryatalberi.com) features

attractive modern Arabian decor and a small but select array of upmarket boutiques, jewellers and other outlets.

Shopping malls

Abu Dhabi Mall
Near the Beach Rotana Hotel, Tourist Club Area, www.abudhabi-mall.com
Abu Dhabi's ritziest mall, with a wide range of designer outlets plus more workaday shops.

Marina Mall
On the Breakwater, near Emirates Palace, www.marinamall.ae
Attractive modern mall arranged around a couple of large courtyards under tent-like roofs. The soaring Burj al Marina (Marina Tower) at the back offers great city views from its top-floor restaurant and coffee shop.

Dubai

Dubai is famous for its shopping – things are particularly lively during the annual Dubai Shopping Festival (Jan–late Feb, www.mydsf.ae), when stores across the city slash prices and the malls are engulfed in crazed consumers.

Souks

Gold Souk, Sikkat al Khail Street Deira. The region's most famous gold souk, selling a vast range of gold jewellery in Arabian and European designs, very competitively priced, as well as other precious stones.
Karama Souk, Karama. Infamous for its designer fakes – although prices are higher than you might expect.
Khan Murjan Souk, Wafi, Oud Metha. Gorgeous modern recreation of legendary Baghdad market, hosting well over 100 upmarket craft shops.
Souk Madinat Jumeirah, Madinat Jumeirah. Lovely modern souk in traditional quasi-Moroccan style. Good, though relatively expensive, handicrafts.
Spice Souk, Deira. A couple of alleyways piled up with huge sacks of

spices and other regional produce – frankincense, saffron, dried lemons, rose petals and so on.

Shopping malls

BurJuman
Khalid Bin al Waleed Roads, Bur Dubai, www.burjuman.com
The biggest mall in the old city centre; the glitzy southern extension is good for designer fashion.
Dubai Mall
Downtown Dubai, www.thedubaimall.com
The world's biggest mall, with a staggering 1,200-odd shops. "Fashion Avenue" is home to the biggest array of designer labels in Dubai, while the in-house "Gold Souk" houses a further 120 shops selling gold, jewellery and Arabian perfumes and artefacts.
Emirates Towers Boulevard
Emirates Towers, Sheikh Zayed Road Small but very exclusive mall stuffed with high-end fashion and jewellery shops.
Festival Centre
Festival City, www.festivalcentre.com
Large, colourfully designed mall at heart of new Festival City development in an attractive Creekside location.
Ibn Battuta Mall
Between interchanges 5 and 6, Sheikh Zayed Road, www.ibnbattutamall.com
Dubai's quirkiest mall.
Mall of the Emirates
Interchange 4, Sheikh Zayed Road, www.malloftheemirates.com
Second-largest mall in the city, full of excellent, largely upmarket shops – particularly good for fashion.
Mercato
Jumeirah Beach Road, Jumeirah, www.MercatoShoppingMall.com
Quirky Italian-themed mall hosts a small but well-chosen range of shops. Good for clothes.
The Village Mall, Jumeirah Beach Road, www.thevillagedubai.com
Small mall, home to a clutch of interesting independent boutiques.
Wafi
Oud Metha, www.wafi.com
This zany Egyptian-themed mall has a good range of shops, and is usually a lot more peaceful than many other places in the city.

Sharjah

Central Souk (also known as the Blue Souk)
Next to Sharjah Creek. Two huge blue-domed buildings full of mainly ordinary shops on the

ground floor, but a treasure trove of antique furniture, carpets and Gulf mementoes awaits upstairs – particularly good for carpets.

Souk al Arsah (Old Souk)
Behind Borj Avenue. Lovely little traditional souk full of handicrafts shops, and with an excellent coffee house.

CHILDREN'S ACTIVITIES

Abu Dhabi

Abu Dhabi Ice Rink
Tel: 02-444 8458; www.zsc.ae/facts/abu-dhabi-ice-rink.html
Off Airport Road near Zayed Sports City Stadium. Olympic-size rink with teachers on hand plus ice hockey lessons at the weekend.

Ferrari World
Yas Island, tel: 02-496 8001; www.ferrariworldabudhabi.com
Huge new theme park featuring all manner of rides, including the world's fastest rollercoaster.

Al Ain

Al Ain Zoo
South of town, tel: 03-782 8188; www.awpr.ae
Spacious, well-run wildlife park.

Dubai

Many of the beachside hotels have dedicated kids' clubs, while most of the larger malls also have children's play areas catering for all ages – these include **Fun City** (BurJuman, Mercato and Ibn Battuta malls), **Magic Planet** (Mall of the Emirates and Deira City Centre) and the **Wafi Encounter Zone** at the Wafi mall.

Aquaventure
Atlantis, The Palm Jumeirah, tel: 04-426 0000; www.atlantisthepalm.com
Superb water park, centred on stunning Ziggurat and the stomach-churning "Leap of Faith".

Dolphin Bay
Atlantis, The Palm Jumeirah, tel: 04-426 2626; www.atlantisthepalm.com
Swim with dolphins.

Children's City
Creekside Park, Oud Metha; www.childrencity.ae
Fun "edu-tainment" complex with displays and interactive exhibits on a variety of themes.

Dubai Aquarium and Underwater Zoo
Dubai Mall, tel: 04-448 5200; www.thedubaiaquarium.com
Spectacular aquarium.

Dubai Dolphinarium

Next to Gate #1 at Creekside Park, tel: 04-336 9773; www.dubaidolphinarium.ae
Twice-daily dolphin shows plus interactive swimming sessions.

Dubai Ice Rink
Dubai Mall, tel: 04-448 5111; www.dubaiicerink.com
Olympic-size rink.

Dubai Zoo
Beach Road, Jumeirah, tel: 04-349 6444
Old-fashioned zoo.

KidZania
Dubai Mall, www.kidzania.com
Innovative attraction based on an imaginary city where kids can dress up and role-play a variety of adult characters, from airline pilot to archaeologist.

Lost Chambers
Atlantis, The Palm Jumeirah, tel: 04-426 0000; www.atlantisthepalm.com
Stunning subterranean aquarium dotted with kooky "ancient ruins".

Sega Republic
Dubai Mall, tel: 04-448 8484; www.segarepublic.com
State-of-the-art indoor theme park featuring a range of adrenalin-pumping rides and other amusements.

Ski Dubai
Mall of the Emirates, www.skidxb.com
Go skiing, build snowmen or chuck snowballs at the Gulf's first ski-slope.

Wild Wadi
Next to Jumeirah Beach Hotel, tel: 04-348 4444; www.jumeirah.com/hotels-and-resorts/Wild-Wadi
Brilliant water park with rides and slides to suit all ages.

Wonderland
Oud Metha, next to Garhoud Bridge; www.wonderlanduae.com
Old-fashioned theme park with a variety of rides and the modest Splashland water park.

Umm al Qaiwain

Dreamland Aqua Park
Ras al Khaimah Road, 17km (10½ miles) past Umm al Qaiwain, www.dreamlanduae.com
Large, well-equipped water park.

TOUR OPERATORS

There are numerous tour operators in Dubai (along with a smaller number in Abu Dhabi and elsewhere), all offering largely the same trips: city tours, trips to neighbouring emirates, desert safaris and dhow cruises. Arabian Adventures is the biggest and best run, although the following are all reliable. It's easiest to book

by phone at most places, as offices are often inconveniently located and tricky to find (with the exception of Arabian Adventures, which has a travel desk in a number of leading hotels in Dubai and at Le Méridien in Fujairah). All operators will pick you up from your hotel.

Abu Dhabi

Arabian Adventures, Emirates Travel Shop, Corniche, tel: 02-691 1711, www.arabian-adventures.com
Desert Adventures, Al Raha Beach Hotel, tel: 02-556 6155, www.desertadventures.com
Net Tours, Khalifa St, near Sheraton Hotel, tel: 02-679 4656, www.netgrouppauh.com
Off Road Emirates, tel: 02-633 3232, Hamdan St, near BHS; www.offroademirates.com
Specialising in tailor-made tours in the desert region.
Orient Tours, tel: 02-667 5609, www.orienttours.ae
Sunshine Tours, tel: 02-444 9914, www.adnh.com

Dubai

Alpha Tours, tel: 04-294 9888, www.alphatoursdubai.com
Arabian Adventures, tel: 04-303 4888, www.arabian-adventures.com
Branches in a number of hotels across the city.
Balloon Adventures Dubai, tel: 04-285 4949, www.ballooning.ae
Hot-air ballooning over the desert.
The Big Bus Company, tel: 04-340 7709, www.bigbustours.com
Double-decker bus tours of the major sights in hop-on, hop-off open-top buses.
Desert Adventures, tel: 04-224 2800, www.desertadventures.com
Net Tours, tel: 04-602 8888, www.netgroupdubai.com
Orient Tours, tel: 04-282 8238, www.orienttours.ae.
Wonder Bus Tours, tel: 04-359 5656, www.wonderbustours.net
Bur Juman Centre, Bur Dubai. Tours of city and Creek aboard an amphibious vehicle – half bus, half boat.

Sharjah

Orient Tours, Al Aruba Street, tel: 06-568 2323, www.orienttours.ae

Fujairah

Arabian Adventures, Le Méridien al Aqah Beach, tel: 09-204 4057, www.arabian-adventures.com

A – Z

A HANDY SUMMARY OF PRACTICAL INFORMATION, ARRANGED ALPHABETICALLY

A

Admission Charges

Admission charges to government-run heritage sites, museums and parks are extremely modest, sometimes free, never more than Dhs5. Conversely, entrance fees to privately run attractions can be stratospheric, particularly for families – excursions to attractions like Ski Dubai, either of the Dubai water parks, the observation deck at the Burj Khalifa or Ferrari World in Abu Dhabi can put a significant dent in your finances, often pushing north of US$100 for two adults and a couple of kids.

Age Restrictions

Car-rental agencies require drivers to be at least 21, rising to 25 and 30 for 4x4, although this is sometimes waived upon payment of a "young driver" surcharge. Children under 10 are not allowed to sit in the front passenger seat of cars, while the minimum age for entry to bars and nightclubs varies between 18 and 21. On the water and in some theme parks, the minimum age for activities is seven or eight, but it also depends on the child's height (often with a minimum of 1.1 metres/3ft 6ins). For diving lessons, the minimum age for junior open-water training is 10, but children can begin learning in a pool from the age of eight.

B

Budgeting for Your Trip

The cost for a standard double room ranges from around Dhs350 per night in a one-star city-centre hotel to Dhs575–1,000 at a four-star hotel and Dhs1,000-3,500 at a five-star hotel. Sandwiches and curries from street-level restaurants can be bought for as little as Dhs5–10. Main courses in most decent Western-style, non-hotel restaurants are between Dhs25–45. For fine dining, allow upwards of Dhs55 per person for mains. Soft drinks start at Dhs1 in shops but are heavily marked up in restaurants. Imported alcoholic drinks tend to be more expensive than in the West.

Generally taxis are significantly cheaper than those in Western cities (although the fare from Dubai Airport comes with a Dhs20 mark-up). Bus tickets offer good value, costing around Dh3, while a creek crossing on an traditional abra is just Dhs1.

Package deals arranged from your home country are likely to be cheaper than separately arranged air travel and accommodation. The best prices occur in low season (July–Sep), when the UAE is at its hottest.

C

Children

Childcare facilities are on a par with those in the West. Most malls have changing facilities in the women's public toilets; many also have supervised indoor play areas. Many of the more upmarket beach resorts also have kids' club and babysitting services.

Climate

Summers are very hot. From **May to September** daytime temperatures are rarely below 40°C (104°F), with humidity up to 90 percent.

From **October to April** there is very good weather (sunny and warm), with temperatures ranging from as low as 10°C (50°F) inland to 30°C (mid-80s°F), with little or no humidity. However, strong winds sometimes bring sandstorms, and it occasionally rains very heavily. The rain usually comes sometime from January to March, and can result in large areas of flooding. The desert inland gets much colder than the coastal regions at night and during the winter months.

What to bring

In the summer months it is extremely hot, so bring a sun hat, sunblock and wear cool cotton clothes. A jumper or jacket is needed at night in the cooler winter months. Women are advised to wear modest clothes in the streets, particularly in the souks, so avoid short shorts and skirts and keep your shoulders covered to avoid unwanted attention and risk offending anyone. Men should not bare their torsos for the same reason. On the beaches swimsuits, shorts or bikinis are fine. In Sharjah, women are only allowed to wear swimwear on private beaches. For business a light suit is useful.

Crime and Safety

The UAE is generally a safe country for both men and women. The crime rate is low: major crimes are relatively rare, and even petty theft is less common than in most other countries. The level of personal security is also high: for women to avoid personal harassment not walking around alone at night is recommended, but there is no real physical danger.

Taxis are safe to take during the day, or at night within towns as long as a woman is wearing demure clothing and knows her route so that she can avoid being taken on a "detour". Fares, except in metered taxis, should be agreed in advance, to avoid arguments at the end of the journey. Inter-emirate registered taxis are fine, and taxi shares are safe for women in the day. At night, lone women are advised not to get a taxi out of town into desert areas, or for a long inter-emirate drive.

Customs Regulations

Duty-free goods can be brought into the country:
400 cigarettes or 0.5kg loose tobacco. Non-Muslims can bring in 4 litres of alcohol (or 12 cans of beer), unless you are arriving in Sharjah where alcohol is prohibited. You are not allowed to bring in alcohol if arriving overland. Check these allowances have not changed when you travel.

Books and magazines are expensive, so it's wise to bring some paperbacks to read, avoiding any that may cause offence. The same applies to DVDs and videos. There are also severe penalties if you are found carrying drugs. This applies not only to carrying drugs but also, potentially, if you have drugs in your bloodstream or any other evidence of being in possession of illegal substances – one man was jailed on account of microscopic quantities of cannabis found in a piece of gum stuck to the sole of his shoe. Prescription medicines can also get you into trouble – either carry a letter from your doctor explaining that these are needed for health reasons or, if at all possible, leave them at home.

D

Disabled Travellers

Many of the country's better hotels now have specially adapted rooms for disabled travellers, while some modern malls also have disabled parking spaces and specially equipped toilets. Dubai is particularly accessible. Dubai Taxi (tel: 04-208

0808) has specially designed vehicles equipped with ramps and lifts, while the metro features tactile guide paths, lifts and ramps to assist visually and mobility-impaired visitors, as well as wheelchair spaces in all compartments. The city's water buses can also be used by mobility-impaired visitors, and staff will assist you in boarding and disembarking, while there are also dedicated facilities for passengers with special needs at the airport. Sadly, but not surprisingly, most of the country's older heritage buildings are not accessible.

E

Electricity

220/240 volts. The majority of sockets accept three square-pin 13-amp British-style plugs. Adaptors for two-pin appliances can be bought in supermarkets.

Embassies and Consulates

As Abu Dhabi, not Dubai, is the federal capital of the UAE, Dubai tends to have foreign consulates rather than embassies. Embassies are usually open 8.30am–1.30pm, with all closing on Friday and some closing on Saturday.

Abu Dhabi

Australia, Al Muhairy Centre, Sheikh Zayed the First Street, tel: 02-401 7500; www.uae.embassy.gov.au
Canada, Abu Dhabi Trade Towers (Abu Dhabi Mall), West Tower, tel: 02-694 0300; www.canadainternational. gc.ca/uae-eau
UK, Khalid Bin al Waleed Street (Street 22), tel: 02-610 1100, http:// ukinuae.fco.gov.uk/en
US, off Airport Road, tel: 02-414 2200; http://abudhabi.usembassy.gov

Dubai (Consulates)

Australia: BurJuman Centre, Khalifa bin Zayed Road (Trade Centre Road); tel: 04-508 7100; www.dfat.gov.au/missions
Canada: 7th floor, Bank Street Building, Bur Dubai; tel: 04-314 5555; www.dfait-maeci.gc.ca.

Emergency Numbers

Police and ambulance, tel: 999
Fire, tel: 997
Dubai Police Headquarters, tel: 04-229 2222
Dubai Police Tourist Security Department, tel: 800 4438

ABOVE: kids paddling on the beach in Ajman.

Ireland: Riyadh, Kingdom of Saudi Arabia; tel: +966 1 488 2300; www. embassyofireland-riyadh.com
New Zealand: Riyadh, Kingdom of Saudi Arabia; tel: +966-1-488 7988; www.mfat.govt.nz
South Africa: Villa Number 202, corner of Airport Road and 25th Street, Abu Dhabi; tel: 02-447 3446
UK: Al Seef Road, Bur Dubai; tel: 04-309 4444; www.britishembassy.gov.uk
US: 21st Floor, Dubai World Trade Centre, Sheikh Zayed Road; tel: 04-311 6000; http://dubai. usconsulate.gov

UAE Embassies

UAE Embassy in London
30 Princes Gate, London SW7 1PT, tel: 020-7581 1281 (9am–3pm); www.uaeembassyuk.net
UAE Embassy in Washington
3522 International Court, NW Washington DC 20008, tel: 202-243 2400; www.uae-embassy.org

Etiquette

Although the UAE is a very liberal country compared with other states in the Gulf region, it is still a conservative Muslim country, and visitors should respect this. Women especially should remember that clothing that is acceptable in a nightclub or on the beach is not appropriate to wear on the street during the day.

Outside the cities, dress more conservatively. Everyone should cover their upper arms and women should wear longer skirts or trousers. Men should not wear shorts in a business situation.

During the holy month of Ramadan don't eat, smoke or drink in public. Never drink and drive as you could end up in jail for a month, and don't offer alcohol to Muslims.

If visiting the home of a UAE citizen it is customary to remove shoes before venturing on the carpets, though increasingly many local families no longer follow this custom. Avoid showing the soles of your feet when sitting down. If you wish to take a present, a box of pastries or sweetmeats is a safe option.

G

Gay and Lesbian Travellers

Homosexuality is not tolerated in the UAE and is officially illegal, so discretion is strongly advised.

H

Health and Medical Care

Travel insurance is advisable as healthcare can be expensive, although there are good government hospitals as well as numerous private clinics.

No special injections are required for the UAE. Cholera and yellow fever certificates are only necessary if you arrive from an infected area. It is wise to drink bottled water. The drinking water is safe, but your system may not have time to acclimatise.

You can buy most items in the UAE, but if you're taking certain medicines then you should bring a supply with you. Just make sure you can also produce a prescription if asked, as certain drugs that are readily available in the West are prohibited in the UAE without one.

There are good government hospitals where treatment is free to health-card holders (only available with residence visas).

Emergency treatment is available to everyone but it is often easier for visitors to visit a private clinic and make a health insurance claim rather than spend time queuing in the government hospitals.

Hospitals

Abu Dhabi

Al Noor Hospital, Khalifa Street, tel: 02-626 5265, www.alnoorhospital.com.

Dubai

Dubai Hospital, between the Corniche and Baraha Street, Deira, tel: 04-219 5000, http://web.dohms.gov.ae/dh.

Rashid Hospital, off Oud Metha Road, near Maktoum Bridge, Oud Metha, tel: 04-562 4000, www.alrashidhospital.org.

Wasl Hospital, Oud Metha Road (just west of Wafi), Oud Metha, tel: 04-324 1111.

Sharjah

Al Zahra Private Hospital, Al Zahra Square (Clocktower Roundabout), tel: 06-561 9999, www.alzahra.com.

Private clinics

Abu Dhabi

Gulf Diagnostic Centre, 30th Street (Khaleej Al Arabi Street), tel: 02-665 8090, www.gdc-hospital.com.

New National Medical Centre, Electra Street (Hamad Centre Building), tel: 02-633 2255, www.nmc.ae.

Dubai

Al Borj Medical Centre, Al Diyafah Street, Satwa, tel: 04-345 4666.

Dubai London Clinic, Al Wasl Road, Jumeirah, tel: 04-344 6663, www.dubailondonclinic.com.

General Medical Centre, Beach Road, Jumeirah, Magrudy Centre, tel: 04-349 5959, www.gmcclinics.com.

Manchester Clinic, Beach Road, Jumeirah, tel: 04-344 0300, www.manchester-clinic.com.

Dentists

Abu Dhabi

Advanced American Dental Centre, behind BMW showroom, Al Bateen, tel: 02-681 2921.

Dubai

American Dental Clinic, Villa 54, next to Dubai Zoo, Beach Road, Jumeirah, tel: 04-344 0668.

British Dental Clinic, Al Wasl Road, Jumeirah, tel: 04-342 1318, www.britishdentalclinic.com.

Sharjah

Al Zahra Private Hospital, Al Zahra Square (Clocktower Roundabout), tel: 06-561 9999, www.alzahra.com.

I

Internet

Internet access is provided by the two national telecoms providers, Etisalat (www.etisalat.ae) and Du (www.du.ae), although access to certain websites may be blocked due to political, religious or sexual content. Internet connectivity is available in the guest rooms and business centres of larger hotels, although often at exorbitant rates. Internet cafés are surprisingly thin on the ground. In Dubai, the easiest place to get online is Bur Dubai (where internet cafés can be found in many of the small roads and alleyways off Al Fahidi Street). One reliable place is the Al Jalssa internet café in the Al Ain Centre. Elsewhere, the Grano Coffee shop in Wafi is one of the few reliable options. Charges are around Dhs10–15 per hour.

Things are a lot easier you have your own Wi-fi-enabled laptop and can access one of the numerous free Wi-fi hotspots around Dubai and other parts of the country, including the whole of the Dubai Mall. You can also get online on the Dubai metro for Dhs10 per hour. Various Wi-fi hotspots are also operated by Etisalat and Du, which offer access at numerous places around the main cities, including many malls, numerous coffee shops and selected hotels, with various pay-as-you-go packages. See the websites for full details of charges and hotspot locations.

L

Lost Property

If you lose your property, call the relevant authority or organisation in the general area where you believe you lost your belongings. This might be the local police station, mall management office, taxi company, hotel or bar. The number for lost property (Baggage Services) at Dubai International Airport is 04-224 5383, or email them via the lost and found form at www.dubaiairport.com. If you leave something in a taxi or on the metro, call the RTA on 800 9090.

M

Maps

Ongoing developments mean that maps of the UAE, Dubai in particular, are often out of date even before they're printed. The best local maps are published by Explorer, which produces a wide range of maps, regularly updated, covering the entire country and all its various cities and which are generally available in bookshops around the country. Good country maps include *Dubai Insight Flexi Map*.

Media

Print

The press in the UAE is not officially censored, although local journalists usually steer well clear of expressing negative or controversial opinions about local matters, making for a rather dull media. Local English-language newspapers are the broadsheet *Gulf News*, *Khaleej Times*, *The Gulf Today*, and the tabloid *Emirates Today* and *7 Days*, although easily the best local paper is *The National*, published in Abu Dhabi. If you want to read foreign newspapers, it is easiest to do so online.

The main sources of information on events, concerts and hotel functions in the UAE are *What's On*, *Time Out Abu Dhabi* (monthly) and *Time Out Dubai* (weekly), available at most bookshops and hotel newsagents.

Note that imported magazines are routinely censored, with any pictures showing nude or incompletely dressed women (or any other material which the authorities deem offensive) struck through with a black marker.

Broadcast media

The main English-language TV stations are Abu Dhabi Channel 2, Dubai's One TV, the Sharjah Channel and Ajman TV. These show imported serials and English-language films, and most have news in English.

International satellite TV stations including CNN and BBC World News are almost always available on hotel TVs, which usually offer a vast range of satellite channels from across Arabia and Asia.

Dubai has a number of local English-language radio stations, including Virgin Radio Dubai (104.4FM; virginradiodubai.com) and Dubai 92 (92FM; dubai92.com), churning out mainstream Western pop and inane chat. In Abu Dhabi, Abu Dhabi Classic FM (www.adradio.ae/abudhabiclassicfm) broadcasts light classics, easy listening and world music at 87.9FM.

The BBC and Voice of America are also available on short- and medium-wave radio, and through PAS4 satellite service.

Money

There are ATMs all over the UAE, most of which accept foreign Visa and MasterCard credit and debit cards. Any currency can be exchanged at one of the many banks or at money exchanges in all major malls. Money changers offer varying rates and are sometimes better value than banks.

Travellers' cheques are sometimes accepted in major shops and are easily exchanged at banks. It is best to have the purchase receipt with you. Credit cards are accepted in major hotels but anywhere else, check first. Smaller shops may add 5 percent to your bill if you pay by credit card. If you plan to bargain, you'll need cash.

Currency 1 UAE Dirham (abbreviated variously as dh, Dhs or AED) = 100 fils. The value of the dirham is linked to the US dollar at the rate of $1=Dhs3.67.

Tipping

A tip of 10 percent is usually sufficient in restaurants, although note that many places automatically add a 10 percent "service charge" to your bill, in which case you might feel that a tip is not necessary. Supermarket employees who carry bags to your car are usually tipped, as are petrol attendants who wash your windscreens.

O

Opening Hours

The UAE runs on an Islamic calendar, with the weekend falling on Friday and Saturday. Government offices usually work from 7/7.30am–1.30pm Sun–Thur. International companies keep the hours of 9am–5pm Sun–Thur. Local companies and shops in souks typically open 9/10am–1/1.30pm and 4/4.30–9/10pm Sat–Thur. Generally, banks are open 8am–1pm Sat–Thur; some also open Fri 8am–noon. Larger shopping malls open from 10am–10pm Sat–Thur and on Fri from around 2pm–late evening. Most shops operate limited opening hours during religious holidays, if they open at all.

P

Photography

Don't photograph men or, especially, women without asking permission first. The best place to photograph local people is at the Heritage and Diving Village in Dubai or Hatta Heritage Village where they are more used to the attentions of camera-toting tourists.

Postal Services

Poste restante facilities are not available in the UAE. The American Express office will hold mail for

Above: an Abu Dhabi camel farm.

cardholders, or you can receive it at your hotel. Mail is usually delivered to a PO Box number, not directly to a residence. The main **Abu Dhabi Post Office** is located on East Road, between Al Falah Street and Zayed the Second Street. The main **Dubai Post Office** is located on Zabeel Road, Al Karama.

Public Holidays

Religious holidays follow the Islamic calendar and vary annually, usually falling 11 days earlier year on year. The main holidays are the Eid Al Fitr (the end of Ramadan), Eid Al Adha (during the month of the Hajj, or pilgrimage to Mecca), the Islamic New Year, the Prophet's Birthday, and the Ascension of the Prophet. Other holidays with fixed dates include New Year's Day (1 January) and National Day (2 December). Some emirates honour their rulers, as in Abu Dhabi where 6 August is a holiday to mark the accession of former president HH Sheikh Zayed.

R

Religious Services

Islam is the official religion of the UAE, with nationals being mostly Sunni Muslims; however, there is freedom of worship for Christians in church compounds. The main services are held on Friday – the local weekend.

Abu Dhabi

St Andrew's Church
Tel: 02-446 1631, www.standrewauh.org. Between Al Khubairat School and Sheikh Mohammed Bin Zayed Mosque, off Airport Road.
St Joseph's Catholic Cathedral
Tel: 02-446 1929, www.stjosephsabudhabi.org. Between Karamah Street and Airport Road, close to Al Khubairat school.

Al Ain

St Mary's Catholic Church
Tel: 03-721 4417, www.stmarysalain.com.

Dubai

A Hindu temple is located in the souk area of Bur Dubai, near the Abra station. The Christian churches are in two main areas, along Oud Metha Road in Bur Dubai, and in a compound near Jabal Ali village.
Holy Trinity Church
Tel: 04-337 4947, www.
holytrinitychurchdubai.org.
United Christian Church of Dubai (UCCD)
Tel: 04-884 6623, http://uccdubai.com.
St Mary's Church (Roman Catholic)
Tel: 04-337 0087, www.
saintmarysdubai.com.

Sharjah

St Martin's Church
Tel: 06-566 3388.
St Michael's Catholic Church
Tel: 06-566 2424, www.
stmichaelssharjah.org.

S

Smoking

In general, the attitude to smoking is similar to that in Western nations. Smoking is banned in all indoor public venues, including restaurants, malls and offices, although you can still smoke in bars and pubs, in most outdoor eating venues, and in most hotel rooms (although a few hotels are now entirely smoke-free). During Ramadan, smoking in public anywhere is forbidden during daylight hours.

T

Telephones

Direct international telephone dialling is available from all phones. Local calls within the same city are free from a subscriber's phone. There are coin- and card-operated public phones on the streets and in shopping malls. Prepaid phone cards can be purchased from local shops and supermarkets and cost Dhs30. Some phones also use credit cards, and in many hotels you can make a call and pay for it at the reception desk. Cheap rates for international calls exist between 9pm–7am and all day on Friday.

Activate the roaming function on your mobile phone if it has one. If not,

you can buy a new SIM card. Mobile phone numbers are identified by the prefix 050.

Faxes can also be sent from many shops, offices or the mail Etisalat offices. The big hotels can usually send a fax for you.

Useful numbers

Calling the UAE from abroad: dial 00 971 followed by city code (minus the initial zero) and number.
City Codes Abu Dhabi: 02; Al Ain: 03; Dubai: 04; Fujairah: 09; Ras Al Khaimah: 07; Sharjah, Ajman and Umm al Quwain: 06. There is no need to use the access code when dialling within an emirate. To phone overseas from Oman, dial 00 followed by the national code of the country you are calling.
Directory enquiries 181.

Time Zone

GMT + 4 hours, BST + 3 hours.

Toilets

The majority of places have Western-style toilets, although you may occasionally find Asian-style squat toilets. Your best bet is to head for the nearest reputable hotel, while there are also toilets in all shopping malls.

Tourist Information

There are no actual tourist offices in the UAE – the best source of information is local travel agents.

There is a growing number of websites covering the UAE. Visit www. uaeinteract.com, www.dubai.com, www.godubai.com, www.sharjah-welcome.com, www.visitabudhabi.ae and follow links from there.

V

Visas and Passports

Visas are required by all nationalities except Gulf Co-operation Council members. Citizens of Australia, Canada, New Zealand, the US, all EU countries and some Asian countries including Singapore, Malaysia and Japan, get an automatic free single-visit visa upon entry – usually valid for up to 30 days, although changing regulations mean that it may be valid for 60. If you're planning on staying for over 30 days, check with your nearest embassy or consulate in advance, or when you arrive in the country.

Other nationalities visiting the UAE

ABOVE: public telephones.

must be sponsored by the company they are seeing on business, by friends or family resident in the UAE or by the hotel they are staying at in the UAE. These 30-day, non-renewable tourist visas should be arranged before entry to the UAE. If a hotel obtains a tourist visa for you, you enter the country on their sponsorship for the duration of your stay. You generally have to stay with them for a few nights and you can then travel freely within the UAE for the rest of your stay. It is very important to keep copies of all paperwork, and of your visa, and useful to carry a photocopy of your passport with you. Entry regulations change from time to time so check before your trip.

W

Weights and Meaures

The metric system is used.
1 inch = 2.54 centimetres (cm)
1 foot = 0.30 metres (m)
1 mile = 1.61 kilometres (km)
1 pound = 0.45 kilograms (kg)
1 American gallon = 3.79 litres (l)
1 British gallon = 4.5 litres

Women Travellers

Unlike in neighbouring Saudi Arabia, in the UAE women are not expected to cover up in public (except when visiting mosques), and they are allowed to drive. Dubai in particular is one of the easiest places in the Middle East for lone women to travel around, and many feel comfortable on their own in the evening.

In terms of personal security, women are generally safe; instances of rape are extremely rare, although not unheard of. Exercise standard precautions and never accept lifts from men met in bars and nightclubs. Dressing modestly will help women avoid unwanted attention.

LANGUAGE

UNDERSTANDING THE LANGUAGE

ABOVE: sign advertising henna hand art in Taqah.

Greetings

Hello or **Welcome**/*Márhaba, ahlan* (**reply**)/*áhlayn*
Greetings/*As-salám aláykum* (peace be with you)
(**reply**)/*Waláykum as-salám* (and to you peace)
Good morning/*Sabáh al-kháyr*
(**reply**)/*Sabáh an-núr* (a morning of light)
Good evening/*Misá al-kháyr*
(**reply**)/*Misá an núr*
Goodnight/*Tisbáh al-kháyr* (wake up well)
(**reply**)/*Wa ínta min áhlu* (and you are from His people)
Goodbye/*Máa Saláma*
How are you?/*Káyf hálak?* (to a man)/*Káyf hálik?* (to a woman)
Fine, thank you/*Zayn, al-hámdu, li-la*
Please/*Min fádlak* (to a man)/*Min fádlik* (to a woman)
Thank you/*Shúkran*
Thanks be to God/*Al-hámdu li-llá*
God willing (hopefully)/*Inshá allá*
Yes/*Náam* or *áiwa*
No/*La*

Useful Phrases

What is your name?/*Shú ismak?* (to a man)/*Shú ismik?* (to a woman)

My name is.../*Ismi...*
Where are you from?/*Min wáyn inta?* (for a man)/*Min wáyn inti?* (for a woman)
I am from: England/*Ána min Ingíltra*
the United States/*Ána min Amérika*
Australia/*Ána min Ustrália*
I have 1/2/3 children/*Andi walad/waladun/thalatha awlaad*
How do you say ... in Arabic?/*Chayf tegool ... bil'arabi?*
May I take your photo?/*Mumkin sura, min fádlak?* (to a female: *Mumkin sura, min fádlik?*)
Do you speak English?/*Btíhki inglízi?/Teh ki ingleezi?*
I speak English/*Bíhki inglízi*
I do not speak Arabic/*Ma bíhki árabi*
I do not understand/*Ma báfham*
Repeat, once more/*Kamán márra*
Do you have...?/*Ándkum...?*
Is there any...?/*Fí...?*
There isn't any.../*Ma fí...*
Never mind/*Ma'alésh*
It is forbidden.../*Mamnú'a*
What is this?/*Shú hádha?*
I want/*Uríd*
I like/*ana bhib*
I don't like/*Ana ma bhib*
I do not want/*Mauríd*
Hurry up/*Yalla/bi súra'a*
Slow down/*Shwáyya*
Go away!/*Imshi!*

What time is it?/*Adáysh as-sáa?/kam as-sáa?*
How long, how many hours?/*Kam sáa?*
You're welcome/*Afwan*
OK/*Tayib/N'zain/Kwayyis*
Not OK/*Mish kwayyis*
Come in/After you/*Tafdal*
Excuse me/*Afwan/lau samaht*
Sorry/*Afwan/Muta'assif*
Can I...?/It is possible?/*Mumkin?*
I don't know/*Mabaraf*
No problem/*Ma fi mushkila*
Perhaps/*Mumkin*
Not possible/*Mish mumkin*
What time is it?/*Kam as saa?*
How much?/*Bikaim?*
How many? /*Cham?*
What?/*Shu?*
What is this?/*Shu hadha?*
I'm ill/*Ana mareed*

Vocabulary

General

embassy/*safára*
post office/*máktab al-baríd*
stamps/*tawábi'a*
bank/*bank*
hotel/*otél/fúnduq*
room/*ghurfah*
museum/*máthaf*
hospital/*mustashfa*
doctor/*doktor*
chemist/*saydaliyeh*
police/*shurta/boulees*
ticket/*tádhkara*
passport/*jiwáz as-sáfar*
good/*kuwáys*
not good, bad/*mish kuways*
open/*maftúh*
closed/*musákkar/múghlik*
old/*kadeem*
new/*jadeed*
big/*kabeer*
small/*saghir*
beautiful/*zayn*
hot/*haar*

cold/*bareed*
open/*maftuh*
shut/*mughlag*

Eating out/drinking

restaurant/*máta'am*
breakfast/*futour*
lunch/*ghadaa*
dinner/*ashaa*
food/*ákl*
fish/*simich*
meat/*láhm*
chicken/*dijaj*
mutton/*ghanam*
milk/*halíb*
cheese/*jabne*
butter/*zibdeh*
eggs/*bayd*
bread/*khúbz*
salad/*saláta*
honey/*'asl*
yoghurt/*laban*
jam/*murabbeh*
dates/*balah*
olives/*zatoon*
delicious/*ladhidh*
coffee/*káhwa*
tea/*shay*
beer/*beera*
cup/*finján*
with sugar/*bi súkkar*
without sugar/*bidún súkkar*
mineral water/*mái ma'adaniya*
glass/*gelaas*
bottle/*zajaja/botel*
I don't eat meat/*Ana ma bakul laham*
I am a vegetarian/*Ána nabbáti* (for a man)/*nabbátiya* (for a woman)
Enough, thanks/*Bas, shukran*
the bill/*al-hisáb*

Getting around

Where…?/*Wáyn…?*
How far is it to…?/*Kam kiloometre ila…?*
downtown/*wást al bálad*
street/*shária*
car/*sayára*
taxi/*táxi*
shared taxi/*servís*
bus/*bas*

ABOVE: road sign in Arabic.

aeroplane/*tayára*
airport/*matár*
petrol, super/*benzín*
diesel/*maazout*
to/*íla*
from/*min*
in/*fi*
right/*yamín*
left/*yassar*
straight/*gida*
here/*hina*
there/*hunak*
near/*gareeb*
far/*ba'eed*
town/*madina*
city/*madinat*
north/*shimaal*
south/*janub*
east/*sharq*
west/*gharb*

Days and numbers

today/*al yoom*
tomorrow/*bokhra*
yesterday/*ams*
early/*mbach'ir/badri*
late/*mit'akhir*
day/*yoom*
might/*layl*
Monday/*yoom al ithnayn*
Tuesday/*yoom ath thalatha*
Wednesday/*yoom al araba'a*
Thursday/*yoom al khamees*
Friday/*yoom al jum'a*

Saturday/*yoom as sabt*
Sunday/*yoom al had*
zero/*sifir*
one/*wáhid*
two/*ithnayn*
three/*taláta*
four/*árba'a*
five/*khámsa*
six/*sítta*
seven/*sába'a*
eight/*tamánia*
nine/*tísa'a*
ten/*áshara*
eleven/*hidáshar*
twelve/*itnáshar*
twenty/*áishreen*
twenty-one/*wáhid wa áishreen*
twenty-two/*ithnayn wa áishreen*
thirty/*thalatheen*
forty/*arba'een*
fifty/*khamseen*
sixty/*sitteen*
seventy/*saba'een*
eighty/*thimaneen*
ninety/*tis'een*
one hundred/*maya*
one hundred and fifty/*may wa khamseen*
two hundred/*mayatayn*
three hundred/*thaltamaya*
four hundred/*rab'amaya*
five hundred/*khamsamaya*
six hundred/*sittamaya*
seven hundred/*sabamaya*
eight hundred/*tamnamaya*
nine hundred/*tissamaya*
one thousand/*alf*

Shopping

market/*souk*
shop/*dukkán*
money/*fulús*
no money/*mish fulús*
cheap/*rakhís*
expensive (very)/*gháli (jídan)*
too expensive/*ktir gháli*
receipt, invoice/*fatúra, wásl*
How much does it cost?/*Adáysh?/Bikaim?*
I like this/*Buhíbb hádha*
I do not like this/*Ma buhíbb hádha*

BELOW: Sohar at night.

FURTHER READING

History and Reference

The Arabs, Peter Mansfield. Broad history of the Middle East, and a look at its recent politics.
A History of the Arab Peoples, A. Hourani. Excellent introduction to the peoples of the region.

The UAE

Dubai Dreams: Inside the Kingdom of Bling, Raymond Barrett. Intermittently entertaining portrait of the 21st-century city, mixing travelogue, history and reportage.
Dubai: Gilded Cage, Syed Ali Dubai. Perceptive look at the role and status of Dubai's massive expat community, from Indian labourers to wealthy Western execs.
Dubai: the Story of the World's Fastest City (published in North America as City of Gold: Dubai and the Dream of Capitalism), Jim Krane. Superbly readable and perceptive portrait of the modern city. Essential reading for anyone interested in the 21st-century Gulf.
Dubai: the Vulnerability of Success, Christopher M. Davidson. Detailed scholarly history of Dubai, accompanied by chapters on the city's social, political and economic workings.
Rashid's Legacy: the Genesis of the Maktoum Family, Graeme Wilson. Depicts the family's history and approach to transforming Dubai.
Sheikh Zayed Life and Times 1918– 2004, through the lens of Noor Ali Rashid. The history of a nation personified in its founder.
Telling Tales: an Oral History of Dubai, Julia Wheeler. Photographs accompany insights from some of Dubai's founding citizens. Written by a BBC Gulf correspondent.
This Strange Eventful History: Memoirs of Earlier Days in the UAE and Oman, Edward Henderson. A good account of how the country evolved.
The Trucial States, Donald Hawley. Historical perspective written by a British ex-diplomat.

Oman

Arabian Album: Travels to Oman, Ronald Codrai. Diary extracts and photographs of Oman before the boom.
In the Service of the Sultan, Ian Gardiner. Gripping first-hand account of the Dhofar rebellion told by one of the British combatants involved in it.
Oman and Its Renaissance, Donald Hawley. Portrait of Oman since the 1970 accession of Sultan Qaboos.
Oman: the Islamic Democratic Tradition, Hussein Ghubash. Excellent academic survey of Omani history, seen through the lens of the country's Ibadi traditions.

People and Society

Bedouin: Nomads of the Desert, Alan Keohane. Definitive study of traditional Bedu life and their changing role in modern Arabia.
Explorers of Arabia, Zahra Freeth and Victor Winstone. Profiles of important early travellers.
The Merchants, Michael Field. Focusing on nine of the Gulf's prominent families; gives a good impression of how society has changed since oil.
UAE – Culture Smart! The Essential Guide to Customs and Culture, John Walsh. Useful guide to customs and etiquette.
Understanding Arabs: a Guide for Westerners, Margaret K. Nydell. Accessible guide to the cultures and customs of the Arab world.
Understanding the Arab Culture, Jehad Al-Omari. Guide to developing successful business relationships in the Middle East.

Women

Arab Women: Old Boundaries, New Frontiers, Judith E. Tucker. Collection of women's writing on the changing lives of Arab women.
Behind the Veil in Arabia: Women in Oman, Unni Wikan. Fairly academic, but a good book on Gulf customs and traditions, and women's role in rural society.
Mother Without a Mask, Patricia Holton. A personal account from a Western woman who lived with a UAE family.
Women of Sand & Myrrh, Hanan al Shaykh. Collection of women's stories.

Coffee-Table Books

Crossing the Sands, Wilfred Thesiger, published by Motivate. Chronicles the five years the writer spent with the Bedu.
Dubai: A City Portrait, Patrick Lichfield. Lavish coffee-table book.
Dubai 24 Hours, by Michael Tobias. The city as experienced by a team of Dubai's leading photographers during the course of a single day.
Dubai: the Arabian Dream, David Saunders. Account of Dubai's rapid development, illustrated with many stunning photographs.
Emirates, Helene Rogers and Kevin Higgins. The seven emirates' natural and man-made wonders.
The Emirates by the First Photographers, William Facey and Gillian Grant. Historical photographs of the region.
Images of Dubai, by Explorer Publishing. Inspiring visual guide to Dubai by various photographers.
The UAE Formative Years, 1965– 75. A Collection of Historical Photographs, Ramesh Shukla.
The UAE: Visions of Change, Noor Ali Rashid. Photographs from 1958 to 1997.
Visions of a Nomad, Wilfred Thesiger. Thesiger's photographs taken over 50 years cover the Arab world as well as Asia and Africa.

Archaeology and Geology

Atlantis of the Sands: The Search for the Lost City of Ubar, Ranulph Fiennes. Account of Fiennes's role in the rediscovery of the legendary city of Ubar.
Field Guide to the Geology of Oman, Samir S. Hanna. Invaluable practical guide to Oman's unique geology, with 17 field trips.
Oman's Geological Heritage, Michael Hughes Clarke. Superb coffee-table book full of photographs of Oman's strange landscapes and geological formations, with informative accompanying text.
The Road to Ubar: Finding the Atlantis of the Sands, Nicholas Clapp. Absorbing account of Clapp's 20-year search for the lost city of Ubar – and far better than Ranulph

Fiennes's account of the same quest (see above).

Islam

Islam and the West, Bernard Lewis. A view on the East–West relationship by the Professor of Arabic at Edinburgh University.
A New Introduction to Islam, Daniel W. Brown. A clear and well-organised look at Muslim beliefs as well as the development of Islamic studies.
Nine Parts of Desire – the Hidden World of Islamic Women, Geraldine Brooks. Based on the author's personal experiences of talking to women in the Gulf.

Travel Writing/Novels

Arabia Through the Looking Glass, Jonathan Raban. An excellent and amusing overview of the different Gulf and Middle Eastern countries.
Arabian Destiny, Edward Henderson. Fascinating autobiography covering Henderson's time in Dubai in the late 1940s and early 1950s and his delicate negotiations with the Omani tribes during the exploration for oil.
Arabian Sands, Wilfred Thesiger. Journeys made from 1945–50 in and around the Empty Quarter of Oman, Saudi Arabia and the UAE.
Dubai, Robin Moore. Blockbuster novel by French Connection author Robin Moore, set in late 1960s Dubai and with a Hollywood-style cast of arms dealers, gold smugglers, oil-prospectors and other soldiers of fortune.
Dubai Tales, Mohammed al Murr. Short stories set in Dubai and area.
The Sand Fish: a Novel from Dubai, Maha Gargash. Dubai and the northern UAE during the 1950s seen through the eyes of a rebellious teenage girl.
Sandstorms – Days and Nights in Arabia, Peter Theroux. Amusing observations of expatriate life.
Sultan in Oman, Jan Morris. Classic account of Morris's journey through 1950s Oman with Sultan Said bin Taimur.
The Sindbad Voyage, Tim Severin. Compelling account of Severin's efforts to build a traditional Omani dhow, and then sail it to China.
The Son of a Duck is a Floater, Primrose Arnander and Ashkhain Skipwith. A collection of Arab proverbs and sayings.
Travels with a Tangerine: a Journey in the Footnotes of Ibn Battutah, Tim Mackintosh-Smith. Beautifully observed account of Mackintosh-Smith's journey through the Middle East following in the footsteps of Ibn Battuta, with two fine chapters on Oman.

Art and Architecture

Architectural Heritage of the Gulf, Shirley Kay and Dariush Zandi. Traditional architectural styles of the UAE.
Forts of Oman, Walter Dinteman, published by Motivate. Pictorial account of the role of the fort in Oman's history. Moved here from Oman section above.

Arabic Language

Berlitz Arabic Guaranteed, an all-audio course comprising simple lessons on four audio CDs. A free downloadable audio script is available.
Berlitz Arabic in 60 Minutes, all-audio course with more than 250 words and phrases. Audio script provided.
Berlitz Arabic Phrase Book & Dictionary, a two-way dictionary of useful words accompanies language on new technologies, business and general conversation.
Very Simple Arabic Script, James Peters. The title says it all.

Wildlife and Flora

Arabia: Sand, Sea, Sky, Michael McKinnon. Natural history of the peninsula's land and shore.
Beachcombers' Guide to the Gulf, Tony Woodward, published by Motivate. Useful for anyone interested in knowing more about what they see on the Gulf beaches.
Birdwatching Guide to Oman, Dave E. Sargeant, Hanne Eriksen, Jens Eriksen. Useful practical guide to birdwatching in the sultanate, with details of top birdwatching sites, bird lists, and photos and maps
Butterflies of Oman, T.B. Larsen. A 1984 reprint of a first edition, with descriptions and colour illustrations of more than 70 species.
Common Birds in Oman, Hanne and Jens Eriksen. Comprehensive background on the country's avifauna, complete with 400 photos.
Mammals of the Southern Gulf, Christian Gross. Photographic account of the amazing variety of sea life.
Snorkelling and Diving in Oman, Robert Baldwin and Rod Salm. Maps and descriptions of the best places to enjoy Oman's ocean life.

Off-Road Driving and Trekking

Off-Road in the Emirates, Dariush Zandi, published by Motivate. Spiral-bound guide to 15 routes.
The Off-Roader's Manual, Jehanbaz Ali Khan.
Oman Off-Road and UAE Off-Road, published by Explorer Publishing. Excellent guides featuring satellite imaging and GPS co-ordinates for 20 routes.
Oman Trekking, published by Explorer Publishing. In-depth routes and maps covering 12 of the country's top treks.

Other Insight Guides

With their expert text and stunning images, the classic Insight Guides inspire and motivate, help with advance planning and provide a great souvenir of your trip. Titles in this region include: Egypt, Jordan and Morocco.

Insight **Step by Step Guides** are a stylish series of self-guided walks and tours, written by local experts and designed to help travellers of every interest and taste get the most out of a destination. Titles include Dubai and Marrakesh.

Insight **Smart Guides** are a series which will satisfy independent travellers looking for comprehensive listings presented in a snappy, easy-to-find way. The listings provide all the information needed to keep foodies, clubbers, culture vultures and keen shoppers busy. Titles include Dubai and Marrakesh.

Send Us Your Thoughts

We do our best to ensure the information in our books is as accurate and up-to-date as possible. The books are updated on a regular basis using local contacts, who painstakingly add, amend and correct as required. However, some details (such as telephone numbers and opening times) are liable to change, and we are ultimately reliant on our readers to put us in the picture.

We welcome your feedback, especially your experience of using the book "on the road". Maybe we recommended a hotel that you liked (or another that you didn't), or you came across a great bar or new attraction we missed.

We will acknowledge all contributions, and we'll offer an Insight Guide to the best letters received.

Please write to us at:
Insight Guides
PO Box 7910
London SE1 1WE
Or email us at:
insight@apaguide.co.uk

ART AND PHOTO CREDITS

INDEX